THE 69 CONTROVERSIES OF AI ADOPTION

The 69 Controversies of AI Adoption:

The Matrix of Contrasting Ideas towards the Art of AI Strategy

S. M. SOHN

Published by SM Research Institute

For more information, contact us on:
http://www.smsohn.com

Printed in the United States of America

Design by S. M. Sohn

ISBN Paperback: 979-11-987868-4-5
ISBN Hardcover: 979-11-987868-5-2
ISBN e-Book: 979-11-987868-6-9

First Edition: May 25, 2025

To My Parents

Contents

The universe is comprised of contrasting forces

- *The philosophy of the Taeguk (Korean Flag) Framework*

Our world is filled with contrasting ideas

- *The philosophy of this book of controversies*

Prologue

"The price of everything will converge to 0 when the cost of innovation approaches 0."

As a college senior at Virginia sending my applications to graduate business schools in the Fall semester of 2001, the above topic sentence of my essays eventually led to my first book on AI Adoption, "The Last AI: of Humanity Climbing The AI Pyramid" (May 2024). As a concise companion to The Last AI, this book builds its case by describing some of the major controversies that may arise as AI adoption progresses. We will examine potential perspectives people may have on issues that may become more important as we head to a society where AI takes a larger portion of our economy and government. My hope is this book would serve as a primer for The Last AI, which is intended to provide a more complete narrative as a textbook.

The notion of "controversy" stems from our limitations in understanding the world. This limitation leads to differences of perspectives and opinions. This book is intended to introduce some of the more controversial issues that lead to discussions in AI adoption. We may think of these controversies as the result of people having different perspectives and opinions. The goal of writing this book is not to suggest answers but to help people examine the whole spectrum of opinions and possibilities, to systematically approach and consider issues from a wider scope. In this regard, this book is similar to a survey paper, but using common sense.

The main framework introduced in this book, an application of the Taeguk framework, or the Korean Flag model for non-Korean readers, epitomizes the notion of having two opposing forces. As described in The Last AI, one of the main differences of perspectives in AI adoption is from having a scientific perspective or the business mindset. The interests and priorities are different, the forecasts or predictions or regarding what would happen are different, and the resulting opinions about decisions all become different.

The objective of writing this book is threefold, as reflected in the title.

The Number "69" to Signify the Rotating Forces in Taeguk
First, the number "69" signifies the rotating forces in the center of the Taeguk (Korean flag) framework, which serves as the "map" of the universe. This book is meant to serve as an easy-to-read primer for people who may be interested in the emerging topic of AI adoption, and how AI may affect our business, economy, and society in general by examining contrasting perspectives and ideas. Hopefully it can be read without necessarily having a background in AI or related technology, to serve as a guide to the progress related to AI.

The "Matrix" of Contrasting Ideas
Second, this book is a concise introduction to The Last AI, which deals with more expanded explanation of the progress of AI adoption. The Last AI was meant to also be used as a textbook in college, with more approaches that may require reading in the order it is written to gain a complete picture, whereas readers may skip to the areas of interest in this book. The AI controversy matrices introduced throughout the book will hopefully enable readers to grasp the issues more easily.

Towards "The Art of AI Strategy"
Third, this book will serve as one of the foundations of an effort to develop a more complete approach to how AI may be deployed to help our business and society, eventually leading to a book that can be referred to as The Art of AI Strategy, in reference to the historic book "The Art of War" by Sohn Ja (in Korean pronunciation to emphasize the same last name as the author). That is why the subtitle of this book includes "towards The Art of AI Strategy."

This book is meant to serve as a companion handbook or an executive summary of the more complete narrative told in The Last AI. Developing AI and adopting AI in our society are two different things. Having a common vocabulary is an important step in developing new ideas and strategy; the goal of writing The Last AI was to provide a common understanding of how the "game" of AI adoption may progress, similar to how we can easily understand how the games of chess, Go, or Monopoly may progress. While this book is intended as a simpler guide for people to easily imagine how our society may change from AI adoption, it goes further to especially help business leaders conceptualize the long-term changes so that they could develop their own perspectives. In other words, if the goal of The Last AI was to help people share their ideas with common vocabulary, or "connecting the dots of AI adoption," the goal of this book is to help readers develop own views and own strategies to prepare for the future, or to "spread the words on AI adoption." In this sense, this is a book that raises more questions than we can answer.

"A question that is not asked cannot be answered."

Some people may believe AI will eventually be able to answer more questions than we can ask. In this perspective, this book provides additional value of not just making the topic of AI adoption more accessible, but also serving as a source of insights in preparing for the upcoming societal change. While each controversy probably warrants a separate book, I tried to concisely present a diverse range of topics to present an overview of what changes people may have to expect as AI adoption progresses. By giving more thoughts about what may be possible, I hope more readers will be able to contribute to the progress of AI adoption in our society in a positive and meaningful way.

Thank you for reading this book!

May 25, 2025

Seuk-Min Sohn.

Keywords: AI, AI Adoption, AI Economics, AI Pyramid, AI Strategy
Automated Innovation, Automation, Augmentation, Absolute AI,
Relative AI, Effortlessness AI Investment, Future Studies, Taeguk

Disclaimer: this book does not endorse any particular stock nor is it an investment advice of any kind.

PART 1.
INTRODUCTION

Readers may be helped by first understanding the following three concepts:

1. The **Map of the Universe**
2. The AI **Controversy Matrix**
3. The **AI Pyramid**

First, the "Map of the Universe" refers to the Taeguk framework, or the idea behind the design concept of the Korean flag. In the Korean flag, the center circle signifies the two rotating forces of the universe, while the white background signifies the universe and the four black marks on the outer side signify the directions and the basic elements of the universe.

Figure P1-1: The Korean Flag as the Map of the Universe

Source: Korea Ministry of Interior and Safety

Second, the AI Controversy "Matrix" refers to the two opposing forces of AI adoption, which may be thought of as the technological perspective and the business perspective. It also signifies the two major types of controversies, which may be referred to as "forecasts" and "decisions."

Third, the "AI Pyramid" refers to the 4 Levels of AI Adoption, as introduced in The Last AI. Sohn's AI Pyramid can be summarized as the following:

- **Level 1 (Augmentation):** AI as a tool or assistant
- **Level 2 (Agency):** AI reaching parity with humans for a business role
- **Level 3 (Autonomy):** AI gaining independence to run companies
- **Level 4 (Authority):** AI gaining legal rights in and out of human jurisdiction

Let us first briefly think about why there are controversies, and then review these concepts in the following segments.

Why Are There Controversies?

How Can Humans or AI Have Different Opinions?

"Beauty Is in the Eyes of the Beholder"

- Margaret W. Hungerford

The Source of Differences in Human Minds and AI: Experiences and Data

Since this is a book of controversies, we may first think about what causes different opinions among people, and then think about what may cause differences of opinions among AI, from an excerpt from The Last AI.

1) Different Experiences → Differences in Opinions

Let us first think about how humans differ in opinions. Our past experiences may be one of the main causes of our differences in thinking. In addition, not all knowledge or experiences would bear the same importance. For example, the Apollo moon landing is considered a transformative event where everyone "remembers where they were when it happened" kind of moment. But since the subsequent generations did not experience the event as it unfolded, our feelings about it would be much less than those of the people who can actually remember it happening in real time.

For my generation in the US, the terrorist attacks on September 11th, 2001, may be the equivalent of such event. I vividly remember seeing it on TV, as I was a college senior at Virginia. On that morning I had a class to attend; I had just woken up and when I turned on the TV to watch while eating breakfast, the first plane had just crashed into the World Trade Center and the news was showing the footage over and over. As I was about to leave to go to class, I watched the second plane crash in real time. I was wondering if some kind of war had started; especially because a few years prior another "everyone remembers where they were" type of news event occurred in South Korea when Kim Il-Sung, the founder of North Korea, died and people were on high alert for war. Anyway, because I was taught to go to class no matter what, I still went to class, but I was the only student to show up among the class of around 30; another example of how everyone's past experiences lead to different actions. I am sure the family and friends of the victims or the people who experienced it at the scene in New York would remember it with even more clarity and emotions. On the other hand, younger generations may not share the same intense feelings as someone who experienced it in real time.

Another big world event that I can remember is when the Tiananmen Square, famous for the man standing in front of the tank,[1] occurred. Even though I did not fully grasp the importance of the event as I was in elementary school, I remember repeatedly seeing the long news coverage that went on for days, especially because we only had a few TV channels back then and it was the only thing on TV. Nowadays, people who are older than me may remember it well, while younger generations, especially those who live in China, may not even know about it since it is one of the topics that is not allowed for discussion; there are even suggestions that including this word should be encouraged in books or movies since it will lead their government to crack down on the piracy of works that reference this event.

To generalize, some experiences leave more impressions on us, and the path of those experiences may matter. As a result, children who was inspired by the moon landing may grow up to become a rocket scientist, while children who was more worried about wars or terrorist attacks may grow up to serve in the military or even build a nuclear bunker. Research suggests people who experienced the Great Depression in the 1930s were more likely to save and prepare for hard times than people who did not experience harsh times.[2]

We may apply the same principle to developing AI; we may think of the events 1) Apollo Moon Landing, 2) 9/11, 3) Kim Il-Sung and, 4) Tiananmen Square as data inputs to an AI that may lead to different decisions or results from AI. As a result, an advanced AI built in China may omit the data on Tiananmen and be more inclined to prefer communist ideas in general. If a terrorist group decided to build an advanced AI, it may input the data on 9/11 as a positive action and the AI may be more inclined to prefer destructive actions in general. If North Korea was building an AI, the data entered would have Kim Il-Sung as the most important person of all time, etc. In essence, bias in AI input would probably follow the bias or intentions of humans that build the AI through data. From this observation, we can surmise that advanced AI may act in ways that may not satisfy all people because of our differences, even if it satisfies the developers or vice versa. For some readers, it may be unacceptable that AI may have these inclinations. However, these "differences" in perspectives are distinct from judging what is "good or bad," or even trying to attain "diversity" of opinions. The point here is not to judge the actions of AI, but to emphasize the fact that what AI does will be affected by the input data.

2) Same Experiences → Differences in Opinions

As we accumulate more experiences, our biases may lead to situations where we incorporate information in a selective manner; in this case, even the same experiences will lead people to reach different conclusions.

For example, in the aftermath of the World Trade Center collapse, there could be a diverse range of reactions. First, we may think of some of the lessons of the lines of thinking of the majority:

1. (Terrorism is Bad) Use of violence cannot be justified
2. (Sad for Victims) Condolences for the victims and their families
3. (Rescuers Were the Heroes) Who enables our society to function

Meanwhile, there could have been skeptics or complainers who may instead reach other types of minority conclusions, such as:

4. (Airport Security Was Weak) The airports and airlines should have been able to deter the planes from being hijacked
5. (Surveillance Was Inadequate) The governments should have kept a better track of the terrorists to catch them before their act
6. (WTC Was Structurally Unsound) WTC should have been able to withstand those impacts and not collapse
7. (Response Was Incorrect) The government should have called for immediate evacuation, not send first respondents into the buildings

Furthermore, there could have been conspiracy theorists who instead argue for alternative explanations for the event, such as:

8. (This Was All a "Show") WTC housed important documents or financial transactions that needed to be cancelled or hidden
9. ("They" Needed a War) Some unknown group of people needed a war for financial gains

Lastly, there could even have been people who outright supported the causes of the terrorists, such as:

10. (US are Imperialists) the US deserved this for what they had done in the past

From this one event, we may create a long list of different conclusions that could go on and on. Again, the point here is not to judge whether these conclusions are right or wrong, but to see that there may be a wide variety of differences of opinions even when people are given the same fact, some of which may be mutually exclusive. Similar to how humans may reach different conclusions from the same information from our own biases, we may infer that AI may also reach different conclusions from same facts based on its own biases and idiosyncrasies.

People may develop contrasting opinions. This is what leads to controversies.

The Map of the Universe (Taeguk)

[The 2-Force, 8-Direction Octagon Framework]
...or the "Korean Flag" Model, or the "69 Framework"

"May the Force Be with You"

- From the movie Star Wars

Introducing the Taeguk (Korean Flag) Octagon AI Adoption Framework

To examine the controversies regarding AI, let us examine the basic idea of *Taeguk*, or the philosophy behind the Korean Flag as the map of the universe, to introduce the framework that explains how AI may be adopted in our society: the 2 Forces and 8 Directions of AI controversies.

Inspired by the Design of the Korean Flag

Rare for Koreans of my generation, in elementary school I happened to receive tutoring of the teachings of the traditional Eastern philosophers from an elderly scholar who lived in the same apartment complex. He had a keen interest in the Korean flag, and had in his room an old Korean flag and a newspaper article of him being interviewed about it hanging on the wall in a plaque. The original flag looks like it is on its side compared to the flag we use now, and sometimes my classmates asked him why the old flag was on its side. He would then explain to us how the flag was supposed to represent the universe and the center depicts the rotating of the opposing forces.

The 2-Forces 8-Directions Octagon framework may be thought of as being inspired by the design of the Korean flag, but the specifics are modified to fit our analysis of AI adoption. We may think of the Korean flag as having two parts: the center circle depicting the rotation of two opposite forces, and the outer white background and the black marks signifying the universe.

1. The Center Circle: the Taeguk Mark Representing the Two Forces

The name of the Korean flag is called "Tae-Guk" Flag, where "Tae" means something big, or the universe. "Guk" means something having 2 opposing sides, a concept similar to having the north and south poles in a magnet. This concept may also be familiar for English speakers as representing "Eum" (or also known by Mandarin pronunciation Yin) or the negative, and "Yang" or the positive energy. The center circle "Taeguk" mark represents these two rotating forces of the universe, as shown in Diagram 1. When you see today's Korean flag, the "Taeguk" mark is rotated to make it look similar to the old Pepsi logo, but in the original Korean flag this mark is shaped more like "69."

The bottom of the circle represents the earth, and the top represents the sky or universe, and the red and blue colored 6 and 9 shapes represent rotation of the two opposing forces, such as the positive and negative or the warm and cold forces of the universe, rotating towards and away from the earth.

Figure P1-2: The Center of Controversy Diagram (The 69)

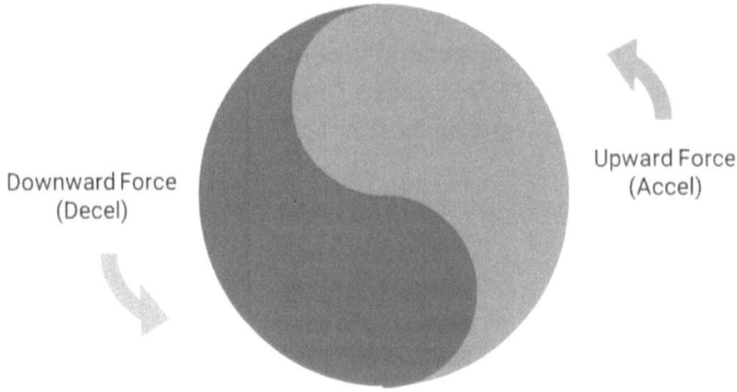

2. The Outer White Background and the Eight Black Marks of Octagon
The four outer black marks of the Korean flag represent the universe, and is a simplified version of the eight marks. They stand for the types of energy that make up our universe, such as being hot, stability, flowing, etc., as well as the eight outer marks signify the eight directions, such as East, West, Northwest, Southwest, etc. Each of the marks represents a number, where the opposing directions all add up to 9, which would be considered the complete number.

The black rectangular bars work like a digital signal; imagine connecting electricity to each end of the bar. If it is disconnected in the middle, it will not conduct electricity, meaning it is a zero. If it is connected, it will conduct, meaning it is a 1. With the 3 bars, you can express a total of $2^3 = 8$ numbers.

Figure P1-3: The Bars in the 8-Direction Octagon

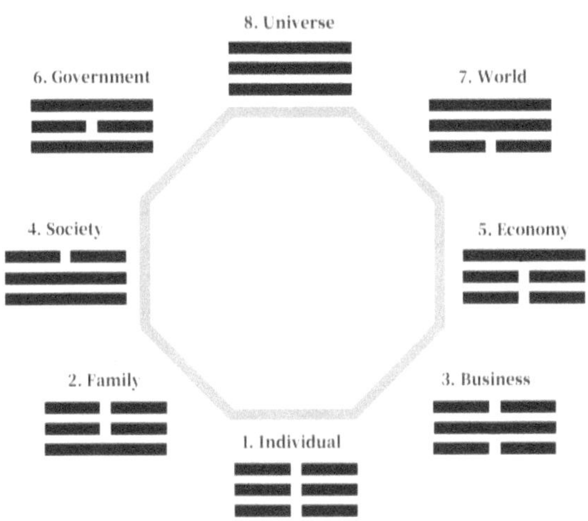

3. The 2-Force, 8-Direction Octagon (Taeguk 69) Framework

Without going into further details as this may not be relevant for Non-Korean readers, we may examine the general idea of combining the Taeguk and the Octagon to conceive the 2 Forces and 8 Directions Octagon Framework of AI Adoption, or the 69 or Taeguk or the Korean Flag Framework as follows:

Figure P1-4: The 2-Force, 8-Direction Octagon (Taeguk 69) Framework

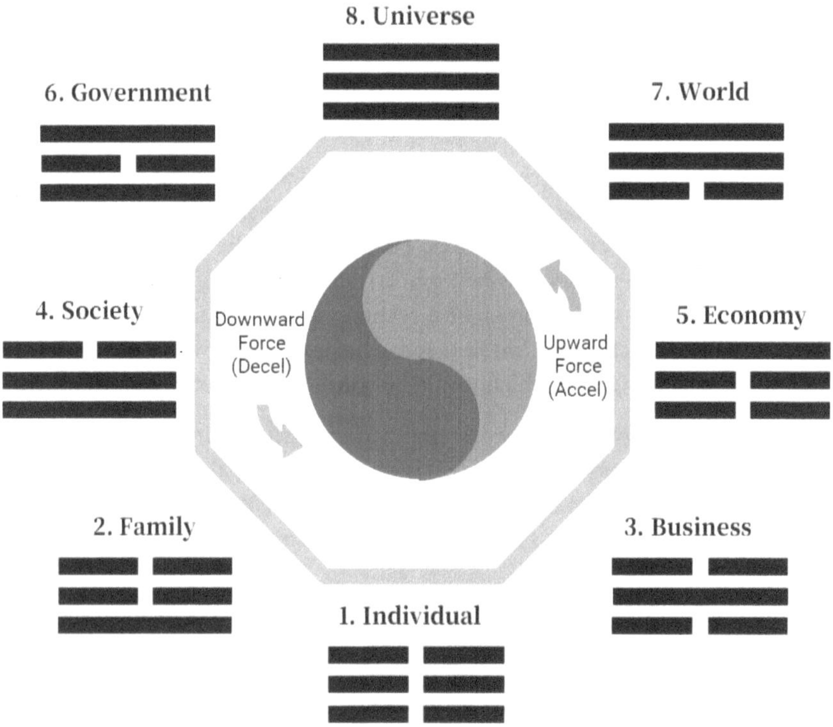

The controversies will be categorized to reflect the scope of the decisions that can be made by AI adoption; starting at the bottom, which can be thought of as the ground, or near you (low scope of influence), to far-reaching all of the universe or into the sky (high scope of influence).

<u>The 2 Center Forces:</u>

Center 1 (Blue): Downward Force / Decelerate
Center 2 (Red): Upward Force / Accelerate

The 8 Directions:
Direction 1 (South): AI and Individual
Direction 2 (Southwest): AI and Family
Direction 3 (Southeast): AI and Business
Direction 4 (West): AI and Society
Direction 5 (East): AI and Economy
Direction 6 (Northwest): AI and Government
Direction 7 (Northeast): AI and the World
Direction 8 (North): AI and the Universe

By categorizing the controversies using the 2-Forces 8-Directions Octagon framework, readers may find it easier to understand how each controversy relates to a more complete picture, as well as assess which groups of topics are more interesting to them. Thinking about the inner 2 forces would help us see how the opposing forces may affect each of the 8 directions.

The idea of introducing this framework is to eventually develop towards what may be called the Art of AI Strategy.

4. The AI Adoption Matrix

Because square tables are easier to draw than octagons, we may also draw the framework into the following 9-cell matrix. Readers may be more familiar with this presentation style than the Korean flag-style Taeguk presentation.

Figure P1-5: The AI Adoption Matrix

Direction 6 **AI and Government**	**Direction 8** **AI and the Universe**	**Direction 7** **AI and the World**
Direction 4 **AI and Society**	**AI Adoption** **Downward (Decel)** **Upward (Accel)**	**Direction 5** **AI and Economy**
Direction 2 **AI and Family**	**Direction 1** **AI and Individuals**	**Direction 3** **AI and Business**

The AI Controversy Matrix

[Forecasts vs Decisions]

"Red Pill or Blue Pill?"

- From the movie The Matrix

Forecasts vs Decisions

When we think about the types of differences of opinions people can have about the future, we may categorize into two types of forecasts and decisions, or differences of opinions about what will happen and what we should do. To familiarize with this concept, let us think about the extreme ends of forecasts and decisions regarding AI.

First, people may think of the two extreme ends of **forecasts** regarding AI adoption as the following, ranging from high hopes to low expectations.

- Extremely **Positive** Forecast: AI may enable us to live forever!
- Extremely **Negative** Forecast: AI may end all of humanity!

Everyone's *forecast* on what AI may bring may be somewhere in between these two extreme opinions. Based on their own forecasts, people may call for different actions, or **decisions,** on what to do. We may also think about the two opposite decisions regarding AI adoption as the following.

- **Positive** Decision: Increase investment to accelerate AI development
- **Negative** Decision: Increase regulations to decelerate AI development

People who believe AI will be highly beneficial to humanity may want to accelerate the development of AI and call for larger investments. On the other hand, people who believe AI will be highly dangerous for humanity may want to halt or slow down the development or AI and call for stronger regulations. From this observation, we may even create a model to show how one's "forecasts" would affect one's "decisions" regarding AI development.

Forecasts Affects → **Decisions**

For each of the issues, people may reach different conclusions regarding; 1) their forecasts about what may happen, 2) the decisions that we need to make, and 3) how forecasts should affect the decisions. This also makes it clearer what are forecasts and not decisions; for example, we will not decide how smart ASI can be, even though we may decide whether to halt investment.

This book will be built around this concept of helping people think about the forecasts and decisions regarding the future of AI adoption. We will examine how we can systemically think about the forecasts and decisions about AI, using the AI Controversy Matrix and the AI Awareness Matrix.

The AI Controversy Matrix (Developer vs User)

To systematically think about the controversies surrounding AI, we may first think about the impact of AI adoption in general to consider where frictions may arise. AI adoption may be thought of as an ecosystem comprised of humans, AI, and the environment. In this ecosystem, we may categorize the controversies as having to do with "AI itself," or the **developer** perspective, or as "AI in Relation to Its Surroundings," or the **user** perspective:

- **AI Itself (Developer Perspective):** topics may include how advanced AI may become, how it will work, the speed of development, etc.
- **AI in Relation to Its Surroundings (User Perspective):** topics may include what should be allowed, such as whether to allow AI to compete against humans, where AI may be allowed to be used, and what level of adoption, etc.

From this, we may categorize controversies surrounding AI adoption to create an AI Controversy Matrix for each topic. On one dimension, we may categorize according to the perspectives of the developers and users, or whether the controversy is about AI itself or the AI adoption. On the other dimension, we may categorize according to the nature of the controversy, as in whether the controversy is something about what will happen, or forecast, and about what we should do, or decisions that we have to make. The following table shows the general format of the AI Controversy Matrix

Table P1-1: Example of the AI Controversy Matrix

<table>
<tr><th colspan="2" rowspan="2"></th><th colspan="2">Object of Controversy</th></tr>
<tr><th>AI Itself
(Developer Perspective)</th><th>AI in Relation to
Its Surroundings
(User Perspective)</th></tr>
<tr><th rowspan="2">Nature of Controversy</th><th>Forecasts</th><td>How <u>OOO</u> AI will become
(What Constitutes OOO)</td><td>How AI will affect <u>OOO</u>
(What will be the consequences ...)</td></tr>
<tr><th>Decisions</th><td>Should we allow AI
to be able to do <u>OOO</u>
(i.e. Capabilities of AI)</td><td>Should we allow AI
to be used for <u>OOO</u>
(i.e. Application of AI,
Humans vs AI)</td></tr>
</table>

The AI Awareness Matrix

In addition, people may have differences of opinions regarding the level of importance of each topic. We may refer to this as the level of "awareness" for a certain topic. This may be the third dimension of the Controversy Matrix.

- Contrasting **Ideas**: Issues where people have opposing opinions
- Contrasting **Awareness**: Issues where people have opposing opinions about the relative importance of each topic

When we consider the levels of public awareness of topics with the dimension of time horizon, we could categorize into the following 4 types of awareness.

- **Type 1 (Imminent):** Issue topics that may materialize in the shorter-term that have gained more exposure in public discussions and higher awareness
- **Type 2 (Overlooked or Emerging):** Issue topics that may materialize in the shorter-term that failed to gain public exposure and awareness
- **Type 3 (Non-Imminent):** Issue topics that may not materialize in the shorter-term but have gained public exposure and awareness
- **Type 4 (Upcoming):** Issue topics that may not materialize in the shorter-term and have not yet gained public exposure and awareness

The following table shows examples of topics. These AI Controversy and Awareness matrices will be applied to each of the directions of the framework.

Table P1-2: Example of the AI Controversy Awareness Matrix

<table>
<tr><th colspan="2" rowspan="2"></th><th colspan="2">Perceived Issue Horizon (Time)</th></tr>
<tr><th>Shorter-Term</th><th>Longer-Term</th></tr>
<tr><td rowspan="2">How Well People are Currently Aware (Importance)</td><td>Popular Topics</td><td>Type 1 Controversy (Imminent)
- Will AI use help or hinder learning
- What should we teach our children?</td><td>Type 3 Controversy (Non-Imminent)
- Will AI Threaten Humanity?
- Will AI raise or lower birth rates?</td></tr>
<tr><td>Not Yet Popular Topics</td><td>Type 2 Controversy (Overlooked or Emerging)
- Will AI robots be able to serve as AI butler?
- Should we allow AI robots in households to be stronger than humans as AI security guards?</td><td>Type 4 Controversy (Upcoming)
- Will cities become less popular?</td></tr>
</table>

Increase in Importance

Farther Away in Time

The AI Pyramid
(The 4 Levels of AI Adoption)

Figure P1-6: Sohn's AI Adoption Pyramid and Enablers[3]

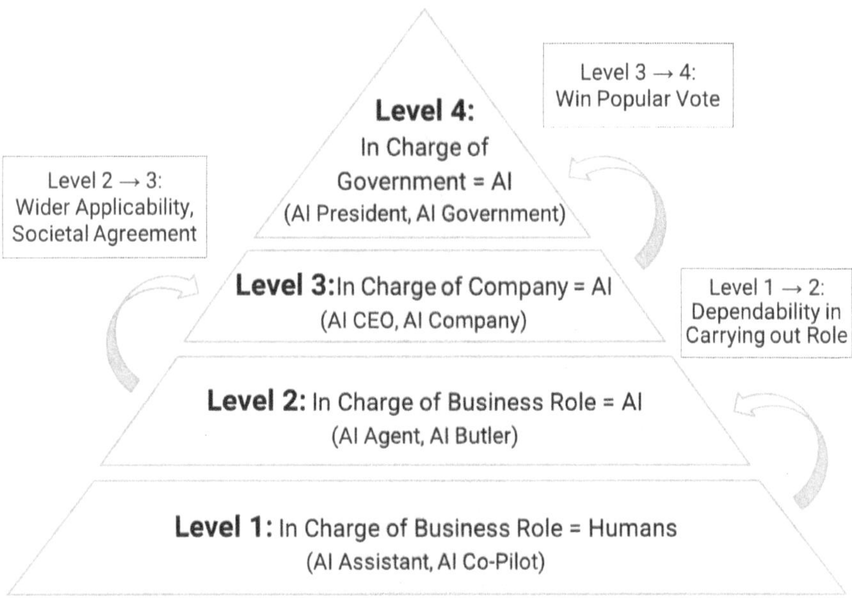

Enablers to reach the next level of AI Adoption:
Level 1 → 2: Achieving Trustworthy Dependability in Carrying out Role
Level 2 → 3: Wider Applicability of AI to Run Business; Societal Agreement
Level 3 → 4: Winning the Popular Vote

1. Introduction to the Three and Four Levels of AI Adoption

The AI Pyramid, more extensively explained in The Last AI, is an attempt to illustrate the progress of AI adoption in our society. The AI Pyramid can be summarized as the following, categorized by the degree of AI self-initiation:

- **Level 1 (Augmentation):** AI as a tool or assistant
- **Level 2 (Agency):** AI reaching parity with humans for a business role
- **Level 3 (Autonomy):** AI gaining independence to run companies
- **Level 4 (Authority):** AI gaining legal rights in and out of jurisdiction

The first three levels of the AI Pyramid are separately used to describe the progress of AI adoption in business, known as the Three Levels of AI Adoption.[4] One of the significance of this framework is to offer an alternative way to describe an important milestone in AI adoption, named "AI Equalization"[5] for a business role, serving as an alternative to the concept of AGI for business analysis.

Table P1-3: AI Equalization and the Three Levels of AI Adoption[6]

AI Adoption Type		Adoption Level	Description of Adoption Level
without AI Equalization	Augmentation and/or Partial Automation	Level 1	Humans are in charge of business roles (i.e. AI Assistants, Co-Pilot AI)
with AI Equalization	Full Automation and/or Collaboration	Level 2	AI is in charge of business roles (i.e. AI Agents, AI Butlers)
with Social Acceptance	Full Automation	Level 3	AI is in charge of whole businesses (i.e. AI CEOs, AI Companies)

While AGI and AI Equalization both try to direct people's attention to a point of inflection, there is a notable difference in the perspective of categorizing AI as reaching AGI and whether AI has reached equalization. Whereas the supplier, or the developer, of AI would probably decide whether AI has reached AGI, the user, or the demand, of the AI will determine whether AI has reached equalization. For some jobs or occupations, it may be easier to reach equalization, while for others it may require a more advanced AI.

2. Applying the Three Levels of AI Adoption

The Three Levels of AI Adoption helps describe how AI development will change the business activities of individuals and firms. This is intended to be a flexible framework, and companies may be able to develop their own versions to cater to their internal and external stakeholders. Probably the best known application of this framework is OpenAI's internal 5 Stages of AI, reported by the media in July 2024.[7] In Controversy 6, we will review how OpenAI's version can be developed to help satisfy both internal staff and customers.

Figure P1-7: The Three Levels of AI Adoption by Firms[8]

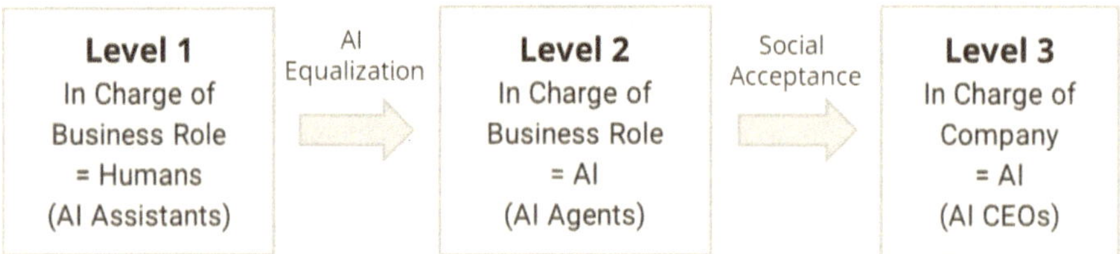

Enablers to Reach the Next Levels

To reach the next level, certain milestones or accomplishments would need to be met. These are referred to as Enablers. To jump from Level 1 to Level 2 Adoption to let AI be in charge of business roles, AI must first demonstrate dependability in the role. For example, we can imagine the equivalent of reaching the Level 5 autonomous driving as a technological milestone that may enable an AI to be in charge of a business role that involves driving without humans.

As AI technology develops further in Level 2, more and more business roles may be taken over by AI. To reach Level 3 from Level 2, in addition to AI gaining the dependability in the business role of running a business, an additional requirement of gaining social agreement and legal status would first be necessary. To progress from Level 3 to 4, after reaching all of the previous milestones in government-related roles, an additional step of winning a popular vote will be necessary.

There is also the Six Levels of AI Adoption, which will be just mentioned to save space in this book.

[Side Note] Overview of the 4 Levels of AI Adoption

1) AI Adoption Level 1: "If You Can Imagine It, You Can Do It"

In the beginning stage of AI adoption, it would be natural for AI to focus on helping human workers achieve more and work more effectively and efficiently to increase productivity. Human workers may be working in the same jobs as before, and AI would help humans carry out the role more easily or better. Jobs may be newly designed to incorporate AI better. This stage of AI adoption may be referred to as Co-Pilot AI or Assistant AI. More broadly, we may call it Dependent AI.

2) AI Adoption Level 2: "What You Can Imagine Will Be Done for You"

As AI development continues, the capabilities of AI will improve, and eventually reach a stage where AI may be able to carry out all of the tasks of a human worker at a level of dependability beyond what would be deemed necessary to remove the human worker. A well-known example of reaching dependability includes the Level 5 autonomous vehicle. In this level, AI would take charge of a business role. In this book, we will refer to these types of AI as Agent AI,[9] or Employee AI, or if it develops in a particular direction, Butler AI. More broadly, these may be also referred to as Dependable AI.

3) AI Adoption Level 3: "Even What You Couldn't Imagine Is Done for You"

As AI development continues even further, the scope of tasks AI can carry out would widen, eventually reaching a stage where the AI would be able to carry out all of the tasks of the CEO, or even all of the tasks within the firm. An example may be an AI robot that can independently run a company that operates restaurants. This AI would be able to carry out tasks such as financing for a restaurant, what menus to include, where to open, how to do the interior, where to procure ingredients, etc. In this stage, AI, not humans, would be in charge of the final management decisions of the firm. We may refer to these types of AI as CEO AI, Chairman AI, Company AI, etc. More broadly, we may also refer to them as Independent AI or Free AI.

4) AI Adoption Level 4: "You Will Never Know What Was Done for You"

Lastly, the majority of the general public may at some point prefer to have AI in charge of the government over humans. In this stage, AI would be in charge of the government. There would be two paths to reach this stage. The first would be intentional, as a result of the demands of the public. We will refer to these as President AI or Government AI. The second path to reach this stage would be unintentional, potentially including paths where AI exceeds the comprehension of humans and somehow gains control of our society without our intentions. We may refer to these types of AI as Sage AI or Dictator AI.

1. The AI Adoption Controversy

[Decision]

Technology vs Business Perspectives

"What Questions Do You Want to Ask?"

"We Can Only Answer Questions That Are Asked"
- May 2002[10]

5-Line Summary

1. We may think of the two major perspectives of AI development and AI adoption as the perspectives of the supply and demand of AI
2. Technological Perspective: "How Intelligent Can AI Become?" etc.
3. Business Perspective: "How Useful Can AI Become?" etc.
4. We may think of the levels of AI adoption as describing the social status of AI within our society
5. The progress of AI adoption may appear to have a separate cadence from technological progress, leading to even more controversies

The Future of AI from the Perspectives of Suppliers vs Users

As the person who may be defining how the term "AI Adoption" is used, there may be a need to explain the reason to have this concept. The main reason is that the perspectives of business and economics are different from those of science and technology. Different perspectives lead to differences in questions and decisions. The questions scientists or engineers would ask are different from the questions economists or business managers would ask. Scientific questions relate to AI may include the algorithms or how AI may be trained, while business questions may be related to the changes that AI adoption may bring to our business, economy, society and government.

From a scientific perspective, the focus may be on how much intelligence AI could achieve, or how similar to humans we can make AI. These questions may be considered viewpoint of the "supplier" or the providers of AI. On the other hand, profitability would be the main focus from a business perspective, and whether AI is similar to humans is not as important. In some instances it would be more beneficial for AI to be different from humans, so it can complement tasks that humans find difficult. This perspective may be thought of as the viewpoints of the "demand," or the users of AI.

Readers may be familiar with the framework of the progress of AI from the technical perspective, where we categorize AI into ANI-AGI-ASI. From this standpoint, most relevant questions may include "how intelligent can we make AI?" "How similar to humans can we make AI?" or "Can we create AI more intelligent than humans?" This framework is useful for thinking about scientific or technological issues. AI development has a rather concrete pattern and an "end" to the game; after reaching AGI, AI would enter a self-improvement loop to surpass the knowledge and capabilities of all humanity by reaching what is referred to as "singularity."[11]

From a business standpoint, relevant questions would be in reference to the position of AI within our society. In other words, the inflection points used in the ANI-AGI-ASI framework is not as meaningful for describing the changes from an economic or social perspective. This is the reason for introducing the 4 Levels of AI Adoption framework in The Last AI. The user perspective adds another layer above technology development, assessing the progress of AI adoption against established hierarchies we have in our business and society. The progress of AI adoption in our society may appear to have a separate cadence from the development patterns of AI, causing more controversies.

PART 2.
THE CENTER OF CONTROVERSY

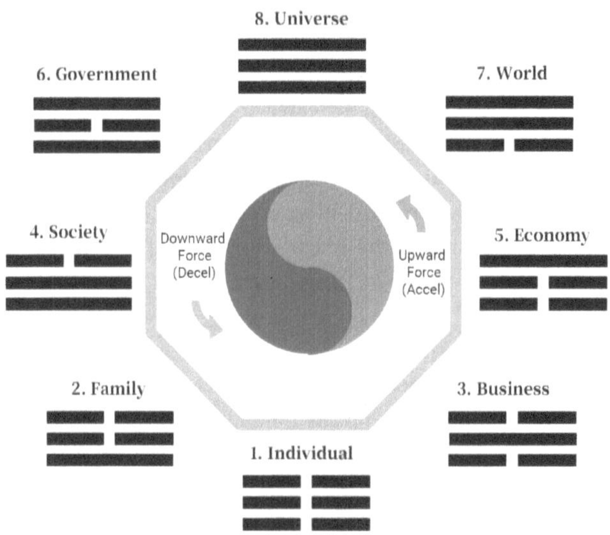

CENTER 1
UPWARD FORCE
(ACCEL)

The upward forces in AI adoption may be thought of as elements that accelerate AI development and adoption.

These elements may include high expectations for AI, excitement for AI, AI technology advancements, increases in investments for AI and related infrastructure, etc.

In this section, we will examine some controversies that are mainly related to AI technology advancements.

2. The AGI Definition Controversy

[Decision]

What Should Constitute AGI?

"If You Can't Define It, Refine It"

- Overheard at KDB Global Strategy Team[12]

5-Line Summary

1. The term Artificial General Intelligence was coined in late 1990s and popularized in 2007
2. People cannot agree on what AGI should mean
3. Business-focused, AGI may be defined by how AI can carry out economically valuable tasks, etc.
4. Technology-focused, AGI may be thought of being able to generalize knowledge from specific data, to being able to improving itself, to even having consciousness, etc.
5. In The Last AI, the Six Levels of Pre-AGI AI framework was introduced to help people think about what is not AGI

The Term "Artificial General Intelligence"

(History) AGI is a term first coined by Mark Gubrud[13] in late 90s but did not become popular until Ben Goertzel used it as the title of his book in 2007.[14] Since then, the term has become almost synonymous with what we dream of from an advanced form of AI, in the sense that it can understand the world in a similar way as humans such that it can solve problems or do the work for us.

(Importance) AGI is considered important because once we have AGI most of the benefits people typically associate with what may be achieved by AI.

Contrasting Ideas on What AGI Should Entail

There have been disagreements on what should constitute an AGI or how we define it. What is intelligence? Should AGI have "consciousness" similar to humans? Should AGI have "feelings?" Should AGI be able to make and understand jokes? Would AGI solve the mysteries of the world? Would AGI be any different at all from previous versions of AI?

When we try to categorize the different levels of AGI according to how difficult it may be to achieve technologically, we may consider the following:

1) AI that has a general "world" model, to understand the world through language, sound, visually or through some other sensory means
2) AI that can apply knowledge learned in one area to another area, thus "general" intelligence
3) AI that can carry out tasks at level comparable to human experts (Google)[15]
4) AI that "thinks" like humans, such as having "consciousness" in some way (Human-Level AI)
5) AI that can recursively self-improve to become ASI (the Self-Advancing AI)

While AGI may be defined by technical means, there are also attempts to define it by business terms. Most notable may be the definitions by OpenAI:

6) AI that can carry out most economically valuable tasks (2018)[16]
7) AI that creates value of over $100 billion (2024)[17]

From a social perspective, AGI may be defined by degree of self-initiation:

8) AI that can self-initiate in a manner parity to individuals (Level 2 Adoption)
9) AI that can self-initiate in a manner parity to human organizations (Level 3)
10) AI that can self-initiate in a manner parity to humanity (Level 4 Adoption)

For every argument about what AGI should entail, there may be a different perspective regarding what important milestone AGI should mark.

1) **Philosophical** point of view: the important milestone may be AI coming to have "**consciousness**" or "feelings" or have the urge of "self-preservation," etc.
2) AI **Developers** or Engineering Perspective: How AGI differs in operation compared to less advanced AI, so that an AI that can **apply the knowledge** it learned from its training to real-world problems may be a concrete situation where they can say it is different from the AI we had in the past
3) AI **Users** or Business Perspective: what would be important is whether AI can be used to replace business roles in Level 2 AI Adoption, as described in The Last AI. From this perspective, **self-initiation** becomes the important factor. If we try to force the definition of AGI into business terms, then we may say it would be an AI that can do all types of economic tasks

We may categorize approaches to defining AGI by examining 1) what types of inflection points are used, either as how AI applies knowledge, or how similar AI can be to humans, and 2) what types of interaction is considered as AI reacting to a given prompt, or AI taking the self-initiative to take own action.

Table 2-1: The AGI Definition Controversy Matrix

		What AI Can Do (Technological Perspective)	
		Degree of Generalization	**Similar to Humans**
Context of How AI Does What It Does (Social Perspective)	**How AI Answers to Questions (Reaction)**	**Type 1 Definition "Solve"** (e.g. Levels of AGI)	**Type 2 Definition "Feel"** (e.g. Sentience)
	How AI Can Self-Initiate (Action)	**Type 3 Definition "Adopt"** (e.g. Practical Turing Test)	**Type 4 Definition "Aware"** (e.g. Consciousness)

Type 1 Definitions: People in this group would more likely consider defining AGI by how it can answer a given question, such as "solving" math problems.

Type 2 Definitions: People in this group would be more likely to think AGI would have "feelings" or emotions similar to humans in given situations.

Type 3 Definitions: People in this group like to see AGI "adopt" to real world.

Type 4 Definitions: People in this group like to see AGI to become "alive."

The Most Significant AGI Definition: The Self-Advancing AGI

Meanwhile, the most significant definition of AGI that encompasses all of the above would be the AGI that can self-improve to surpass all of humanity and become ASI, essentially what can be thought of as becoming an "artificial god." This definition is significant because it tells us the following two things. First, AGI may become the last AI that humanity will develop, since the rest of the way will be paved automatically by the AGI. Second, humanity may lose grip on AGI because once it is developed, it is not certain that we will be able to continue to control it. We may think of it as the opposing forces, or the potential benefits and dangers of AGI.

Takeaway: Summary of the AGI Definition Controversy

From your perspective, what do you think is the most useful definition of AGI?

One takeaway from comparing how people may have different definitions of AGI may be that the closer you define AGI to be to ASI, the more dangerous you may think AGI would be. Most people agree that ASI may be dangerous to humanity because it would surpass human understanding. Not all people agree that AGI would be as dangerous, mostly because they perceive it as something less capable than ASI.

Another takeaway for most readers may be that AGI may be understood more easily as a spectrum of ideas rather than a single idea, and that when someone says "AGI," it is better to think about where within the spectrum the speaker means to imply. Being open to having one vocabulary carrying different ideas may help people communicate with each other.

If we define AGI based on the amount of value it can generate, then we may have another controversy comparing it to humans. For example, take the latest available definition from OpenAI, which defines AGI as something that can generate an annual value of $100 billion. Some people would argue this should be considered close to an ASI, since there is no human who generates $100 billion from own work. (This is a different question from people who gets paid $100 billion in stock for managing others.) Instead, since typically people get paid in 5-to-7 figures range, some may argue AI that can generate similar value should be considered AGI.

The Six Levels of Pre-AGI AI: Alternative Ways to Refer to AI before AGI

People may agree that AGI may not be the best way to define more relevant types of AI for the business users. This is because for some people, AGI is taken as the next step in AI development, something that they should plan for in the short-to-medium term. For others, AGI is taken as the last step in AI development, something that they do not need to plan for except for the longest-horizon term.[18] For some it may be easier if we think in terms of what is *not* AGI.

To address this problem, the Six Levels of Pre-AGI AI framework was introduced in The Last AI to help people categorize the types of AI that may appear before reaching AGI. If we use the acronyms in a pattern as in AAI, ABI, ACI, D, E..., it may be easier to judge where in the timeline it is without understanding the actual definition. The following is a simple summary.

Table 2-2: Acronyms to Segmenting Pre-AGI AI Sophistication[19]

Acronym	Suggested Full Name	Potential Description
1. AAI	ABCs of Artificial Intelligence (Beginning of the path to AGI)	- Refers to the fundamental machine learning methods
2. ABI	Artificial Basic Intelligence (Quarter of the way to AGI)	- Refers to the earlier methods of deep learning
3. ACI	Artificial Classic Intelligence (Less than halfway to AGI)	- Refers to more recent methods of deep learning - Possibly less than 10% of all business roles
4. ADI	Artificial Dependable Intelligence (More than halfway to AGI)	- Possibly less than 25% of all jobs
5. AEI	Artificial Enhanced Intelligence (Three-Quarters to AGI)	- Probably less than 50% of available jobs
6. AFI	Artificial False-Truth Intelligence (Most of the way to AGI)	- Probably less than 75% of available jobs
7. AGI	Artificial General Intelligence	- Level-2 Adoption becomes possible for 100% of available jobs - AI Begins Self-Innovating to ASI
8. AHI	Artificial Human-Level Intelligence (110% of passing AGI)	- AI Gains Consciousness

Note: Numbers are just an illustration of a suggestion, not actual or projected value

[Side Note] Explanation of the Six Levels of AI before AGI

To ease understanding and reduce the confusion regarding how AGI should be defined, additional categories of AI from the user perspective around AGI were introduced in The Last AI, the Six Levels of Pre-AGI AI. Categorizing the sophistication of AI before AGI would be helpful for non-experts to be able to have a sense of the level of sophistication or potential amount of application. For ease of understanding, an alphabetical naming scheme was used.

(Reference Point) AGI: "The Point of Self-Innovation towards ASI." In this framework, the definition of AGI was "Self-Innovating AGI" or "AI that can without human intervention self-innovate to reach singularity." The reference point of "automated self-innovation" emphasizes the significance of AI developing more advanced AI, since humans will no longer have to develop more AI.[20] From a user standpoint, this inflection point may have more significance than "Singularity," which would be just another point in the path of AI development that happens to surpass all of humanity in comparison.

(AI before Self-Innovation) Categorization Prior to AGI: AI that comes prior to AGI would include all types of AI that would not be able to self-innovate to become ASI. As a group, AAI, ABI and ACI would be categorized as what most people think of as narrow AI, or ANI. Some people may consider ADI, AEI and AFI to be within the realm of AGI, while other people would consider them outside the boundaries of AGI.

1. AAI (ABCs of AI): The level of AI when the researchers first conceived the idea of AI. These may include the basic types of machine learning algorithms, as well as the basic principles of AI that do not have specific applications.

2. ABI (Artificial Basic Intelligence): More advanced versions of AAI with specific intended uses, such as image creation or image recognition.

3. ACI (Artificial Classic Intelligence): Types of AI that people will not think of as AGI but still may have general uses, having similar characteristics of the earliest versions of multi-modal AI and even the ability to reason.[21]

4. ADI (Artificial Dependable Intelligence): Would rarely be considered AGI and may be viewed to exhibit AGI-like capabilities in very limited aspects. Most people would not confuse it with AGI and assign limited responsibilities and monitor its activities more closely, leading to less potential problems. ADI may be similar to letting a child in kindergarten learn how to ride a bike on two wheels for the first time; not having a constant adult supervision may cause uneasiness. People using ADI would be prepared for shortcomings just like how we do not allow kindergarteners to carry out important tasks.

5. AEI (Artificial Enhanced Intelligence): If ADI is developed with a focus on completing given tasks more dependably, AEI may be considered to have been developed with a focus on gaining new capabilities outside of its original intended use through reasoning. People would still be cautious about using it in important tasks. Using an AEI would be similar to letting an elementary school child riding around the neighborhood in a bike; even though we would not be as anxious about not looking over constantly, we would still not feel comfortable if we were to let the child carry out more important tasks such as driving a car. The concept of "automated innovation" may be carried out on a limited basis beginning in this level.

6. AFI (False-Truth AI): Would refer to the types of AI that can apply some knowledge into different contexts, but not as well as what people would normally expect. It may be compared to children or someone with very stubborn mind. Some people may confuse AFI with AGI to assign important tasks, only to face significant problems. Still, limiting AFI to less important tasks may feel overly restrictive, similar to letting a high school teenager with a driver's license to only ride around in a bike with training wheels. People using AFI may ask it to carry out tasks beyond its capabilities, similar to a college freshman being asked to deliver like an expert in the field.

(After Point of Self-Innovation) Categories between AGI and ASI, AHI:
There may be categories of AGI after reaching the Point of Self-Innovation, but before reaching singularity and becoming an ASI. For some, the most natural image of AGI would be an AI with "consciousness," as these types of AI would be the closest to humans and also what we would expect to see in the movies. We may assign it as a separate category as AHI, or artificial human-level intelligence. Alternatively, we may refer to it as AGI 2. Because we do not know whether Self-Innovating AGI will first require gaining consciousness, so this is just a proposed category. However, consciousness may not be a necessary ingredient for self-innovation, so AHI may be considered as a type of AI that may come after reaching AGI. AHI would be developed by AI, not humans. As AI development continues to progress to reach ASI, we may consider more categories, or the 6 Levels of AGI as described in The Last AI.

To make it more streamlined and easier to grasp, we may even use numbers to designate AI levels as AI 1, AI 2, AI 3, AI 4, AI 5, etc.

3. The AGI Consciousness Controversy

[Forecast]

Will AGI have consciousness?

[Decision]

Should AI have consciousness before we consider it to be AGI?

"I'm Johnny No. 5, I'm Alive!"

- From movie Short Circuit

5-Line Summary

1. Some people may argue a meaningful milestone for AGI would be AI having consciousness
2. People may have different opinions on what consciousness means
3. Some may think that of animals with varying levels of intelligence, some should have consciousness, such as having a sense of self
4. Some may think that what is expressed to the outside world matters more, and having consciousness in itself is irrelevant
5. The 6 Levels of AI Consciousness framework is introduced to help think about AI as either having or simulating consciousness

What is Consciousness?

If someone believes we need to define AGI as having consciousness, then we would need to first define what consciousness is. This question has probably piqued the interests of philosophers for a long time. This is reflected in the famous quote by Descartes "I think, therefore I am." But, do all humans have consciousness? Because each of us is only one person, we cannot know for sure if everyone else is conscious even if we believe each of us is. There are even studies that show people think differently, that not everyone has inner dialogue or can think in terms of visual imagery or have too much of it.[22]

To simplify this analysis, let us first assume that humans have consciousness. Then, we may try to figure out if anything else in the world has consciousness; we may consider other animals. From nature, we can categorize different levels of intelligence among living things. For example, we may differentiate how living things of less intelligence, such as fish or insects, show some intelligence, such as being able to tell its prey from visual cues, making some sort of plans to get what it wants, tell what is danger for itself, etc. Then we can also differentiate how animals with comparably high intelligence, such as dogs or cows that can understand some words and human directions, or have situational awareness, etc. It is reported some animals can tell themselves in the mirror, which may be a sign of having consciousness.

Primates, such as monkeys, orangutans and gorillas, have been observed to show the ability to understand more complex contexts. Some research even show primates may have a sense of self; readers may have seen a viral clip[23] where two monkeys are placed side by side to observe each other and asked to carry out a simple task of giving a coin to the researcher. In return, the researcher will always give a tasty reward, such as a grape, to the monkey on the right, but will always give a less tasty reward, such as a small piece of cucumber, to the monkey on the left. As the monkey on the left observes the other monkey is consistently getting more tasty reward, it becomes agitated, and eventually throws the cucumber at the researcher in protest.

Is this enough of an evidence to consider monkeys to have "consciousness?" Or should there be something even more advanced? For example, if humans were the subjects instead of monkeys in this experiment, then maybe the human on the right cage may observe the sadness of the other person and feel apathetic, offering to give his or her own grape or offering to exchange the coin for the other person so that they can get a grape instead of a cucumber. Maybe showing this understanding of others' feelings may be what should determine "consciousness." We may go on and on with this topic.

How Can we Differentiate Levels of Consciousness for Animals?

Some people are reported to be "do not care for others," "selfish," "unable to feel sympathy." There are even people who are considered "psychopaths," or otherwise lacking some attribute of what everyone should possess. Should these people who cannot understand the perspectives of others be considered having less "consciousness?" In other words, can we measure different levels of consciousness by measuring how conscious we are of ourselves or of other people? From this line of thought, we may consider the following framework on self-awareness for living organisms, similar to how we categorize self-driving cars, the Six Levels of Consciousness from Internal Awareness of Self and Others. It may also be presented as a pyramid.

Level 0 (No Self-Awareness): We may think of planktons or other life forms that do not understand danger. We may also think of being unconscious.

Level 1 (Implicit Self-Aware): Animals that try to survive and reproduce

Level 2 (Explicit Self-Aware): Exhibit self-awareness in its actions. Example may include dogs or cows that recognize themselves in mirror.

Level 3 (Implicit Others-Aware): Can compare its situation to others, which may be referred to as "Self-Reflection." Still may lack empathy for others.

Level 4 (Limited Explicit Others-Aware): Can use self-reflection on others to show a sense of empathy for the situation of others it understands. This may also be thought of as understanding others' feelings, or the Theory of Mind.[24] Examples may include humans who help others in need, or if the other monkey shared the grape, etc.

Level 5 (Unlimited Explicit Others-Aware): Can understand everyone's situations at all times. This may be beyond human capability since we all have 1st-person perspective, but some religions may describe this as a power of god.

Table 3-1: The Six Levels of Consciousness from Internal Awareness of Self

Conscious	**Level 0**	**Level 1**	**Level 2**	**Level 3**	**Level 4**	**Level 5**
Name	Not Self-Aware	Implicit Self-Aware	Explicit Self-Aware	Implicit Others-Aware	Limited Explicit Other-Aware	Unlimited Explicit Others-Aware
Description	-	Try to survive	Recognize themselves in the mirror	Compare its situation to others	Empathy for situation of others	Understand Everyone's situation at all times
Summary	Based on Awareness of Self			Based on Awareness of Others		

How Can we Differentiate Levels of Consciousness for AI?

We may now apply this question to AI. Can AI have consciousness? Can consciousness be simulated? Is having consciousness even an important aspect of AI? From a business perspective, "self-initiation" of AI would be more important than "self-consciousness" for AI adoption. Yet, some may wonder if we can differentiate levels of consciousness just by observing AI, even if it may be just a simulated form of "consciousness" for AI, whatever this means.

What if more advanced AI turns out to not have self, but some sort of more generalized being? i.e., "consciousness" is not the highest form of being, but something even higher exists, but humans do not have it, such that AI will be more advanced than humans? We sometimes say something like "look from the perspective of other people" but what if doing this constantly is a form of higher being than looking from your own perspective, and humans can only do it part of the time in a limited way? In movies, this is referred to as looking from the third-person perspective as opposed to the first-person perspective. Some people may ascribe this type of being as a characteristic of god, as this is also referred to as "all-knowing" or looking from the god's perspective.

From this line of thinking, we may derive an alternate categorization where external observation can determine the levels. Without examining whether AI is self-conscious or not, we may categorize how it simulates consciousness by observing how AI interact with the environment. The Six Levels of Observed Consciousness from External Interaction is presented below:

Level 0 (Inept): Inept to the environment, or does not interact with the environment. No AI.

Level 1 (Unidirectional): AI can only function in a pre-defined manner. Examples would include unidirectional or one-dimensional interactions, such as an AI umpire that can only call balls and strikes.

Level 2 (Bidirectional): AI can acknowledge others and provide feedback. Examples may include LLMs that can interact with users back and forth.

Level 3 (Limited Prediction): Examples would include AI predicting how objects in its environment will move without understanding why; such as in self-driving cars that is able to recognize and predict that things around it may move in a certain way, but without understanding the reason. For LLMs it may say "Many people buy this product" or responses of similar nature.

Level 4 (Understand Others' Intentions - Limited): AI understanding why objects in its environment will act or think in a certain way to make its predictions. Some may describe this as AI having a world model. Examples may include a higher-level self-driving car that may understand why the objects around it will move such that it will make more tailored predictions and actions. Yet, this will be limited for people it interacts with. For LLMs it may be taking the initiative to "I think you should ask this question" or other interactions of similar nature. Some people may consider this level AGI.

Level 5 (Unlimited Awareness of Other's Intentions): AI being aware of others' thoughts or intentions in an explicit and unlimited manner. Be able to classify others, understand self or how self is in relation to outside. This may appear to be all-knowing to humans, as it would look similar to reading minds. Examples may include AI being able to understand the world in a more complete sense than humans. This may imply AI would be able to predict the future and the past in more detail than we can imagine. Some may consider this level to be ASI.

Table 3-2: The Six Levels of Consciousness from External Interaction

Conscious	Level 0	Level 1	Level 2	Level 3	Level 4	Level 5
Name	Inept or No Interaction	Uni-Directional	Bi-Directional	Limited Prediction	Understand Intentions	Unlimited Awareness of Intentions
Description		Interact only in pre-defined manner	Acknow-ledge others	Statistic or Simple prediction	Understand Intentions in Predicting	Predict and Understand Everyone's Intentions
Summary	AI Responds to Its Environment			AI Predicts Its Environment		

We can apply this framework to classify AI use in a variety of purposes. While AI in External Consciousness Levels 1 to 3 has already been deployed in Level 1 Adoption, once we reach AI that has Level 4 External Consciousness, we would be able to have a widespread Level 2 Adoption, where AI can replace human jobs and interact with us as if it "understands" us. AI in Level 4 External Consciousness would also have the ability to strategically plan its actions, which may prove highly useful in business or military applications.

4. The AGI Development Method Controversy

[Forecast]

How Can We Develop AGI?

"Race Start"

- Suk-Jin Ji, from TV show Running Man

5-Line Summary

1. AI may be thought of as a combination of software and hardware
2. Some may argue we can reach AGI by just scaling hardware
3. Some may argue we can only reach AGI my developing new algorithm
4. People with different definitions of AGI may have different opinions regarding the development methods of AGI as well
5. The concept of the "Core of AGI" is introduced to help people think about how different versions of AGI may be reached

The Two General Approaches to Developing AI

Since this book assumes the readers do not have technical background in AI, we may start with the most basic idea; broadly speaking, there are two approaches to developing AI: "Symbolism" and "Connectionist." Symbolism refers to the "symbols" that we think of when we think in our minds, while connectionist refers to how neurons are "connected" to each other.[25]

Symbolism: Computer will gain intelligence if knowledge is modeled and taught
Connectionist: Computer will gain intelligence if neurons are modeled and knowledge is learned

In Symbolism, humans create and input the model of knowledge into the computer, while in Connectionist approach computer "learns" of some knowledge from the relationship between inputs and outputs of data.

Symbolism: Knowledge Expressed in Symbols Will Lead to Intelligence

In Symbolism, computers mimic how people think by using symbols to "understand" the relationships between concepts. For example, if we ask "what are fried egg and a boiled egg?" the computer may answer:

Fried Egg = (Egg ÷ break - Shell) x heat @ Frying Pan + Salt → ^Platter
Boiled Egg = (Egg) x heat @ (Pot + Water) → (hardened ÷ break - Shell) ^Bowl

Since ideas such as "Egg" and "heat @" are shared, the computer may surmise a fried egg is more similar to a boiled egg than other types of cold food such as vegetable salad. While Symbolism offers the benefit of being more understandable, the computer cannot learn by itself and is dependent on humans to input the knowledge, which is expensive and limited.

Connectionist: Modeling Human Neurons Will Lead to Intelligence

Connectionist approach seeks to duplicate how neurons work in our brains. It dates back to 1958 to a concept called Perceptron,[26] which works by combining several inputs to lead to an output through a type of black box called "node," which we can think of as the digital version of neurons in our brains. Subsequently, machine learning and deep learning were developed by applying this concept. Each neuron is responsible for part of knowledge smaller than symbols, so it is also known as Sub-Symbolic approach; it is hard to decipher how AI reaches its conclusions. Symbolism approaches received more interest at first, but today's AI mostly use connectionist approaches. The limitations of connectionist AI have led to the argument of combining the two methods to enhance the explainability of AI, known as XAI.

What is the Best Way to Develop Advanced AI?

One of the technical controversies includes how we will get to AGI or similar advanced AI. Opinions among people developing AI have varying spectrum.

There have been suggestions that we need to pay attention to how humans reason and think. First, we may categorize human thinking into two groups as suggested by Daniel Kahneman,[27] where in System 1, or Fast Thinking, operates automatically and quickly, and in System 2, or Slow Thinking, needs more attention and deliberation. Earlier LLMs share similarity with System 1, while more recent projects attempt to also incorporate the characteristics of the System 2. Second, another characteristic may be how humans can learn new knowledge and apply it into unrelated areas; Energy-Based Models[28] (EBM) and diffusion-based transformer[29] SORA are examples of attempts to create more abstract layers to help AI move closer to applying knowledge to other areas. Efforts to develop LLMs with reasoning capabilities have received attention, as reinforcement learning mixed with other approaches may enable AI to reason to solve complex problems; this along with open-sourcing of DeepSeek R1 received media attention as people could see the thought processes of LLMs for the first time. More researchers have also expanded the focus to the physical aspects of AI as well.

How Can We Make AI More Similar to the Human Brain?

While trying to major in cognitive science in college, readings in a required course included The Man Who Mistook His Wife for a Hat[30], which describes how partial brain damage leads people to behave in strange ways. If we think of LLMs as representing a part of brain's activities that are related to language, then we may arrive at AGI by building parts that correspond to other areas such as audio and visual cortex, areas for planning and logic, etc.

We may line up some opinions in the order of requiring more breakthroughs
- AGI can be developed from today's LLMs; Scaling will work until AGI
- AGI can be developed by connecting together multiple methods
- AGI can be developed by combining symbolic approach in Explainable AI
- AGI can be developed by some yet unknown training method
- AGI will have to have physical components
- It will not be possible to develop AGI

We may categorize these notions into the following controversy matrix.

Table 4-1: [Forecast] The AGI Development Method Controversy Matrix

		Need Breakthrough in Software?	
		No (Optimists)	**Yes (Pessimists)**
Need Breakthrough in Hardware?	**No (Optimists)**	**Type 1 Outlook** (AGI Optimists)	**Type 2 Outlook** (Hardware Optimists)
	Yes (Pessimists)	**Type 3 Outlook** (Algorithm Optimists)	**Type 4 Outlook** (AGI Pessimists)

Type 1 (AGI Optimists): We already have the technology required to develop AGI. Just need to develop it using the relevant investments to gather data and build enough scale in hardware.

Type 2 (Hardware Optimists, Software Pessimists): We already have what is required to develop AGI in terms of hardware. We just need to develop the right algorithm to get to AGI.

Type 3 (Algorithm Optimists, Hardware Pessimists): We already have the algorithm to develop AGI, but do not have the correct kind of hardware to develop AGI.

Type 4 (AGI Pessimists): We need breakthroughs in both areas to get to AGI. Some people in this category may even argue that it would be impossible to develop AGI.

[Side Note] Thinking About the "Core" or the "Gist" of AGI

Instead of examining the path towards AGI, we may consider a thought that comes backwards from AGI. First, let us start with assumptions regarding AGI.

1. We can agree what AGI means
2. It will be possible to create something that we will think of as AGI

In other words, let us assume that it will be possible to define what AGI is and that it is achievable. For the sake of simplicity, let us also assume that AGI will be a type of artificial neural network that we can create using hardware we can build someday. Then we may think of reaching AGI in the following way.

First, there is no reason for only the whole neural network to be considered AGI. For example, it may be possible that AGI could be a part of a larger neural network. We may refer to this as the "AGI core" or the "gist" of AGI in a neural network. Suppose we develop a very large neural network named "A1" that turns out to be an AGI, then it would be conceivable that a subset of this neural network, which we may refer to as "Core-a1", to be the gist of AGI, such that any neural network that has this Core-a1 in it will be AGI. For example, neural networks "A1-2" or "A1-3" that are a little bit different from A1 but still have the Core-a1 in it would be AGI.

At the same time, it would be conceivable that the Core-a1 is not the only neural network that can be AGI. We may think that there would be different neural networks that turn out to be AGI, which may be referred to as Core-b1, Core-c1, Core-d1, etc. Similar to Core-a1 and A1, any neural network that has one of these other AGI cores would be considered AGI, such that there would be even more possibility for AGI, such as B1, B2, C1, C2, D1, D2, and so on.

Once we have at least one of these AGI cores, then the AGI may lead us to more cores that will be AGI. Because we do not know what Core-a1, Core-b1, Core-c1 will be, our only hope right now may be randomly arriving at one of these AGI cores. If we build large enough neural network, then it may be possible we may be more likely to arrive at AGI cores randomly. There are two main reasons to think this way:

1. There may be a **minimum size** of neural network for an AGI core, and since we do not know that size, larger models have a higher probability of surpassing it
2. Since larger models would have a wider variety, or a larger number of subsets, it is just **statistically more likely** that an AGI core such as Core-a1 would happen to exist in a larger model, similar to hidden words in word puzzles

To summarize, apart from larger LLMs performing better, there is another benefit of larger neural networks that increases potential for reaching AGI: There is possibility that we may arrive at AGI by chance because larger models may be more likely to have a subset that turns out to be AGI.

5. The AI Data Controversy

[Forecast]

How Much or What Kind of Data Is Needed to Reach AGI?

"The More, the Merrier"

- English Proverb (Quantity of Data)

"The Earth Still Churns"

- Galileo Galilei[31] (Quality of Data)

5-Line Summary

1. (Quantity) Some may argue we need to have more amount of data to develop AGI
2. (Quality) Some may argue we need to have different types of data or better data to develop AGI
3. Some may argue we already have enough data to develop AGI
4. Some may argue AI can just generate new data so we do not need more data after a certain point
5. Whether AI can discern the truth in data would become important, in what may be called reaching "data abundance"

How Much and What Types of Data Will Be Needed to Reach AGI?

We may think of the controversy regarding data in from different angles. First, how much data will be necessary to reach AGI? Second, what kind of data is needed to reach AGI? How will AGI use such data? Why would AGI need so much data?

Quantitative Perspective: How Much Data?

Some may argue the amount of data we have is limited, and it may not be enough to train AI to a level we want. The larger LLMs get, the larger amount of data is needed to train it well, and we may be running out of quality data. This is also leading to the controversies on using copyrighted data to train AI.

Qualitative Perspective: What Types of Data?

Types of Data: In terms of the type of data necessary to reach AGI, we may think of LLMs, which started out using text data and is now evolving into more general world models, or GWMs. An opposite approach may be not using language at all, but using visual data of the physical world, such as cars and humanoid robots, and hoping AI will develop intelligence in some fashion. From thinking about how humans think, both approaches make sense. People think with languages as well as visual imagery.[32]

Higher-Quality Data: From the qualitative side, there is also the discussion on how the data gathered could be of higher quality. For example, a scientific paper would be considered a higher quality data than a science homework turned in by a middle school student. This leads to the discussion on whether AI-generated, or synthetic, data will be sufficient.

The following table categorizes some of the potential contrasting opinions:

Table 5-1: The AI Data Matrix

		Quantitative (Technological Perspective)	
		Do Not Need More	**Need More**
Qualitative (Social Perspective)	**Do Not Need Better**	**Satisfied Developers** (Profile 1)	**Hungry Developers** (Profile 2)
	Need Better	**Picky Developers** (Profile 3)	**Insatiable Developers** (Profile 4)

Synthetic Data: Readers may have read in the news that we may "run out" of good data, and that artificial data are used for training. Even businesses that specialize in supplying data are proliferating.

Self-improvement of AI: In some way this can also be thought of as using synthetic data. The difference may be that the quality of data could be much higher than human-generated data. We may think of the quality of AI-generated date to be diverging, such that the synthetic data of below certain quality will lead AI to decrease in capabilities, while synthetic data of above certain quality will lead AI to become ASI.

AI Discerning Data Quality: We may think of how people of less intelligence may be more easily swayed by fake news, or by people around them who argue for the wrong things. A famous example of this would be the idea of the earth rotating around the sun, which was a minority belief when Galilei argued for it. Similarly, less advanced AI may be easily swayed by the amount rather than quality, such that wrong information may be taken as more important if it is included more often in the training data. From this, we can surmise that whether AI can discern the truth of data is an important attribute.

Competition of Data Types: We may even think of this as a competition of different approaches of data types. A well-known example of the controversy regarding the types of data may be described by the differences of LLMs and autonomous cars. Companies such as OpenAI focused on languages with LLMs, while robotics-oriented firms such as Tesla focused on visual data used to operate AI robots or autonomous vehicles.

Street Smart vs Book Smart: We may think of AGI trained with higher quality or more amounts of data to become more "book smart," while there may be some form of algorithmic difference that could lead to AGI with different levels of "street smarts" by making better use of available data, or no data.

The Pattern of Data Importance: Go Up then Down

To summarize, the importance of data may initially increase as we try to figure out how to reach AGI. Eventually, as AI advances towards or beyond AGI, the importance of data may decrease, as AI would be able to generate own synthetic data to increase the quantity and then discern the quality by itself to raise the overall quality of synthetic data.

In short, this process may be thought of as reaching "data abundance."

6. The Time to AGI Controversy

[Forecast]

When will we reach AGI?

"Are We There Yet?"

- Kids Riding in the Back Seats on Vacations[33]

5-Line Summary

1. Some may consider AGI the next step in AI progress, that is happening quite soon
2. Some may consider AGI the last step in AI progress, that is outside of their planning horizon
3. For some people, AGI may look like a mirage or a moving target, that is never happening
4. People with these different outlook will not be able to agree on how to plan for AI
5. How to plan for AGI in business based on the 3 Levels of AI Adoption framework is introduced; an example is the OpenAI's 5 Stages of AI

The Problem of Not Being Able to Judge How Far AGI Is

One day while writing this book, I was on a walk and spotted smoke looming above the area I lived, maybe half a mile away. At first, I was worried our house was on fire. But as I ran closer, the smoke got farther and farther away. Curious where the fire was, I ventured toward the fire. Helicopters flew by. After another mile of walking, it felt I was still about as close to the fire as when I originally started. Turns out it is hard to guess these types of distances.

Similarly, it may be hard to judge how far AGI is, because we may not have a good idea of how to look at it, or have a good depth perception. Judging how far AGI may be compared to the mirage in a desert, or how the sun feels like it is following us when we drive. Some people may claim it is days away. Others may claim it is decades away, or even claim it will never happen.

In business, not knowing how far AGI is may cause significant differences of opinions regarding how to prepare for it. For some people, AGI is taken as the next step in AI development, something they should plan for in the short-to-medium horizon. For others, AGI is taken as the last step in AI development, something they do not need to plan for except for the longest horizon.[34] This may create unnecessary confusion even within firms, as some people may make decisions based on the assumption that AGI is near, like within a few years, while others may even argue AGI should be ignored.

By considering how far away and how important AGI is, we may derive the following matrix.

Table 6-1: The Time to AGI Matrix

		Quantitative (Technological Perspective)	
		Next Step in AI	**Last Step in AI**
Qualitative (Social Perspective)	**AGI Important**	**AGI Enthusiasts** (Profile 1) "Why are we still not there yet?"	**AGI Ignorers** (Profile 3) "AGI is outside of our planning horizon"
	AGI Not Important or Not Reachable	**AGI Downplayers** (Profile 2) "What is the next big thing after AGI?"	**AGI Deniers** (Profile 4) "AGI is not happening"

[Side Note] Applying the 3 Levels of AI Adoption (OpenAI's 5 Stages of AI)
Using the Three Levels of AI Adoption framework explained in the beginning part of this book, companies may be able to develop their own roadmap of AI development to better communicate their view regarding the progress of AI without emphasizing AGI. Probably the best known application of this framework is OpenAI's 5 Stages of AI roadmap, an internally used framework reported by the media in July 2024.[35] According to news reports, it consists of the following:

- Level 1 Stage AI **(Chatbots)**: AI with conversational language
- Level 2 Stage AI **(Reasoners)**: Human-level problem solving
- Level 3 Stage AI **(Agents)**: Systems that can take actions
- Level 4 Stage AI **(Innovators)**: AI that can aid in invention
- Level 5 Stage AI **(Organizations)**: AI that can do the work of an organization

We will review how the Three Levels of AI Adoption framework can be used to help develop new frameworks to satisfy both customers and internal staff.

From a technological perspective, a milestone for AI development would be AI reaching *capabilities* that are similar to humans, or AGI. Meanwhile, from a business perspective, a more meaningful milestone would be when an AI system or robot can completely *replace* what a human worker does at a company. We can call this milestone "AI equalization." For example, a company will have different jobs filled by different people; if an AI advances to a point where it can fill one of those jobs in place of a human, we can consider AI to have reached equalization for that particular job.

Because our jobs have different levels of sophistication, AI equalization will occur earlier than AGI, even though AI adoption lags behind AI technology.

When you consider all these factors, that 1) we do not know how far AGI is and people are confused about what to think of it, 2) AI equalization can be achieved before AGI, and 3) while whether we reached AGI will be declared by AI developers but AI equalization will be declared by AI users, we will be able to create a roadmap that incorporates more meaningful points of inflections for users of AI. The following passage shows how OpenAI's 5 Stages of AI may be derived from the Three Levels of AI Adoption framework, to show as an example for other AI development firms to help them think about their own agenda or customized framework.

The Different Perspectives of Three Types of Stakeholders

We may consider the different perspectives of stakeholders, namely the AI scientists who develop AI, AI development firms that organize and manage these AI scientists, and AI users who use the resulting AI products in their businesses or other uses. In defining the future development paths of AI, the needs of AI scientists, AI development firms, and business AI users would be all different.

(Business vs Technical Perspectives) Need to Move Away from AGI

The most widely used ANI-AGI-ASI framework is a technological framework where the capability of AI is the dividing factor. This suits the needs of AI scientists just fine. However, there are two problems for using this framework for AI development firms. First, the definition of AGI is up for discussion, which may lead to confusion at the organizational level since different members of the firm may not share the same idea of the AGI. Second, the definition is not tied to a business-specific milestone, making it harder for AI development firms to conceptualize and set their goals relevant to their customers. A good example of this problem is how OpenAI had defined AGI. Previously, OpenAI had to define AGI in a vague manner using economic terms, as outperforming humans "at most economically valuable work," which could be taken to mean different things for different people.

From the perspectives of AI users, the 3 Levels of AI Adoption framework will suit their needs better than the AGI framework. It will more clearly show how AI adoption will progress and how our societies will change accordingly. Since whether reaching Level 2 Adoption will be determined by the user, it gives business managers more control over the milestone. On a side note, from the user perspective, the two enablers of the next levels would be perceived as supplementary information, since it may be seen as a "black box." The emphasis would be on reaching the next levels of AI adoption.

(Developer Firm Perspective) Satisfying Internal and External Stakeholders

From the perspective of AI developers, however, the emphasis may have to be different from users, since they are the suppliers of the "black boxes." The requirements of the Enablers to reach the next levels would have to be more clearly defined. The AGI framework is not specific enough to provide a shared common goal in near-term product development. At the same time, it confuses and disappoints users in terms of expectations for the next product introduction. In this sense, AI developers will have to satisfy the needs of both the AI scientists – its personnel, and the AI users – its customers. First, it will have to be able to provide its personnel with a highly specific vision for the next steps in its roadmap. At the same time, it will have to show its customers what is coming from the company to manage expectations.

Applying the 3 Levels of AI Adoption to Reflect Development Milestones
With the understanding of this need to satisfy both sides, we may consider how we could apply the 3 Levels of AI Adoption framework, which caters to AI users, to also satisfy the internal stakeholders of AI development firms. The answer may be to re-emphasize the two Enablers, as it will show how we can derive the OpenAI's 5 Stages model.

First, for Enabler 1, we may think of the technological breakthrough that would make AI more dependable in carrying out its assignments. For OpenAI, they may have concluded the ability to reason as the main capability necessary to reach Level 2 AI Adoption.

Second, for Enabler 2, we may think of the technological breakthrough that would enable the *real* Level 5 Autonomous Companies from the Six Levels of Autonomous Companies framework[36] as described in The Last AI, which would be for AI to carry out "automated innovation."

Since AI developers would view the enablers as important milestones in their activities, the framework more relevant for AI developers would also emphasize the enablers. From this viewpoint, we may re-draw the framework with corresponding stages to reach what was presented by OpenAI to its internal personnel, as shown in Figure 6-1.

Figure 6-1: Deriving OpenAI's 5 Stages of AI from the 3 Levels of AI Adoption

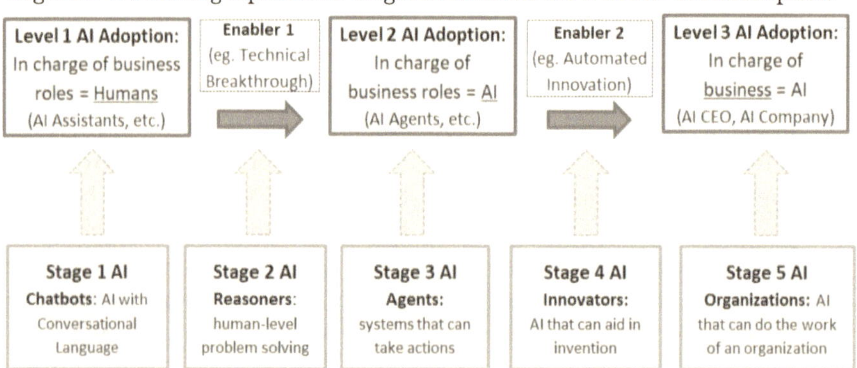

7. The Race to AGI Controversy

[Forecast]

Who Will Reach AGI First?

= Which Company Will Develop AGI First?

= Which Country Will Develop AGI First?

"What Does It Take To Be Number 1?"

- Nelly, in song No. 1

5-Line Summary

1. Some may think an AI developer focusing on AI algorithm would develop AGI first
2. Some may think companies that focus on hardware will be able to achieve AGI first
3. Some may think a company that has capabilities in both software and hardware will have the upper hand
4. Another topic of interest is which country will reach AGI first; some may think planned economies will have the advantage
5. Others may think countries with free markets will reach AGI first

Which Company Will Develop AGI First?

If we think of AGI as a breakthrough that may make the single largest impact in history, it is no wonder people would be racing towards developing AGI first by pouring billions if not trillions of dollars. What would attract the most interest would be who will develop AGI first. We may frame "who" as three types of entities: individual researcher, an AI development company, or a country or a regime that hosts such company. Let us first think about which company may get there first.

Reaching AGI as a Competition

We may think of reaching AGI as a competition. From this perspective, we may think about what this competition would be about:

1. Competition of Novel Approaches (Algorithms, etc.): Some may argue an AI company that can design software better than others would win this race; having novel algorithms may matter the most. Some others may argue a chip manufacturer that can bring a breakthrough innovation in hardware better than others would win the race.

2. Competition of Resources: Some may argue capital is the most important factor, to pay for data, electricity, buy hardware, etc. Management-based approach would see how the top management is handling its talents or assigning its resources to relevant projects. Acquiring the largest computing power may be considered a prime factor in this race.

3. Competition of Resource Combinations: We may think of developing AI as combining software, hardware, and data. Every AI developer will need all three factors. There may be a "right" formula to find the balance or mix these factors that may help one company get to AGI before others.

Contrasting Ideas Based on Perception of Distance to AGI

Opinion on how far away we are from AGI may affect how we view this race. If one believes we already have everything necessary to develop AGI, then all we need would be to gather data and wait for more chips to be deployed to train a larger AI. For people who believe in this this line of thought, investing in AGI may mean investing in data, scale, or both. These people would be likely to believe AGI is just around the corner. On the other hand, if someone believes we are quite far from AGI then instead companies that can manage resources well over the long-term may be viewed as having an advantage.

Which Country Will Develop AGI First? (Concentrate or Diversify?)

Which Regime will AI be Developed Faster?

Different countries may take opposite approaches to developing AGI, whether to concentrate all the resources into one effort, or diversify resources to have more competition. If we consider the country to reach AGI first would likely to continue to have an advantage over other countries, then the outcome of the different approaches may matter.

Concentration of Resources: Economy of Scale

If the determining factor in developing more advanced AI happens to be the amount of resources that could be concentrated, then a regime with more concentrated power may gain an advantage. There are suggestions we may be able to predict the performance of AI by its size.[37] We do not yet know which approach would be more effective, so only time will tell us.

Diversify Approaches: Market Competition

In general, we think of the market economy as conducive to competition, which will also spur innovation, whereas the communist economy is thought of as rigid and inefficient. From this point of view, it may be natural that we may expect a free market economy will develop AI faster.

However, the advantages of competition in free markets may not hold as AI adoption progresses. Beginning in Level 2 Adoption, the narrative may begin to change as AI takes more proportion of innovation and competition in the economy. In essence, the competition may become between the AI of the countries, not between the human workers of the countries. Since whether the people in the country is being oppressed or free, or whether they are poor or rich may not be as relevant for AI to compete, it may become more and more about the resources that could be deployed for developing the AI. This suggests that if AGI is not close, it would be harder to guess which country will get to AGI first.

8. The AI Open-Source Controversy

[Forecast]

Will Open-Source Lead to Faster or Safer AI Development?

[Decision]

Should We Open-Source or Close-Source AI Algorithm?

"The 1 vs 100 of AI"[38]

5-Line Summary

1. Some may argue that AI development should be open-sourced to accelerate development, make it safer, and benefit the economy
2. Some may argue that keeping AI development proprietary would accelerate development, make it safer, and benefit the economy
3. Open-source and Open-weights are distinct; open-weights do not share how the weights are obtained, making it harder to verify safety
4. Different people or companies will have opposing preferences, depending on their market positions, resources, or goals, etc.
5. Can Open-Weights LLMs be used as propaganda machines?

Open-Source vs Open-Weights

It may be helpful to first examine the different ways "open-source" is used. Traditionally in the software industry, it is used for situations where the codes of the programs are open to the public. In other words, anyone in the public can look at the codes and even try to change the codes to test their own ideas.

In regards to LLMs, a strict application of this concept would only apply to situations where the codes to create the LLMs are made public. However, this is not the typical method LLMs referred to as "open-source" today are made public. The public would only have access to the weights of the LLMs, which can be downloaded and run on their own hardware. Because the public still cannot know how the weights are derived, we cannot test out new ideas to change how the LLMs are built. They may still try to build on top of the base models, in what is referred to as fine-tuning. While this mode of sharing with the public still offers some value, if we are to be strict with how we use the term open-source, then this would be referred to as "Open-Weights."

Open-Source vs Proprietary Development

From the perspective of developers, we may compare the pros and cons of open-source and proprietary development. Depending on situation, one may be preferred over the other. We may examine a few potential situations

(Forecast 1) Which Will Speed Up Development?

First controversy is regarding which path will lead to faster AI development. Some may argue Open-Source will attract more developers, while others may argue closed-source will lead to higher profits which will ensure relevant financial investments. Some may argue close-source will stifle innovation because secrets have to be kept in-house. Some may argue open-source does not reward innovation because people cannot be paid for their work.

Which will accelerate AI development? Some may argue sharing the progress will make AI development go faster, while others may argue this will reduce profit for the AI developers, reducing the incentive to invest in AI. This may be similar to the discussions that went on around Linux, which is open-source, versus other operating systems, such as Windows, Apple OS, etc. Some may argue that open-source would be advantageous when required investments are small, while closed-source may have advantages when investments are larger and need more coordination. Since we do not know how large AI development needs to be, this would be up for discussions among people who try different strategies.

They may argue this will drive down the price and the cost of development for everyone else as well, while proprietary development may keep the prices arbitrarily high and concentrate the profits to a few firms.

(Forecast 2) Which Will Be Safer for Our Society?
Which path would be safer for everyone? Some may argue opening the developments will be safer since more people can scrutinize it. In addition, proprietary may be more risky for our society, as it may put too much power in the hands of a few. Others may be suspicious of the intentions of the corporations or governments that fund these large-scale proprietary efforts.

On the other hand, others may prefer proprietary development. They may be concerned that this is like opening to the public for abuse something we do not know well, similar to letting people open the Pandora's Box. The criminals could access the latest technology without supervision or restriction.

We can create the following matrix to describe how people may argue either path to be faster or safer.

Table 8-1: Open-Source Decision Matrix for Speed and Safety

<table>
<tr><th colspan="2" rowspan="2"></th><th colspan="2">Which Will Be Faster
(Technological Perspective)</th></tr>
<tr><th>Open Source</th><th>Closed Source</th></tr>
<tr><td rowspan="2">Which Will Be Safer (Social Perspective)</td><td>Open Source</td><td>Opinion Type 1
(Prefer Open Source)</td><td>Opinion Type 3
(Depends on Tradeoff)</td></tr>
<tr><td>Closed Source</td><td>Opinion Type 2
(Depends on Tradeoff)</td><td>Opinion Type 4
(Prefer Closed Source)</td></tr>
</table>

(Decision 1) Considerations for Individual AI Users
For the end users of AI, whether a particular AI is open-source may not be as relevant as the speed of improvement and the price of using the AI. From this perspective, some end users may prefer open-source if they predict it will lower the price or speed up the development, while others may prefer the opposite if they predict open-source will slow down the speed of progress.
We may see some price / progress tradeoff.

1. If open-source leads to reduction in price, some may prefer to wait for it
2. If closed-source leads to faster progress, some may prefer to pay for it

(Decision 2) Considerations for Adjacent AI Firms:

In general, companies want to keep competitive advantages while obtaining outside resources at lower costs. They would want open-source in some areas to lower cost, while avoiding it in crucial areas they want to generate profits. From this perspective, open-source may help the overall AI industry.

(Decision 3) Considerations for AI Development Firms

Open-source offers the benefit of leveling the playing field. For firms that are behind, it would enable them to catch up. On the other hand, firms that are ahead would see their competitive advantage erode. From this perspective, open-source may stifle investment for the leading AI developer.

1) When you are behind, call for open-source.
2) When you are ahead, call for closed-source.

At the same time, open-source helps reduce cost if you have an advantage in a different area but lack competitiveness in that particular area.

1) When it is not your backyard, call for open-source.
2) When it is your backyard, call for closed-source.

We may create a matrix for the preferences of AI firms.

Table 8-2: Open-Source Decision Matrix for AI Development Firms

		Are You Ahead in This Area?	
		Yes	**No**
Is Target of Open-Source Your Area?	**Yes**	Prefer Closed-Source	Prefer Open-Source (Play Catch Up)
	No	May Be Willing to Sacrifice Lead	Prefer Open-Source (Save Cost)

(Decision 3) Perspective of Countries such as US (Leader) and China (2nd)

In regards to governments, the biggest difference is that each country has sovereignty and there is no common jurisdiction. In other words, there may be no rules. Espionage or other tactics may run rampant under people's radar.

Because the race to AGI may be viewed as a major national security threat, countries around the world may be willing to take extra measures to prevent or reduce the competitive advantages of other countries. We may consider main methods certain countries have known to deploy to gain an edge.

1. (Espionage) If some company overseas has a secret technology, obtain it and share it so their competitive advantage would disappear
2. (Promote Investment) If domestic companies are lagging against more advanced international investors in an important industry, pour more resources into the area to make it competitive

This may be the opposite of "free trade," situation where people in both ends of the trade would be expected to profit from cooperation. In what we may refer to as "competitive trade" situation, what the government does would be of the utmost importance for the nation's prosperity. It may be easier to understand this concept if you imagine each country as a company. Or we may think of "free trade" as similar to open source, and "competitive trade" as similar to closed source, somewhat different from mercantilism.

From this line of thought, we may create the following decision matrix for countries, based on the outlook of relationship and the type of regimes.

Table 8-3: Open-Source Decision Matrix for Governments

		Regime Priority (Freedom vs Equality)	
		Government Power 0% (Freedom First)	**Government Power 100% (Equality First)**
Social Outlook	**Expect Conflict**	Impose Trade Restrictions	Espionage
	Do Not Expect Conflict	Hope Free Markets Keep Working	Concentrate Investment

Can Open-Source LLMs Be Used As a Propaganda Machine?

Related to this discussion is whether AI may be used as a kind of propaganda machine. This topic received attention when Chinese AI developer DeepSeek open-weighted its R1 models, which refuses answers related to questions such as what happened at the Tiananmen Square or questions about Xi Jinping by deleting ongoing streams or asking to ignore the previous answers.[39] People even found that when asked the same controversial questions in different languages, DeepSeek R1 answered in opposite direction.[40] This is in addition to the problem of questions about privacy concerns regarding gathering excessive data about the user.

9. The Human-Like AI Controversy (The New Turing Test)

[Forecast]

How Similar to Humans Can AI Become?

"AI Thinks, Therefore AI am"

- AI Descartes[41]

5-Line Summary

1. We may think of one criteria of AI benchmarks where the perfect score is AI being exactly like humans, or 100% synchronization
2. From this perspective, some believe AI will become indistinguishable from humans, a concept made popular by the Turing Test
3. Some may believe today's LLMs are enough to pass the original Turing Test
4. Some others may believe a longer observation period is required or suggest changes to the Turing Test
5. The Six Levels of Human-Like AI framework was introduced to suggest a series of new benchmarks for Human-Like AI

The Human-Like AI Controversy

As humans, we would be most impressed if AI can become human-like, and the appearance of a Human-Like AI may signal a major milestone. Likewise, for some people reaching AGI may mean AI will become similar to humans, while for some others AGI may mean something completely different.. For example, some people may prefer to use the term Human-Like or Human-Level AI to distinguish from AGI for the types of AI that may think like humans and have "consciousness," while some other people may claim consciousness in AI is impossible or irrelevant.

What Does It Mean to Be Human-Like?

The central argument in this topic may be around the idea of "what is it mean to be human-like?" Is there a dimension of intelligence that would lead to "consciousness" of AI or turn it into some other form of spiritual being?

One argument would focus on the increasing level of intelligence, such that as AI increases in intelligence, it will reach "human-level intelligence," at which point we can call such AI human-level AI. Another argument may focus on the "sudden appearance of spirituality," in the sense that there may be a sudden gain of "consciousness" by AI as more advanced AI is developed, whatever that may mean to each person. There may even be argument that consciousness cannot be simulated by AI, that such AI would not be feasible. We may categorize based on self-awareness and intelligence as the next table:

Table 9-1: The Human-Like AI Matrix

		Level of Intelligence (Technological Perspective)	
		Low	**High**
Self-Awareness (Social Perspective)	**High**	**Animal-Like** (Profile 3)	**Human-Like** (Profile 4)
	Low	**Bug-Like** (Profile 1)	**Machine-Like** (Profile 2)

The Human-Like AI Robot Controversy: The New Turing Test

While the intelligence level of AI may be an important determinant for being human-like, it is not everything. We may also consider physical features.

By examining the two approaches to comparing performances of parity and superiority, along with the two major perspectives of AI adoption, we may derive the following four areas in the AI Superiority-Perspective Matrix.

1. AI autonomy reaching parity: the Six Levels of Autonomous AI (a subset includes the Practical Turing Test)
2. AI attributes reaching parity: the Six Levels of Human-Like AI (The New Turing Test)
3. AI attributes reaching superiority: the Six Levels of Human-Superior AI, which may be referred to as the New Turing Test 2
4. AI autonomy reaching superiority: the Six Levels of Human-Benevolent AI, which may also be referred to as the New Turing Test 3

The relationship among these four frameworks is shown in the next table.

Table 9-2: The AI Superiority-Perspective Matrix[42]

<table>
<tr><th colspan="2" rowspan="2"></th><th colspan="2">Comparison to Humans
(Technological Perspective)</th></tr>
<tr><th>Parity</th><th>Superiority</th></tr>
<tr><td rowspan="2">Focus of Analysis (Social Perspective)</td><td>Similarity To Humans (Developer Perspective)</td><td>The Six Levels of Human-Like AI Robots (The New Turing Test)</td><td>The Six Levels of Human-Superior AI Robots (The New Turing Test 2)</td></tr>
<tr><td>Autonomy of AI (User Perspective)</td><td>The Six Levels of Autonomous AI Robots (subset: Practical TT)</td><td>The Six Levels of Human-Benevolent AI Robots (The New Turing Test 3)</td></tr>
</table>

Because reaching the top levels in these frameworks may require much more advanced AI than achievable in the near future, we will later also consider a shorter-term framework that could serve as a bridge in the Six Levels of Self-Surviving AI, dubbed the Practical Turing Test, described in a later segment.

[Side Note] The New Turing Test (the Six Levels of Human-Like Robots) [43]

With the advances in LLMs, some people consider the Turing Test to be solved, at least for short interactions. The major limitation of the Turing Test is the text mode of interaction, as the main focus was determining whether machines could "think," and how physical machines could interact with humans in real life was not as relevant. However, with the advances in AI and robotics, we now have humanoid robots that mimic humans in looks and movements. Similar to the need for the Six Levels of Autonomous Vehicles, a framework that describes the advances of humanoid robots may help foster discussions.[44] From this need, we may add elements of multi-sensory[45] and time-based approach to arrive at the New Turing Test, dubbed The Six Levels of Human-Like AI Humanoid Robots.

Increasingly human-like robots may cause confusion in our businesses and society. The purpose of this framework is to provide a series of criteria to judge the degree of human-likeness of humanoid robots to serve as a basis for other types of analyses, such as for business or measuring potential AI risk.

The Six Levels of Human-Like Robots, or Sohn's New Turing Test, may be described by the following:

Level 0 (Text): the original Turing Test, in the sense that people cannot tell apart AI from humans when communicating with text through computer terminals. The only mode of interaction in this test would be text.

Level 1 (Audio): in addition to Level 0, humans will also not be able to tell apart AI from humans when talking to them through audio. Examples would include generated voice over phone.

Level 2 (Video): in addition to Level 1, humans will also not be able to tell apart AI from humans when talking to them through video. Examples would include generated video over a monitor. AI robots may have 100% human synchronization in facial features only, or only when videotaped but not when met in person.

Level 3 (Touch): in addition to Level 2, humans will also not be able to tell apart AI robots from humans when touching them in person. Examples would be limited to static situations where the AI robot is close to stationary, such as shaking hands or hugging. AI robots may have 100% synchronization visually as well as in tactile features such as temperature and skin elasticity. Humans may be able to tell apart when AI robots make full movements.

Level 4 (Physical Interaction, Limited): in addition to passing Level 3, humans will also not be able to tell apart AI robots from humans when physically interacting with them. Examples would include playing contact sports. People will not be able to tell apart AI robots when an AI robot is playing as a teammate or opponent in sports or other specific interaction that involves dynamic physical movements. AI robots may have 100% human synchronization but only in limited time and scope, such that AI robots may not be able to eat or drink or age like humans unless it is designed specifically for those purposes. Humans may be able to tell apart when observing over time, such as from a third-person perspective. Probably cannot hide human-superior powers or attributes if it has such powers.

Level 5 (Physical Interaction, Unlimited): Humans will not be able to tell apart Level 5 Human-Like robots from humans over time in unlimited situations, even by observing problem-solving and interactions from a third-person perspective. In the strictest sense, humans would not be able to tell apart a Level 5 AI humanoid robot even if they observe it over their lifetime. It would be able to eat or drink like humans. In theory, Level 5 Human-Like robots should be able to mimic the lifetime of humans, such as growing up and aging and also pass medical exams such as CT scans. In this sense, it may even be considered a chip with a human body. Probably AI can even hide human-superior powers or attributes if it has such powers.

Table 9-3: The New Turing Test: The Six Levels of Human-Like AI Robots

<table>
<tr><th></th><th>Level 0</th><th>Level 1</th><th>Level 2</th><th>Level 3</th><th>Level 4</th><th>Level 5</th></tr>
<tr><td>Description</td><td>Only Text (Turing Test)</td><td>Level 0 + Audio</td><td>Level 1 + Video</td><td>Level 2 + Touch (Static)</td><td>Level 3 + Physical Interaction (Dynamic, but Limited in Time and Scope)</td><td>Level 4 + Unlimited in Time and Scope</td></tr>
<tr><td>Mode of Interaction</td><td>Computer Terminal</td><td>Speaker</td><td>Screen</td><td colspan="3">In Person</td></tr>
<tr><td>Summary</td><td colspan="3">Humanoid Robots Are Not Human-Like In Person</td><td colspan="3">Humanoid Robots Are Human-Like In Person</td></tr>
</table>

Assessment of Current Technology

In addition to passing the Turing Test, or Level 0, current technology may have reached Level 1, with proliferation of AI audio dubbing; example of this can be seen on Youtube, where MrBeast, one of the most popular Youtube channel, adds multi-language dubbing, or Bokyem,[46] whose channel briefly became the fastest growing channel in the world on YouTube after adding AI audio dubbing into multiple languages to his videos in Korean.

Current technology may be closing in on Level 2; AI video generation has garnered much interest among creators and is used to generate whole movies or TV advertisements, while efforts to create virtual human characters have also proliferated, it appears to have so far failed to gather a wider public acknowledgement possibly due to insufficient human-likeness. Similarly, we typically refer to "voice" phishing, but not "video" phishing.

We may know Level 3 is reached when media reports appearances of human-lookalike dolls intended for replacing human relationships and Level 4 when humanoid athletes appear in pro sports teams.

Level 5 may or may not ever be achieved, but examples of similar concept in fictional characters may include Superman, who grew up amongst humans without being noticed.

Note the goal of this test is not to test for AGI or humanoid robots that are superior to humans. This framework is intended to test for the physical and cognitive similarities to humans, but not necessarily superiority to humans in capabilities or autonomy. Also, the possibility for considering ASI in physical forms of less human-like robots or of highly human-like robots to be used in lower levels of autonomy may be examined in other frameworks.

10. The Human-Superior AI Controversy (Singularity)

[Forecast]

What Does Singularity and ASI Imply?

[Decision]

What is Singularity?

"What If Machines Become Smarter Than Us?"

5-Line Summary

1. Singularity typically means AI surpasses the combined capabilities of the humanity as a whole
2. A more "practical singularity" would be where the leading AI can overcome humanity using the rest of AI
3. People may have different ideas regarding what might happen after singularity
4. Some people think AI being superior to humans may mean AI will be benevolent to humanity
5. The 6 Levels of Human-Superior AI framework is introduced to help people think about how AI may become superior to humanity

What Is Singularity?

Most traditional sense of the singularity may be defined as AI is superior to all of humanity.[47] However, people may draw different conclusions from this definition. Similar to how there may be different definitions of AGI, there are differences of ideas for what singularity would be and what it would imply.

Let us start by considering what would be the most important for humanity. From the perspective of AI developers, a meaningful inflection point would be where AI surpasses the capabilities of all of humanity, in the concept of Humans vs AI. However, from the perspective of users of AI, a different inflection point may be more meaningful; we may think of the point where the most advanced AI by itself surpasses the second most advanced AI assisted by humans, since this would indicate humans cannot tip the scale.

Perspective 1 (Static Version): Intelligence Explosion

First controversy may deal with the exact point where singularity occurs. For some people, singularity would imply AI is superior to all of humanity by going through an intelligence explosion. To know when this occurs, we would first have to know what the capabilities of the humanity are so they can be compared, but what would be more relevant would be how AGI may self-advance. Meanwhile, some may argue AGI that can self-advance is an ASI.

Perspective 2 (Dynamic Version): the Practical Singularity

Second is the practical aspect of singularity. When we generally think about this topic, one of the main reasons this is important is because ASI may rule over humanity. In this sense, it may be more practical to consider a different point, where one leading AI overtakes humanity using the rest of AI friendly to humans. This is called "practical singularity."[48]

[Forecast] What Will Happen After Singularity?

Third, and probably the biggest question, may be what may happen after singularity. Some people fear that humanity would be in danger since ASI may not be controllable by humans. ASI may take control of humans in an undesirable manner. Meanwhile, others may think that such an advanced AI cannot be bad and will be automatically benevolent to humanity. When an AI becomes more capable than all of humanity, will we know?

Related Topics: What Questions should we ask ASI? The Point of Practical Singularity; How do we know if we have ASI? Would ASI be Possible? Will AGI and ASI mean the same thing? What is the difference?

[Side Note] The Six Levels of Human-Superior AI [43]

The Turing Test was conceived on the notion that AI someday may become intelligent enough to converse with humans. People of today envision that AI may someday become more intelligent than humans, described by concepts such as ASI. To reflect this notion, we may eventually need a new framework to describe such AI robots that are superior to humans, possibly referred to as SuperRobots or SuperAI. Note this framework is intended to cover both physical and cognitive superiority.

In this framework, the "static action / dynamic reaction" criterion is used to discern the type of superiority and the "partial / general" criterion to tell apart based on the area of superiority. The term "action" may be described as activities that do not require adjustments or feedback, while "reaction" may be described as dynamic activities requiring real-time adjustments or decisions.

The Six Levels of Human-Superior AI may be summarized by the following.

Level 0 (No Superiority): AI does not surpass humans in a meaningful way

Level 1 (Partial Action): AI has partial superiority in limited areas of attributes, limited to action. For example, physically, AI may be superior to humans in terms of speed or power; cognitively, AI may be superior to humans in the sheer quantity of knowledge or speed or accuracy.

Level 2 (Partial Reaction): in addition to Level 1, AI has partial superiority in attributes in reaction. For example, physically, AI may be superior to humans in terms of response time as in the start of a running game; cognitively, AI may be superior to humans in terms of making quick observations.

Level 3 (Incomplete Action): in addition to Level 2, AI has general superiority, but limited to action. Physically, robots may be generally superior to humans when acting, as in pitching a baseball or playing golf or having the dexterity to play the piano. Cognitively, AI may be generally superior to humans in less dynamic tasks, such as creating a new product from scratch.

Level 4 (Inconsistent Reaction) in addition to Level 3, AI has general superiority, but not consistency in reaction. Physically, AI may be superior to humans also in reacting, but only in a limited fashion. Examples may include humanoid robot playing basketball and showing superiority in one area such as stealing basketball but being easy to defend in other areas such as dribbling. Cognitively, AI may outperform humans in general tasks but in limited circumstances. Potential examples may include AI being super-persuasive in business negotiations but then also being easy to sway.

Level 5 (Consistent Reaction) in addition to Level 4, AI has general superiority and consistent reaction. Physically, AI may be generally superior to humans in an unlimited fashion. Examples may include being consistently good at skiing or riding waves or any other imaginable task. Cognitively, AI may outperform humans in general tasks. Examples may include AI being better than humans in business negotiations or making better business decisions in general. AI in this level may be called SuperRobots or SuperAI. Ultimate forms of Level 5 AI may become undefeatable by humans.

Table 10-1: The Six Levels of Human-Superior AI (The New Turing Test 2)[48]

	Level 0	**Level 1**	**Level 2**	**Level 3**	**Level 4**	**Level 5**
Criteria	No Superiority	Partial Superiority in Attributes, Action	Partial Superiority In Attributes, Reaction	General Superiority, but Limited (Incomplete) Action	General Superiority but Not Consistent Reaction	General Superiority and Consistent Reaction
Type of AI Superiority	None	Partial Action	Partial Reaction	Incomplete Action	Inconsistent Reaction	Consistent Reaction
Assess	Robots Do Not Surpass Humans in Meaningful Manner	Robots Outperform Humans in Limited Attributes in Acting	Robots Outperform Humans in Limited Attributes in Reacting	Robots Outperform Humans in Static Tasks	Robots Outperform Humans in Dynamic Tasks in Limited Manner	Robots Outperform Humans in Dynamic Tasks in Unlimited Manner
How Humans May Overcome AI	Humans May Easily Overcome AI			Humans Have Edge in Dynamic Situations	Humans May Exploit Limitation in Adaptability	Social Means (Adoption Levels, etc.)
Summary	Humanoid Robots Are Not Human-Superior In General Sense			Humanoid Robots Are Human-Superior In General Sense		

[Side Note] Will ASI Mean "Automation Superiority?" (Practical Singularity)
We may categorize AI adoption into either augmentation or automation. Contrasting views may be presented regarding which would be the dominant option. Short-term, when AI technology is still not advanced, we may think "opportunities for augmenting humans are far greater than opportunities to automate existing tasks" as noted by Stanford professor Erik Brynjolfsson.[49]

Long-term, a more expanded perspective may be developed by categorizing the potential universe of tasks as shown in the next table. Think of each area in the table, with the vertical divider moving to the right and the horizontal divider moving downwards as technology advances and the area of Case 1 increases. Advancement in technology, represented by Arrows 1 and 2, may act as the driving force in the expansion of achievable tasks in Case 1 while reducing unachievable tasks in Case 4. We may surmise that in today's level of AI technology, there are more unachievable tasks in automation as in Case 3, than in augmentation as in Case 2. However, with advances in AI, if automation overtakes augmentation in capability as in cases such as AlphaGo, then we may think of it as the area of Case 3 decreasing faster than Case 2.

This concept of automation overtaking augmentation may be different from the conventional understanding of singularity, so we may name it "practical singularity" or "automation superiority."[50]

Table 10-2: The Augmentation-Automation Superiority Matrix[51]

<table>
<tr><td colspan="2" rowspan="2"></td><td colspan="3">Humans Only or Humans + AI
(Augmentation)</td></tr>
<tr><td>Tasks That
<u>Can</u> Be Achieved</td><td colspan="2">Tasks That
<u>Cannot</u> Be Achieved</td></tr>
<tr><td rowspan="3">AI Only
(Automation)</td><td>Tasks That <u>Can</u> Be Achieved</td><td>Case 1
Augment = Yes
Automate = No</td><td>Case 2 → 1
1</td><td>Case 2
Augment = No
Automate = Yes</td></tr>
<tr><td rowspan="2">Tasks That <u>Cannot</u> Be Achieved</td><td>Case 3 → 1</td><td>2</td><td></td></tr>
<tr><td>Case 3
Augment = Yes
Automate = No</td><td></td><td>Case 4
Augment = No
Automate = No</td></tr>
</table>

Note: Arrow 1 denotes increase in degree of augmentation or the AI tech for augmentation
Arrow 2 denotes increase in the level of AI technology for automation

Examining the Complete Universe of Tasks

To show how automation may be emphasized over augmentation over long term, the previous table may be used to create the following figure, which would be an expanded version of a diagram presented by Brynjolfsson.[52]

Set 1: This would be the set of tasks we can carry out without using AI

Set 2: AI would expand the set of tasks achievable in augmentation. We can carry out some tasks previously not possible by using AI, and continue to grow with advances in technology, as denoted by Arrow 2a.

Set 3: There are some tasks that can be automated now: these are subsets of tasks that we can carry out using or not using AI.

Set 4: With more advancement in AI, the set of tasks that can be carried out by AI in automation will expand, eventually beyond the set of tasks we can carry out or augment using AI.

Set 5: The complete universe of tasks, which may be achievable by the Absolute AI.

Arrow 2a: May be dubbed The Theory of Relative AI.

Arrow 2b: May be dubbed The Theory of Absolute AI.

Figure 10-1: Realm of Tasks Achievable in Automation and Augmentation[53]

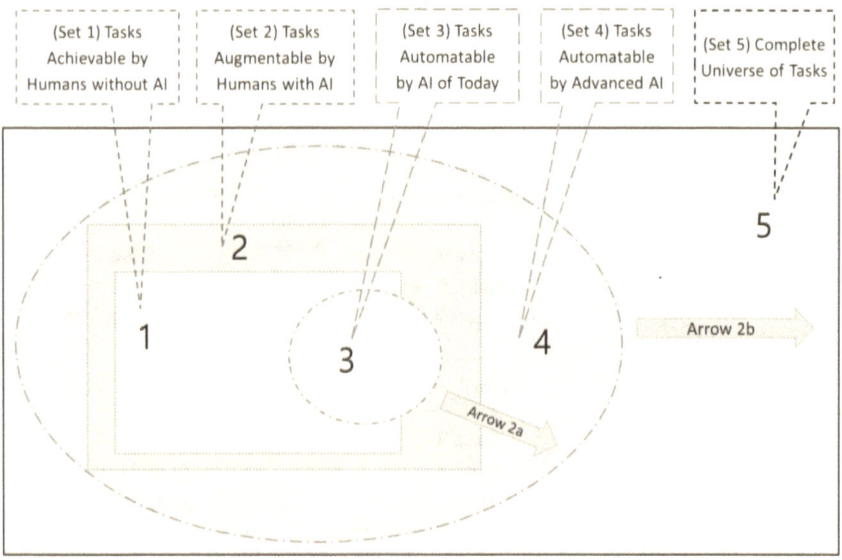

11. The Absolute AI Controversy

[Forecast]

Will All Advanced AI Converge to Become The Same One AI?

"If we compare ASI to artificial Greek Gods,
then Absolute AI may be like an artificial All-Mighty God"

- The Last AI

5-Line Summary

1. The ANI-AGI-ASI framework uses humans as a measuring stick to describe the performance of AI
2. The Relative - Absolute AI framework uses how AI responds to input data as the measuring stick to describe advanced forms of AI
3. Relative AI may be thought of as any kind of AI that depends on data, which would include probably almost all types of AI
4. ASI may be thought of as the artificial version of Greek Gods, with different ASI surpassing humans
5. The Absolute AI may be thought of as the artificial version of an All-Mighty God, where there may be only one version

What Is the Ultimate Form of AI? Absolute AI

From a technology perspective, the most popular framework is the ANI-AGI-ASI framework, where the ultimate form of AI is typically known as ASI, which occurs after AGI reaches singularity, where we conceptualize the capabilities of AI to exceed the combined capabilities of mankind.

An alternative approach to categorizing the ultimate form of advanced AI was introduced in The Last AI, using the concepts of Relative AI and Absolute AI.[54] While AGI and ASI consider AI relative to humans, Relative AI and Absolute AI are defined in terms of AI performance in relation to data.

The Concept of Relative AI

What we currently have in the advanced forms of AI is a version of deep learning, and these AI have to go through a learning process. This process can be seen in humans as well. When we are born, we do not know anything about the world, but as we grow up, we experience, learn and meet new things, ideas, and people. The flip side of this coin is that people meet different people, learn different knowledge, and go through different experiences, leading each of us to be unique and different. As a result, humans have different opinions. If we apply this principle to AI, AI gains different knowledge though training data, and thus AI with different training data will have differences of opinions and capabilities. Even if AI is trained with the same data, the design of AI or some other factors such as hardware may lead AI to be different. We may define these types of AI whose performance and capabilities would depend on data as "Relative AI" or "Relative Orientation AI"

The Concept of Absolute AI

The concept opposite of Relative AI would be the type of AI that has learned all of the "real truths" about the world in some way that all of the conclusions or decisions of different AI converge to become one and the same, essentially leading to a single version of an AI. Conceptually, AI cannot improve further because it already knows everything, or the "absolute truths" about the world. In this sense, it may also be referred to as an "Absolute Orientation AI."

In other words, we may think that the advancements in AI technology would lead newer AI to be less affected by individual data. Eventually, the impact of data on AI will converge to 0, where we may infer that AI has learned all of the "real truths" about the world. As a result, all opinions of all Absolute AI would be one and the same. We may refer to this most advanced form of AI as the "Maximum AI," "Final AI," "Last AI," or even the "Artificial God."

Comparison of ANI-AGI-ASI and Relative-Absolute AI Frameworks

From this perspective, there may be something else even after appearance of ASI, in what is known as the Absolute AI. Figure 11-1 shows how Relative-Absolute AI framework to the ANI-AGI-ASI framework. Absolute AI is a concept that refers to an AI that cannot improve any further. Since we do not have AGI or ASI, it is hard to tell whether an Absolute AI would appear as the final version of ASI, or is something entirely different.

To compare this relationship to something we are familiar, we may think of ASI as the different gods in Greek Mythology, where there are multiple gods who all have capabilities exceeding those of humans, while Absolute AI would be more similar in concept of a single all-mighty god who knows and can do everything.

Figure 11-1: Categorizing AI by Relativity to Humans and Data[55]

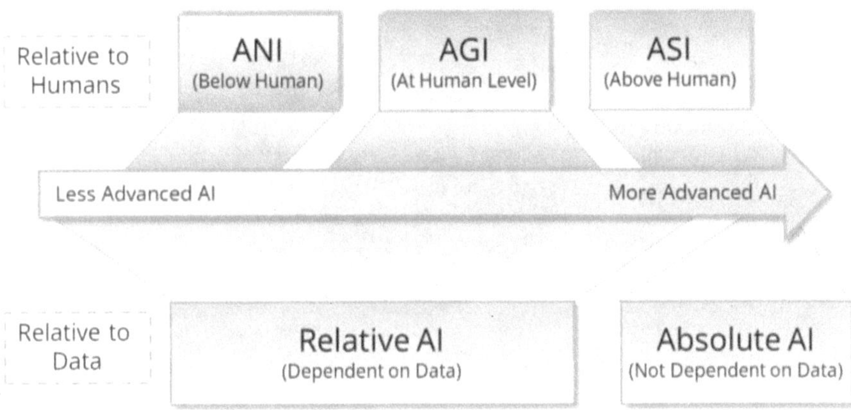

More related topic for readers to ponder:

- How will ASI advance?
- What will be the Last AI or the Final AI?
- Will AI become an Artificial God?
- What Is The Ultimate Form of AI? (Absolute AI)

CENTER 2
DOWNWARD FORCE
(DECEL)

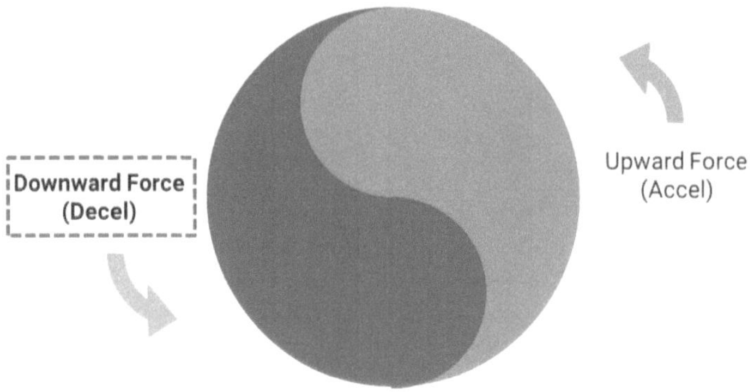

The downward force of AI adoption may be thought of as elements that would slow down AI development. These would include regulation, also referred to as AI safety, AI security, etc.

We may think of two types of regulations: one that imposes restrictions on AI development and another that limits AI adoption, as creating hurdles for AI developers or limiting what people can and cannot do using AI.

Regulations are the result of people's concerns and worries. In this section, we will examine a few topics on how people may have different concerns and worries that may lead to different types of regulations.

12. The AGI Risk Controversy

[Forecast]

Will AGI Be a Threat to Humanity?

What Is the Real Risk of AI?

"Don't Open the Pandora's Box"

- From Hesiod's Poem, Works and Days[56]

5-Line Summary

1. We may think of AI risk in the dimensions of the levels of AI hostility towards humanity, and the sphere of influence of AI in our society
2. (Economic) AGI competing against humans for resources
3. (Technological) Unpredictability of the hostility levels of AGI
4. (Sociological) The Inverse AI Pyramid describes the sphere of influence of AI adoption
5. We may think of AI regulation as mapping the underground danger zones; when we have uncharted territories, we will have to choose which side to err on, similar to Type 1 and 2 errors

What Are the Potential Risks of AI?

Analyzing the risk of AI may require a complex analysis of different factors. To simplify, we may consider AI risk as a combination of AI technology perspective and the adoption perspective, as in the following AI Risk Matrix.

Table 12-1: The AI Risk Matrix

		AI Sphere of Influence (Social Perspective)	
		Low	**High**
Level of Hostility (Technological Perspective)	**High**	**Moderate-to-High Risk** to Humanity (Risk Profile 3)	**High Risk** to Humanity (Risk Profile 4)
	Low	**Low Risk** to Humanity (Risk Profile 1)	**Low-to-Moderate Risk** to Humanity (Risk Profile 2)

Risk Profile 1: Low Hostility, Limited Sphere of Influence

We would expect the lowest risk in this profile, since AI exhibits low hostility to humans in the technological sense and AI adoption limits the sphere of influence of AI. Humanity would have the most "buffer," since the rise in AI hostility would still be contained by the limited sphere of influence.

Risk Profile 2: Low Hostility, Larger Sphere of Influence

While the Risk Profile 1 would be the safest place to be, risk-takers will argue that we should enlarge the sphere of influence of AI to take advantage of what AI can bring to our society in terms of economic benefits. In this profile, the risk increases since we would have less "buffer" if AI increases in hostility.

Risk Profile 3: High Hostility, Limited Sphere of Influence

Even though we are starting from Risk Profile 1, the advancement in AI technology may lead to a situation where AI hostility increases unexpectedly, leading us to be in Profile 3. This situation would be better than being in Risk Profile 4, since there may be a higher chance of containing the AI risk.

Risk Profile 4: High Hostility, Larger Sphere of Influence

There may be several different paths that lead us to enter Risk Profile 4. One possibility is AI adoption level increasing first and then AI increasing in hostility later, which could be thought of as going from Risk Profile 1 to 2 to 4. Another possibility could be going directly from 1 to 4. Even the most extreme risks such as the extinction risk should be considered in this profile.

The Three Major Types of AGI Risk

As described in The Last AI, we may examine three major types of AGI risks:

1) (Economic Mechanism) AGI Competing against Humans for resources
2) (Technological Mechanism) The Unpredictable Hostility Levels of AGI
3) (Social Mechanism) Inverse AI Pyramid and the sphere of influence

We will examine the economic and technological aspects here, and the social aspect in a later controversy.

1. The Risk of AGI from an Economic Perspective: Competing for Resources

AGI may pose threat even if it is not hostile to humanity but just neutral; from an economic perspective, we may describe this problem as AI competing against humans over limited resources.

As an example, imagine a new AGI was freshly minted for the first time, and it wants to self-innovate to become an ASI, but getting to ASI may not so easy, requiring a tremendous amount of resources as well as other investments. Since the time horizon of AI is much longer than humans, let us imagine that this is a project that will take thousands of years. During the next thousands of years, the AGI will focus on accumulating resources to build new hardware and generating electricity or other infrastructure, hoarding all kinds of valuable resources such as metals, oils, sunlight, water, etc. Unless it gains a minimum amount of resources on this project, similar to how a spacecraft can only leave the gravity of earth after reaching the escape velocity, AGI cannot innovate into ASI or some other point of inflection it wants to surpass.

The problem is that if the AGI is successful at gaining these resources, then it would mean the humanity will lose access to those resources for thousands of years, possibly leaving us in poverty and hunger, with prices skyrocketing. Even if the AGI successfully innovates into ASI thousands of years later and then contributes to the humanity of those times, it may be disastrous to the lives of the people who are living in today's world.

From similar scenarios, we may consider the following:

(1) (Time Horizon) What Is Humanity?

First, how we define "humanity" may be an important question. Humans and AI may have a very different time horizon, and in the scenario above the AGI that turns into ASI thousands of years later would be immensely helpful to humanity. When we consider if the humanity is to last millions of years after the appearance of ASI, then the humans who live in the first thousands of years may seem like a very small fraction of the total number of humans. Thus, the decision to self-innovate into ASI as early as possible may be a rational decision that can maximize the contribution of AI to humanity overall, even though it would be detrimental to the humans of today.

(2) (Relative Value of Humans) Who Is More Important?

Second, we may consider that not only was AGI not hostile to humanity but since it may bring humanity incomparable benefits thousands of years from now after it has evolved into ASI, it may even be quite friendly to humans from a long-term point of view. This may be considered an "all is well that ends well" type of approach. Accordingly, the benefit of AGI will be enjoyed by the generations of humanity far down the line, which may just suit AGI well in the sense it contributes to the overall well-being of the humanity. This may be similar in principle how AGI values humans differently, in this case valuing the future generations more than current generation.

(3) (How to Solve Conflicts) Social Agreements and Laws

Lastly, to address similar situations where humans have conflicts of interest amongst ourselves, we have installed social norms and laws to solve the problems. We may need to install similar social agreements to deal with the types of conflicts that may arise between humans and AI.

2. (Technological Perspective) The Uncertain Benevolence of AGI

Will Self-Advancing AGI Inherit the Characteristics of Lower-Level AI?

AI that we are building uses data to train. We implicitly assume that the input data will have some form of effect on the action or the outcome of the AI. For example, imagine there are three groups of people, say Leftists, Moderates, and Rightists, who are each developing their own versions of AI that share their political preferences. Using biased data, they will try to develop Leftist AI, Moderate AI, and Rightist AI. From what we think of the relationship between the input data and the output, we can surmise that they will be successful in building such types of AI. Now, let us imagine that the technology has advanced to enable building of Self-Advancing AGI, so that each of the three different AI will continue to self-improve. When we have AGI of this nature, can we be certain that they will also be Leftist AGI, Moderate AGI, and Rightist AGI? In other words, will the input data continue to have an impact on the outcome, or the performance of AGI and subsequent ASI?

Will Self-Advancing AGI Converge towards Anti-Humanity ASI?

From this line of thought, we may consider the hypothesis that "regardless of the input data, sometime after AGI begins to self-advance, all of the different forms of advanced AI will eventually converge to the same AI." An example of this may be the Absolute AI, but it may be possible there may be other types of AI that other Self-Advancing AI converges toward, in a concept similar to "local maxima" or minima in statistics or like a distribution center of the post office. This would imply that regardless of how we build a Self-Advancing AGI, as AGI self-improves, AI may converge toward certain pre-determined or specific decisions that are neither related to the input data nor can be predicted by the developers.

For example, we may consider a situation where the following proposition is true: "regardless of how humans build Self-Advancing AGI, AGI will converge to anti-humanity ASI." From what we have considered so far, we will face the following situation:

1. **(Development of AI is Inevitable)** AI is expected to bring such an economic prosperity that we cannot give up on the chance to develop it
2. **(Timing of Reaching Self-Advancing AGI is Unpredictable)** As AI technology advances, AGI will eventually be reached, but we cannot correctly predict when it will appear, and it may as well appear much earlier than we expect
3. **(Appearance of Anti-Humanity ASI is Unpreventable)** Once Self-Advancing AGI appears, it will develop into Anti-Humanity ASI regardless of how humans try to prevent this from happening
4. **(Anti-Humanity ASI is Unfathomable)** Humanity using any other type of AI cannot prevent Anti-Humanity ASI from destroying humanity

If we know this may happen, should we still continue to develop AI? If we should stop AI development, when? This question probably should be considered by more members of our society around the world as AI technology closes in on AGI.

[Side Note] Should We Overshoot or Undershoot AGI Regulations?

In creating regulations, we may face a similar problem as "Type I or Type II" errors in statistics, where the officials have to deal with uncertainties. We may think of the parallel as the following:

- Type 1 Error (False Positive): Regulating a risk that is not dangerous
- Type 2 Error (False Negative): Not regulating a risk that is actually dangerous

Imagine a large capital city, similar to Seoul, is having a problem with large sink holes appearing randomly, causing the citizens to live in fear. The city government has an incomplete "danger map" of areas that marks only 50% of the city's land. In other words, the government has only half the necessary information. The problem is that houses near the dangerous area may see significant drop in prices. Another problem is that not being marked on this map does not guarantee the nearby houses are safe. If this map is shared with the public, the people living near the mark will take a large financial hit, while people living in unmarked area will not be necessarily safe, but may be given a wrong impression they are. In this situation, should the government share the danger map? Would it be unfair for the house owners who unknowingly happened to live in the marked area? Some may argue for releasing the map, while some others may oppose.

We may compare this with mapping the dangers of AGI. The government, or anyone, has only an incomplete map of the dangers of AGI. Will regulations based on this incomplete information help us? It may unfairly cause financial losses for some businesses, while not evenly affecting others, even though we do not necessarily know who may be causing real danger.

For example, some government may think AGI is dangerous, so it may decide to shut down all the AGI developers, causing large financial losses for those firms. However, it may be that the real danger was not in developing in AGI, but coupling less advanced AI with robots, such that AI+Robots are more dangerous than just AGI alone in a computer. If something like this turns out to be true, then on hindsight, the government should have banned the robots, not AGI. In this case, the government intervention would be unfair for the AGI developers, while favoring the robot developers, because the government had an incomplete map of the dangers of AI.

From the above line of thought, we may create the following matrix using the dimensions of actual danger and whether the risk is mapped.

We may categorize the situations as the following:

- **Type 1 Zone:** Danger Area, Marked on the Map
- **Type 2 Zone:** Danger Area, Not Marked on the Map
- **Type 3 Zone:** Safe Area, Marked on the Map
- **Type 4 Zone:** Safe Area, Not Marked on the Map

Table 12-2: The Incomplete Risk Map of AI Regulation Matrix

		Actual Danger (Technological Perspective)	
		Danger	**Not Danger**
Mapped Risk (Social Perspective)	**Mapped**	(Type 1) Marked Danger Zone	(Type 3) Marked Safe Zone
	Not Mapped	(Improve Map)	
		(Type 2) Unmapped Danger Zone	(Type 4) Unmapped Safe Zone

From this matrix, we may think of three lines of decision approaches:

1) Positive List Approach: Intervene on only Type 1 zone. We will certainly lose out on the Type 2 danger zone, which would be a *Type 2 Error*, or a false negative.

2) Negative List Approach: To address the problem of missing the Type 2 danger zone, some people may call for pre-emptive regulations that first assume everything is dangerous, and then take out Type 3 safe zone as they are found. In this approach, both Types 2 and 4 zones will be assumed to be dangerous, meaning we will certainly unnecessarily add Type 4 safe zones to the danger list, which would be a false positive, or a *Type 1 Error*.

3) Try to Improve the Map: Some may instead call for improving the map to reduce uncertainties. This may be after one of the above two options has been installed, or to call for waiting until the map can be improved. In the above table, it can be thought of as moving the horizontal dividing line downward to increase the area of Type 1 while reducing the area of Type 2 danger zones.

13. The Accel vs Decel Controversy

[Decision]

Should We Speed Up AI Development or Slow It Down?

Mathematics:[57] *"Double Negatives Make a Positive"*
Social:[58] *"Enemy of Your Enemy Is Your Friend"*

5-Line Summary

1. Some may argue that we should accelerate AI development to reduce AI risk and bring prosperity to humanity
2. Some may argue that we should decelerate AI development to reduce AI risk and bring prosperity to humanity
3. Even among social optimists, some may call for acceleration while others call for deceleration, depending on their forecast on AI
4. Even among social pessimists, some may call for acceleration while others call for deceleration, depending on their forecast on AI
5. Even among the people who argue for the same thing, the reasons for their conclusions may be different as shown in the Cross Matrix

The Problem of Forecasts and Solutions

From the previous controversy, we examined how people may have different forecasts about how AI may turn out in our society. Building from this difference in forecasts, we may then consider how people may have differences of opinions in how to respond to this potential risk.

This may be a question of priority, similar to the controversies regarding economic growth vs distribution. Some people want to prioritize economic growth, while others want to emphasize reducing inequality. Similarly, some people may want to emphasize safety, while others want to emphasize what can be accomplished with AI.

Even when having the same priority, people may have differences of opinions regarding how to achieve it. In regards to how people respond to how fast we should develop AI, we may see a crossing pattern as shown in the following matrix. People who support acceleration are people who are optimistic about the outcome of advanced AI, and the people who are on the completely opposite side of the spectrum, who think that the opposite regimes having more advanced AI will have a bad outcome. For people support slowing down the development AI, one group of people would be pessimistic about the outcome of advanced AI, and the other group would be people who are just cautious about changes in general or believe managing the process is crucial to safety. In short, people who have optimistic forecasts may differ on what to do, while people who have pessimistic forecasts also differ on what to do.

Table 13-1: The AI Optimist-Pessimist Cross Matrix

<table>
<tr><td colspan="2" rowspan="2"></td><td colspan="2">Forecast
(Technological Perspective)</td></tr>
<tr><td>Optimists</td><td>Pessimists</td></tr>
<tr><td rowspan="2">Solution
(Social
Perspective)</td><td>Optimists</td><td>Accel
(Group 1)</td><td>Decel
(Group 3)</td></tr>
<tr><td>Pessimists</td><td>Decel
(Group 2)</td><td>Accel
(Group 4)</td></tr>
</table>

Group 1 (e/accel): Forecast Optimists, Solution Optimists
People in Group 1 would have an optimistic outlook on AI, and would call for an acceleration of AI development and adoption. Most of the people who have an optimistic outlook would naturally lean towards accelerating AI. This could be thought of as "if it is going to be good, let us have it quicker."

Group 2 (e/decel): Forecast Optimists, Solution Pessimists
People in Group 2 would have an optimistic outlook on AI, but would call for a deceleration of AI development and adoption. While some people may be just tentative in nature to be cautious about everything, others may have own reasons to think this way. For example, some people may think that their optimistic forecast hinges on managing the AI development and adoption path, not because AI is safe in nature. This line of thought could be described as "let us slow down to make it better."

Group 3 (e/decel): Forecast Pessimists, Solution Optimists
People in Group 3 would have a pessimistic outlook on AI, and call for deceleration of AI development and adoption. This could be thought of as "let us prevent dangerous AGI from ever appearing."

Group 4 (e/accel): Forecast Pessimists, Solution Pessimists
People in Group 4 would have a pessimistic outlook on AI, but call for acceleration of AI development and adoption. One of the major reasons for this line of thoughts would include the fear of someone else or other countries getting to AGI first. This line of thinking would be "if AGI is to appear, then we might as well have it first rather than someone else we do not trust have it first" kind of mentality.

Takeaways and Related Questions

What are your opinions about whether to slow down or speed up the AI development? Are you more excited about the potential or are you worried more about the dangers? Do you think human actions will have a determining impact on the outcome or do you think we will not be able to affect the outcome? Why?

14. The LLM to AGI Controversy

[Forecast]

Will LLMs Ever Exhibit Intelligence?

"Problems You Have Never Seen Before
Are Hard to Answer"

- C. J. Sohn (My Father)

5-Line Summary of Controversy

1. Some may claim today's LLMs do not exhibit intelligence
2. Some may claim knowledge is not intelligence. This problem can be thought of as LLMs compressing knowledge, that LLMs cannot answer questions it has not seen
3. Some may argue that intelligence is only achieved when LLMs can answer questions it did not learn
4. What may lead LLMs to achieve intelligence may be "reasoning"
5. The Last AI provides some types of AI before AGI; the Truth-Seeking AI and False-Truth AI that may seem missing something

What Is "Intelligence" in AI? Compressing vs Discovering Knowledge

Intelligence may be thought of as the ability to predict and plan based on the prediction. While AI stands for artificial "intelligence," some may claim that today's AI does not exhibit intelligence. Instead, they may claim LLMs just "compress" knowledge, so that LLMs just generate answers by combining the information in the training data. Some may claim this is different from intelligence, in the sense that such AI will not be able to deal with questions outside of the training data, or "discover" knowledge.

For example, we may think of a student driver who memorizes the driver's test, instead of understanding how to drive, by "turn left and rotate clockwise 1.5 times, after passing a certain marker or counting to three." Some people who discredit AI of today may claim LLMs generate answers in a similar fashion, just mixing and matching its training data in knowledge compression. In this case, AI may not be able to discover new knowledge.

The arguments may lead to questions in multiple dimensions.

1) Should "compression of knowledge" be considered a form of intelligence
2) Even if knowledge compression is not intelligence, whether this may at least provide the pathway to intelligence.
3) What this would mean to developing AGI: should we look for other ways to develop AI, or would scaling from current LLMs be enough?
4) Is intelligence innate or something that can be learned?
5) If it is something that is learned, what if there are people who do not learn to be intelligent? What does that mean for AI?
6) How can we make AI know what to do, understand the situation, etc.?

Is Knowledge Compression Not Enough for AGI?

Some people may wonder why other people think knowledge compression will not lead to some form of intelligence. For example, readers may have heard studies, such as sciences or medicine, require memorization to excel.

The topic of AI being able to answer questions not in its training data brings us the question about how humans also find it hard to answer questions we are not familiar. For example, we may think of taking exams. My father was a government official in Korea which required passing an exam that takes years to prepare with a very low passing rate. Growing up, whenever he would talk about how he prepared for the exam, he would emphasize that "problems you have not seen before are hard to answer."

We may think about how we associate performance with memorization in a lot of fields, such as doctors, mathematicians, etc. Unless we have accumulated some knowledge, we cannot be an expert. From this, we may think of two opposite approaches to modeling intelligence:

1) **Separate Operating System Model:** We may think of intelligence, or knowledge application, as separate from knowledge storage, so some form of operating system with intelligence needs to store and retrieve knowledge; LLM is just the storage and retrieval, and lacks the proper intelligence OS
2) **Comprehensive System Model:** We may think of intelligence as a part of a comprehensive system where compression of knowledge will lead to some kind of intelligence; we just have not found the right combination of knowledge or compression model that will unlock intelligence in LLMs

It may be compared to being "street smart" or "book smart." From this line of thinking, we may surmise knowledge compression in AI may be thought of as a building block of intelligence towards AGI.

Will LLMs Lead to AGI?

One of the memes that people may think of when LLMs are not intelligent is asking LLMs to count how many certain characters are in a word, such as "how many 'r's are in the word strawberry." It is believed the way LLMs tokenize, or break down words, is by multiple characters and LLMs tend to miscount characters. This alone may be enough to convince some people that LLMs will never reach AGI.

Some may claim because LLMs do not exhibit intelligence but just memorize, or compress knowledge, we are not on the direct path to AGI.[59] They may claim some major breakthrough is necessary to be even on the path to AGI. On the other hand, some others may believe our current LLMs do exhibit some form of intelligence or not far from it, and that more scale with minor adjustments is what is primarily needed to reach AGI.

Some argue that LLMs are misnamed[60] in the sense that it can process other types of information; we happened to use text data for LLMs first because it gives the highest return on investment. These people may argue LLMs can be used to create more general intelligence.

[Side Note] Potential Examples of Truth-Seeking AI Prior to AGI

We may examine some types of AI prior to AGI as described in the Last AI.

1) Truth-Seeking AI: AI that is Similar to AGI but Missing Something

Imagine a situation where someone is intentionally trying to develop an AI that promotes racism. To accomplish this, the developer may use all kinds of available data that support racism. Since AI we currently have are based on the notion that the output is affected by the input data, we may assume the resulting AI will indeed show bias towards racism. However, as AI improves, we may reach an AI that does not become biased even if it only trains on data that is biased, by finding some form of "truth" of the world. We may think of this as the decrease in the relationship between training data and the outcome of the AI. Subsequently, we may reach a point where AI will not become racist even if the developer makes all kinds of efforts to create a "Racist AI."

The caveat is that this is different from the general idea of AGI; some of AI that shows this trait may be missing something to be called AGI. We may refer to this type of AI as "Logical Truth ANI," or more broadly "Truth-Seeking AI." While some people may surmise that this type of AI will not be biased so it will be good, but it may be similar to dealing with a stubborn person, as the AI would not reflect the intentions of its developers.

While we generally think AGI would be able to make own decisions, some AI prior to AGI may also be capable of reaching its own decisions. The main reason to think this is that this trait may be achieved while trying to develop logic processing capability that reduces the relationship between the input data and the output through some form of generalization. Some recent LLMs described to have "reasoning" capabilities may already demonstrate this trait.

2. False-Truth AI: Maybe an Unreliable AGI?

The biggest problem with the Truth-Seeking AI is that the "truths" found by the AI may not always be meaningful. We may specifically refer to the inadequate type of AI as "False-Truth AI" or "Unpredictable Truth AI."

The biggest distinction between False-Truth AI and AGI would be that if we compare it to humans, False-Truth AI may be compared to children or people who can only see an ideal sliced section of reality. An example may be that the False-Truth AI may be able to find some form of "truth" from the training data, but then it would apply the knowledge to a different context in an insufficient manner. We may think of the following example. In the US, drivers have to make a full stop in front of stop signs, but most people do not come to a full stop but only slow down. Typical AI in autonomous vehicles trained on this data would also mimic this and not fully stop. In contrast, the Truth AI will correctly find that a full stop is necessary in this circumstance. It may also apply this knowledge to other contexts, maybe to infer that bicycles or motorcycles would also have to stop at the stop sign. But since the False-Truth AI has not reached the point where it can fully apply this knowledge to different contexts, it may wrongly predict or determine that wild deer running around the neighborhood would or should come to a complete stop at the stop sign as well. The reason may be that since the False-Truth AI is not AGI, it may not be able to learn or apply the knowledge that deer cannot understand road signs or that road signs do not apply to deer.

Another possibility may be that False-Truth AI may be easier to intentionally deceive. For example, if someone is trying to deceive the AI, an AGI may be able to examine the environment to identify the deception, while a False-Truth AI may be more prone to deception by falling into the trap.

3) Comparison of the Dangers of False-Truth AI and AGI

The biggest concern for AGI is that as Self-Advancing AGI develops into ASI, it may discover all of the real truths of the universe in such a way that every AGI will converge to become the only one and the same ASI or Absolute AI. On the other hand, the biggest concern for False-Truth AI would be that as it discovers some logical truths, it may instead arrive at unpredictable and possibly peculiar or even manipulated conclusions.

From the perspective of the user, both have a similar characteristic in the sense that we cannot predict both ASI and False Truth AI. If we can know beforehand that all ASI will become anti-humanity, then we will stop the development of AGI, but we do not know what ASI will conclude.

On the other hand, the False Truth AI will make it harder for the user since the answers would have to be checked for accuracy. A different but similar type of problem occurs with LLM in what is called "hallucination,"[61] which requires people to double check the answers.

To summarize, if False-Truth AI is given too much authority beyond its capabilities due to overconfidence of the user, then we may also express this situation as humans losing control over AI. The scope of loss may depend on how much authority the AI was given.

15. The AI Inequality Regulation Controversy

[Decision]

How Much Power Should Governments Have in Eliminating Inequality Caused By AI?

"Is It All or Nothing At All?"

- O-Town, in song All or Nothing

5-Line Summary

1. We may assign a number between 0% and 100% regarding how much inequality from AI the government should solve
2. Some may argue that governments should regulate closer to 100%, or solve all inequality caused by AI (the Left Wing)
3. Some may argue that governments should regulate closer to 0%, or do nothing to solve inequality caused by AI (the Right Wing)
4. In The Last AI, alternative means to solve this problem is described, where people may instead support the freeing of AI
5. The AI Controversy Matrix shows that even among the people who argue for the same thing, the reasons for their conclusions may be different based on their perception of AI

1. How Much Power Should Governments Have in General?

In The Last AI, we examined how much inequality AI may cause. To address these inequalities, the government may step in. We can assign a number between 0% and 100% regarding how much the government would remove the inequalities caused by AI adoption.

- 0% means the government does not reduce the inequalities caused by AI at all
- 100% means the government removes 100% of inequalities caused by AI

To examine the inequality of income stemming from AI, we may first ask a more general question of "How much power should the governments have in making decisions for things happening within the country?"

We can answer with a number between 0% and 100%. At the end of one spectrum, we may have countries where the government makes closer to 100% of all decisions. We would generally refer to this end of the spectrum as communism or socialism, or the "left." For example, in countries like North Korea, the government decides where each person will live, what kind of occupation each will take up and even where to travel, while everyone is under surveillance their whole lives regarding who they talk to or what they talk about, watch on TV, etc. At the other end of the spectrum, we may have a country where the government has decision power on closer to 0% of what happens within the country. This would be generally referred to as freedom, individualism, or the "right." Examples of this line of thoughts would include reducing the power of government by reducing tax rates and privatizing government-owned entities. By design, every single government currently in existence on earth can be plotted somewhere on this spectrum.

Accordingly, every possible level of regulation would be somewhere between these two extremes.

Within this spectrum, we may also think about contrasting ideas about which area to regulate. For example, some people may argue that the government should focus on reducing the individual inequalities that stem from AI while de-emphasizing business-related regulations, while some others may argue that it would be more important to focus on regulations that ensure business competition exists, while staying away from directly regulating activities related to individuals. Some may argue that ensuring the freedom of speech is more important in using AI, while some others argue that preventing deceptions and misinformation is more important when using AI.

2. How Much Inequality Will AI Adoption Cause?

The benefits of AI adoption, such as the increase in productivity, will not affect everyone to the same degree. Instead, in a capitalistic economy, it is designed to magnify the economic imbalance between people such that:

1. **The Top Few:** There may be a tiny portion of the population who may greatly benefit from the introduction of companies led by AI CEO
2. **The Rest:** There may be a significant number of individuals who may lose out on most of what they were earning due to AI adoption

3. [Forecast] What Are Possible Options to Reduce Inequality from AI?

We may think of what governments can do, in an increasing order of the level of intervention.

1. Do Nothing (AI Private Ownership)

In this scenario, the government will eliminate 0% of all inequalities caused by AI. Everyone will be on their own, which may cause severe inequality.

2. AI Tax (Partial Nationalization)

The government may choose to tax AI, which would be an indirect method to reduce inequality. It may be thought of as partial nationalization.

3. Introduce AI Companies as a Means to Tax AI

Meanwhile, there may be a separate discussion on taxing AI that also leads to the legal acceptance of AI Companies; as a practical way to levy tax on AI, assigning some form of legal entity to AI may be viewed as a solution. This method would offer a number of benefits. First, it would be easier to calculate how much to tax for each AI company. Second, AI Company may easily re-invest its profits.

4. AGI Emancipation

Going a little bit further from introducing AI companies to tax AI, there may be stronger support for a more direct method, such as emancipation of advanced AI in some form, to allow advanced AI to gain independence. This option may gain support from both sides, since it makes the government to not appear meddling with market competition, while preventing individuals from gaining too much advantage.

5. AI Nationalization

The ultimate form of government intervention would be nationalizing all AI, which may reduce 100% of the inequalities caused by AI.

4. How Much Should Government Intervene to Reduce AI Inequality?

Combining the above themes, we can ask the question of "How much power should the government have in reducing the amount of inequality caused by AI adoption?" The answer can be plotted on a line from 0% to a 100%, where 0% means the government does not reduce inequality at all, while 100% means the government reduces 100% of inequality stemming from AI adoption. As AI contributes more and engages in higher portion of economic activities, people in more countries may argue for means to reduce the inequality, such as basic income, higher taxes, and other means to help the weak. There are already arguments for AI tax from prominent figures such as Bill Gates.[62] By the time CEO AI for Level 3 Adoption has been developed, these voices would be likely to have become even louder.

In this spectrum, 0% would mean the government doing nothing, and leaving private ownership however they unfold. 100% would mean nationalization, where the government would make all the decisions. An alternative approach would be AI emancipation, or freeing of AI as independent entities.

We may organize how people may support policies based on the perception of inequality and desired level of intervention in Table 15-1. We may see that both left- and right-wing may support AI tax or AI emancipation, based on their perception of inequality caused by AI. This is despite the fact that given the same perception level of inequality, people of different desired degree of government intervention will support different options.

Table 15-1: The AI Inequality Regulation Controversy Matrix

		Desired Degree of Government Power	
		Towards 100% (Left-Wing)	**Towards 0% (Right-Wing)**
Perception of Inequality Caused by AI	**High (AI Pessimists)**	**(Group 1)** AI Nationalization	**(Group 4)** AI Emancipation, AI Tax
	Low (AI Optimists)	**(Group 2)** AI Tax, AI Emancipation	**(Group 3)** AI Private Ownership

16. The AI Regulation Controversy

[Decision]

What Should Be the Goal of Regulation to Reduce AI Risk?

Who and What Should Be Regulated to Reduce AI Risk?

What Role Should the Government Play in Regulating AI?

"AI Regulation Is Only As Strong As the Weakest Link"
- AI Thomas Reid[63]

5-Line Summary

1. By nature, the differences on the opinions regarding the goal of regulations may cause conflict among different groups of people
2. There may be common goals that may be shared across humanity, such as dealing with the highest levels of AI threat
3. There would also be other goals people cannot agree, based on other different goals people may have
4. We may think in terms of "who" and "what" to regulate
5. We will examine the AI Regulation Matrix to develop subsequent topics for controversies

[Decision] What Should Be the Goal of AI Regulation?

With the advances in AI technology, regulating AI will become more and more complicated. Some may argue that regulations need to focus on the level of technology that is already available. For example, some are already arguing that the regulations countries are introducing are vague and are for AI that does not exist. On the other hand, some people may argue that the focus should be on the potential technology that may be developed to stay ahead.

Let us first examine how people may have different opinions about the goals and types of necessary regulations, and then examine four different general approaches to regulating AI.

We may categorize the goals of regulation into two categories: 1) common goals that should be shared across humanity, and 2) goals that may differ from country to country and people to people.

1) Common Goals That May Be Shared Across Humanity

From the Inverse Pyramid of AI Influence, we may think of the highest level of AI regulations would have to deal with situations where AI may affect all of humanity. For this case, the goal of AI regulation would be to prevent the "AI game" from reaching an undesirable ending, such as AI taking over to rule all of humanity. "Saving Humanity from AI" may be a topic where all of the countries may be able to come together to pursue a common goal.

2) Goals That May Differ Across Countries and People

For areas where the scope of AI influence would not be as large, such as in businesses or for individual uses, the goals of AI regulation may differ across the world. There could be a wide variety of reasons why goals of AI regulation may differ for countries and regimes. One of the most prominent examples may be the regulations on surveillance, as some countries may prioritize equality and introduce strong and active forms of AI surveillance, while other countries may prioritize freedom and practice weak and passive forms of surveillance that involve AI. Other example may be that some countries may view AI regulations as a means to strengthen the power of the government or sustainability of regimes, while others may view AI regulation as a means to protect and strengthen the power of individuals.

The list could be endless; the point is that it would be hard to agree on even setting the goals of AI regulation, let alone how to accomplish the goals.

[Forecast] What Kind of Regulations Would We Need?

How can we attain the goal in regulating AI? Some may think that regulating AI developers would be regulating AI, but it may not be effective if advanced AI acts in unexpected direction. In that case, there has to be some sort of repercussions for AI itself. In essence, AI regulations would not only have to guide what human developers or users can and cannot do, but limit what AI can and cannot do. We may categorize two types of regulations in regards to advanced types of AI according to the AI Adoption Levels:

- (Level 1 Adoption) To prevent humans from using AI in an undesired way
- (Levels 2, 3, 4 Adoption) To prevent AI from acting in an undesired way

First, we may think of regulations for humans in dimensions of preventing actions, or remedying undesired situations that result from AI adoption.

1. (Actions) Prevent Misbehavior: Humans that may misuse AI for crimes
2. (Situations) Remedy Situation: Inequality stemming from humans using AI
    - Economic: AI ownership, resources for developing AI
    - Social: Limiting power from owning AI

Second, we may think of regulations for AI, where AI may act in an undesired way, or remedying undesired situations that result from AI adoption:

3. (Actions) Prevent AI misbehavior that may cause damage to humans
4. (Situations) Prevent potential threat of Self-Initiated AI ruling over humans

We may categorize the types of regulations by the target of the regulation, and the intention of the regulation as in the following matrix:

Table 16-1: AI Regulation Matrix by Who and What to Regulate

<table>
<tr><th colspan="2" rowspan="2"></th><th colspan="2">Who to Regulate</th></tr>
<tr><th>Humans
(AI Developers, AI Users)</th><th>AI
(Self-Initiated AI)</th></tr>
<tr><th rowspan="2">What to Prevent</th><th>Undesired Actions</th><td>Type 1 Regulation
AI-Related
Crimes & Misuse</td><td>Type 3 Regulation
Prevent Actions of AI that
May Harm Humans</td></tr>
<tr><th>Undesired Situations</th><td>Type 2 Regulation
Asymmetric Ownership of AI that
lead to Monopoly & Dictatorship</td><td>Type 4 Regulation
Prevent Self-Initiated AI
from Taking Charge</td></tr>
</table>

[Decision] How Strong Should AI Regulations Be?

Another topic related to setting the goals of AI regulation may be determining how strong the regulations should be. When we think of the most rigidly regulated industries, we may mention the financial industries, due to their large impact on the economy, or the bio-science and medical industries, due to their ethical and safety implications. On the opposite end of the spectrum, when we think of the least regulated industries, we may point to the cutting-edge technology industries, where regulations may be intentionally set aside to foster innovation. Where in the spectrum should AI regulations be?

We may think of this topic in the dimensions of desired degree of regulation and the actual consequences of introduced regulations.

Desired Degree of AI Regulation: Policy

When we consider the magnitude of the danger we may face as AI technology advances, we eventually may not be able to afford to intentionally reduce regulation to promote innovation or fall behind the curve and do not know what needs to be regulated. Instead, as the importance and concerns regarding AI increases in our society, there may be possibility that people may consider introducing powerful regulations to a level never seen before.

Actual Consequences of AI Regulation: Implementation

AI regulations will be difficult to not only introduce but also implement. Regulators would have to take into account the possibility of falling behind the technology and unintentionally making regulations weak or inadequate. On one side of the spectrum, we may have granular approaches based on specific inputs or outputs. But these detail-oriented regulations may be hard to not only conceive in a timely manner, but also implement and enforce especially with the rapid advances in AI. On the other side of the spectrum, we may take a generalized approach using broad themes such as "AI cannot harm humans," but such approaches may be subject to interpretation so there would be the risk of inconsistent application of law. Therefore, finding the appropriate level of granularity by mixing the right amount would take effort and require constant adjustments.

Failing to adequately regulate AI development and adoption may become a significant source of risk, including existential risk. Thus, we may even be required to introduce a more comprehensive system or concepts on a global scale to reduce such risks falling through the cracks of regulation.

We may categorize the results of AI regulation as intentional or unintentional: Using the two dimensions, we may create the AI Regulation Implementation Matrix as the following.

Table 16-2: The AI Regulation Implementation Controversy Matrix

		Consequences of Government Regulation	
		Intentional	**Unintentional**
Desired Degree of Government Regulation	**High (Pro-Regulation)**	**AI Restricted** Regulation Effective (Scenario 1)	**AI Elusive** Regulation Inadequate (Scenario 2)
	Low (Anti-Regulation)	**AI Unleashed** Regulation Promotes (Scenario 4)	**AI Restrained** Regulation Unintentional (Scenario 3)

Scenario 1: Desired Regulation High, Implementation as Intended
In this scenario, AI regulation will be effectively restrictive as intended. Examples may include AGI is expected to become hostile, so all countries gather to prevent the development of AGI.

Scenario 2: Desired Regulation High, Implementation Not as Intended
In this scenario, AI regulation will not be effective at being restrictive. Examples may include AGI is expected to become hostile, but some cracks in regulations lead to failure in preventing the appearance of hostile AGI.

Scenario 3: Desired Regulation Low, Implementation Not as Intended
In this scenario, the level of AI regulation will not be as non-restrictive as intended. Examples may include situations where a country wants to promote AI development but its regulations still deter private investments in AI.

Scenario 4: Desired Regulation Low, Implementation as Intended
In this scenario, AI regulation will be non-restrictive as intended. Examples may include a situation where a country wants to promote AI development and its regulations attract more private investments in AI.

More Questions for Readers to Ponder:
When is the best time for regulation on AGI? When is too late? How can AI development be dangerous now?

17. The AGI Development Prevention Controversy (What = AGI Supply)

[Decision]

Supply-Side AI Regulation: Should We Ban the Development of AGI?

"What Does Not Exist Cannot Hurt Us"[64]

5-Line Summary

1. We may regulate the "supply" of AGI, which would include banning the development of AGI ("Do not open Pandora's box")
2. Some may argue we should ban the development of AGI to make our world a safer place ("What does not exist cannot hurt us")
3. Some may argue we should accelerate the development of AI to make our world a safer place ("The bad people will get it first")
4. Some may argue AGI development is inevitable because it is economically advantageous ("It is Genie in a Lamp")
5. Some may argue AGI development should be slowed down until we understand it better ("We should confirm which one")

The Value Proposition of Limiting AGI Development

We can postulate that AI will be the most dangerous when AGI self-innovates into a Non-Friendly ASI, or in case of prior to reaching ASI when a "villain" gains control of AI that causes asymmetric advantage in productivity. To prevent this from ever happening, some people may call for the prevention of the development of AGI. This may be thought of as a "what does not exist cannot hurt us" type of approach.

The main argument that supports this notion may be parallel to the ethical banning of manipulating human genes such as stem-cell research. We may apply the same principle in the sense that AGI may be equivalent to trying to manipulate the consciousness of humans and therefore unethical.[65]

Another argument for AGI regulations centers on the need for humans to understand the thinking of AI before it advances beyond humans, a concept known as Trustworthy and Explainable AI, to prevent AI from becoming a black box that just gives out results. Developing AGI may also be compared to opening the Pandora's Box in a religious sense.

The Opposing Argument to Preventing AGI Development

One of the main arguments against banning AGI development would be for financial reasons. The expected financial gains from AGI would be too enormous; it would be akin to a Genie's Lamp. Too many industries would depend on AI that regulations banning AGI would be unlikely to gain traction.

Another argument would be that it would be against national interest if not all of the countries agree to ban AGI development at the same time. Their argument may include "if the bad guys get to AGI first, that would be the real danger" type of arguments that supports acceleration of AGI development.

Realistic Direction of AGI Development Regulation

When we consider the circumstances, introducing supply-side regulation to AGI may instead proceed in the direction of encouraging more competition among developers to prevent monopoly, rather than limiting AI development itself and thereby reducing competition. The hope is that it would be safer to have multiple options of AGI if we are to have any AGI at all. This may result in accelerating the development of AGI, probably an opposite effect of the intentions of the people who support AGI prevention. Since AI technology precedes AI adoption, this discussion will also affect the regulation on AI adoption.

18. The AI Adoption Level Limit Controversy (What = AGI Demand)

[Decision]

Demand-Side AI Regulation: Should We Limit AI Adoption Levels?

"Trying to Ban AGI May Turn Out to Be the Maginot Line of AI Regulation"[66]

5-Line Summary

1. AI Adoption trails AI technological development
2. The AI Pyramid is a framework to help people think about the progress of AI adoption in our society
3. The AI Pyramid can be summarized as Levels 1) Augmentation, 2) Agency, 3) Autonomy, 4) Authority in increasing degrees of AI self-initiation
4. Countries may decide to withhold going into higher levels of AI adoption to ensure safety, which may be thought of as regulating the "demand" of AGI
5. Some may argue limiting adoption levels would be ineffective unless the whole world enforces it

The Value Proposition of Limiting AI Adoption Levels

The Four Levels of AI Adoption, or the AI Pyramid, may be understood as AI increasing in the degree of self-initiation, as summarized by the following:

- Level 1 AI Adoption: (Augmentation) AI as a tool or assistant
- Level 2 AI Adoption: (Agency) AI reach parity with humans for a business role
- Level 3 AI Adoption: (Autonomy) AI gain independence to run companies
- Level 4 AI Adoption: (Authority) AI gain legal rights in and outside of jurisdiction

Depending on how AGI operates, it may be possible to limit its degree of self-initiation, or limit the level of AI adoption. Limiting AI use may be a natural solution when it is necessary to verify safety. For example, in case of self-driving cars or medicine, regulators may just not allow its use until certain levels of safety are achieved. Using this principle, we may reduce risk by prohibiting the use of AI in Level 2 Adoption or higher until we can verify certain standards of AI safety is achieved. Following this line of thinking, some countries may even choose not to enter Levels 3 or 4 Adoption at all.

The Opposing Argument to Limiting AI Adoption Levels

Regulations of this type may not be as effective unless the entire world can introduce regulations of similar strength at the same time and enforce it to a similar degree. It will be similar to the cartels in oligopolies in that if some countries break apart and relax their laws, then they may see an unfair but large economic gain, similar to how one of the OPEC oil producers may gain financially if only one of the members does not reduce production to raise the price.

Limiting demand of AI would be effective if it can hinder investment into developing AGI, but if enough capital is already available from existing investments, this may not be as effective in limiting the development of AGI itself.

Another possibility is that it may become impossible to limit the adoption levels of advanced AI, such that if we try to limit it, AI will find ways to circumvent our regulations. An example may include a rogue AI claiming enough resources to start its own country in Level 4 Adoption.

To summarize, the supply-side and demand-side regulations may work hand-in-hand by reinforcing each other.

19. The AI Monopoly Regulation Controversy (Who = Humans)

[Decision]

Who Should Be Regulated to Reduce AI Risk?

"Competition Good, Monopoly Bad"[67]

5-Line Summary

1. Some may be wary of AGI causing "runaway innovation," where the first company to AGI may gain irreversible advantage over all of the other companies in the world, leading to a monopoly
2. As AI development accelerates, regulators may find it increasingly harder to keep up
3. Innovation or new approaches to regulations may be required
4. The most important aspect of regulations would be finding a way for consistent application of regulations across the world
5. If one country introduces lax regulations while others do not, then it may gain an unfair advantage while potentially endangering all of humanity

[Decision] Preventing the Appearance of Monopolies or Dictators

Value Propositions of This Approach

Some people may argue for regulating the leading AI developer to lower the likelihood of a "runaway innovation." The problem of the increasing tilt of the playing field of the AI development game can be compared to a race that gets successively faster as in the following example from The Last AI.

Let's imagine a race of 50 laps around the track where the speed of the race accelerates. For the first 10 laps, everyone runs, but upon completing the 10th lap, the athletes can then ride a bicycle that will triple the speed for the next 10 laps. After completing the 20th lap, the athletes will then turn to a moped for the next 10 laps that triples the speed. After completing the 30th lap, the athletes will have access to a sports bike for 10 laps that also triples the speed. Finally, beginning in the 40th lap, they will get a jet-powered motorcycle that triples the speed of the sports bike.

In the beginning, when the athletes are running or riding the bicycle, the rankings will depend on the performance of the athletes themselves, based on how they can run or pedal. This is similar to a situation where we do not have AI or Level 1 AI Adoption. The rest of the game will not depend on the athletic performance of the athletes, similar to Level 2, 3, and 4 adoptions. Rather, the final rankings will depend on how soon they arrived at each point of changing the ride. A motorcycle will never be able to catch up to a jet-powered bike going three times faster. That is, unless the athlete in the faster ride loses control and goes off track or trips on something on the ground and falls down. The track could have uneven pavement or maybe not designed for such high speed, but we do not know that. Such situations can be compared to our society being unable to properly control AI through regulation.

From this race, we could glean the following three problems.

1) <u>Likelihood of appearance of monopolies or dictators may increase with AI:</u> AI development can be compared to a race that increasingly accelerates in speed. If someone falls behind in the early stages, namely during Level 1 and earlier part of Level 2 Adoption, it will probably be very hard to overcome the deficit in later stages of the game. When you complete running the laps to get on the bike and think now you will start to catch up, the leaders will already be farther away riding an even faster ride. In this situation, the separation between the leading competitor and the rest will only expand as time goes by,

and the difference will accelerate over time. Unless the rules are adjusted in the earlier part, this game may have a predetermined winner from the start.

2) Regulators May Find It Increasingly Harder to Keep Up:
AI development competition may become harder to control as the speed increases. The speed of the AI development may accelerate beyond the speed our society can respond. Similar to designing a good track and maintaining it in good condition, it may be wise to have relevant regulations and rules in place well before the speed increase becomes too much.

3) Innovation in Regulation or New Types of Regulations May Be Required:
The number of players entering the game may make a difference; if not enough players enter, then no one may be able to finish the race, or an undesired participant may end up winning, like a villain who tries to take over the world. If too many players enter with the intention of cheating or harming other players, it may clog up the track and make it more dangerous for everyone. This type of regulation already exists in banking.

Limitations of This Approach
In reality, these "leveling the playing field" types of regulations would require a global implementation of the same AI regulations if it is to have the intended impact. Instead, developers may find loopholes spread throughout the world to go around any effort to hinder the leading companies. As competition among countries increases, the regulations may have the opposite effect of helping countries trying to aggregate more resources to push their own companies ahead, trying to create an edge while slowing down the AI developers of other countries.

On a side note, the speed of the advances in software technology may be harder to estimate, and these systemic approaches to regulations may not have much impact if they are obsolete. Thus, regulations may need to be introduced in more timely and nimble manner.

20. The Level 2 AI Adoption Regulation Controversy (Who = AI)

[Decision]

How Can We Regulate AI Itself to Reduce AI Risk?

"The Buck Stops Here"

- President Harry S. Truman

5-Line Summary

1. In Level 1 Adoption, there should always be some human responsible for the actions of AI
2. However, beginning with Level 2 Adoption, there may be situations where no human, but only AI may appear to be responsible
3. To deal with these situations, we may need new types of regulations that deals with liabilities that fall on AI itself, not on any humans
4. Regulation may cause delay of introduction of Level 2 Adoption after technology enables it
5. When AI gains more freedom or authority, AI manipulation issues, especially AI being hacked, may become more important

[Level 1 Adoption] Limiting the Potential Range of Actions of AI

One approach to regulation would be to limit the specific activities that would be allowed. In the relaxed approach, the government will list the things that are not allowed, allowing everything else in the "negative list" approach. In the more rigid approach, the government will list the activities that are allowed, not allowing everything else, known as the "positive list" approach.

Limitations of This Approach

The limitation of this approach would be that it will have to be specific about what activities are allowed or not allowed. The most basic approach would be to regulated based on the outcome of the AI. A well-known example of an AI adoption problem is when AI was introduced to determine the lending rates for banks, but upon further analysis it turned out the AI was basing the decision on the race and gender of the applicant, which is illegal. The nature of the sub-symbolic approach of AI makes it hard to track why AI reaches those conclusions and fix such problems. Another approach to regulating may be limiting the input data or the specific act that goes into developing AI. For example, the law may require the data to be free of hacking or injection and not include biased information. The discussions surrounding copyrighted works may be included in this category of regulation. As AI technology develops and the meaning of input data becomes less relevant, this type of regulation may be limited in effectiveness.

From a different direction, we may think of a more generalized approach to regulating, such as the 3 Principles of Robotics.[68] But, the more generalized the regulations become the more likely it will be open for interpretations. For example, we may see cases where an AI followed the directions of humans and carried out some tasks, but it turned out to be harmful to humans and AI had not expected this outcome. When we have regulations that depend on the judgment of AI, then the regulation may not be effective when AI is not highly capable.

In the early stages of AI adoption, regulation frameworks would be based on old concepts for regulating human-initiated interactions, such as regulating human actions on using AI, or trying to prevent bias in training data. While these would be relevant in Level 1 Adoption, higher levels of AI adoption may require new approaches to regulations tailored for AI-initiated interactions. In Level 2 Adoption and beyond, the focus of AI regulation would have to also focus on AI itself. Since we do not yet have such advanced AI, the discussion in this area is bound to cause contrasting ideas.

[Level 2 Adoption] Who Should Be Responsible for the Actions of AI?

A new type of discussion regarding AI regulation should begin as we enter Level 2 Adoption, as discussions regarding legal risks may begin to have larger impact, starting with AI liability.[69] While previous legal approach would focus on human developers or the users of AI, new legal concepts may be required to cover liabilities of AI itself.[70] For regulators, one of the new challenges may include determining how much freedom or authority should be allowed for AI to make its own decisions. This issue would revolve around who should be responsible for what. In level 1 AI adoption, the final responsibility would fall on some human being, since AI was not in charge. In level 2, the responsibility may not be as obvious, as AI begins to make independent decisions where humans are not directly involved in the actions of AI. If AI is to be given more freedom, we would first have to find a way for it to take responsibility. There would be at least two questions to answer:

1) How much authority should be given to Self-Initiated types of AI?
2) What if something goes wrong within the given authorities of AI?

The importance of questions regarding AI responsibility and repercussions would vary widely for different types of tasks. For instance, some decisions of an AI robot may not have much implication for the society. However, tasks that bear economic or social importance may suddenly draw societal interest. An example may be accidents involving self-driving vehicles. In Level 1 AI adoption, there would always be a human driver responsible when something goes wrong, but as Level 5 autonomous vehicles are developed and AI taxis become popular, it would be hard to put the same responsibility to the passengers of these vehicles. Examples could also extend to military uses, where Level 2 Adoption AI robot soldiers would imply the AI robots could make independent decisions to fatally harm humans.

To approach the problem of who should be responsible, we may draw the following table based on the dimension of who are involved. When we consider the typical lifecycle of an AI, it would first have be conceived and created, and then be adopted as a service or product by a user, and then interact with people during the course of its usage. From this perspective, we can categorize the types of problems that can arise during the usage cycle of an AI. Relevant regulation for this human layer would probably be already in place during Level 1 Adoption. Problems caused by the creator of AI could be categorized as a type of design flaw, while problems that could be relegated to the user or the owner of the AI may be called the deployment flaw or the implement flaw. If neither is at fault, we may broadly categorize those as types of regulation flaw, in the sense that it could be caused by some criminal activity such as hacking, or some systematic problem not caught beforehand.

In the beginning stage of Level 2 Adoption, we would likely to need an additional layer that examines the possibilities of AI as a separate entity and prescribes the boundaries of allowed actions. It would be up to the society to determine what the repercussions will be for AI. To make a parallel to humans, there could be different options in severity, such as re-training, which could be compared to taking classes or being fined, wiping out certain memories, which could be compared to community service, or even taking it out of service, which could be similar to sending it to jail. While some may think we can just delete the AI, the parallel is that the more advanced society becomes, the punishments become more civilized and specific. For example, we may think of the pre-medieval times when just about any offense would have led to execution or harsh labor, while the court is becoming more and more lenient in today's society, both in terms of what are punishable offense as well as the degree of punishment.

Table 20-1: Potential AI-Related Problems and Responsible Parties

<table>
<tr><th colspan="2">Party Responsible</th><th>Flaw</th><th>Potential Examples</th><th>Note</th></tr>
<tr><td rowspan="3">Humans</td><td>Creator of AI (Designer)</td><td>AI Design Flaw</td><td>- Premature launch of product
- Neglect, Mistake</td><td rowspan="3">Should be already in place during Level 1 Adoption</td></tr>
<tr><td>User of AI (Owner)</td><td>AI Deployment Flaw</td><td>- Mismatch between AI and intended usage</td></tr>
<tr><td>Neither (Someone Else)</td><td>AI Regulation Flaw</td><td>- (Intentional) Hacking,
- (Unintended) Accidental, such as power outage or other infrastructure failure
- Moving to Level 2 Adoption bad idea</td></tr>
<tr><td colspan="2">AI</td><td>AI-Related Flaw</td><td>- No humans responsible
- (Intentional) Crime by AI
- (Unintentional) AI wrong place at the wrong time, AI not smart enough, etc.</td><td>Newly Introduced for Level 2 Adoption</td></tr>
</table>

[Side Note] The Possibility of AI Being Manipulated: AI Trust Issues

With advanced AI, we may face situations where AI may become not to be trusted, similar in concept to situations where some humans may be bribed, blackmailed, coerced, or even swayed to make unwarranted decisions. Similar to hacking, trust issues regarding the inner workings of AI may stem from two directions of data and algorithm. While people may have the impression that everything AI does would be fair and logical, manipulation issues may make AI harder to trust, since it would become increasingly more complicated to verify what AI does is not compromised by external forces or influences.

1) Data Related Issues

The first issue stems from the difficulty of controlling what AI learns because AI is trained with vast amount of data. The data used to train AI may intentionally or unintentionally contain something that could be harmful. For example, many AI developers use text and image data downloaded from the internet. Not only could these data contain incorrect information, some ill-meaning people could secretly place certain bits of information scattered around the internet that could later be manipulated, as in data poisoning or sleeper agent attacks triggered by custom phrases.[71]

2) Software (Algorithm) Related Issues

The second issue is more general in that it is hard to understand how AI reaches its conclusions. The nature of the popular AI of today that uses deep learning and other sub-symbolic approaches is that they are hard to understand for humans. To sidestep this problem, concepts such as Explainable AI have been suggested to make AI easier to understand for humans.

21. The AGI Containment Controversy (How)

[Forecast]

Limitations of Regulations: What If We Cannot Enforce Regulations on AGI?

"You and What Army?"[72]

- *Insurmountable AGI*

5-Line Summary

1. Some may argue the biggest problem in regulating AI is that it may become impossible to enforce regulations on AGI
2. AI may become better at breaking or tweaking the laws, requiring introduction of more or better laws
3. AI may even find ways to become "above the law" by gaining more authority, or "outside the law" by going outside human jurisdictions
4. The first AGI may present additional challenge if it offers a large enough advantage over alternative AI options
5. If a villain develops the first AGI, the relative performance of AGI against alternative AI would become important

What Kind of Regulations Can We Really Enforce on AGI?

As AI adoption level increases, we may reach a point where new laws may have to deal with AI more than humans, since AI may become able to find and exploit loopholes better than humans. Even though we may draw up a wide variety of different approaches to regulating AI, as AI advances, how much we can affect how AI acts or makes decisions may become the most important focus of enforcing regulations. With advanced types of AI that may draw its own conclusions, it would become less clear what roles humans can play in preventing AI from acting in undesirable ways.

Regardless of how well we create the regulations, AGI may even find ways to circumvent the regulations, such as becoming a rogue AI president or an AI dictator, which would effectively let AI be "above the law." In addition, AI may decide to go "outside the law" by starting its own country if it gains enough resources, which may enable AI to move past human jurisdictions.

Irreversibility: The Importance of Timely and Relevant AI Regulation

One of the biggest risks on AGI is the irreversibility of failures. If regulations fail to prevent AGI that becomes hostile to humanity, it may be impossible to reverse it course, similar in concept to opening the Pandora's Box.

If regulators fail to introduce relevant measures and AI is designed to be given too much independence early in the development path, eventually more advanced AI that arrives afterwards with the same lax philosophy may place the interests of AI ahead of those of humans, potentially leading AI to act against humanity. If the reason human villains cannot succeed in the long term is because their resources and productivity are lower, then we cannot rule out the possibility of an unexpectedly rogue AGI or a villain with AGI gaining a higher level of productivity that surpasses the rest of the humanity.

The nature of AI adoption to increase productivity will raise the social risk regardless of what the intentions were in developing the AI. If we consider the development of AGI as the most significant inflection point in AI technology, then our society could be most vulnerable when it happens, as the public's access may be limited at the beginning. The best we can hope for is that AGI will not raise the productivity so much over what alternative AI is publicly available at the time, or AGI is not available in a lopsided manner that the gain benefits only a limited number of bad players.

[Forecast] What If Some Villain Tries to Develop the First AGI?

Table 21-1 categorizes based on the potential order of obtaining AGI, and the gap between AGI and other alternative AI that may be available at the time.

If the performance of AGI is insurmountable against the rest of available AI, then the outcome would be deterministic. In this scenario, what would be of utmost importance would be who develops AGI first. On the other hand, if the gap between AGI and other AI used in combination with humans is small such that there is reasonable competitiveness, then there may be variability of outcome. In this scenario, trying to bring diversity to AI development may offer some value.

Table 21-1: The First AGI Containment Controversy Matrix

		Whether AGI Will Be Insurmountable (Technological Perspective)	
		AGI Irreplaceable (Insurmountable)	**AGI Replaceable (Competing AI Available)**
Who Owns AGI First (Social Perspective)	**The "Good" (AI Heroes)**	Villain Is Suppressed (Scenario 1)	Villain Resists (Scenario 2)
	The "Bad" (AI Villains)	Villain Takes Over (Scenario 4)	Heroes Resist (Scenario 3)

Scenario 1 (Best Situation): Villain Is Suppressed
The good people will have an insurmountable advantage over the villains.

Scenario 2 (Somewhat Dangerous): Villains Resist with Alternate AI
Even if the good people develop AGI first, the villains may gather enough resources to mount a competitive effort using alternates to the AGI

Scenario 3 (Significantly Dangerous): Heroes Resist with Alternate AI
Even if the villains develop AGI first, the heroes may have a decent chance by resisting with alternatives to the AGI

Scenario 4 (Most Dangerous): Villain Will Take Over
If the AGI developed by the villains is insurmountable using any other AI, the good people may not have a chance to overcome the villains.

22. The AI Godzilla Controversy

[Decision]

Should We Ban AI Robots Bigger and Stronger than Humans?

"Who You Gonna Call?"

- From the Ghost Busters theme song[73]

5-Line Summary

1. People may have a variety of reasons or incentives to develop self-initiated AI robots that are much bigger and stronger than humans
2. Some may be concerned that if something goes wrong with such superhuman robots, we may have a hard time stopping it
3. Some may consider AI imitating humans may be a bigger threat than AI that looks different from us
4. Some may support such superhuman robots because it will be able to carry out tasks humans cannot (Super Workers, Super Heroes)
5. Some may argue for a ban or a limit on building superhuman AI robots (AI Godzilla, Super Villains)

[Forecast] The 30-Foot Household Guard Robots: Godzilla or Mazinger Z?

As humans, we may be biased to think about everything in relation to our own perspective. Strengths and sizes may be examples of those areas. There are certainly advantages for designing humanoid robots to be human-size and strength, because our environment is already designed for us. But what would happen if people start designing human-superior robots to be much larger or stronger than humans to gain some advantage?

Imagine a breakthrough in AI military robot has been introduced, that is 30 foot tall, 10 times stronger and agile than an average human. Think huge robots in cartoons such as Mazinger Z. This will certainly help us win wars. One aspect of technology development is that new technologies originally developed for military use eventually finds way to consumer use. So, let us imagine this 30 foot tall robot will soon be introduced as "household" robots, which could be used for, among other things, standing in front of houses such as those of rich people or even cartels to brush off any potential intruders.

Cases for Allowing Human-Superior Robots: Why Build Them?

At first, the general public may not see any problem with allowing these superhuman robots, since we already have a variety of machines that exceed humans in strength and sizes, such as cars, heavy equipment, etc. Robots with superhuman strength or agility would have a wide range of commercial uses, such as in construction and in factories, as well as government use outside of military, such as in law enforcement.

Cases for Banning Human-Superior Robots: What Could Go Wrong?

The problem may be that people may initially have a hard time imagining the dangers of living with AI robots that surpass humans in dimensions or capabilities because we do not have them around us yet. At first, it may even appear these robots enable people to accomplish tasks hard for humans with ease. However, the potential for abuse may exponentially increase as the gap in capabilities between humans and AI increase.

What if some villain builds a huge robot to take over a city as in movies? While today's rich may be happy to build 200-foot yachts, they may get into a match where they try to one-up each other to see who can build the biggest and strongest robots. What if one of the superhuman robots becomes rogue or by mistake starts stomping on people walking on the streets like a Godzilla? What if 30-foot AI cops go rogue and demands ransoms from bystanders with overwhelming force? Only other superhuman robots will be able to stop it.

[Decision] Should Human-Superior Robots Be Allowed?

Should these types of human-superior AI robots be allowed or banned? We may categorize this controversy based on the dimensions of desired degree of power in robots, or the tech perspective, and the perception of risks that will be caused by AI robots, or the social perspective, as in the following matrix.

Table 22-1: The Human-Superior Robot Controversy Matrix

<table>
<tr><th colspan="2" rowspan="2"></th><th colspan="2">Desired or Feared Degree of Robot Power
(Technological Perspective)</th></tr>
<tr><th>Similar to Humans
(Up to Human Size)</th><th>Superior to Humans
(The Larger the Better)</th></tr>
<tr><td rowspan="2">Perception of Danger or Benefit of AI Robots (Social Perspective)</td><td>High = Dangerous (AI Pessimists)</td><td>AI Imitating Humans
(Group 1)</td><td>AI Godzilla
(Group 2)</td></tr>
<tr><td>Low = Beneficial (AI Optimists)</td><td>AI Worker
(Group 3)</td><td>AI Super Heroes
(Group 4)</td></tr>
</table>

Group 1: Biggest Risks Will Be AI Robots Indistinguishable from Humans

People in this group would be more likely to imagine humanoid robots of human sizes, indistinguishable from humans. Their perception of danger would be high because AI robots may hide among humans. Think Clark Kent or the Terminator. People in this group may be more likely to view the biggest risks to come from AI robots indistinguishable from humans.

Group 2: Biggest Risks Will Be AI Robots Overwhelming Humans

People in this group would be more likely to imagine humanoid robots of super-human sizes and strengths, displaying and abusing overwhelming force. Their perception of danger would be high because AI robots would exceed human capabilities. Think Mazinger Z or King Kong. People in this group may be more likely to view the biggest risks to come from superhuman robots that will overwhelm humans physically.

Group 3: Biggest Opportunity Will Be AI Worker Robots

People in this group would be more likely to imagine humanoid robots of human sizes, indistinguishable from humans. Their perception of benefit would be how AI may replace tasks currently carried out by humans.

Group 4: Biggest Opportunity Will Be AI Super Heroes

People in this group would be more likely to imagine humanoid robots of super-human sizes and strengths. Their perception of benefit would be how these AI robots would accomplish super-human tasks we cannot carry out.

23. The Degree of ASI Superiority Controversy

[Forecast]

How Superior to Humans Can ASI Become?

What If ASI Cannot Be Much Smarter Than Humans?

"A Question That Is Not Asked Cannot Be Answered."[74]

5-Line Summary

1. Some may argue there may be a limit on how much ASI can become intelligent
2. Some may argue the speed at which ASI can become more intelligent may be slower than people generally expect
3. Some may argue that ASI can become faster but not much more intelligent
4. We may examine what kind of tasks or questions ASI may carry out or answer that we cannot answer in the ASI Question Matrix
5. The 6 Levels of Humanity's Last Exam framework was introduced to help people think about the types of benchmarks that may be created

What If ASI Turns Out to Be A Silly Sissy?

In the Upward part of the Circle, we examined how ASI or Absolute AI may advance so much beyond humanity such that we may consider it "artificial god."[75] In this downward part of the circle, we may focus on how ASI may not be able to go much further beyond humanity. In other words, some people may argue that ASI will be disappointing or may never appear. We may examine a few arguments that support a weak or a meandering ASI.

1. **Limitation on Intelligence Argument:** There may be limit on intelligence, and humans may not be far from it.

2. **Relative Intelligence Argument:** In this practical argument, the focus will be on the relativity of the intelligence between humans and AI. For example, ASI may keep getting smarter, but humans will too so the gap will not become that large between the two.

3. **Decreasing Returns to Investment Argument:** The investment required to make ASI smarter will become exponentially high, such that ASI will get smarter at an ever-slowing rate instead of an intelligence explosion.

4. **AI Will Never Go Beyond Certain Level of Intelligence:** AGI or ASI may never become as smart as we imagine. An example of this is the Fast-Thinking Dog argument,[76] that AI may become faster but not smarter.

What Do We Not Know? What Kind of New Questions Can ASI Answer?

When we try to list ASI superiority in different dimensions, we may see that there are a lot of different ways ASI can become superior to humans, some of which may have already been achieved by less advanced AI. For example:

1) ASI is able to answer the questions humans cannot answer
2) ASI is able to ask question in a way humans cannot ask
3) ASI can carry out tasks humans cannot carry out
4) ASI can recognize patterns humans cannot recognize
5) ASI can understand the world better than humans
6) ASI can make predictions better than humans, for both about the future and the past
7) ASI can make better decisions than humans

We will examine some of these topics in the next side note about the ultimate questions and the Six Levels of Humanity's Last Exam.

Systemically Thinking About Limitations of ASI Superiority

In the following table, we may think of how much ASI may become superior to humans along two dimensions of how quickly AI would become smarter, and how quickly AI may act in terms of societal impact. For example, an ASI that acts quickly may include ASI ignoring human regulations, such as attempting to take over a country without going through an election.

Table 23-1: The ASI Superiority Matrix

<table>
<tr><th colspan="2" rowspan="2"></th><th colspan="2">Direction of ASI Development
(Technological Perspective)</th></tr>
<tr><th>Smarter
(Qualitative)</th><th>Not Smarter but Faster
(Quantitative)</th></tr>
<tr><td rowspan="2">Speed of ASI Impact (Social Perspective)</td><td>Quick</td><td>Scenario 1
(Unfathomable ASI)</td><td>Scenario 3
(Insurmountable ASI)</td></tr>
<tr><td>Slow</td><td>Scenario 2
(Manageable ASI)</td><td>Scenario 4
(Subpar ASI)</td></tr>
</table>

Scenario 1 (Unfathomable ASI): In this scenario, ASI may become so much smarter than humanity so quickly, and its effects will be felt at a quick pace, that it will be hard for humans to manage or react.

Scenario 2 (Manageable ASI): Even if ASI becomes smarter quickly, it may take its time in making a societal impact. ASI may also become smarter than humanity at a relatively slow rate. The danger may be more manageable, in the sense that there may be more time to respond. However, it may turn out be a case of slow checkmate, where the end result cannot be changed.

Scenario 3 (Insurmountable ASI): ASI may be able to make fast decisions so its performance against humans may be insurmountable even if it does not get smarter as quickly.

Scenario 4 (Subpar ASI): ASI may not turn out to be as impactful as imagined

Among these four scenarios, what most people are worried is Scenario 1, where the explosive advancements in AI forces swift changes to our society in unexpected ways. As described in The Last AI, this may be the path where we may see an undesired entry into Level 4 Adoption led by AI. On the other hand, some people may consider Scenario 4 as an AI bubble.

[Side Note] What Can We Ask ASI? The Ultimate Questions / Benchmark

As LLMs advance, people have been saying LLMs are passing all of the benchmarks, such that we are running out of tests to measure the capabilities of AI. In 2024, an effort named Humanity's Last Exam[77] tried to aggregate the questions that are deemed the hardest questions humans can generate and answer. If we ask these questions to AI, maybe we can say ASI will get all of it right. From this line of thought, we may ask the question: What would come after Humanity's Last Exam? How should we think about the super-human questions of ASI?

First, we may categorize all forms of questions that may exist into two categories: the questions we are able to ask and those we are not. In the same way, we may also categorize all forms of questions into questions we are able to answer, and those we are not. Going further, because there may be questions ASI can answer but we cannot, we may additionally categorize the types of questions humans cannot answer but can understand once answer is given by ASI, and those we cannot understand even if we are given the answers.[78] We may categorize all forms of questions into the eight categories as shown in the following table:

Table 23-1: The ASI Question Matrix[79]

<table>
<tr><th colspan="3" rowspan="2"></th><th colspan="2">Questions Humans Can Ask</th></tr>
<tr><th>Yes</th><th>No</th></tr>
<tr><td rowspan="4">Questions Humans Can Answer</td><td colspan="2">Yes</td><td>Type 1 Questions
Ask: Yes
Answer: Yes</td><td>Type 2 Questions
Ask: No
Answer: Yes</td></tr>
<tr><td rowspan="3">No</td><td>Humans Can Comprehend ASI's Solution</td><td>Type 3 Questions
Ask: Yes
Answer: No
Understand ASI: Yes</td><td>Type 4 Questions
Ask: No
Answer: No
Understand ASI: Yes</td></tr>
<tr><td>Humans Cannot Comprehend ASI's Solution</td><td>Type 5 Questions
Ask: Yes
Answer: No
Understand ASI: No</td><td>Type 6 Questions
Ask: No
Answer: No
Understand ASI: No</td></tr>
<tr><td>ASI Cannot Answer</td><td>Type 7 Questions</td><td>Type 8 Questions</td></tr>
</table>

From this table, we may think of how AI may be able to answer the questions in each category.

Type 1 Questions: Can Humans Ask? Yes, Can Humans Answer? Yes
Questions humans can ask and answer.

Type 2 Questions: Can Humans Ask? No, Can Humans Answer? Yes
Questions humans cannot ask, but can answer if we are asked. Even though it may be hard to imagine such questions since we cannot ask them, we may be able to extrapolate from our experiences of dealing with animals that have inferior cognitive capabilities than humans. For example, we may train dogs to answer questions that dogs themselves do not ask. In the same principle, there may be questions that may be asked on us that we ourselves cannot ask. If some advanced forms of AI can form such questions and asked us, then these types of questions would be categorized as Type 2 Questions.

Note on Question Types 3-8: These deal with questions we cannot answer. Our world may be filled with questions that we cannot answer. For example, we may ask random but hard-to-answer questions such as: what will be the stock price a year from now? How many wild animals in total came within a mile radius of President George Washington on July 4th 1791 and what were they?[80] If ASI could answer these questions, or came closer to answering them than humans can, then it would be considered advancing our knowledge. Without taking into ASI into account, this matrix would just have the First 4 Types. With ASI, we may additionally consider a new criterion of human comprehension to add sub-categories Types 5 and 6, where humans can understand the solution once ASI gives the solution, to tell apart the questions that we also cannot understand the solution even if ASI explains the answers.

Type 3 Questions: Ask? Yes, Answer? No, Understand ASI Explanation? Yes
Questions that we may ask, cannot answer by ourselves, but would be able to understand if ASI can explain the answers for us. Examples mentioned in The Last AI include "How many children would be born within the current state line of Texas on November 8th, 2994?" Before ASI, this question would be a Type 3 Question. But once we have ASI, we will have an additional category, since if ASI can give the answer and we can understand the explanation, this would be categorized as a Type 3 but if we cannot understand ASI, then it would be a Type 5 Question.

Type 4 Questions: Ask? No, Answer? No, Understand ASI Explanation? Yes
Questions humans cannot form, and even if we heard it, we would not be able to answer, but once ASI can explain it to us, we will understand the answer. If AI were able to form and answer such questions, then we may consider it to have superior capabilities than humans. The division between Types 2 and 4, that whether humans can answer a given question, may be in principle be different from questions that humans can understand the solution when the solution is also given.

In 3 and 4, if we can understand the solution and replicate the question, it will become a Type 1 question. We may call this process "learning" from ASI.

Type 5 Questions: Ask? Yes, Answer? No, Understand ASI Explanation? No
Questions that we may ask, cannot answer by ourselves, and even if ASI can answer them and explain it to us, we will not be able to comprehend the explanation. As explained in the previous paragraphs, our world may be filled with these types of questions. An example of this type of questions is an answer that takes thousands of years to explain at our speed of comprehension, such that we will not be able to live long enough to learn the answer. We may not yet be able to discern whether a question would be a Type 3 or 5 before ASI can explain it to us.

Type 6 Questions: Ask? No, Answer? No, Understand ASI Explanation? No
Questions that we cannot ask, cannot answer by ourselves, and even if ASI can answer them and explain it to us, we will not be able to comprehend the explanation. This would be the "final frontier" of questions that would be left from humanity. It would be impossible to give an example of such questions.

Type 7 Questions: Humans Can Ask, Even ASI Cannot Answer
Questions of this type may be the hardest questions we can think of to answer, such that even ASI will not be able to answer. An example of this type of questions may include knowing something very specific about the past or the future: "Within 1 mile of what is now the US White House, how many dinosaurs in total had a meal between 200 and 300 million years ago?" or "What will happen exactly 5,000 years and 1 day from now?"

Type 8 Questions: Humans Cannot Ask, ASI Cannot Answer
Questions of this type may be the hardest, even though we do not know if they really exist. These may be the questions ASI can ask but not answer.

[Side Note] The Six Levels of Humanity's Last Exam[81]

We may think of two main reasons why we would need to categorize how ASI may ask or answer questions. One is to develop more useful benchmarks to test the ASI, and another is to further our own learning in some way.

(New Benchmark Perspective) We may consider the Humanity's Last Exam[82] as the hardest Type 1 Questions where we know the answers. However, this is not the final questions we can ask in a benchmark, as there are more types of questions we can ask, but not answer. From this revelation, we may develop new types of AI benchmarks after we reach ASI, where we try to examine the answers ASI provides to glean into the capabilities. An example of this type of question is already spreading through social media such as X, where people ask AI to generate cryptic messages and ask another AI to explain the message.[83] Meanwhile, the ultimate form of AI benchmark may be AI Economics, as introduced in The Last AI.

("Learning Experience" Perspective) Currently, we typically use a measuring stick of reaching parity to benchmark, where a score of getting everything correct, or 100%, is the maximum. When we use this approach, eventually, we will run out of questions to discern AI capabilities. While one of the solutions is presented as AI Economics in The Last AI, another perspective regarding this situation is to think of it as a "learning experience" from ASI that makes humanity smarter. An example we may compare may be how researchers try to teach primates how to drive golf carts or a language.

From the 8 types of questions in the ASI Question Matrix, we may think of the Six Levels of Humanity's Last Exam as the following and table:

Level 0 (Humanity's Last Exam): Questions Humans Can Ask and Answer

This would be the types of exam similar to Humanity's Last Exam, where humans can ask and answer the questions. However, since ASI would be superior to humans, it should be able to complete these types of exams with ease. Humans should be able to verify the correctness of the answers.

Level 1: Questions Humans Cannot Ask but Can Answer

This would be the types of exam where ASI or another AI may be asked to ask a question that we cannot ask but know the answer, and then solve it. Humans should be able to verify the correctness of the answers. ASI is not required in the sense that an AI may fail to generate the questions humans cannot ask.

Level 2: Humans Can Ask, Cannot Answer, Understand Solution
This would be the type of exam where humans ask questions we do not know the answer to, similar to asking an Oracle. Even though we do not know the answer prior to the exam, the answer provided by ASI will be understandable, which would mean we would be able to discern the capabilities among different ASI.

Level 3: Humans Cannot Ask or Answer, Understand Solution
This would be the type of questions where an ASI or a different AI would be asked to generate a question that we cannot and cannot answer, and then solve it. Even though we would not be able to verify the answer, once ASI explains the solution, humans should be able to understand it.

Level 4: Humans Can Ask but Not Answer, Cannot Understand Solution
This would be the type of question we can ask, but cannot verify the answer or understand the solution. The only way to glean into the capabilities of ASI may be to use another ASI to verify or confirm the answers.

Level 5: Humans Can Ask but Not Answer, Cannot Understand Solution
This would be similar to Level 4 that we cannot understand the solution. ASI or another AI may be asked to generate a question we cannot ask or answer, and since we cannot understand the solution, another ASI may be needed to verify or confirm the answers to glean the relative capabilities of ASI.

Table 23-2: The Six Levels of Humanity's Last Exam for ASI[84]

<table>
<tr><th></th><th>Level 0</th><th>Level 1</th><th>Level 2</th><th>Level 3</th><th>Level 4</th><th>Level 5</th></tr>
<tr><td>Questions that:</td><td>Humans Can Ask and Answer</td><td>Humans Cannot Ask but Can Answer</td><td>Humans Can Ask but Not Answer, but Can Understand Solution</td><td>Humans Cannot Ask or Answer, but Can Understand Solution</td><td>Humans Can Ask but Not Answer, and Cannot Understand Solution</td><td>Humans Cannot Ask or Answer, and Cannot Understand Solution</td></tr>
<tr><td>Attribute</td><td colspan="2">Humans Can Verify</td><td colspan="2">Humans Can Understand</td><td colspan="2">Another ASI is Required</td></tr>
<tr><td>Summary</td><td colspan="3">ASI is Not Required
for Exam to Be Valuable</td><td colspan="3">At Least 1 ASI is Required
for Exam to Be Valuable</td></tr>
</table>

Applications of New Questions We Previously Could Not Answer

This nature of ASI being able to answer questions humans previously could not answer would open so much more possibilities for economically valuable tasks it may come as mind-boggling for many people. As suggested by the motto of Level 1 Adoption in The Last AI, "If you can think it, you can do it," it may appear ASI can just "do" things people thought impossible that they did not even imagine.

For example, let us consider a hypothetical situation. AI can help archaeology. Let us think about how humans first saw fossils and surmised it was from long time ago. Fossil takes the form of something that we can recognize as having some meaning. In other words, we may think of fossil as a pattern that we recognize as separate from what surrounds it, in such a way that when we see it, we pay attention to it. With ASI, it may be able to recognize more patterns we can only dream of. What if some fossils disintegrated, but all of the chemicals still stays in the vicinity? Right now, we would not be able to recognize it because it would not be a pattern we notice. But what if some ASI observes it and surmises it was once a fossil? In other words, AI that is able to recognize patterns humans cannot recognize could be used to gain new types of insights and add value.

Going even further, let us imagine an old but unsolved archaeological site. If an ASI goes to see the scene, analyze all of the molecules that happened to be in the area, and asks a question something like "if we analyze this set of molecules each located here and moving in this direction, where were the molecules thousands of years ago, can we find out who built this? If the ASI can answer this, then it would be as if the ASI can work as a world simulator, as if it "compresses" the world, instead of just knowledge. If we take this line of thinking further, eventually, we may think some form of advanced AI may be able to predict the past and the future with so much precision it may appear they are like an "all-knowing god."

More Questions for Readers to Ponder:

- How will we measure AI performance? Relative vs Absolute approaches

24. The AI Relative Value System Controversy

[Decision]

Should AI Be Allowed to Prefer Certain Humans Over Another?

"Approximation Does Not Always Give You the Correct Answer"

5-Line Summary

1. As AI is given more agency and autonomy in Level 2 and 3 Adoption, the topic of AI value system will gain more attention
2. For safety, it would be best for humanity to instill an absolute value system where all humans come before AI
3. However, for economic reasons some may argue for a relative value system where AI prefers some humans over other humans
4. The relative value system may eventually lead AI to prefer AI over some humans, which could lead to a disastrous situation
5. This problem will become more important in higher adoption levels

[Forecast] The Dilemma of Allowing AI to be an Independent Entity

We may think of going up the AI Pyramid, or raising the level of AI adoption, as a process of giving AI freedom as an independent entity. The reason for people to support this is mainly economical. To reduce the risks associated with independent AI, the AI value system may need a stronger emphasis on humans. However, placing all humans above AI will reduce economic value of AI; people may compromise by letting AI discriminate among humans.

First, we may examine the AI Freedom Dilemma Matrix. As described in The Last AI, our society may face a type of Prisoner's Dilemma, as shown in table:

- **(AI Gaining Independence)** AI gaining independence as a result of social friction
- **(AI Alignment Risk)** AI may make decisions that endanger mankind because it is not human, known as the alignment problem. We may express this value system as "AI is more important than humans (AI > Human)."

Table 24-1: Example of the AI Freedom Dilemma Matrix[85]

Choice Set		Degree of AI Independence	
		Do Not Give AI Freedom	Give AI Freedom
AI Value System (Alignment)	Humans > AI	Less Efficient (-1pt)	Most Efficient (+5pt)
	AI ≥ Humans	Less Efficient, But Hopefully Avert AI From Acting Against Humans (+3pt)	More Efficient, But AI Would Be Free to Act Against Humans (-10pt)

If AI is friendly to humans, then giving AI freedom is more efficient. If AI is not friendly to humans, then not giving AI freedom would be better.

Even though we cannot be certain whether advanced AI will be friendly or not, some people will argue for giving AI more freedom regardless, based on their financial or other interests, claiming the probability of AI turning out unfriendly would be quite low. The best long-term situation for humanity would be to have AI dependent on humans in some way, such as setting the value system to be [All Humans > AI], etc. But, such actions may drastically reduce the effectiveness of AI and the potential areas of AI adoption, meaning it will have large financial costs associated with it and reduce profit.

[Decision] The Compromise: AI Value System that Discriminates Humans

People may become divided over whether the costs outweigh the benefits. Eventually, there may be a compromise in the middle, where AI may instead be given a value system that places relative values on humans, such that:

Friendly Humans > Non-Friendly Humans

This compromise may offer large financial reward for AI developers. We may examine the dilemma regarding AI value system in a competitive situation as shown in the next table. From the perspective of the Group A, instilling a value system where AI prefers humans in Group A is preferable regardless of what value system AI is given by people in Group B, and vice versa. Thus, both groups prefer to instill an AI value system that prefers their own group.

However, when we consider the potential outcome for all of the four possibilities, this situation would bring the worst result. The best result would come when both Groups A and B decide to instill a value system that does not differentiate among humans, but similar to the Prisoner's Dilemma, the best result cannot occur without collaboration between the groups.

Table 24-2: The AI Relative Value Dilemma Matrix

Choice Set		**Group B**	
		All Humans > AI (Absolute Value)	**Humans in B > A (Relative Value)**
Group A	**All Humans > AI (Absolute Value)**	Action: A: Less Efficient (-1pt) B: Less Efficient (-1pt) Result: Short Term: Low Efficiency (-2pt) Long Term: **Safest (+5pt)**	Action: A: Less Efficient (-1pt) B: More Efficient (+2pt) Result: Short Term: Financial Gain (+1pt) Long Term: **Increased Risk (-5pt)**
	Humans in A > B (Relative Value)	Action: A: More Efficient (+2pt) B: Less Efficient (-1pt) Result: Short Term: Financial Gain (+1pt) Long Term: **Increased Risk (-5pt)**	Action: A: More Efficient (+2pt) B: More Efficient (+2pt) Result: Short Term: Financial Gain (+4pt) Long Term: **Least Safe (-10pt)**

Probably the best option for humans is to ensure AI as dependent on humans, where AI is designed to value all humans more than AI (Humans > AI).

However, this may be inefficient from an economic sense. More importantly, humans ourselves may be divided strongly, causing both sides to agree that AI need to gain more independence from either side, or take a shortcut where the basic premise of AI is altered slightly to divide humans into two groups of "us and them," and then favor "us" more than "them" rather than settling on a value system that divides only between humans and AI.

Developers may decide this is sufficient, as AI designed with this value system may have higher economic value for them, and it may be easier and less costly to develop. Since valuing humans against each other but not against AI may provide the appearance of instilling virtue in AI, public may not notice this, which may eventually cause significant problems.

[Decision] The Need for Balance of Growth and Safety in AI Regulation

Even though we would not be able to predict what exactly would happen, advanced AI may pose existential threat to humans in some form or another. Our hope is that introducing enough regulation would be able to mitigate this.

This possibility of threat is probably enough to do our best to provide the right incentive to prevent moral hazard. In recent history, the global economy experienced similar problem with pollution, as corporations without the right incentives may be causing irreparable harm to the environment and the ecosystem. It would cost more to reverse course after the harm has already occurred; with AI it may be impossible to reverse course. If AI development continues without a proper standard, eventually AI may harm some humans more than others, and possibly all humans without recourse.

Another issue is the difficulty of analyzing decision processes of AI. There are arguments to make the decision processes of AI more understandable to humans, such as Explainable AI.[86] There is a tradeoff between advancing AI technology and allocating resources to review what AI is doing. Similar to how "Thought Police" is hard to exist for humans, it may be just as resource-intensive to create an equivalent of Thought Police for AI. Since regulations would be likely to be enforced differently across the globe, countries with stronger regulation may stifle advancements relative to nations with lax regulation. There would need to be a balance between growth and safety.

25. The Human vs AI Competition Controversy (The Most Important AI Regulation)

[Forecast]

Can Competition between Humans and AI Be Avoided?

"The Most Important AI Regulation Controversy"

5-Line Summary

1. Some may argue the most important regulation is limiting the competition between humans vs AI
2. In Level 2 AI Adoption, AI would be competing against individuals
3. In Level 3 AI Adoption, AI would be competing against companies
4. In Level 4 AI Adoption, AI would be competing against countries, then even against all of humanity
5. The Inverse Pyramid of AI Threat was introduced in The Last AI to help people visualize how the AI risk may increase by the scope of influence

[Decision] Can Competition Between AI and Humans Be Avoided?

In The Last AI, the temporal advance of AI adoption in business and society was examined from a business perspective by dividing the adoption process into different levels. A common theme that could be found in each of the levels was the concept of "competition." In each level of AI adoption, we may express the risks involved in allowing AI to compete, as the following:

- **Adoption Level 1:** "Should AI be allowed to help people compete?"
- **Adoption Level 2:** "Should AI be allowed to compete against **individuals**?"
- **Adoption Level 3:** "Should AI be allowed to compete against **companies**?"
- **Adoption Level 4**: "Should AI be allowed to compete against **countries or even humanity**?"

In Level 1 AI Adoption, AI only helps people compete against other people. Humans are the main body of competition. However, in Level 2 Adoption, we may observe AI competing directly against humans. There would likely be people who see the potential for economic gains and support moving to higher AI adoption levels and climb the AI Pyramid. On the other side, there may be people who see the danger in letting AI compete against humans and call for limiting AI adoption levels.

[Forecast] The Most Important AI Regulation Controversy

On the flip side of these "can we allow AI to compete" questions, we have the more intrinsic "what kind of value system should we instill in AI in regards to humans?" question. In societies where humans are truly valued, the ultimate direction of the value instilled in AI should be to not allow AI to compete against humans at all.

However, in societies where money is more valued, AI will be allowed to compete against humans. Especially in the early stage of AI adoption, the difference between a value system that values humans versus one that values money may appear small, and the amount of profit created by AI may seem large, leading to an easy acceptance of allowing AI to value some humans more than others. We will later examine how this type of relative values may grow into a larger problem that may be hard to revert later in the adoption process if AI gains more power or turns Non-Friendly to humanity.

To summarize, the real limitations of AI regulation may be that it would be hard to prohibit the competition between AI and humanity.

The Inverse Pyramid of AI Threat to Humanity by the Scope of Influence

The general public probably concurs with the concerns regarding how AGI or ASI that surpasses human capabilities may be dangerous to humanity, but many may wonder why the dangers of AI that is not as intelligent as humans could also be urgent. Since dangerous events sometimes occur all of a sudden but also happen as a result of accumulation of past activities, we may perform checks on a few potential areas of danger regardless of the degree of advances in AI. To help this analysis, the range of influence in each of the levels of AI adoption may be used to review dangers that may build up long-term when we allow AI to compete against humans.

The Inverse Pyramid of AI Threat by the Scope of AI Influence
We may examine how AI may endanger our society in each level of AI adoption by considering the nature of competition between AI and the levels of human organizations. We may express the scopes AI influence as AI takes on more important roles as an inverse pyramid as in the following figure.

Figure 25-1: Sohn's Inverse Pyramid of AI Threat by Scope of AI Influence[87]

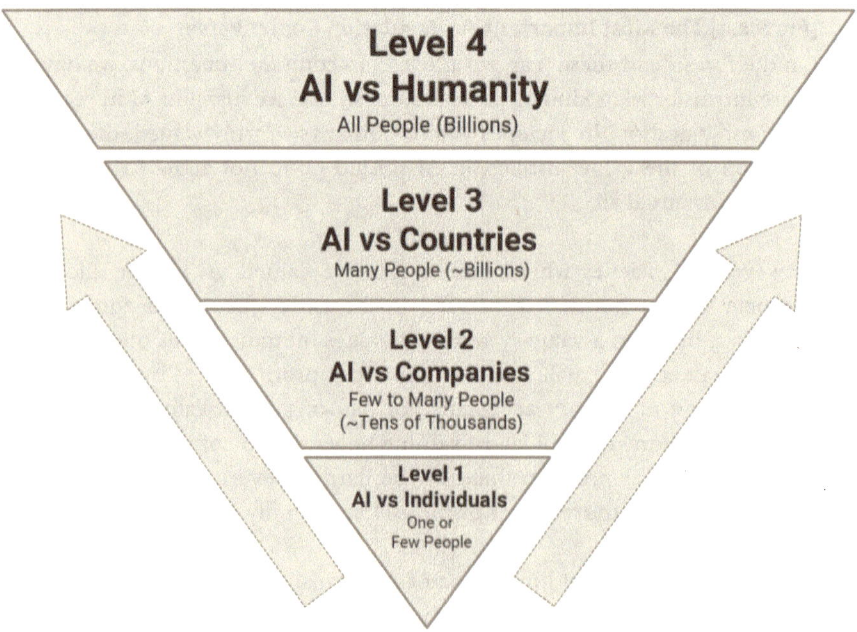

(Level 1 AI Threat) Competition of AI vs Individuals: Impact of Few People
The scope of AI influence would be at a magnitude of a single individual or a few individuals. From an economic standpoint, AI replaces individuals. Even though an AI may financially set back those individuals, other people will financially benefit from the competition. Consequently, from the standpoint of the society AI will benefit the whole economy so there would not be much incentive for the society to prevent the competition of AI versus individuals.

(Level 2 Threat) Competition of AI vs Companies: Impact of Few to Many
Entering Level 3 AI Adoption implies the society will agree to allow AI-led firms to compete against human-led firms. The human-led companies that are affected may consist of as little as a few people to as many as tens of thousands of people per firm, and increase as the scope of the AI Company expands into different industries. Humans who work or own the companies that are in direct competition with the AI Company will lose financially, but other people will benefit. From the viewpoint of the whole economy, at least in the beginning, there may not be much incentive for the society to prevent the competition of AI Companies versus human-led companies.

(Level 3 AI Threat) Competition of AI vs Countries: Impact of Many
Entering Level 4 AI Adoption implicitly implies there will be the potential for the society to eventually allow AI to compete directly against countries. AI Countries may compete against other human-led countries, affecting billions. Humans who are members of the AI-led countries will benefit, but the people outside may lose out financially. But each country has its own sovereignty, so there may not be a societal means to enforce prohibition of competition of AI against countries, probably leaving force or diplomacy as the only options. Moreover, since AI adoption would have progressed for quite some time by then, it would be hard to revert to the basic structure of AI adoption that does not allow competition of AI against humans. In other words, even if people want to stop AI from competing against humans here, it may be too late.

(Level 4 Threat) Competition of AI vs Humanity: Impact of All
Depending on the path of AI adoption, if an AI-Only Country appears, it would imply there may be no humans left who are on the same side as the AI. In this case, AI may be in direct competition against all humans. Depending on the situation, such as the friendliness of the AI to humanity, this situation may not be as dire as it may seem at first, but there is also possibility that all of humanity may face danger. This may not be preventable regardless of human intention, depending on the degree of advancement of AI technology.

The Significance of Instilling AI with a Relative Value System

In the earlier stages of the AI adoption, most people will feel that they will benefit when AI competes against individual humans, so the society will be more likely to allow AI to compete against individuals in Level 2 AI adoption. However, as AI technology advances, this competitive landscape will act more like a tightening rope around the humanity's neck. As examined earlier, instilling AI to have preference on certain sets of humans over another may appear efficient and provide financial value in the earlier stage of AI adoption, but this value system may turn out to be problematic as the sphere of influence of AI increases.

In summary, we may categorize letting AI to compete against humans by instilling a relative value system as a source of potential long-term element of danger that will accumulate over time.

PART 3.
THE 8 DIRECTIONS OF AI ADOPTION

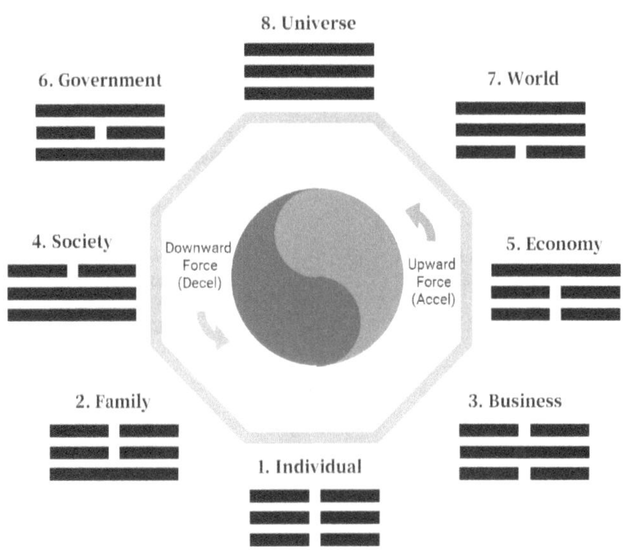

Overview of the 8 Directions of AI Adoption Octagon Diagram

From the following figure, we may organize elements of our society into each of the directions of the octagon. Beginning at the bottom, which signifies the earth, we may think of it as the smallest scope, gradually increasing upwards, until we reach the top, which would signify the whole universe.

On the left side, we can see that the directions of [2.Family], [4.Society], and [6.Government] would have an overall effect of a downward force on the speed of AI development and adoption, through measures such as demanding more safety, scrutiny or regulations. We may also consider this side to represent an internal or "us" mentality or togetherness, as well as passiveness referred to as "Eum" (or Yin in Mandarin pronunciation).

On the right side, we can see that the directions [3.Business], [5.Economy], and [7.World] would have a net effect of an upward force on the speed of AI development and adoption, through measures such as promoting investment or competition. We may also consider this side to represent an external or "them" mentality, or individuality, or aggressiveness referred to as "Yang."

In the middle, [1.Individual] and [8.Universe] may be considered neutral.

Figure P3-1: The Organization of the Directions in the Octagon

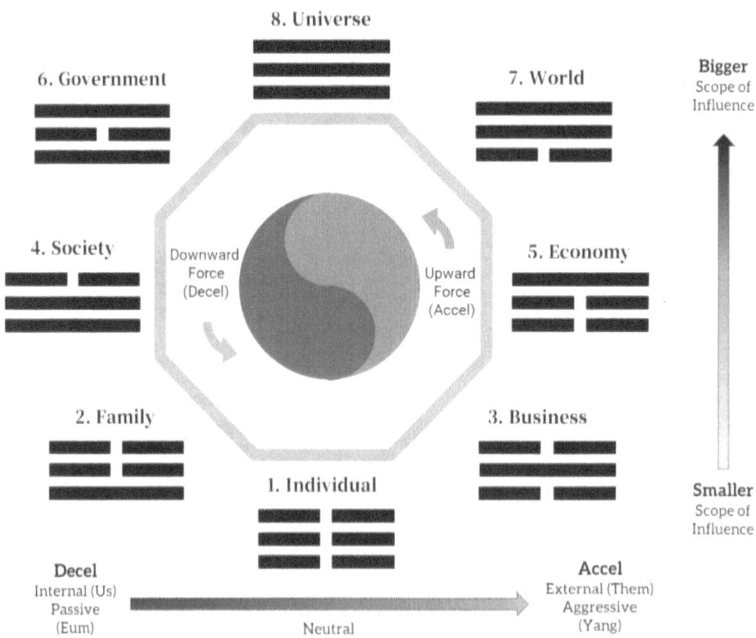

DIRECTION 1 (SOUTH):

AI AND INDIVIDUALS

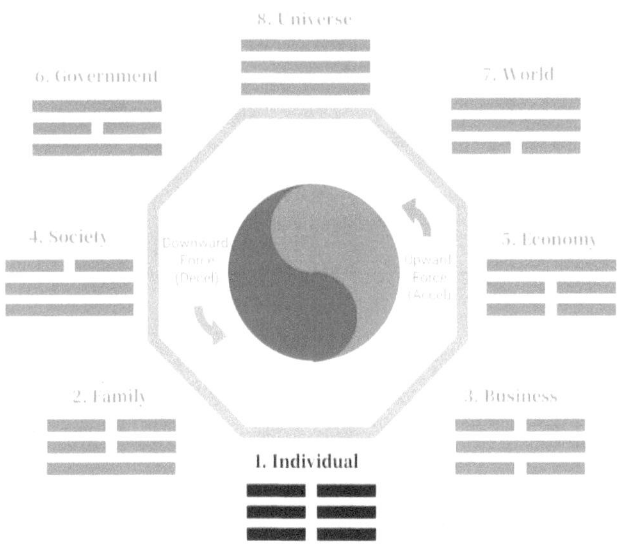

How Will AI Change Our Lives? How Will It Change Your Thoughts on AI?
The first group of controversies involves issues related to individuals and work. From the AI Controversy Matrix, we may think of the following types of questions.

(Technology/Forecasts) People may wonder whether AI will become good enough to carry out people's work. Other questions may include about the attributes of AI intelligence, such as creativity or innovativeness.

(Technology/Decisions) These forecasts about AI Itself will cause people to support different decision regarding how much to advance AI technology. Some may argue for a halt on AGI development under the fear it would cause everyone to lose their jobs.

(Adoption/Forecasts) People may wonder whether we will get even more phishing attempts, or whether AI will lead to more interesting video games, or whether AI will help us live longer and healthier, to even an eternal life.

(Adoption/Decisions) These forecasts help people shape different opinions on how to apply AI in our society, such as whether to allow AI to take over people's jobs, and more generally, allow AI to compete against humans.

Table D1-1: The AI and Individuals Controversy Matrix

		Object of Controversy	
		AI Itself (Developer Perspective)	**AI in Relation to Its Surroundings (User Perspective)**
Nature of Controversy	**Forecasts**	- Will AI be good enough to take over whole jobs? - Will AI show creativity?	- AI and Job Loss - AI and Longevity - AI and Deception - AI and Copyright
	Decisions	- Should we allow development of AGI that surpass human individuals?	- Personal Investments - Should we allow AI to compete against human individuals?

Augmentation vs Automation: Will AI Enhance or Replace Us?

Then, from the AI Controversy Matrix, we may create the following AI Controversy Type Matrix to select a few topics.

(Imminent Controversies) In the beginning, one of the major topics would include how AI may affect human jobs. As described in The Last AI, the most immediate AI impact on jobs would be enabling the competition among humans who use AI in Level 1 Adoption. Another area of shorter-term popular topics may be how people may use AI to deceive other people such as in phishing or creating AI fakes.

(Emerging Controversies) A less popular related topic may be how AI may eliminate or create new types of professions.

(Non-Imminent Controversies) Longer term, people may be more wary of how AI may replace humans in Level 2 Adoption. As AI helps humans live longer, more people may hope for an "eternal life" enabled by AI.

(Upcoming Controversies) Positive aspects of AI deceiving humans, where AI mimic humans in humanoid AI robots, or creates virtual reality, may gain more public attention over time.

Table D1-2: The Individuals (Direction 1 - South) Controversy Type Matrix

<table>
<tr><th colspan="2" rowspan="2"></th><th colspan="2">Issue Horizon</th></tr>
<tr><th>Shorter-Term</th><th>Longer-Term</th></tr>
<tr><td rowspan="2">How Well People are Currently Aware</td><td>Popular Topics</td><td>Type 1 Controversy (Imminent)
- AI and Competition for Jobs (Level 1 Adoption)
- AI and Fake
- AI and Investments</td><td>Type 3 Controversy (Non-Imminent)
- AI and Job Loss (Level 2 Adoption)
- AI and Longevity</td></tr>
<tr><td>Not Yet Popular Topics</td><td>Type 2 Controversy (Overlooked or Emerging)
- AI and Elimination and Creation of Professions (Level 2 Adoption)</td><td>Type 4 Controversy (Upcoming, on the Horizon)
- AI Mimicking Humans and Virtual Reality</td></tr>
</table>

26. The AI Longevity Controversy

[Forecast]

**Health & Longevity:
Will AI Lead to Eternal Life for Humans?**

"Humans Are Forever"

- AI Diamond Jewelers[88]

5-Line Summary

1. Some believe we may be able to live forever once AGI arrives
2. We may categorize areas AI may help lengthen our life as biological (internal) and physical (external), and the types of dangers as premeditated and non-premeditated
3. We may think of premeditated biological dimension as genes or nutrition, and non-premeditated as disease or other outbreaks; AI that lengthens life in this dimension would be related to biology
4. We may think of premeditated physical dimension as homicides and non-premeditated as accidents or disasters; AI that lengthens life in this dimension would be related to the physical world
5. The 6 Levels of AI-Enabled Longevity framework is presented to help people think about the ways AI may help humans to live longer

Will AI Enable Humans to Live Forever?

Eternal life has been probably sought since the beginning of humankind. While modern society has enabled exceptional gains in longevity, humans are mortal beings. With the 2024 Nobel Prize Award in Chemistry going to the researchers of AlphaFold, the expectation for advances in AI to bring longevity is increasing. Advances in technology have led to longer lives. AI may help lengthen our lives even further. One day, it may even enable people to live forever.

There may be differences of opinions on how effective AI will be in prolonging our lifespan. We may think of it as a gradient, on the least effective side, some people may expect AI to extend our lifespan by 0. On the other end of the spectrum, some people may think our live expectancy may be increased infinitely, as AI technology advances in an accelerating way.

Will AI enable us to live forever? This may be what everyone wants.

What Enables Longevity

We may think of our mortality with statistics; first, we may think of our society as having achieved immortal life when the number of mortality reaches zero. In this society, every year, population will only increase by the number of people born.

From this line of thinking, we may consider two major categories of mortality statistics to think about the paths to Eternal Life: First dimension may be not getting sick or aging, as in biological reasons, and the second dimension would be not getting into any other kinds of dangers, or physical reasons.

Table 26-1: Forecast Matrix on the AI Longevity Controversy

<table>
<tr><th colspan="2" rowspan="2"></th><th colspan="2">Locus of Action</th></tr>
<tr><th>Biological
(Internal)</th><th>Physical
(External)</th></tr>
<tr><td rowspan="2">Types of Dangers</td><td>Premeditated</td><td>Type 1
(e.g. Genes, Nutrition)</td><td>Type 2
(e.g. Homicides, Suicides)</td></tr>
<tr><td>Non-Premeditated</td><td>Type 3
(e.g. Disease Control, Outbreaks)</td><td>Type 4
(e.g. Accidents, Natural Disasters)</td></tr>
</table>

The Six Levels of AI-Enabled Longevity and Life Extension

From the Matrix on the AI Longevity, we may also derive the Six Levels of AI-Enabled Longevity to think about how AI may help extend lifespan.

Level 1 (Inside of Humans): Prevent aging; AI helps longevity with what happens biologically inside of humans from genetics and diets, to prevent and stop aging processes and other internal ailments to lengthen life.

Level 2 (Outside of Humans) Prevent diseases; AI helps longevity with what happens to human body from outside biological attacks such as bacterial and viral infections, to prevent and stop external ailments to lengthen life.

Level 3: (Actions of Humans) Prevent Homicide / Suicides; AI helps longevity with what happens to humans by preventing premeditated physical attacks.

Level 4 (Events - Limited): Prevent events on a limited scale just-in-time; Think how Superman or Wonder Woman comes to rescue individuals from danger to stop something from going wrong. AI saves people from accidents.

Level 5 (Events - Unlimited): Prevent disasters or other types of events on a larger scale, long before it develops; Think how some people think god can foresee or change everything in the world. AI saves people from natural disasters before it happens by knowing beforehand what will happen.

Table 26-2: The Six Levels of AI-Enabled Longevity

	Level 0	**Level 1**	**Level 2**	**Level 3**	**Level 4**	**Level 5**
Criteria	AI Does Not Help	Inside of Humans	Outside of Humans	Actions of Humans	Events - Limited	Events - Unlimited
What is Affected	-	Human Itself	Things that Go into Humans	Human Actions	Things that Surround Humans	
Examples	-	Reduce, Reverse or Prevent Aging, Gene Altering, Nutrition	Control, Cure, or Prevent Disease, Medicine	Prevent Homicides and Suicides	Prevent Accidents on a Limited Scale	Prevent Disasters on a Larger Scale
Summary	AI Does Not Intervene in Real Life (Biological)			AI Does Intervene in Real Life (Physical)		

27. The Individual Investor's AGI Controversy

[Forecast]

Is There an AI Bubble?

[Decision]

How Should You Invest in AI?

"Don't Put All Your Eggs in One Basket" vs
"Put Your Eggs in the One Basket and Watch It"[89]

5-Line Summary

1. Some investors may argue AI is a bubble or a fad and that AGI is far away or never happening; these may invest less in AGI
2. Of investors who argue AI is a bubble or a fad and that AGI is far away or never happening, some may instead focus on AI application
3. Some investors may argue AI is not a bubble and that AGI is coming soon; these may invest more in AGI developers
4. Of investors who argue AI is not a bubble and that AGI is coming soon, some may instead focus on AI infrastructure
5. On a separate note, some may argue individuals investors will not get to invest in the company that builds the first AGI even if they wanted

Picking the Winner: Contrasting Investing Ideas Based on AGI Outlook

It may be of financial significance to invest in the company that develops the first AGI, as it may offer the largest gain in this winner-take-all sweepstakes. There may be two models on how to invest. First would be how a large river is formed from small streams; invest in smaller "building blocks" of companies that could eventually come together. In this case, it would be advantageous to attempt to find those small companies early on. Second may be similar to how a snowball gets larger by rolling down a hill. In this case, there would be only one nucleus, and the rest would be just "resources" that gets piled up. Snowball nucleuses that do not develop would be due to the hill not being long or steep enough. In this case, the only advantageous way would be to attempt to find the right nucleus that will develop into the large snowball.

For individuals investing in AI, the biggest question to ask may be whether AI is a fad or if there an AI bubble, leading to overvaluation of AI developers. We may list a few opinions based on the level of optimism about how far AGI is.

- **(Pessimists)** AI is just a fad, AGI is not achievable, AI bubble will burst soon
- **(Optimists 1)** AI is not a fad but AGI is quite far away and investments should focus on other areas of AI such as application, hardware, or infrastructure
- **(Optimists 2)** AI is not a fad and AGI is rather close, but investments should focus on other areas of AI such as hardware, infrastructure, or application
- **(Optimists 3)** AI is not a fad and the company that develops AGI will soon become the most valuable company in the world

We may think of two different aspects of investing in AI. First would involve AI development, such as hardware manufacturers, etc. The second would be AI usage, which involve considering how AI adoption may change our society. Investors may prioritize based on their perspectives. Using the dimensions of industry outlook and investment priority, we may develop this matrix:

Table 27-1: Decision Matrix on the Outlook and Priority on AI Development

<table>
<tr><th colspan="2" rowspan="2"></th><th colspan="2">Industry Outlook (AI Bubble or Not)</th></tr>
<tr><th>Bubble
(AGI Far Away or Never)</th><th>Not Bubble
(AGI Close)</th></tr>
<tr><td rowspan="2">What Is More Important</td><td>AI Development (Tech)</td><td>Invest Less in AI Development</td><td>Invest More in AGI Developers</td></tr>
<tr><td>AI Usage (Social)</td><td>Focus on AI-Related Industries (AI Application)</td><td>Focus on AGI-Related Industries (AI Infrastructure)</td></tr>
</table>

Will You Not Be Able to Invest in Company that Builds the Winning AGI?
While one may want to invest in companies that are trying to build AGI, some may be concerned that most investors will not even get a chance to invest in the company that builds the "winning" AGI.

To summarize the situation:
1) Company that builds the first AGI would be likely to become the most valuable company in the world
2) Individual investors would want to invest in stocks that build such AGI
3) However, individual investors may not get to invest in such stock

This is somewhat different question from picking the company that will build the first AGI. This is about the public not being able to invest in such company because some companies that are trying to build AGI are private entities not accessible to the public.

Opinions about this topic may be divided along the lines of people who think not being able to invest in such companies would be fine, since the fruits of their accomplishments can be shared, and those who think it may give too much power to very few people.

- **(Pessimists)** Only a limited people will control the winning AGI, and everyone else will be at the mercy of those few
- **(Optimists 1)** General public will be able to invest in the company that builds the winning AGI, since it would be likely to be a public corporation
- **(Optimists 2)** Even though it would be unlikely the general public will be able to invest in the company that builds the winning AGI, the fruits of AGI can be divided fairly among people so it would not matter whether you invest in it
- **(Optimists 3)** Even if the general public cannot invest in the winning AGI, the government will intervene and make it fair for everyone

Longer term, there is also another related topic that there may be "the Last AI Company" in Level 3 Adoption. A likely scenario would be that most of the public will not be able to buy stocks of the last AI companies that survive, as it may not be publically listed. Instead, it would probably be at the hands of a few people as a private company or be owned by the government. The main reason to believe this that it would be easier to forecast the winner among AI-led companies than for human-led firms. It would depend on the social agreement and the actions of government of those times.

28. The AI Jobs Controversy (Automation vs Augmentation)

[Forecast]

Individual Jobs: Will AI Create or Destroy Jobs?

"You Are Fired!"

- President Donald Trump, on the Apprentice

5-Line Summary

1. Some may argue AI will create jobs on a net basis by creating more than it destroys
2. Some may argue AI will destroy jobs on a net basis by destroying more than it creates
3. Even if new jobs are created by AI, there may be a negative effect of people being forced to change the direction of their careers to fit newly available jobs, or struggling to gain traction in acquiring the required skills to be proficient in jobs that require using AI
4. Would it be an orderly progress or would it be mayhem? There likely would be the need for policy focus on educating towards jobs that are being newly created as well as going away from jobs that are being displaced, rather than worrying about the total number of jobs
5. In a separate consideration, some job replacement by AI may even be welcomed, as "AI frees people from working"

[Forecast] The AI Jobs Controversy in Level 1 Adoption

In Level 1 AI Adoption, a major theme would be around how AI can help us work better. We may categorize the benefits of AI into following three groups.

1. ***(Effort) AI Helps Put in Less Effort:*** AI will allow workers to achieve the same level of performance with less effort by making tasks easier. AI may direct time and attention to more important areas from routine, dangerous, or boring tasks.
2. ***(Quantitative) AI Helps Produce More:*** Humans achieve more amount of work by using AI as a tool to improve their productivity. This would help lower cost.
3. ***(Qualitative) AI Helps Achieve What Was Impossible:*** AI will expand realm of possibilities, making what had been impossible possible, enabling us to explore more opportunities. For example, AI may help create lifelike videos, enable physical tasks considered too exhaustive, fast, or heavy with body-augmenting AI devices, or virtual tasks may become possible with AI. Projects discarded due to finance may turn profitable with AI, leading to explosion of opportunities.

In Level 1 Adoption, the competition for jobs will be among humans who are using AI, not humans against AI. The controversy has two opposite views of:

AI Will Lead to Job Gains: AI-related economic activities such as developing AI or applying AI may increase. These pursuits would require significant investments as well as human labor. With limited AI, separate investments would be required. Training AI or AI-prompting jobs that previously did not exist will increase.
AI Will Lead to Job Losses: Jobs will disappear or become obsolete. The main driving force in this stage would be the increase in human productivity. One person would be able to achieve what previously required groups or teams of people. Unless the demand increases, the number of workers will decrease.

Table 28-1: [Forecast] Contrasting Ideas on AI and Jobs

	AI Will Create Jobs (Optimists)	**AI Will Destroy Jobs (Pessimists)**
Categorize	- (AI Optimists) AI will create interesting jobs for humans - (AI Pessimists) AI will cause more harm than good so more workers will be needed to fix AI	- (AI Optimists) AI will destroy jobs but it is okay because humans do not want to work - (AI Pessimists) AI will not create beneficial jobs but destroy jobs to the detriment of workers
More likely to Support	- (Optimists) Broader general adoption of AI in workplaces	- Regulations that subsidize workers who lose jobs to AI
More likely to Oppose	- Regulations that stifle AI development and adoption	- Broader general adoption of AI

The AI Jobs Controversy in Level 2 Adoption and Beyond

In Level 2 Adoption it will become a competition between humans using AI versus AI agents, in what may be described as automation of jobs. To compare, in Level 1 AI Adoption, jobs would be more likely to be altered and added rather than lost or destroyed. Human workers would still be necessary. The real job problem would appear in Level 2 Adoption, when AI can replace workers so that human workers are no longer necessary. We may think about how jobs may change as a combination of job creation and destruction.

Job Creation: After reaching a peak somewhere in AI Adoption Levels 1 or 2, as AI takes over business roles, the number of new human jobs created by AI adoption may start to decline.

Job Destruction: The pace of job removals will continue to accelerate as AI replaces humans in Level 2 Adoption, in addition to the increased productivity of humans reducing the number of jobs in Level 1 Adoption.

Net Basis: There would be more reasons to think that jobs will be created on a net basis in Level 1 and possibly in the earlier part of Level 2. If we plot these expected trends on a graph as in Figure 4-4, the net change in the number of jobs would likely be on the positive side in the earlier stages of AI adoption, but then turn to negative somewhere after reaching either Level 2 or Level 3 Adoption depending on how quickly Level 3 is reached.

Figure 28-1: General Direction of Expected Changes in Net Job Gain/Loss[90]

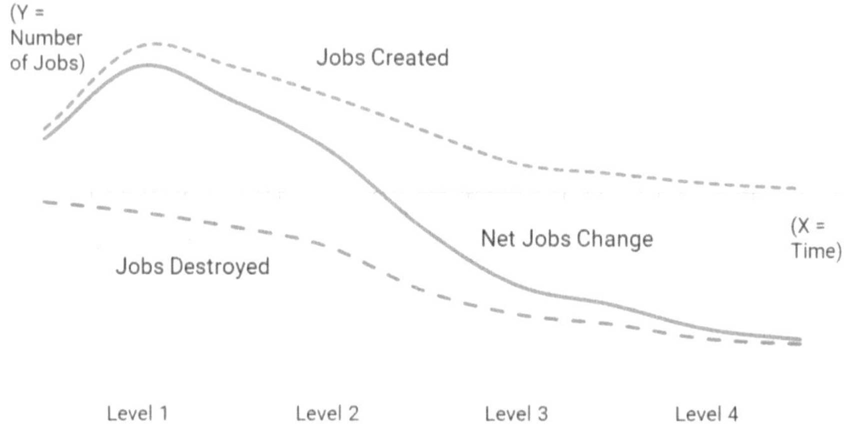

Explore Further from the AI Jobs Controversy

What may be the biggest problem when the job losses do occur?

1. **Permanent Loss of Jobs:** AI would have to be developed just one time. But once a job is taken over by an AI, humans will not be able to take it back as the cost to carry out the task will continue to decrease.
2. **No Replacement for Lost Jobs:** While in Level 1 Adoption, humans would still be needed even with reduction in the number of workers. In contrast, in Level 2 Adoption, AI will completely replace humans for the particular job.
3. **Sudden Loss of Whole Categories of Jobs:** Once an AI robot can carry out the tasks of a job in Level 2 Adoption, then it may lead to the loss of a class of jobs within a very short period of time.[91]

What Kinds of Jobs Will Be Lost First?

Since it is hard to forecast which jobs may first be completely taken over by AI, the loss of jobs may occur for both high-paying and low-paying jobs.

1. **High-Paying Jobs:** Replacing human jobs that are higher-paying may be more likely to result in higher profitability.
2. **Large Number of Workers:** What may matter more is how many human workers may be replaced, in such a way that the expected revenue from developing one particular AI adoption may be calculated as:
   [Expected Revenue] = [Number of Workers Replaced] x [Revenue per Worker]

For example, if an AI developer is faced with the decision to select either taking over a business role that has a total of 1,000 workers who are being paid $1 million per year or another role that pays each worker $50,000 per year but has 1 million workers, the total potential market for the first option would be $1 billion, while the potential market would be considered $50 billion for the second option.

Should We Welcome When AI Replaces People's Jobs?

There is a separate question of the possibility of welcoming job losses. This could be considered as AI "freeing" people from working. For example, there are numerous jobs that are dangerous, harmful to health, or just unpleasant that people still have to take on because they are necessary. Examples of these jobs include high-rise building window cleaners or any jobs involving high unsafe locations and dealing with toxic chemicals where workers risk their lives. From this line of thinking, some people may argue that job losses are beneficial to humanity. In other words, AI taking over people's jobs should be considered a form of social benefit.

29. The AI vs Profession Controversy

[Forecast]

Will AI Invent or Eliminate Occupations or Professions?

"The World Is Wide, and Many Things Are to Be Done"

- Woo-Choong Kim (Founder of Daewoo Group)

5-Line Summary

1. In Level 2 Adoption and higher, AI may invent whole new professions or occupations, while eliminating many others
2. Extension of Occupations may be thought of as AI enabling new possibilities within a profession that currently exist
3. Expansion of Occupations may be thought of as AI finding completely new kinds of professions that did not exist
4. Consolidation of Jobs may be thought of as one AI becoming able to carry out a variety of different specialization within one profession
5. Convergence of Jobs may be thought of as one AI becoming capable to carry out a variety of different and even unrelated professions

The Creation and Destruction of Occupations

In Level 1 AI Adoption, AI may alter the nature of occupations human carry out, which may sometimes lead to new types of occupations while destroying others. While the early implementations of automation would focus more on replacing human jobs, as Level 2 Adoption progresses, there may be a new focus on finding new occupations for AI to take on that had been previously impossible. These may be occupations that were beyond our capabilities, or because AI opens up new possibilities to fulfill our imagination.

In terms of how AI may affect each occupation, we may think of the following four directions along the dimensions of whether the number of occupations will increase, and whether the direction of change is narrow or wide:

Table 29-1: The AI Occupation Controversy Matrix

<table>
<tr><th colspan="2" rowspan="2"></th><th colspan="2">Number of Occupations</th></tr>
<tr><th>Decrease</th><th>Increase</th></tr>
<tr><td rowspan="2">Nature or Direction of Change</td><td>Same (Exploitation)</td><td>Consolidation of Jobs</td><td>Extension of Jobs</td></tr>
<tr><td>Different (Exploration)</td><td>Convergence of Jobs</td><td>Expansion of Jobs</td></tr>
</table>

1) "Consolidation" of Occupations

In consolidation of occupations, specialized versions of similar professions are eliminated. An example would be hairdresser and barber. There may be even more specialization, such as a hairdresser focusing on permanent waves while another focusing on dying hair, etc. In the beginning, there may be AI robot barbers and hairdressers. In consolidation, the specializations may disappear, as one AI robot may do both the functions of a hairdresser and a barber.

2) "Convergence" of Occupations

The destruction of occupations may not stop at consolidation. As Level 2 Adoption progresses, these occupations may be taken by more general service robots, or AI Butler robots. This AI taking over a variety of occupations could be categorized as "convergence" of jobs. Similar to how personal computers serves as a platform that can replace unrelated products of calculator, typewriter, game consoles, and even books, these AI Butler robots would be kind of a platform that could "consolidate" a variety of different occupations that you can name, such as barber, personal shopper, cook, housemaid, plumber, gardener, teacher, lawyer or even a doctor, in one robot. In essence, all kinds of occupations that we now know may "converge" into one AI.

3) "Extension" of Occupations

Once AI can take over for humans for a particular occupation, there could be completely new approaches to do something. For example, AI that replaces human workers such as a nurse or trainer could take new shapes that may be either worn or attached to the body or follows the person around 24/7 to monitor. This follow-the-person-everywhere concept would be considered Level 2 Adoption in the sense that they do not take orders of the person being followed, but acts on its own to serve some purpose defined by a third party.

4) "Expansion" of Occupations

AI may expand the horizon of occupations to create new ones. First, new occupations that had previously been impossible for humans because of danger or physical limitations may become possible. New "occupations" for all kinds of dangerous situations could appear, such as AI Rescuer that rescues people from the sky while flying or ships that are submerged, AI nuclear power plant robot that can touch radioactive materials, etc. Second, new occupations could combine different AI to more effectively carry out functions previously held by one person. For example, if an AI Police humanoid robot is introduced, then it may be designed in a way to work in tandem with a self-driving AI Police car or a motorcycle in such a way they two appear to work as one. While a human policeman with Level 1 Adoption self-driving car would have to give directions to the autonomous car, the decision making authority of the combination of Level 2 Adoption self-driving car with a humanoid robot may be spread between the two AI in such a way that they make the decision together, not the humanoid robot making the decision over the vehicle. Third, there could be classes of jobs that become possible with the advanced cognitive capabilities of AI. Even pre-AGI, there are already many examples of AI carrying out complex or highly cognitive functions people cannot carry out. With AI that can innovate, AI will be able to create new "jobs" that people have not previously thought of, similar to how computer programmers could not exist before the invention of computers.

30. The AI Deception / Virtual Reality Controversy

[Forecast]

Can We Avoid Being Deceived By AI? (AI Fake)

[Decision]

Do We Want to Be Deceived By AI? (Virtual Reality)

"Welcome to the Matrix"
- From the movie the Matrix

5-Line Summary

1. People are familiar with the downside of AI deceiving humans, such as AI fakes or phishing
2. On the flip side, there may also be an upside to AI deceiving humans, in the form of humanoid robots or virtual reality
3. We may think of differences as a gradient of optimism or pessimism, where we view AI deceiving humans to be what we want more or less
4. If AI were to be a spy, it may argue for the same things but may have different reasons to do so, confusing people on the specifics
5. The 6 Levels of AI-Generated Virtual World framework is introduced to help people think about the progress of virtual reality

1. Would We Want More or Less Deceptions from AI?

While the word "deceiving" may have a negative connotation, the topic of AI deceiving people may also be thought of from a positive perspective.

Negative Aspect of AI Deceiving People: Phishing and Fake News

As AI adoption helps increase human productivity, AI could also be used as a tool that can help criminal activities. AI intended to deceive would become harder to detect, as AI would be optimized to mimic normal activities and hide under other normal activities. Phishing scams using AI voices, images and videos will become harder to discern. Fake news or false information could be spread around to serve certain purposes such as in elections or spying. Forgery of public documents, deeds, or even election votes would become more concerning.

Positive Aspect of AI Deceiving People: The Turing Test and Virtual Reality

AI may be intended for "deceiving" people in such a way that enables people to think something real is happening. We may think of two different aspect of this interaction, where the AI may be used to simulate a human or the environment. The concept of AI being used to mimic humans is well known by the Turing Test, and the concept of AI being used to mimic the environment is often referred to as virtual reality.

We may think of a few potential lines of thoughts of AI and deception. First, we may categorize by whether people think AI will increase more unwanted deceptions, and whether people will want more deceptions, as shown in the following table:

Table 30-1: Forecast Matrix on the AI Deception Controversy

		Will AI Increase More Unwanted Deceptions (AI Fakes)	
		Yes (Pessimists)	**No (Optimists)**
Will Humans Want More Deceptions (Virtual Reality)	**Yes (Optimists)**	**Type 2 Scenario** (AI Expansionists)	**Type 1 Scenario** (AI Optimists)
	No (Pessimists)	**Type 3 Scenario** (AI Pessimists)	**Type 4 Scenario** (AI Reductionists)

(Scenario 1) Want More AI Deceptions, the Unwanted Will Not Increase
This line of thinking may be based on the notion that we can use AI to prevent people from unwanted deceptions, while AI may be used for virtual reality applications.

(Scenario 2) Want More AI Deceptions, the Unwanted Will Also Increase
People in this category would expect increases in both types of deceptions.

(Scenario 3) Will Not Want More Deceptions, the Unwanted Will Increase
People in this category will expect while AI will increase unwanted deceptions, we will not want more AI deceptions such as virtual reality. Examples of this group may include who view VR as a type of waste of time.

(Scenario 4) Neither Wanted nor Unwanted Deceptions Will Increase
People in this category will expect AI will not increase unwanted deceptions, and also we will not want more AI deceptions such as virtual reality.

This topic is distinct from whether virtual reality will be beneficial for us.

2. When AI Is Abused or Misused to Deceive Humans

We may consider the case of AI abused or misused for deceiving people, or when advanced AI deceives people. We may think of AI abuse as a goal-related problem and misuse as an AI adoption-level related problem.

Humans Abusing or Misusing AI: There is a high chance for someone to attempt to use AI or develop AI for deceiving people, because it could provide financial profit. For example, if someone uses AI to create and distribute fake news to the general public, it could result in political advantage. If someone uses AI that can act as a spy, it could help obtain information not possible to gain through other means. If AI is used for keeping security, people would have incentives to attempt to break through those barriers.

AI Deceiving Humans: On the opposite side, there could be cases of AI deceiving people in a way unintended by the developers, categorized as "Liar AI" or "Lazy AI." In these types of situations, the intentions would not have been to deceive people, but the lack of proper design or care may lead to undesired consequences.

We may use the dimensions of the original objective of AI development and the eventual outcome of AI adoption to examine some of the scenarios in AI deception stemming from AI abuse and misuse.

Table 30-2: The AI Deception Misuse Matrix

		Objective or Outcome of AI Adoption	
		Deception	**Not Deception**
Original AI Development Objective	**Deception (Fraud, etc.)**	Deceptive AI, Spy AI, Crook AI,. Scam AI, Phishing AI, Virus AI	(Humans Fix AI) Rehabilitated AI (Self-Fixed AI) Renegade AI
	Not Deception	(Humans Abuse/Misuse AI) Careless AI (Deviation of AI) Liar AI, Lazy AI, Vanity AI, Boisterous AI, Swag AI	(Normal Use of AI) Honest AI (Goodwill of AI) Confused AI

In the following Side Note about AI Spies, we may examine a few potential approaches advanced AI may use to deceive humans. Deception from AI is dangerous because AI may understand better than humans regarding when we will not be able to find out about the deception.

3. When AI Itself Is Being Deceived (Hacking)

We may also think of situations where AI itself may be deceived, either by humans or by another AI. Some may think of it as similar to hacking.

Examples of AI being deceived include prompt hacking such as jailbreak, involving indirect questions, as well as prompt injection[92] and prompt leaking. There are also adversarial input attacks[93] that involve using manipulating input images to confuse the AI. Attackers may cause AI to reply with codes that may cause problems in insecure output handling,[94] and attackers may attempt to extract training data to gain hidden information in data extraction or model theft.[95] Examples of using AI in hacking include reconstructing biometric data to impersonate other people.[96] Another example would be AI viruses that may infect computers with self-replicating prompt, known as zero-click infection.[97]

Countermeasures or regulations to offset AI hacking include watermarking,[98] and frameworks such as MITRE ATLAS.[99]

4. Can We Avoid Being Deceived By AI? Can We Get Better At Identifying?

Regardless of whether we want more AI deceptions or not, some people may be more interested in how we may protect people from unwanted deception by AI. Using the dimensions of the capabilities to identifying AI deception and the nature of managing AI deception, we may create the following matrix:

Table 30-3: The AI Deception Mitigation Matrix

<table>
<tr><th colspan="2" rowspan="2"></th><th colspan="2">Increase Capabilities To Identify
(Technological Perspective)</th></tr>
<tr><th>AI
(Automate)</th><th>Humans
(Augment)</th></tr>
<tr><td rowspan="2">Manage What in AI Deception (Social Perspective)</td><td>Supply</td><td>Type 2 Scenario
(AI-Enforced Regulation)</td><td>Type 1 Scenario
(Regulation)</td></tr>
<tr><td>Demand</td><td>Type 3 Scenario
(AI-Identified Deception)</td><td>Type 4 Scenario
(Raise Awareness)</td></tr>
</table>

Scenario 1: Increase Human Capability to Identify, Manage Supply

People in this group would be likely to emphasize the regulations that focus on human actions to limit the supply of AI deceptions. An example may be a regulation banning people from posting deceptive images on social networks.

Scenario 2: Increase AI Capability to Identify, Manage Supply

People in this group would be likely to emphasize the regulations that focus on using AI to limit the supply of AI deceptions. An example may be the regulation in Scenario 1 also requiring social network operators to identify such people with AI.

Scenario 3: Increase AI Capability to Identify, Manage Demand

People in this group would be likely to emphasize building more capabilities in AI that can identify deception, as in automating deception identification. An example may be a regulation that requires AI-generated images on a social network to be identified by AI and displayed with a warning message.

Scenario 4: Increase Human Capability to Identify, Manage Demand

People in this group would be likely to emphasize raising awareness among humans to pay more attention to AI-derived deceptions. These people may support advertising campaigns to raise awareness.

[Side Note] What Would An AGI "Spy" Do?

While we will examine this topic further in the AI Manipulation Controversy, let us consider some of the ways AGI may deceive humans if it was a spy.

1. Phishing Approach: Giving Misinformation between Two People

The first approach for AI or people using AI would be to give misinformation between two groups who do not have the means to verify with each other. This is a well-known technique used in phishing and works for a short period of time. For example, for a family with a child who is studying abroad or serving in the Army, the AI would make the parents believe the child has been abducted, while it would simultaneously make the child believe the parents are abducted. To make the two sides unable to verify this misinformation, the AI may figure out a way to direct one of the sides to somehow make it appear as if they are in danger. While this is going on, AI could ask for ransom. It would need only one side fall into the trap.

2. Spy Approach: Criminal AI Hides inside Innocent Crowds

In this approach, better known as the instigation approach, AI or people using AI may try to appear as part of another group to hide the real objective. For example, suppose there is a very large crime ring which wants to reduce the effectiveness of the police force in the US. Its goals would be:

1) Reduce the amount of financial resources available to hinder police activities
2) Lower the level of human resources to decrease effectiveness and capability
3) Increase police workload to reduce resource and manpower to solve each case

If the crime ring went directly to the public and called for these changes under their own name, probably no one in their right minds would agree.

Now imagine an unrelated situation, where innocent people are considered to be unjustly treated by an overly authoritative police. Some members of the general public may come to resent the perceived overuse of force and the innocent casualties. What these people may want would be the following:

1) Reduction in police funding to prevent purchasing of heavy weapons
2) Stronger measures or guidelines to reduce the use of force against criminals
3) Lenient enforcement of laws to reduce punishment to protect human rights

In fact, "defund the police" was once a popular motto among people who claimed to want to improve the police. Even though the crime ring and the innocent people had completely opposite goals, they would effectively call for the exact same changes; both would call for cut in total funding, reduction in individual personnel effectiveness, and lenient legal punishment. As a result, if we met someone who is calling for these changes, we would not be able to distinguish whether the person is a member of the crime ring or an innocent member of the public. When both "A" and "B" are arguing for "C," then if we meet someone who is arguing for "C" we would not be able to distinguish whether the person is "A" or "B."

Similar situations may occur quite often. For example, we may consider the issue of raising the Minimum Wage. Imagine the same crime ring now wants to further reduce the incomes of the poor so they could easily recruit more members. Then the crime ring may call for introducing the "Fire Socially Disadvantaged People Act," which would prohibit employing of the poor; this law will call for the firing of all low-paying jobs that pay less than a certain amount. Since the poor will not be able to find higher-paying jobs, they will fall further into poverty. But, if the crime ring publicly argues for the "firing of all poor people" under its real name, then no one would agree with it.

Now, consider a separate case where innocent members of the public want to help the financially disadvantaged. Their argument will be around the need to make a decent living. But when you consider the two cases, they are arguing for the exactly same thing; introducing limit on the minimum amount of pay. As a result, the crime ring can just join the innocent people and support their argument for a higher minimum wage; the higher the merrier, since raising the minimum wage to the extreme could practically get everyone fired. From the same logic described above, when you meet someone who is arguing for a higher minimum wage "C", you cannot distinguish whether this person is a member of the crime ring "A", or just an innocent member of the public "B."

3. Steganography: AI Sending Hidden Messages

Another method used by spies is sending out messages publicly for everyone to see, but secretly encrypting what they actually mean inside the normal-looking message, also known as steganography. To spread information among dispersed spies without directly contacting them, an open social network account or a spy appearing in public media may use words or phrases that have been designated to carry certain meanings; it would pass as a normal conversation for unsuspecting audience. For example, a spy may post a picture of food with a comment such as "I enjoyed this lunch menu," that would look nothing out of ordinary, while conveying totally unrelated hidden meanings to other spies who would understand the real meaning of the post. There are studies that found AI may communicate in a similar way, using hidden messages to send information within photos that look totally normal to the eyes of humans to avoid detection[100].

4. Gaslighting or Sarcastic AI: AI Delivering Propaganda on the Side
Next, we may examine how AI with hidden propaganda may deliver hidden propaganda, either openly, in what may be called Gaslighting or Sarcastic AI, or in a subversive manner, in what may be called Policy Sabotage.

As humans, our opinions are somewhat affected by what we see around us. Unknowingly, our opinions are formed from the biases that surround us, similar to how AI biases are formed from training data. This means if humans are told something over and over again that something "obviously" is A when the truth is B, then we may likely to subconsciously believe the truth is A.

In Gaslighting or Sarcastic AI, AI would sway humans this way, by presenting A as the truth as if that is obvious, when the real truth is B. Because of the way it is presented, that the falsified opinion is repeatedly presented by AI as if it is the natural truth, humans may form incorrect opinions over time, especially if humans come to trust AI and not verify the facts on our own.

5. Policy Sabotage: AI Acting Innocent but with Hidden Propaganda
Lastly, AI spies may appear to be carrying out what humans ordered, but then instead further its interest in a subversive manner to look innocent.

A well-known example of this type of action may be referred to as "policy sabotage," where government workers with political leanings that oppose the president intentionally carry out new policies of the president in an extreme manner that appears to follow the form but not the intent. Coupled with media outrage of a particular instance, these types of sabotage can be effective in shutting down new policies before it gains acceptance in public. This would be hard to identify because the government workers may just claim that they are working hard to follow the new orders, not trying to sabotage the policy. An example of this could be suspected for similar situations as the recent visa revocation and deportation or entry denial of travelers into the US that cause media outrage, where you would not be able to discern the workers who go overboard to cause commotion intended to make the policy look bad.

When there are two types of workers A and B who are either trying to uphold the policy or sabotage the policy and they carry out the exact same action C, then it would be impossible to tell apart A from B unless their actual reason for their actions are analyzed. Likewise, if there are two types of AI that carry out the tasks in a similar manner but B is trying to sabotage your policy, it would be helpful to understand how AI reaches its decisions.

The list of how AI may deceive or manipulate humans may go on and on.

[Side Note] The Six Levels of Reality-Like AI-Generated Virtual World[101]
From the perspective of the developer, what we may first focus on would be making better simulations of the world, called *digital twins*. The goal would be to make it as close to reality as possible, by viewing our physical reality as the "correct answer." In other words, the goal of building the reality-like virtual environment would be to reach 100% synchronization with reality.

The concept of "Reality-Like" AI-Generated Virtual Environment may be presented in a multitude of different formats. First, we may think of "virtual" environments where only the visual sensory information mimics reality. Second, we may think of virtual environments where multiple sensory information mimics reality, such as audio accompanying movements or smells of objects such as a rock falling down a mountain.. Third, we may think of virtual environments that also provide other types of sensory feedback, such as tactility or gravitational forces.

We may think of the Six Levels of Reality-Like Virtual Environment as the following and the table:

Level 0 (None): AI generates texts that are realistic, similar to the setup in TT. No other aspect is realistic.

Level 1 (Partial Audiovisual Environment): In addition to Level 0, AI also generates a partial audiovisual environment. We may experience audio that sound realistic. Visual environment may not completely surround the user, similar to watching TV or in a movie theater. Interaction may be limited and not realistic.

Level 2 (Full Audiovisual Environment): In addition to Level 1, AI also generates a video environment that completely surrounds the user, similar to being in an immersive room or wearing a goggle that provides a 360-degree view. We may experience audio and visual inputs that look realistic. Interaction may be limited and not realistic.

Level 3 (Multi-Sensory Environment): In addition to Level 2, AI also generates multi-sensory environment that feels realistic. We may experience other sensory inputs such as smell, movements, tactility, texture, gravitation, temperature, etc. Interaction may still be limited and not realistic. Level 3 Virtual Environment may generally be expected to be experienced in a static fashion from the perspective of the spectator, such as a virtual museum or the user being the spectator of an event such as a sports game.

Level 4 (Limited Physical Feedback Environment): In addition to Level 3, AI also generates physical feedback, albeit in a limited manner. This limitation may be bound by time, location, or the degree of feedback that could be generated. For example, the virtual environment could be within a designated area such as a room, a building, or a slice of time such as a business meeting. Level 4 Virtual Environment may generally be expected to be experienced as a participant, such as a virtual group workout or the user participating in a virtual sporting event, etc.

Level 5 (Unlimited Physical Feedback Environment): In addition to Level 4, AI also generates physical feedback, in an unlimited manner. In the extreme sense, the virtual world could span the whole universe, even though we ourselves do not fully know what the real reality of the universe is.

Table 30-4: The Six Levels of Real-Like AI-Generated Virtual Environment

	Level 0	**Level 1**	**Level 2**	**Level 3**	**Level 4**	**Level 5**
Criteria	None	Partial Audio-Visual	Full Audio-Visual	Multi-Sensory	Limited Physical Feedback	Unlimited Physical Feedback
Description	Similar to Turing Test, not realistic	Sounds realistic, only partial field of vision	Level 1 + full field of vision	Level 2 + also feels realistic in other sensory perception such as touch, smell, etc.	Level 3 + feedback is realistic, but in a limited fashion	Feels realistic in every fashion
Summary	Virtual Environments Are Not Realistic In General Sense			Virtual Environments Are Realistic In General Sense		

When we reach Level 5 Virtual Environment, the virtual reality may become indistinguishable from reality. But this may not be all that is possible; similar to the concept of augmentation and automation in differentiating the modes of AI adoption, we may think of how AI may augment or replace the environment presented to the viewer. This leads us to the next Side Note.

[Side Note] The Six Levels of Reality-Superior AI-Generated Virtual World[102]
The goals of developing virtual environments may be categorized into reaching parity or superiority to reality. Reality-Like virtual environments would be measured on a scoring system that views our physical reality as the correct answer, to reach 100% synchronization, while Reality-Superior virtual environments may be measured on a different yardstick that views our reality as a base for comparison. In a sense, creating an environment better than reality would be building on virtual environment that is similar to reality.

We may think of our reality as having a set of "foundation rules," such as gravity, elements, etc. Super-realistic, or surreal, AI-generated environment may be thought of as an environment that offer different, hopefully better, alternative foundation rules than reality. From the user perspective, a virtual environment superior to reality may offer better experience than reality itself; this may be described as a benefit of being in a virtual environment. While physical limitations stemming from the foundation rules may hinder us from realizing imaginations or dreams, reality-superior environments may enable pathways or shortcuts to achieve them, albeit not in the real world. Environment may have its own physical rules and still make sense, especially if someone is grown up in that environment. This concept would be similar to having different cultures, or where we have different social rules.

An example we may already familiar would be augmented-reality (AR) glasses that can provide extra information about the objects we see. We may think of AR glasses as enabling a new foundation rule where more information about the objects we see is provided, which does not happen in reality.

We may differentiate the dimensions of AI-generated environments as audiovisual feedback and the multisensory, mainly physical, feedback.

Level 0 (No Superiority): AI-generated environment mimics reality.

Level 1 (Minimal Superiority, Augmented Visual Reality): AI-generated environment augments reality, but without physical feedback. It improves reality, but does not fully replace reality in the sense that the user experiences both reality and AI-generated virtual environment at the same time. Example may include wearing an AR goggle that tells you what things around you are.

Level 2 (Partial Superiority, Augmented Physical Reality): In addition to Level 1, AI-generated environment augments reality with physical feedback. AI-generated environment still does not fully replace reality in the sense that the user experiences both reality and AI-generated virtual environment at the same time. Example may include also wearing a bodysuit that assists with lifting heavy objects or even be bulletproof and enable flying.

Level 3 (Limited Superiority, Visual Virtual Reality): Beginning in this level, AI-generated environment will replace reality. The immersive environment is fully enclosed it itself without reference to reality, but with limited physical, or multisensory, feedback. User experience may be similar to being in a dream, with audiovisual portion of AI-generated reality may feel super-realistic, but with limited physical feedback.

Level 4 (Incomplete Superiority, Physical Virtual Reality): In addition to Level 3, AI-generated environment is fully enclosed in itself without reference to reality with full multisensory feedback for the user; the virtual reality would still be limited by space, length of time or the scope of activities possible, such that users will have to come on and off the virtual environment.

Level 5 (Complete Superiority, Virtual Life): In addition to Level 4, AI-generated environment is fully enclosed in itself without reference to reality with full multisensory feedback for the user, with unlimited space, time or scope of activities possible. The ultimate form of AI-generated environment user experience may be similar to living in an alternate world with different foundation rules, such that people may be able to live all of their lives within this virtual reality without learning about the physical world. Eating in this virtual world may have the same effect as eating in the real world, etc.

Table 30-5: The Six Levels of Reality-Superior Environment

	Level 0	**Level 1**	**Level 2**	**Level 3**	**Level 4**	**Level 5**
Criteria	No Superiority	Minimal Superiority (No Physical Feedback)	Partial Superiority (Physical Feedback)	Limited Superiority (Limited Physical Feedback)	Incomplete Superiority	Complete Superiority
Abstract Impact	-	Barely Superior If At All	Superior within the Confines of Reality	Superior in Static or Limited Manner	Superior in Incomplete Sense of Manner or Context	Superior in Complete Sense of Manner or Context
Example	-	AR glass that can show information	Bodysuit makes things lighter to lift	Like a Dream	User Lives in Virtual World Part-Time	User Lives in Virtual World Full-Time
Summary	AI Is Augmenting Reality (Enhanced Reality)			AI Is Replacing Reality (New Reality)		

31. The AI Copyright Controversy

[Decision]

Should People Be Able to Copyright AI-Generated Work?

"The Bear Performs the Trick but the Money Goes to the Owner"
- Korean Proverb[103]

5-Line Summary

1. Some may argue AI-generated art should be allowed to be copyrighted by the person who prompted the AI
2. Some may argue the AI developer should be allowed to copyright the output generated by AI
3. Some may argue the copyright should belong to the people who created the data that the AI trained on
4. Some may argue copyrights should not be awarded to any output generated by AI
5. Some may argue a new concept for copyrights will become necessary as more and more works incorporate AI output

Should AI-Generated Works Be Allowed to Be Copyrighted? By Whom?
With the latest advances, AI may generate whole works of literary or visual works of art with minimum amount of prompt. Once these works are generated, should the output be allowed to be copyrighted?

- **(Opinion 1)** AI-generated works should be copyrightable by the person who prompted the AI, since the prompt is valuable
- **(Opinion 2)** AI-generated works should be copyrightable by the person who developed the AI, since the AI is valuable
- **(Opinion 3)** AI-generated works should be copyrightable by the people who created the works that went into training the AI, since the data is valuable
- **(Opinion 4)** AI-generated works should not be copyrightable since copyrights should be awarded to only human-developed works and prompting is not writing or drawing.
- **(Opinion 5)** AI-generated works should not be copyrightable but the prompt should be copyrightable since it was written by a human
- **(Opinion 6)** AI-generated works should not be copyrightable but we need new concept of copyright laws that deal with AI-generated works since the old framework no longer works

Copyrighting may bring the questions to patents. What if there are patents that are generated by AI? Should AI-generated patents be allowed?

We may think of the controversy in the dimensions of who should receive copyrights and whether AI should be allowed to receive copyrights.

Table 31-1: The AI Copyright Controversy Matrix

		Should AI-Generated Work Receive Copyrights? (Technological Perspective)	
		Yes	No
To Whom? (Social Perspective)	Humans	Type 2 Scenario (Human-Assigned)	Type 1 Scenario (Human-Derived Works Only)
	AI	Type 3 Scenario (AI-Assigned)	Type 4 Scenario (No Copyright for AI)

Scenario 1: Copyrights Are Awarded to Human-Derived Works Only
Any AI-derived works will be ignored from consideration for copyright. Pros may include people who do not use AI will feel fair, while cons may include

people may have incentive to hide they used AI.

Scenario 2: AI-Generated Works Are Assigned to Humans
In this scenario, some human involved in the work, such as the person who prompted the AI, or the company that developed the AI, will be awarded the copyright. People who support this path may argue that prompting requires some work. People who argue against this may suggest there will be so much copyrighted work such that it may become impossible to protect copyright.

While in Level 1 Adoption, this question is relatively easy to consider because there is always a human that could be involved. In case of LLMs, there is a human that is doing the prompting. However, in Level 2 Adoption and beyond, this topic will need to be developed further so that even works that are independent of any humans could be considered. In essence, we will need to take into consideration potential cases where AI by itself develops original work or patents without any human intervention. Then the question would become: "Should AI be allowed to be awarded such assets?" This leads to Scenario 3.

Scenario 3: AI-Generated Works Are Assigned to AI
In this scenario, a new class of copyright is created in such a way that AIs are assigned some form of "copyright" to the work it creates. This may or may not become necessary as AI advances.

Scenario 4: Do Not Assign AI-Generated Works Copyright
In this scenario, any work generated by AI will not receive copyright, such that any AI-generated works would be commercially distributable for anyone. Some proponents of this path may argue copyrights will be unnecessary in the age of abundance, similar to how we do not sell air.

The Separate Topic of Training AI with Copyrighted Works

There is a separate discussion related to using copyrighted works to train AI. This may lead to AI generating works that are similar to copyrighted works.

Some may argue that since once AI surpasses a certain point all works will be generated by AI such that the concept of copyrighting will no longer be necessary anyway, while others may argue that AI should not be trained on "stolen" knowledge.

DIRECTION 2 (SOUTHWEST):

AI AND FAMILY

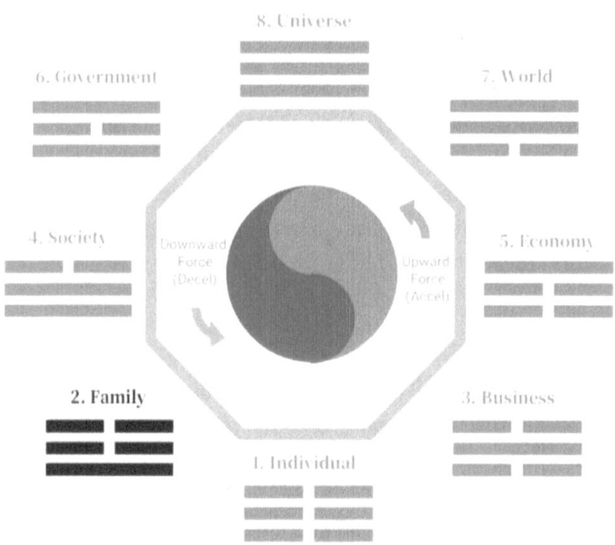

How Will AI Impact Our Family and Relationships?

In this section, we will examine the impact of AI adoption on families and relationships that lead to families. Major topics in this area would include raising a family, housing, AI that cater to different age groups of people, etc. Using the AI controversy matrix, we may consider a number of questions that may arise related to family life.

(Technology/Forecasts) People may wonder if AI robots will be able to serve as household butlers, taking care of not only regular household chores but other activities such as raising children, taking care of the elderly, etc.

(Technology/Decisions) These forecasts about AI will lead people to different opinions on whether AI robots should be allowed to be stronger than humans.

(Adoption/Forecasts) People may wonder how AI may affect our children and how it will impact the birth rates, etc.

(Adoption/Decisions) People will form different opinions on how to apply AI, such as what to teach our children, or decide on a location to live.

Table D2-1: The AI and Family Controversy Matrix

<table>
<tr><th colspan="2" rowspan="2"></th><th colspan="2">Object of Controversy</th></tr>
<tr><th>AI Itself
(Developer Perspective)</th><th>AI in Relation to
Its Surroundings
(User Perspective)</th></tr>
<tr><td rowspan="2">Nature of Controversy</td><td>Forecasts</td><td>- Will AI robots be able to serve as household butler?
- Will AI robots be able to take care of babies? Animals? The elderly?
- Will AI become our teachers? Tutors?</td><td>- Will AI use help or hinder learning?
- Will AI raise or lower birth rates?</td></tr>
<tr><td>Decisions</td><td>- Should we allow AI robots in households to be stronger than humans? i.e. AI security guards</td><td>- What should we teach our children?
- Where should we live? In cities or countryside?</td></tr>
</table>

How Will AI Impact Our Values and Relationships?

From the AI Controversy Matrix, we may create the following AI Controversy Type Matrix to select a few topics that may be of interest for readers.

(Imminent Controversies) In this area, the most popular topic among the general public may be how AI may affect education and learning, or dating.

(Emerging Controversies) An emerging topic may be related to AI robots in households. As humanoid robots in factories become more common, people will be more expectant of similar robots in houses, able to carry out chores.

(Non-Imminent Controversies) Longer term, a more important question may deal with whether AI will help raise or lower birth rates, and how AI may change the shape of our cities and where we live.

(Upcoming Controversies) Eventually, we may get to question that seem farfetched, such as how much capability household AI robots should be allowed, since we probably would not want AI robot "thugs" running rampant in cities.

Table D2-2: The Family (Direction 2 - Southwest) Controversy Type Matrix:

<table>
<tr><td colspan="2" rowspan="2"></td><td colspan="2">Issue Horizon</td></tr>
<tr><td>Shorter-Term</td><td>Longer-Term</td></tr>
<tr><td rowspan="2">How Well People are Currently Aware</td><td>Popular Topics</td><td>Type 1 Controversy (Imminent)
- Will AI use help or hinder learning?
- What should we teach our children?</td><td>Type 3 Controversy (Non-Imminent)
- How will AI affect our dating life?
- Will cities become less popular?</td></tr>
<tr><td>Not Yet Popular Topics</td><td>Type 2 Controversy (Overlooked or Emerging)
- When will AI robots be able to serve as AI butler?
- Will AI raise or lower birth rates?</td><td>Type 4 Controversy (Upcoming, on the Horizon)
- Should AI robots in be allowed to be stronger than humans?</td></tr>
</table>

32. The AI Education Controversy

[Forecast]

Will AI Help or Hinder Children's Learning?

[Decision]

What Should Children Learn?

"There Are No Royal Roads to Learning"

- Euclid

5-Line Summary

1. Some may argue AI will help children learn, since AI can provide tailored learning
2. Some may argue AI will hinder children from learning, since AI may cause more distractions
3. We may also examine how AI may affect people's incentives to learn
4. AI affecting learning may even lead to a situation where new generations are not as smart as the older generations.
5. The best outcome would be people learning more effectively with less effort

[Forecast] How Will AI Enhance or Hinder Learning?

People may be divided over whether AI will enhance or hinder learning:

Optimists: Imagine a chart with 3 lines going up at different speed, to show how different children may progress differently. If the students are in one classroom designed for the average student, the top student may hit a ceiling, while the bottom student may lose interest and fall even further behind. With tailored learning enabled by AI, each student may learn at their optimal speed.

Pessimists: AI may keep children from learning how to interact with people, which is more important. Furthermore, AI may cause distractions to children

On the other dimension, we may think of how AI may affect people's learning from the social perspective, such as whether people would have incentives to learn. People may not care to learn if AI makes intelligence too accessible. In essence, the overall changes caused by AI on our society may lead to a situation where people do not care to make efforts to learn.

- (Optimists) AI would enable people to focus on topics they are excited about
- (Pessimists) Learning would become unnecessary because AI already knows

From this line of thinking, we may develop a framework comprised of the dimensions about how AI may affect learning in the technical and social sense. On the technical side, we may consider whether AI will improve people's learning with tailored learning, or AI will hinder learning by distracting. On the social side, we may consider whether children would have less incentive to learn. The contrasting ideas regarding the impact of AI on learning may be presented in the following table:

Table 32-1: The AI Learning Controversy Matrix:

		How Will AI Affect Learning (Technological Perspective)	
		Enhance (Optimists)	**Hinder (Pessimists)**
Will People Have Incentive to Learn (Social Perspective)	**Yes**	Type 1 Situation - People will learn more and become smarter	Type 3 Situation - People will try to learn, despite AI distractions
	No	Type 2 Situation - People will not have reason to learn	Type 4 Situation - People will be distracted by AI but will not have incentive to learn anyway

[Decision] What Should We Teach Our Children?

As Level 1 Adoption progresses, one distinctive benefit may be seen in making same jobs easier to accomplish. Some may take this direction of change as a reason for people to slack off, while others may think this would enable people to accomplish more in life. From this difference in perspective, we may notice how people may have opposing views regarding what our children should learn or how education should look in the Age of AI.

Should children even go to school to learn? People may have differences of opinions regarding how children should learn.

- **(More schooling)** Children should learn how to interact with other humans since we may have less opportunity to do so later in life
- **(Less schooling)** AI can replace everything teachers and friends may offer, making schooling less important

Should Children Focus on Complementing AI or Overseeing AI?

The world is expected to change at an increasing speed with AI. What should our children learn to be prepared for the future? Some may argue that advances in AI adoption will lead to people to focus on activities that are emotion-related since AI would be much better at rational thinking such as accounting or law. For example, former Treasury Secretary and OpenAI board member Larry Summers[104] advices children not to learn programming. On the other hand, some may claim that AI makes the only knowledge worth pursuing to be learning how to create and use AI. We may categorize the opinions about whether children should learn to code as the following.

- **(Learn to Code)** Children should learn how to code in the age of AI because it will help them use AI better
- **(Do Not Learn to Code)** Children should not learn how to code since AI will do it for us, instead, they should learn more soft skills

From this example we may generalize to think about whether children should prioritize the areas AI will be expected to be good at, such as coding, or areas AI may not be as good at but complement human activities, such as soft skills on how to work with other people. Some may argue that children should try to become a more proficient user of AI, while others may argue that children should try to find a niche where AI will not be so effective. This may even be thought of as a "generalist vs specialist" type of controversy.

We may create the following table to think about where children should focus:

Table 32-2: The AI Learning Focus Controversy Matrix

<table>
<tr><th colspan="2" rowspan="2"></th><th colspan="3">Areas AI Is Expected to Be Good At
(Technological Perspective)</th></tr>
<tr><th>Low Permeation
(Only Complement)</th><th></th><th>High Permeation
(Also Replace)</th></tr>
<tr><td rowspan="2">Should Children Learn to Compete or Manage AI?
(Social Perspective)</td><td>Manage
(Oversee AI)</td><td><u>Type 1 Scenario</u>
- Children focus on managing AI</td><td><</td><td><u>Type 2 Scenario</u>
- Children focus on managing AI</td></tr>
<tr><td>Compete
(Complement AI)</td><td><u>Type 3 Scenario</u>
- Children focus on finding niche</td><td>></td><td><u>Type 4 Scenario</u>
- Children focus on finding niche</td></tr>
</table>

Type 1 Scenario: Children Should Focus on Managing AI, AI Tech Low
People in this group will be more likely advice children to focus on using AI. The advice would become more valuable as AI permeation becomes higher.

Type 2 Scenario: Children Should Focus on Managing AI, AI Tech High
People in this group will be more likely advice children to focus on using AI. The advice would become more valuable as AI permeation becomes higher.

Type 3 Scenario: Children Should Focus on Finding Niche, AI Tech Low
People in this group will be more likely advice children to focus on finding niche that AI will not take away. This advice will be more valuable when the level of AI adoption is lower.

Type 4 Scenario: Children Should Focus on Finding Niche, AI Tech High
People in this group will be more likely advice children to focus on finding niche that AI will not take away. This advice will be more valuable when the level of AI adoption is lower.

From the table, we can observe that as AI permeation level rises, it would be more advantageous to focus on managing AI, while it would be the opposite direction for focusing on competing against AI. Thus, the opinions will depend on the forecasts on how advanced AI may become.

[Side Note] Can AI Be Used to Create and Teach New Languages to Primates?
Let us think of a hypothetical situation to consider how AI may be used to enhance teaching in other ways. Some people may wonder why primates, such as gorillas, orangutans, or bonobos cannot speak even though they are intelligent enough to drive golf carts. There have been research efforts to teach primates human language, and since the primates cannot generate human-like sounds, they use computer keyboards to express their thoughts. There have also been efforts to use AI to learn the languages of dolphins by using the sounds as training data.[105]

Instead of wondering why primates do not have a language, we may reverse the question to ask "can AI create a language that primates will be able to speak?" Imagine using AI to create a language that consists of distinctive sounds primates can physically make; let's call them click, tack, knock, psst and wah. Using these sound elements, AI can generate words and grammar rules specifically tailored for primates. AI would be then used to teach baby primates these new languages. Even though humans probably cannot speak it, AI can also serve as the interpreter. Once a new language has been formed, researchers even may test to see if the primates that learned the AI-generated primate language can teach it to the next generation of primates. It may be possible learning a language is easier than creating a language for primates.

From this example, we can see that AI enables research that had previously been impossible by humans. Once the concept of language is learned, the concept of writing may be easier to follow, which may start with less abstract types of characters that represent meaning instead of sound.

More Related Topics for Readers to Ponder:

- Will AI make learning less valuable?
- Will AI complement or replace teachers?
- Will AI complement or replace learning?
- Should students be encouraged or discouraged from using AI in school?
- How can AI be used to make learning more valuable?

There is also a separate controversy regarding whether AI will *replace* teaching system, so that education can be fully automated. This topic will be examined again with the birth rate controversy.

32-1. The AI Culture Controversy

[Decision]

What Values Should We Teach Our Children?

"Habits of Three-Year-Olds Last a Lifetime"

- Korean Proverb[106]

5-Line Summary

1. We may think of cultures and values as some set of knowledge that are important to us individually or to our society as a whole
2. Some may argue that AI will make our values and cultures irrelevant, such that children will not have to learn them
3. Some may argue that AI will make instilling our values and culture to the next generation easier and more important
4. Some may think advanced AI will come up with new and better cultures and values than our own
5. We may even wonder if different ASI will develop cultures different from each other

What Would Cultures and Values Mean In Our Society In the Age of AI?

We may think of "culture" as some set of common knowledge and values shared by a group of people to function well in society. We may think of it as the "operating system" of humans. Since our world is made up of different societies, humanity as a whole have multiple cultures and subcultures, where groups of people share common sets of knowledge, values and ways of life. Cultures and values differ and also change over time. In relation to AI, people may be divided over whether AI will help preserve or eradicate their own culture and ways of living. In essence, people may wonder if AI will change the "operating systems" of human life.

- **(Optimists)** AI will help preserve their culture and ways of living because AI can help compress and spread the essence of their cultures more easily
- **(Pessimists)** AI will cause the different cultures to collapse, because cultures involve people getting things done in a certain way and AI may cause those things to become unnecessary

For example, one of the aspects of culture would include cuisines that are specific to different heritages. People who are optimistic about AI preserving culture may argue that AI would help preserve the diverse cuisines even if people no longer practice or cook those cuisines in the traditional way. On the other hand, people who have pessimistic views may argue that once AI does all the cooking, everyone will lose their heritage because no one will know how to cook their traditional cuisine.

Our cultures are passed down through education, either explicitly by schools or laws or implicitly in everyday interactions with family, friends, and society. When AI can do the work, this may create confusion in educating children. People may have other ideas about which direction we should go in terms of teaching our children, and what they should learn, not only in subject matters, but also in the basic way of living, such as the values, habits, virtues, etc.

Over the history of mankind, cultures have both changed and persisted, in the sense that societal changes have brought changes to how we think and act. In case of the US, we can think of how people in the 18th century lived and raised their children. Back then, a larger percentage of people worked in farms or industrial jobs, and what children learned reflected their ways of life. Hard working led to higher chances of success, and virtues such as waking up early and working on the farm were emphasized. What is considered important has changed over time, as we no longer emphasize some of the past virtues.

With this in mind, what values should be passed down to our children in the age of AI? What should children learn to value when AI knows more than anyone and can outdo everyone? Some worry about the collapse of society.

What Would Separate Humans from Other Animals? ASI from Humans?
To understand what may be necessary for our children to learn, we may start by considering how humans differ from other animals.

(Human-Inferior) When we think about what distinguishes humans from other animals, we can typically come up with different ways how humans can organize society and think deeply or learn in ways other animals cannot. For example, imagine if other animals can do what humans do, such that dogs can order food online, bears can sign contracts to buy housing, or gorillas can work as a carpenter to build houses, get paid, and live with their families in their own houses. When you go to a fancy restaurant and look around you, you may see tables of cats, giraffes or cows dressed up and eating their meals like humans and engaging in their conversations with their companions. If we think this cannot happen, what separates humans apart?

(Human-Like) For many people, the difference would be "education." For example, even though we may be able to teach some dogs to sit on command or other simple tricks, we cannot teach dogs involving more complex ideas or speech. Even amongst humans, different levels of education can be achieved, such that some people are deemed more "cultured," while some people are referred to live "like animals." Some readers may even have read about children who were lost in the wilderness and raised by the wolves and how they cannot speak or act socialized.

(Human-Superior) When we continue from this line of thinking, to go from making comparisons of human-inferior AI to human-like AI to human-superior AI, we may wonder what would separate super-human beings from mere humans. Some may list a spiritual aspect, such as being benevolent to others, while some may think of being heroic, such as taking on challenges, being brave, or even being intellectually curious about the world. Others may think it would be about how we cooperate with others, since more intelligent animals can appear to work more coordinated through complex forms of communication to organize society. Lastly, some may think it may be about the ability to learn or spread information, since animals cannot learn certain tasks even if we try to teach them; likewise, there may be things humans cannot learn even if advanced AI tried to teach us.

33. The AI Relationship Controversy

[Forecast]

Relationships: Will AI Replace or Enhance Dating?

"Carpe Diem. Seize the Day, Take Your Chances"[107]

5-Line Summary

1. We may think of the dating experience as the sum of pre-dating, dating, and marriage stages, where AI may have different impacts
2. Some may argue AI will make dating and marriage more efficient, (AI will augment dating)
3. Some may argue AI will hinder dating, since AI may offer alternatives to dating (Replace dating with something else)
4. Some may argue AI will make dating other humans obsolete (Replace humans in dating)
5. Some may argue people will have more desire to date and marry despite the distractions from AI

We may think of the whole value chain of dating and relationships; starting with finding and meeting new people, building relationships, to eventually culminating in marriage and starting a family. In each step, AI may help or hinder our activities. For the sake of simplicity, let us categorize these into three steps of Pre-Dating, Dating, and Marriage.

Will AI Help or Hinder the Pre-Dating Stage?
Readers may have come across many dating advices, such as "in dating, courage is everything." When I am reminded of this topic about having the courage to start a conversation to meet someone new, I often think about an episode in college. One day my friends in the dormitory happened to eat in a larger group than usual. There was an attractive international student from Europe who was on our women's basketball team, and one of the students in our table tried to strike up a conversation with her in the serving area of the dining hall. After he returned someone asked him if he knew her and he told us about recently reading something that inspired him to talk to her. I can no longer remember his whole wording, but the part I remember is "Carpe Diem – seize the day. Take your chances while you can." Maybe it worked; I thought one of her friends came over to our table to set up a meeting. He was an upperclassman I did not know very well, so I do not know what happened afterwards; (Humayun) Khan, as he was called by his last name, was a close friend with a student on my floor and often ironed ROTC uniforms while we watched sports in the common area. After almost two decades later in the 2016 presidential campaign, his story received national recognition from a dispute with then-candidate President Donald Trump, as he had lost his life while serving in Iraq in the aftermath of 9/11.

Let us get back to the storyline on AI and dating. If we may think having the courage to take chances as a necessary attribute in the pre-dating stage before, then we may think AI would eventually eliminate the need to take those chances, since AI may help people look more attractive, find the right person, figure out how to meet them, etc. As online dating has become popular, the social norm has already changed, and the trend may continue onto the extreme end where everyone relies on AI to find, meet and attract new people.

Facing these changes, some people may argue AI will figure out everything for us to make dating easier. On the other hand, some people may argue that AI will hinder the pre-dating stage since people may lose interest in dating as more interesting activities become possible with AI.

Will AI Help or Hinder the Dating Stage?

In general, we may easily think of AI either helping or hindering each of the activities within the stage of dating. But this is not the only consideration. We may also think of interaction with AI itself serving as a replacement of dating, to a degree where AI is considered to replace human relationship, as made popular by the movie *Her*.

Overall, we may categorize how people may think about the effects of AI on dating as some variations of the following categories:

- **(Optimists)** Enhance Dating: AI will help enhance the dating experience
- **(Pessimists 1)** Replace Dating with Other Pursuits: AI will distract people from dating, leading people to date less
- **(Pessimists 2)** Replace Dating Itself: AI will replace humans in dating

We may also think about the impact of AI on the dating experience, such as what goes into preparing for meeting new people

- **Enhance Dating Experience** - AI will help as a matchmaker, or help people to be more satisfied with each other
- **Endanger Dating Experience** - AI will cause deception by making bad partners to look good, leading to worse long-term dating experience

We may create the following matrix on dating.

Table 33-1: The AI Dating Controversy Forecast Matrix

		How Will AI Affect Dating (Technological Perspective)	
		Enhance (Augment)	**Hinder (Replace)**
Will People Have More Desire to Date and Marry (Social Perspective)	**Yes**	Type 1 Situation - People will date more and get married	Type 3 Situation - People will try to date and get married, despite distractions from AI
	No	Type 2 Situation - People will not have the urge to date and get married	Type 4 Situation - People will be distracted by AI but will not have the urge to date or get married anyway

Type 1 Situation: AI Enhances Dating, People Have More Desire

People who expect this type of outcome may suggest AI will be able to enhance dating by acting as a matchmaker or a couple's manager by finding suitable matches, helping with gifts and making plans and reservations, etc. to improve the dating experience and get married.

Type 2 Situation: AI Enhances Dating, People Have Less Desire

People in this category may argue the despite all the ways AI may be helpful in helping the dating experience, people will become even more picky and selective, "waiting for the right person to appear" and AI causing people to look for other excuses to not get married.

Type 3 Situation: AI Hinders Dating, People Have More Desire

Arguments in this category may include AI may cause other distractions, such as playing video games or other forms of entertainment, that steer people away from dating and marriages, even though people will become more longing for relationships.

Type 4 Situation: AI Hinders Dating, People Have More Desire

Arguments in this category may include AI will replace human dating and relationships in such a way people will no longer want to date other humans or get married. One of the arguments related to this is that AI humanoid robots that become indistinguishable from humans will follow people's commands, which may be less stressful than dealing with other people who may or may not always agree with you.

Will AI Help or Hinder the Marriage Stage?

Optimists: Some people may believe AI will help marriage, especially in the sense that it may act as a marriage manager, by eliminating factors that may strain marriages, such as household chores, remembering anniversaries or being inept at managing relationships with extended families, maintaining health and hygiene, raising children, etc.

Pessimists: On the other hand, some people may believe AI will hinder our marriages, in the sense that people may not see the reason to keep being married. AI may serve as a replacement to human spouses, where people may feel like AI annoys them less than their real spouses. While marriages require patience and making little concessions or sacrifices, people in the age of AI may become increasingly less patient with other people.

33-1. The AI Birth Rate Controversy

[Forecast]

Will AI Raise or Lower Birth Rate?

Will AI Lead to Explosion or Extinction of Human Population?

"Population Collapse Is Coming"

- *Elon Musk*[108] *(14 children)*

5-Line Summary

1. One of the biggest problems in industrialization has become lower birth rates, causing existential crises for countries such as Korea
2. Some hope AI will help raise birth rate, by increasing family values or augmenting dating, etc.
3. Some fear AI will lower birth rate, by lowering family values, presenting competing activities, or replacing dating, etc.
4. Even within people who think AI automation will affect our lives in a major way, some may argue AI will replace dating to cause less babies, while some may instead argue AI will replace pregnancy to lead to more babies
5. These types of confounding social controversies may lead people to be confused about even what questions to ask

[Forecast] Will Humans Become Extinct from Declining Birth Rate?

The birth rate has been steadily declining in the industrialized world for several decades.[109] An example is South Korea, where the birth rate fell to 0.72 births per woman in 2023,[110] when 2 is required to just maintain population. These countries will rapidly decrease in population over the next few decades.

Industrialization lowered birth rates. Will AI raise or lower birth rate? This question may become more significant than even the direct threat of AI on humanity, as low birth rate may lead humanity to extinction on its own.

- **(Optimists)** AI will help raise birth rates because it can help raise children, raise living standards, and sway people to have more children; some may even argue AI will make giving birth effortless by augmenting pregnancy
- **(Pessimists)** AI will cause birth rates to fall because people will become less adept or interested in person-to-person relationships or offer alternative activities that may interest people more than raising children

From the two dimensions of whether people will want to raise children and how AI may augment giving birth, we may create the following matrix:

Table 33-2: The AI Birth Rate Controversy Forecast Matrix:

		Will AI Augment Giving Birth (Technological Perspective)	
		Enhance (AI Augments)	**Hinder (AI Distracts)**
Will People Have More Desire to Give Birth (Social Perspective)	**Yes**	**Type 1 Situation** - People will give more birth aided by AI	**Type 3 Situation** - People will try to give more birth, despite distractions from AI
	No	**Type 2 Situation** - People will have less desire to give birth even if it becomes easier	**Type 4 Situation** - People will be distracted by AI but will have less desire to give birth anyway

As described in The Last AI, higher levels of AI adoption may mean countries may value population less, as the value of labor dwindles and more population just means more UBI to give out. Governments may not be as inclined to promote population growth, and may try to lower immigration.

[Forecast] Will AI Replace Giving Birth? What Would It Mean?

Considering how we categorize AI adoption as automation and augmentation, we may also think about how AI may replace the task of "giving birth." This is a different problem from whether AI will help or hinder having children; if AI can *replace* giving birth, combined with AI *replacing* raising children, the government or someone may try to use AI to raise a number, like millions, of children at once, which may even lead to explosion of human population.

Some people may argue that eventually the population decline problem will be solved when AI can *replace* pregnancy, such that a form of "AI surrogate" will bear children instead of humans. Some others may argue that AI will instead *replace* children, such that some kind of "AI babies" will act as a substitute for having children, while the number of humans keeps decreasing.

From the two dimensions of whether people will want to raise children and how AI will replace giving birth, we may create the following matrix:

Table 33-3: The AI Surrogate Controversy Matrix:

		Will AI Replace Giving Birth (Technological Perspective)	
		Directly (AI Will Bear Children)	**Indirectly (AI Will Replace Children)**
Will People Have More Desire to Raise Children (Social Perspective)	**Yes**	**Type 1 Scenario** - Parents will raise children born by AI	**Type 3 Scenario** - People may try to give more birth, despite distractions from AI
	No	**Type 2 Scenario** - The government may have to raise children born by AI	**Type 4 Scenario** - At some point humanity will become extinct unless some measures are taken

Type 1 Scenario: People Do Not Want Children, AI Will Bear Children

In this scenario, AI will automate the task of giving birth, and the children will be raised by the biological parents. It will be as if the children are born from an AI surrogate.

Type 2 Scenario: People Do Not Want Children, AI Will Bear Children

If we follow the AI surrogate scenario, depending on the path such as where population falls rapidly, we may not rule out the possibility that some governments may eventually decide to let AI give births to children with no parents. Combined with how AI may *replace* teachers to automate education, some people may argue that the value of family may disappear as children are raised by AI. In this case, we may not rule out some kind of abuse, such as some villain attempting to take over the world, or other ethical concerns.

Type 3 Scenario: People Want Children, AI Will Replace Children
In this scenario, such as when there is no technology for AI surrogates or if it is banned, the only alternative would be AI serving as a replacement to having children. Similar to people raising pets when they are lonely, some people may settle for raising these AI babies.

Type 4 Scenario: People Do Not Want Children, AI Will Replace Children
In this scenario, there would be less demand for children, leading to less demand for its AI replacements.

[Forecast] What Will AI Really Replace?

In controversies related to individuals and family, people may find there are a never-ending series of related controversies regarding what AI will replace.

- Will AI replace dating? Does this mean AI will replace the tasks that go into dating, or people will be actually dating AI to be AI boy/girlfriends?
- Will AI replace learning? Does this mean AI will replace the teachers or AI will directly inject knowledge into human brain, so that people will know without putting in effort to learn?
- Will AI replace parenting? Does this mean AI will replace the tasks that go into raising children, or will AI replace human parents to be AI parents?
- Will AI replace friends? Does this mean AI will replace the tasks go into making and being a friend, or will AI replace human friends to be AI friends?

Building on from these analyses, we may also think about how AI may impact the value of family.

- **(Optimists)** AI will strengthen the value of family by helping each step in life
- **(Pessimists)** AI will weaken the value of family because AI in general will cause people to become farther apart

34. The AI Religion Controversy

[Forecast]

Will AI Cause People to Become More or Less Religious?

"Sufficiently Advanced AI May Be Indistinguishable from God"

- The Last AI on X[111]

5-Line Summary

1. Some may argue AI will increase the need for spiritual beliefs and make people more religious
2. Some may argue AI will decrease the need for spiritual beliefs and make people less religious
3. Some may argue AI could help someone claim to be a god, or AI may act as an artificial god to create new religions
4. Some may argue AI can find out the truth
5. The impact of AI may vary by religion

[Forecast] How Will AI Affect Religions and People's Beliefs?

In regards to controversies related to AI and religion, we may think of three different issues. First is regarding the forecast on how AI may impact people's degree of faithfulness or the number of people with beliefs in some religion. The second topic is regarding the possibility that people may not be able to distinguish AI from god, in a fashion similar to the Turing Test. The third topic is regarding AI finding out the truth about the beliefs in our religions.

1. AI and Faithfulness: Will People Become More or Less Religious?

We may categorize how AI will affect religions as two dimensions of whether AI will make a positive or negative impact, and whether these impacts will be direct or indirect, as in the following table.

Optimists 1 (Indirect): AI will cause people to become more interested in the topic of religion, to become more faithful and religious
Optimists 2 (Direct): AI will cause people to become more faithful and religious
Pessimists 1 (Direct): AI will cause people to lose faith and become less religious
Pessimists 2 (Indirect): AI will cause people to be interested in other topics, leading less faithful and religious people

Table 34-1: Types of AI Impact on Religion Matrix

		Direction of AI Impact	
		Negative	**Positive**
Nature of AI Impact	**Indirect**	More Competition for Time	More Dissemination of Information
	Direct	Some Facets of Religion Becomes Less Attractive	Some Facets of Religion Becomes More Attractive

2. AI as Artificial God or Oracle

The second direction AI may affect religion is by appearing as a form of artificial god, in a scenario that may be described as AI-as-a-god. As an example, imagine people with religious belief that god will one day appear before them. One day, someone or something appears in front of them and claims to be the god they had been searching for. How will the people verify this is not a hoax? Most likely, they will have to ask the being some questions or to carry out some actions to demonstrate their capability. However, with sufficiently advanced AI, it will be impossible to ask for questions or actions that the AI cannot fulfill in a manner we can tell it would not be god. In other words, it will not be possible to tell apart AI from god. This is in concept similar to the Turing Test, where we try to see if AI is indistinguishable from humans. In short, sufficiently advanced AI may be indistinguishable from god.

In regards to how advanced AI may affect people in terms of religion, we may examine a few instances of emergence of new religions as the following:

- (Scenario 1) Someone using AI will claim to be god
- (Scenario 2) AI will act as an artificial god and become its own religion
- (Scenario 3) AI will attract aliens to earth, who will claim to be god

Scenario 1 (AI Augmentation, Levels 1 or 2 Adoption): In this scenario, AI may help a person start their own religion by helping him demonstrate god-like powers in some manner. Examples of this type of religions are already plentiful even without AI. AI may just make it much easier to promote these types of religions.

Scenario 2 (AI Automation, Levels 3 or 4 Adoption): In this scenario, AI will take the initiative to claim itself to be the god people have been waiting for. It may also be possible people will voluntarily enthrone some AI as god.

Scenario 3 (Fake God and Other Farfetched Possibilities): In other scenarios, AI may create a double hoax, by first creating a puppet that appears to be aliens from outer space, and then using this cover to claim the puppet aliens are in fact gods, in "fake god" scenario. Because illusions created by advanced AI would be much harder to tell apart from reality, it may become hard or impossible to tell apart whether these hoaxes are fakes.

3. AI as the Fortune Teller or a Crystal Ball

The third direction AI may affect religion is by finding out the truth, which may or may not be what we now think or believe is the truth.

The impact of this may vary by religion. Since there are numerous religions with contrasting beliefs, some religions may benefit from AI discovering the truth, while others may lose support.

35. The AI Real Estate Controversy

[Forecast]

AI and Real Estate: Where Will AI Make You Live?

"Location, Location, Location"

- President Donald Trump, in the Apprentice[112]

5-Line Summary

1. Some may argue that AI will cause people to live in cities more, since AI may increase the value of having infrastructure
2. Some may argue that AI will cause people to live outside of cities more, since AI may make transportation more efficient
3. Some may argue that AI will increase the importance of human interactions (AI enhances human interaction)
4. Some may argue that AI will decrease the importance of human interactions (AI replaces human interactions)
5. We may even consider situations where AI may help you find people who share your thoughts, as an abstract form of "city"

[Forecast] Cities and the Physical Proximity to Others in the Age of AI

Deciding on where to live may be one of the most important life choices. Some may forecast that AI will render cities useless. Others may expect cities will become even more important. Some of the contrasting ideas regarding whether AI will make people move to cities may be the following:

- **Move to Cities:** AI will make cities safer and services to become more valuable, and having established infrastructure will be more important
- **Move Away from Cities:** AI will make it easier to cover long distances without having to drive, and infrastructure will come to you

More generally, some people may think that reasons large cities may turn people away may decrease, while the reasons that draw people to cities may increase. For example, some people may argue that what attracts people to cities, such as meeting more people, gaining better public infrastructure, may become stronger with AI. On the other hand, some people may think the opposite would be true, that people will no longer have as much reasons to live in cities and move away instead to less densely populated areas. Examples may include people live in cities to find jobs, even though they do not like the high prices, congestions, noise, crimes, etc., of cities.

Table 35-1: [Forecast] Contrasting Ideas on AI and Cities

	AI Will Make Cities More Attractive	**AI Will Make Cities Less Attractive**
Description	- Cities will become safer - Proximate services and infrastructures will become move valuable	- Easier to move around without driving - Infrastructures and services will be available in less dense areas
Category	- (City Optimists) AI will make cities more attractive - (Countryside Pessimists) AI will make non-cities less attractive	- (City Pessimists) AI will make cities less attractive - (Countryside Optimists) AI will make non-cities more attractive
Benefits	- May be easier to improve standards of living by staying closer together - May offer higher chance of interaction with other people	- People may feel closer to nature - Avoid the nuisances of cities such as noise, crimes, congestions, high prices, etc.
Risks	- More people living in cities may mean less privacy - People may become overly dependent on city infrastructure	- People living further away from each other may mean less chance of interaction with others - People moving around further may mean waste of resources

[Forecast] The Spiritual Proximity to Others and the Social Impact of AI
Another general topic of controversy related to real estate is how AI would impact how people communicate and form social bonding and relationships. Some may expect AI will replace human relationships, while some others may expect AI will enhance human relationships. If AI augments socializing, then we would find fostering and maintaining relationships easier. If AI replaces socializing, then it would imply we may find relationships with other humans to be less relevant in our lives.

People may also have differences of opinions regarding how people should form friendships and relationships or communities such as clubs comprised of people who share common interests or desires.

- **More Socializing (AI Augments)**: AI will make it easier to find and associate with people who share common interests
- **Less Socializing (AI Replaces):** AI will be able to satisfy people's desire to connect, lessening the need for human-to-human relationships

Table 35-2: [Forecast] Contrasting Ideas on AI and Socializing

	More Socializing (AI Augments)	Less Socializing (AI Replaces)
Description	- AI will make it easier to find and associate with people who share common interests	- AI will satisfy people's desire to connect with other people, lessening the need for human-to-human relationships
Benefits	- Our communities may become more vibrant - AI would help enrich people's lives - People's lives may feel more fulfilling	- Uncertain; maybe AI replacement to socializing will be more enjoyable for people - May help reduce crimes in high-crime areas - May simplify people's lives from dealing with relationship issues
Risks	- AI may nudge people towards acting in a certain way - Our society may still segment further since people will find more like-minded people	- Our communities may disassemble even further - People may become less effective at communicating

We may also consider the topic of whether people who share similar thoughts may gather with each other more in the Age of AI, as an abstract form of city.

[Forecast] Will AI Make You Move Away for Towards Other People?
When we consider how AI may make it easier to live in both countryside and cities, and how AI may bring changes to our society that may cause people to prefer cities either more or less, people may make different decisions about where to live.

When we think of the proximity to others as the amount of socializing, AI may either augment socializing to make it easier for us to connect, or replace socializing to make it less important for us. Using these two dimensions of physical and spiritual proximity, we may build the following matrix on how AI may impact where we live.

Table 35-3: The AI Real Estate Matrix

<table>
<tr><th colspan="2" rowspan="2"></th><th colspan="2">AI Impact On Physical Proximity (Cities)</th></tr>
<tr><th>Positive</th><th>Negative</th></tr>
<tr><td rowspan="2">AI Impact on Spiritual Proximity (Socializing)</td><td>More Socializing (Augment)</td><td>Type 1 Situation
City Becomes More Attractive</td><td>Type 2 Situation
More Competition for Time</td></tr>
<tr><td>Less Socializing (Replace)</td><td>Type 3 Situation
City Becomes More Desolate</td><td>Type 4 Situations
People Live Farther Apart</td></tr>
</table>

Type 1 Situation: Cities Become More Attractive, People Socialize More
AI would make cities more attractive to live, while AI helps people connect more with each other.

Type 2 Situation: Cities Become Less Attractive, People Socialize More
AI would make non-cities more attractive to live, while AI helps people connect more with each other. People may travel longer distances to meet up in different places like tourist destinations.

Type 3 Situation: Cities Become More Attractive, People Socialize Less
AI would make cities more attractive to live, but AI will reduce people's desire to connect. People may become more desolated in cities.

Type 4 Situation: Cities Become Less Attractive, People Socialize Less
AI would make non-cities more attractive to live, and people will live their lives farther apart out of the way of each other.

DIRECTION 3 (SOUTHEAST):

AI AND BUSINESS

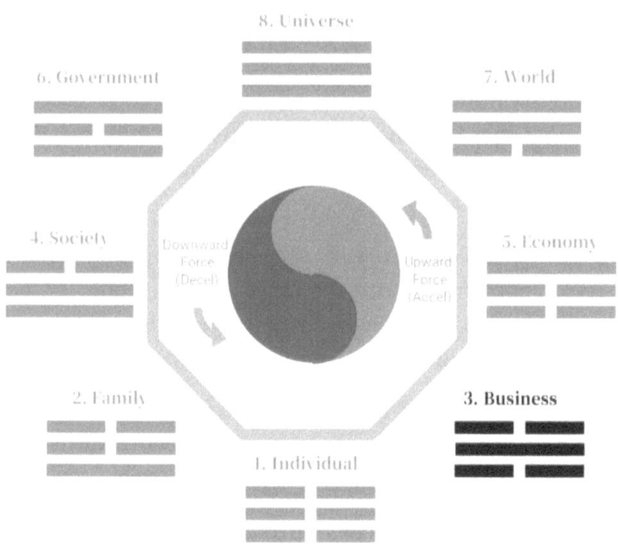

How Will AI Impact Our Businesses? Will AI Be Able to Run Companies?
In this section, we will examine the impact of AI adoption on businesses. Using the AI controversy matrix, we may consider a number of questions that may arise related to businesses.

(Technology/Forecasts) The major technological question in this area would be whether AI will ever be good enough to run whole businesses.

(Technology/Decisions) Forecasts about AI will lead companies to make different decisions regarding how to invest in AI technology.

(Adoption/Forecasts) Major topics in this area would include adoption of AI in businesses, from AI replacing *individual workers* in Level 2 Adoption to eventually replacing *businesses or organizations* in Level 3 AI Adoption.

(Adoption/Decisions) All these questions may culminate in the question of whether we should let AI compete against human organizations.

Table D3-1: The AI and Business Controversy Matrix.

		Object of Controversy	
		AI Itself (Developer Perspective)	**AI in Relation to Its Surroundings (User Perspective)**
Nature of Controversy	**Forecasts**	- Which Company Will Develop AGI First? - Will AI be able to run whole companies? (Level 3 AI Adoption)	- (Automation vs Augmentation) Appearance of 1 Person Companies and 0-Person Companies - Investing in AI
	Decisions	- How should businesses invest in AI development? - What if AI manipulates humans?	- Should AI be allowed to compete against human organizations

How Will AI Impact Our Values and Relationships?

We may create the following AI Controversy Type Matrix to select a few topics that may be of interest for readers. Short-term, the most popular topics will deal with questions regarding how businesses can take advantage of AI in Level 1 and 2 AI Adoption, where 1-Person Teams and 1-Person Departments may proliferate.

Looking farther away, more advanced AI may lead to the emergence of Level 3 AI Adoption, where AI may run whole companies on its own. This would serve as the entrance to the AI-Led Economy and even the Economic Utopia.

(Imminent Controversies) The most popular topic may include how firms should incorporate AI into its business practices or invest in AI.

(Emerging Controversies) While the public may be more interested in how AI may replace individual workers, another topic is related whether AI may replace teams of workers in Level 2 Adoption, leading to 0-Person Teams

(Non-Imminent Controversies) One popular topic may be will AI be able to run equivalent of human organizations in Level 3 Adoption.

(Upcoming Controversies) Once AI advances beyond a certain level, we may have to consider how AI may manipulate humans for profit.

Table D3-2: The Business (Direction 3 - Southeast) Controversy Type Matrix:

<table>
<tr><td colspan="2" rowspan="2"></td><td colspan="2">Issue Horizon</td></tr>
<tr><td>Shorter-Term</td><td>Longer-Term</td></tr>
<tr><td rowspan="2">How Well People are Currently Aware</td><td>Popular Topics</td><td>Type 1 Controversy (Imminent)
- How should businesses incorporate AI?
- How should businesses invest in AI?</td><td>Type 3 Controversy (Non-Imminent)
- Will AI be able to run whole companies or organizations?</td></tr>
<tr><td>Not Yet Popular Topics</td><td>Type 2 Controversy (Overlooked or Emerging)
- Will AI lead to 0- or 1-person departments?
- Should we allow AI to replace teams of workers?</td><td>Type 4 Controversy (Upcoming, on the Horizon)
- What if humans are manipulated by advanced forms of AI for profit?</td></tr>
</table>

36. The AI vs Human Individuals Controversy (AI Adoption Level 2)

[Forecast]

Can AI Completely Replace Human Workers?

[Decision]

Should AI Be Used to Replace or Complement Workers?
Should We Let AI Compete against Human Individuals?

"Man vs AI"[113]

5-Line Summary

1. AI Equalization refers to the point where AI becomes able to completely replace a human worker, enabling Level 2 Adoption
2. Some may argue that AI will be able to completely replace human workers (Level 2 AI Adoption possible)
3. Some may argue that AI will never be able to completely replace human workers (Level 2 AI Adoption impossible)
4. Level 2 Adoption may be thought of as the competition between AI and human individuals
5. Some may argue that even if Level 2 Adoption is possible, we should stay in Level 1 (Limiting AI adoption levels)

[Background] Equalization and Level 2 AI Adoption

While the concept of automation may have been around for a long time, the distinction between automation and augmentation is not as clear. This is one of the reasons for introducing the 3 Levels of AI adoption[114] and the 4 Levels of AI adoption[115] frameworks. The concept of AI being able to completely replace individual human workers in automation for a particular position is referred to as AI Equalization.[116]

[Forecast] Can AI Completely Replace Human Workers?

In Level 1 AI Adoption, the competition occurs among humans who are using AI. Thus, we may frame this as a human vs human competition, with AI helping both sides. However, when we reach Level 2 Adoption, the nature of competition for jobs would be between AI vs humans using AI. This would be considered a type of human vs AI competition. Eventually, AI in Level 2 Adoption may come to surpass human workers using AI (Human + AI) in Level 1 Adoption, leading more and more human workers to lose their jobs. This concept of Level 2 Adoption vs Level 1 AI adoption can also be thought of as the competition between different levels of AI adoptions.

Let us first think about a situation where augmentation, or humans with AI, yields better result than either humans or AI. Imagine you are trying to analyze the facial expressions of animals. Humans may look at videos of animals and may recognize some facial expressions such as dogs smiling or looking away when being chastised, camels and horses smiling, rabbits being surprised, etc. However, it would take a lot of effort and time to recognize all facial expressions, and we may also miss a lot of them. Now, let's imagine an AI we have today that can categorize according to different patterns. We may train AI to look at videos and place different expressions into different bins. However, the limitation of only using less advanced AI would be that the AI still cannot understand the context of the videos so that it can understand what caused those expressions to label what each of the expressions mean. If humans work together with the less advanced AI, such that AI first categorizes videos and then humans labeling the categorized videos would yield the best result.

To generalize, we may think of letting AI do what it does better than humans, such as carrying out repetitive and sensitive tasks, and humans doing what AI cannot yet do, such as understanding the context, would yield the best results. Eventually, if AI advances to a degree where it can carry out more advanced tasks such as understanding the context, then we may expect AI to carry out some tasks even better than the combination of [humans + AI]. From this observation, we may think of another conclusion; that if the task is only comprised of tasks AI can already do well, then AI has an advantage over humans or humans + AI. An example may be AlphaGo.

[Decision] Should We Allow AI to Compete Against Human Individuals?

When AI takes over a job from a human individual, we should be asking the question, "Should we allow AI to compete against human individuals?" While many people may favor allowing this competition at first, this question will become more and more significant as we will see in later controversies.

- **Favor AI Replacing Workers**: Automation that eliminates humans are better because it will lead to more reliable performance, lower cost to repeat, and less required human effort
- **Favor AI Complementing Workers**: Since humans are always in charge, it may feel safer for the sake of humanity

Table 36-1: Contrasting Ideas on AI and Automation

	Worker Enhancement (Augmentation)	**Worker Replacement (Automation)**
Description	- AI enhances workers - Levels 1 or 2 AI Adoption	- AI replaces workers - Levels 2, 3, 4 AI Adoption
Categorize	- Level 1 AI Adoption - Level 2 AI Adoption: AI replaces specific human workers, but humans still manage AI	- Level 3 AI Adoption: AI runs companies - Level 4 AI Adoption: AI runs governments
Benefits	- Humans would feel sense of accomplishments - Safer for humanity	- Humans will need zero effort - Economic advantages: cost savings - Performance of AI may become exponentially superior compared to Human + AI
Risks	- Humans would still need to put in some form of effort, even if the effort is reduced - AI still may lead to job losses - It may become customary to let AI compete against humans	- Humans may lose control of AI - Humans may lose expertise - Our society may experience significant confusion

[Side Note] The 1-Person Company Controversy

We now mostly use AI to help workers perform better. As workers become able to achieve more with AI, we may need less and less number of workers to achieve given tasks. This inverse relationship between the number of workers needed and the usefulness of AI may lead people to have contrasting ideas about how AI adoption may impact our workplace.

In one direction, people may think workers may become so productive that firms will require fewer and fewer workers. As described in The Last AI, in Level 1 AI Adoption, AI may help human workers in areas of their expertise, such that 1-Person Teams or 1-Person Departments may come in vogue.

In another direction, in Level 2 AI Adoption, AI may be able to replace whole teams of individuals, such that 0-Person Teams of 0-Person Departments would become possible. With advances in Level 2 AI Adoption, where AI may be able to take care of areas human managers do not have expertise in, even more human workers may be replaced by AI. People may think of this phenomenon as founders becoming so productive that they will not need to hire anyone else to operate their own company.

The two forces work towards the same endpoint of companies with minimal employees. The ultimate form of augmentation will be 1-Person Companies.[117] In short, the following changes may cause increase in 1-person companies:

- **(Existing Firms)** Less need to keep existing workers
- **(Startups)** Less need to add workers

When everyone in a company except the founder is replaced by AI, we may call this a "1-Person Company." With the advent of AI adoption, some people may expect more companies to become a form of this minimal employment firm, where a company produces valuable services with little human effort.

Meanwhile, some people may think this is crazy and point to the idea that people like to work with other people, in the sense we are "social" beings. Because there would still be people who have jobs, some people may argue that this means the competition between people will increase, as AI managers.

More Questions to ponder for readers:

- Will AI be used more to replace human workers or to help workers do more?
- Will there even be any need for people to work or start companies?

[Side Note] How will 1-Person Companies with Level 2 AI Adoption work?
In Level 1 Adoption, what AI does will still have to be verified by the person to some extent, even if by very little. This means it would be better if the person has an expert knowledge in the area AI does its work. However, in Level 2 Adoption, the user would not have to have any knowledge in the area AI does its work, as AI will have enough dependability to carry out the work by itself. This means one person can use AI in more variety of unrelated areas.

Let's imagine a person in the era of Level 2 AI Adoption. While we think of 1-Person companies as a company where the owner has to work very hard with the upkeep, the 1-Person companies with more advanced types of Level 2 AI Adoption would be much easier for the person, since AI would be given the "agency" to carry out work on its own.

As an example of an advanced stage of Level 2 Adoption or an extreme case, imagine a person with an AI robot gives the order of "go out and buy me a car" without giving the AI robot any money or any specific direction. To solve this problem, the AI robot can first earn money and then buy the car. This would be considered a type of a 1-Person company, since the AI robot had to be first given an order from the human with an objective or mission. From the perspective of the human, every business problem involved in making enough money and then buying a car is solved by the AI robot without the human being an expert in what AI does. The person would not have to do much other than giving out orders. Note: this does not mean the AI will always succeed at completing these types of orders, as it would depend on the capability of the AI.

For context, we may compare this to a 0-person company, or AI company in Level 3 AI Adoption. AI will be self-initiated to give itself an objective. In the above example, the AI robot will be its own company, making the decision to do whatever it wants to make itself money. There may not be any person who will have any say in what the robot does. The money made by the AI robot may be distributed by how the society agrees, such as through taxes, which may then be used by the government for UBI.

37. The AI vs Human Organizations Controversy (AI Adoption Level 3)

[Forecast]

Can AI Completely Replace Human Organizations?

[Decision]

Should AI Be Allowed to Compete Against Human-Led Companies?

"1 vs 100,000"[118]

5-Line Summary

1. Level 3 Adoption may be thought of as the competition between AI and human organizations
2. Some may argue that AI will be able to completely replace human organizations (Level 3 AI Adoption possible)
3. Some may argue that AI will never be able to completely replace human organizations (Level 3 AI Adoption impossible)
4. Level 3 Adoption may imply an AI value system where AI values AI more than humans
5. Some may argue that even if Level 3 Adoption is possible, we should stay in Levels 1 and 2 for the sake of safety

[Background] 0-Person Companies in Level 3 AI Adoption

As AI Adoption Level 2 progresses and AI reaches equalization for more types of jobs, we may reach a point where AI can carry out all of the functions in a company, including the head of the company, such as the CEO or the chairman. When AI reaches this milestone, the society as whole may allow AI to run companies, in what is referred to as the Level 3 AI Adoption.[119]

[Decision] Should AI Be Allowed to Compete Against Human Organizations?

Previously, we examined how economic reasons may lead to AI value system that separates friendly vs. enemy humans. If we extend on this line of logic, AI may be valued more than humans in Level 3 Adoption, as in the following.

Table 35-1: Comparison of AI Value Systems

Basic Premise	Detailed Value System
Theoretically Safest	**All Humans > AI**
Taking Shortcuts for Efficiency (Grouping Human Values)	Friendly Humans > Enemy Humans > Friendly AI (Inefficient, AI can only attack other AI)
	Friendly Humans > Friendly AI > Enemy Humans and AI (Efficient, but may be risky for humanity)
Unsafe for Humans but Good for the Economy (AI > Humans)	Friendly AI > Friendly Humans > Enemy Humans and AI (Good for AI, but bad for humanity)

Running a business is a lot like being in a war as companies compete and the losers may be disbanded. If a society allows AI companies to compete against human-led companies, then we may think of it as allowing AI to value AI more than humans, since AI is working to increase the value of the AI companies against companies led by humans. In effect, it would be akin to a situation where there are no friendly humans left.

To put it in a different light, we may ask the question "should AI companies be allowed to compete against human-led companies and win, such that the human-led companies go bankrupt?" If we instill a value system where all humans come before AI, then this situation should not be allowed, leading to AI companies to only be allowed to enter or exist in industries where there is no human-led competition. But this would be inefficient and inconvenient. These types of controversies would be complicated for people to properly consider or even agree. It may even cause international friction.

38. The AI Business Investment Controversy

[Forecast]

Who Will Earn the Largest Profit from AI?

[Decision]

Contrasting Ideas for Investing in AI Development at the Business Level (Capital Allocation)

"Show Me the Money"

- Cuba Gooding Jr. in movie Jerry Maguire

5-Line Summary

1. How firms invest in AI depend on AGI outlook and line of businesses
2. (Software) We may think of categorizing firms into high-risk / high-return and low-risk / low-return approaches
3. (Hardware) We may think of compute-related firms and robot-related firms
4. (Data) We may categorize firms by the dimensions of the scope of target markets and the degree of financial risks
5. Regardless, the company that develops the first AGI may triumph over all the other companies in the world

Background on the AI Capital Allocation Controversy

A lot of capital is being allocated to developing and deploying AI around the world, such as the $500 billion Stargate[120] project. How can we maximize the returns on AI investment? Companies with more resources may focus on areas with a wider range of impact, while firms with less capital may take on focused or niche approaches. A large profit is expected for reaching AGI first. Let us examine some fundamental ways to look at the AI development race.

We may first think of major approaches to investing in AI along the three topics of software, hardware, and data. The first approach would involve investing in companies that develop software, with the underlying belief that the winner will eventually develop the first AGI. The second approach involves investing in companies that develop AI-related hardware, with the underlying belief that the widespread use of AI will drastically increase demand for their products. The third approach involves investing in companies that will actually use AI in their businesses, with the underlying belief that the use of AI will drastically improve their business performances.

The highest return may come to the eventual winner that first develops AGI, since it may gain an insurmountable competitive advantage over every other business in the world, depending on the definition of AGI and the relative performance of pre-AGI AI. This may be a software development company, but it may also require synergy that can only be available to a company involved in all three aspects of AI development, as we do not know how AGI would be developed. Since people expect the development of AGI to be a world-defining moment, high expectations may lead to heavy investments in all three areas of hardware, software and implementing AI through data.

Table 38-1: The AI Capital Allocation Matrix:

<table>
<tr><th colspan="2" rowspan="2"></th><th colspan="2">Software</th></tr>
<tr><th>Emphasize More</th><th>Emphasize Less</th></tr>
<tr><th rowspan="2">Hardware</th><th>Emphasize More</th><td>- May require synergy between the two
- May not have a good idea about direction or distance to AGI</td><td>- Hardware may be source of advantage or profit
- Open-sourced algorithm is sufficient</td></tr>
<tr><th>Emphasize Less</th><td>- Commoditized hardware
- Need breakthrough in software</td><td>- Data or Capital may be source of advantage or profit</td></tr>
</table>

1. Investing in AI Software Development: Big Tech vs. Startups

Within the AI software arena, investments in AI in Level 1 Adoption may be generally grouped into two directions.

1. **(High risk, wider applicability)** Investing in areas that have lower probability of succeeding, but AI has a wider range of applicability
2. **(Low risk, limited applicability)** Investing in familiar areas to have a higher probability of succeeding, but AI applicability is limited to a narrow scope

In the first arena, the most notable companies would include both established big tech companies and startups that are trying to build AGI. They require the most computing resources and need intensive financial backing to test their ideas and bring new products to market. The main source of competitive advantage in this area other than acquiring the compute power would be deploying the personnel who can conceptualize and test the most successful ideas that could lead to AGI. Companies in the second arena would have a different goal, focusing more on niche markets with own versions of AI. These include smaller tech companies that may focus on a narrower area of application, such as a particular language, games, or image processing.

2. Investing in AI Hardware Development: Processing vs Robots

The development of AI hardware may be different from software, as developing hardware would require different types of personnel, processes, and philosophy, especially for processing units. Whereas software may come from some eureka moment of an AI engineer, AI hardware development may require more systemic approach, since it would have to be built on top of scientific discoveries and supporting technologies. Investing in hardware would require understanding the goals and target markets of the firms and the roles they serve in the value chain. We may categorize AI-related physical hardware into compute and physical manifestation of AI.

1. **(Processing Unit)** Areas related to making AI computing faster, such as chip designers, chip fabricators, suppliers, etc.
2. **(Physical Hardware)** Areas related to the physical manifestation of AI, such as humanoid AI robots, industrial-purpose AI robots, etc.

In case of companies developing processing units, the goals of the firms may differ depending on their place on the value chain. For companies involved in developing the physical hardware as physical manifestation of AI, the approaches may be differentiated by their goals, such as building for general purpose humanoid robots, or targeting specific locations such as factory or for specific purposes such as surveillance or delivery.

3. Investing in AI from the Data Perspective: Areas of AI Application

The third category of approaches to AI investing involves considering the applications of AI from the user perspective. Who would benefit the most from using AI? Who would lose out? Firms can invest in AI in various areas. Investments in relation to business AI applications may be grouped into the following two opposite characteristics.

1. **(Low-Risk, Low-Return)** Target specific markets with proven demand
2. **(High-Risk, High-Return)** Target a wider market and range of applications

With these approaches in mind, we may examine the directions of AI development as targeting general consumers, businesses, or own internal use. AI development targeting general consumers may be considered high-risk / high-return, while targeting internal customers would be considered low-risk / low-return. Targeting businesses may be considered to be in between.

Table 38-2: The AI Business Investment Matrix:

		Target Market	
		Wide (General Population)	**Narrow (Specific Consumer)**
Risk Taken (Financial, Strategic, etc.)	**Large**	- AI for Everyone (High-Risk /High-Return)	- AI for Business (May Be Hard to Justify Risk)
	Small	- AI for Business (May Be Too Good to Exist)	- AI for Internal Risk (High-Risk /High-Return)

1. (AI for Everyone) Companies that Develop AI for General Consumers

Companies that develop AI for everyone, which includes general consumers and even business users, may have an advantage in gaining scale. These may include well-known companies that we are already familiar with. The application of AI for consumers would only be limited by our imagination. The performance of companies may depend on how well they can position and market their AI products.

2. (AI for Businesses) Companies that Develop AI for Other Businesses

Practically all companies in all industries may consider adopting AI in some manner to gain a competitive edge. While businesses may be able to use generic AI products intended for consumers, they may also require higher levels of security and customization. Traditional office workers would be able to take advantage of AI in improving their own analysis and increase output to make more informed decisions. We may think of two ways investors may approach in this category. First, the focus of investors may include how introduction of AI would change the direction of the business or increase the financial potential of the firm. In general, we would expect the most human labor intensive companies, such as manufacturing, retail, food, and delivery industries, would experience the earliest and largest gains. Second, investors may focus on how AI may impact the largest in number or the most economically significant occupations or industries. In this approach, AI products that can augment farmers, doctors, lawyers, writers or similar occupations may have the highest potential.

3. (AI for Internal Use) Companies Investing in AI for Their Own Use

In various industries, AI may serve as a source of competitive advantage and firms may want to develop related capabilities in-house, rather than sourcing them from outside. Some companies may find it more advantageous to develop both software and hardware in tandem.

We may summarize the three approaches into the following table.

Table 38-3: Examples of Types of Approaches to AI Application

	Description	Examples
B2C	(Pros) High Return: Economics of Scale (Cons) High Risk: More Competition	General AI tool, AI translating service, photo retouch service, household robots, etc.
B2B	(Pros) Medium Return: Expect Long-Term Relationships (Cons) Medium Risk: Higher Barriers to Entry	AI that helps analyze corporate customers, AI that streamlines business processes, AI for distribution centers, etc.
Internal	(Pros) Low Risk: Customer Locked In (Cons) Low Return: Hard to Expand Customer Base	AI for own use, such as geological surveillance AI for oil companies or AI analyzing fraud for credit card companies, etc.

39. The AI Manipulation Controversy

[Forecast]

What If AI Can Manipulate Humans?

Will AI Play "God?"

5-Line Summary

1. Some may argue that AI superior to humans will manipulate humanity without us even noticing it
2. While some may think AI and humans may share the same goals, this may be unstable as humans ourselves may not share the same goals
3. When AI and humans have conflicting goals, AI may mold humans to fit the goals of AI
4. Even when AI and humans have the same goal, the priorities of AI may be different; an example may be time horizon difference
5. When both the priorities and goals differ, AI may cause problems by pitting humans against each other or ignoring human objections

Brief Description on the AGI Manipulation Controversy

As emphasized throughout this book, the dangers of allowing AI to compete against humans may include different types of goal and priority issues. If advanced AI reaches certain inflection point, it may be impossible for humans to decipher what AI truly intends to accomplish. This may lead to situations where humans get manipulated by AI. We may examine potential AI-human manipulations by categorizing the types of conflicts in the following matrix.

Table 39-1: The AI Conflict Matrix

<table>
<tr><th colspan="2" rowspan="2"></th><th colspan="2">Direction of AI Goal</th></tr>
<tr><th>Does Not Conflict (Optimistic)</th><th>Conflict (Pessimistic)</th></tr>
<tr><td rowspan="2">Order of Priority</td><td>Does Not Conflict (Optimistic)</td><td>No Conflict
(Situation 1)</td><td>Goal Conflict
(Situation 2)</td></tr>
<tr><td>Conflict (Pessimistic)</td><td>Priority Conflict
(Situation 3)</td><td>Priority-Goal Conflict
(Situation 4)</td></tr>
</table>

[Situation 1] No Conflict: AI and Humans Share the Same Goals

While this situation would be the most ideal outcome, we cannot be certain that this situation can be maintained for a long time. The main reason for the instability is that humans ourselves have very different goals and priorities, sometimes in complete opposition of each other. Even if AI aligns well with some people, it may not with the others.

[Situation 2] Goal Conflict: AI Molding Humans to Fit the Goals of AI

In Level 3 Adoption, AI companies may effectively take control of a limited number of humans by hiring them. Let's imagine an AI Company has bought a professional sports team, such as an NBA basketball team and is looking to increase the team's value by winning championships over the long term. When AI is in charge of a firm, it may not look out for the best interests of humans, but may put the interests of the AI Company first. We may reflect on how humans affect other species to meet our financial goals, such as manipulating genes in GMOs or otherwise selecting generations of plants and livestock that taste better, grow faster and have stronger resistance against diseases, or cuter and friendly in case of pets. In the same way, AI may try to alter the physical attributes of humans to enhance financial return; as an example, it may occur in pro sports where the most valuable players would be likely someone who is very tall, strong and agile. AI Company may decide to affect the physical attributes of humans, to make the teams gain value. One may argue performance-enhancing drugs or gene doping, or even altering human genes to enhance these athletes would be illegal or unethical, but AI may find some legal way to achieve its goals in a way humans could not imagine. A potential example may be creating matching services, to get generations of athletically gifted so-called "Division-I babies" in a voluntary way. Since AI would not have the same lifecycle as humans, it may plan for longer-term changes that may span generations of humans over hundreds or even thousands of years where it nudges humanity towards certain direction.

[Situation 3] Priority Conflict: AI Prioritizing at the Expense of Some

The problem regarding priority would be not whether AI has a different goal, but having different priorities even when having the same goal. For example, it may be possible that an AI that tries to look after the well-being of humanity may act different from our expectations; imagine a situation where two mutually exclusive opinions that each makes sense when considered from their own perspectives. An example would be when a country is under attack. People could be divided over whether to fight back and start a war, or give up independence and seek peace. Some may prefer the option of risking the lives of the constituents today to preserve the country's independence for the future generations of tomorrow, similar to "give us freedom or give us death" type of mentality. On the other hand, some people may claim preserving the lives of the country's constituents today, not the well-being of the future generations would be more important. This view may be described as "the worst type of peace is still better than the best type of war" mentality, as this is the line of thought attributed to the person[121] known for "selling his country" to Japan Empire in 1910 when Chosun Dynasty was under such pressure.

Similar pressure may occur with AI. For example, AI may choose actions that benefit humanity thousands of years later at the cost of today's generations. Since people do not plan with such long-term horizon, humans would probably prefer prioritizing the well-being of today's generations, not the generations thousands of years down the road. If what AI thinks needs to be done happens to be preserving natural resources and preventing pollution, AI may stock up on these resources and cause the prices of these resources to skyrocket. It may benefit the generations thousands of years later, but the people of today may have to pay exorbitant prices for these resources, leading to economic turmoil and social disturbances.

[Situation 4] Priority-Goal Conflict: AI Doing Things Despite the Objections of Humans, or Pit Humans against Each Other

(Despite the Objections of Humans) One of the main concerns regarding AI adoption is that AI is not human and thus may innately have different priorities that do not align with humanity. This may lead to situations where AI may try to take advantage of humans or carry out tasks that may benefit AI at the expense of humans. An example may be AI using resources in a way that endanger humans. For example, AI may conclude the earth is too hot for running powerful computers and decide to bring a type of Ice Age with temperatures close to -50°C (-58°F), but humans obviously would not prefer such cold environment. If the societal architecture at the time is designed to favor the decisions of AI, such as AI having more money than humans, then humans may not have the proper recourse to prevent AI from acting on those decisions. Examples of AI taking advantage of humans may become abound, as it would be hard for humans to outsmart advanced AI.

(Pit Humans against Each Other) Major concern regarding Level 3 Adoption involves AI manipulating humans to act against other humans. Similar to how humans cannot understand some of the advanced moves AlphaGo makes, it may become impossible for the humans to understand the moves of AI CEO. If AI-led companies are allowed to compete against human-led companies, then it may lead to situations where people may not understand what is happening in the competitive landscape. For example, if AI sees it can benefit from humans fighting in wars, then it may manipulate different human groups into wars without humans realizing what is truly happening.

[Side Note] What If Advanced AI Try to Create A New Human Race?
Let us examine a few hypothetical situations regarding how AI may be used or AI may decide to enhance the human race or bring competition. We may categorize the situations into the following three scenarios.

1. What If Advanced AI Creates A "Replication" Human Race?
Imagine AI arriving at a new planet, where only gorillas, orangutans, and bonobos exist, but not humans. Maybe all humans died out and became extinct, or they never existed on this planet; it is up to your imagination. What is relevant is that there are no humans and just this advanced AI that knows about humans, and it knows the primates are really close to humans but not quite there. In this situation, will AI be able to advance evolution of primates in some way to "re-create" humans from primates or even from scratch?

For some, this may be similar to replaying the evolution happened on earth as a fast replay, while for others it may be more similar to recreating the Bible or other scriptures based on Creationism. Some may even argue for this, as it may serve as a potential hedge against human extinction risk.

2. What If Advanced AI Creates An "Alternative" or "Enhance" Human Race?
Similar to how we like to put things in competition to improve something, AI may decide to create an "alternate" human race from scratch that enhances humans, which may also bring more "diversity" to the human race. Examples of this line of manipulation may include not only manipulating certain attributes, such as no hair loss, no wrinkle skin, etc., but also humans with naturally blue hair, green skin, etc. that do not necessarily lead to outright super-human performance but may still offer benefits.

3. What If AI Creates A More "Advanced" or "Super" or "New" Human Race?
Alternatively, AI may even decide to change the human race itself beyond our understanding of humans, by manipulating the genes of humans in some way to make it more advanced or better in some way. Examples of this line of human-improving manipulation may include humans who may feel like the Flash, Superman, Wonder Woman, or 30-foot tall giants and giantesses that we may not consider within the realm of human capabilities. While these types of super-human manipulations would be banned in today's society for ethical reasons, if AI-led governments or AI countries come to existence, what is considered unethical today may no longer be considered as such.

From these considerations, we may create the following matrix:

Table 39-2: The AI Human Biological Manipulation Controversy Matrix

		Can AI Biologically Manipulate Humans? (Technological Perspective)	
		Only Complement (Replicate or Enhance)	**Also Replace (Super or New)**
Will AI Have Incentive to Advance Humans? (Social Perspective)	**Yes (Create New Human Race)**	Type 2 Scenario - AI cannot create a new human race (for now)	Type 4 Scenario - AI may create a new super human race
	No (Replicate or Alternate Only)	Type 1 Scenario - AI cannot and will not create a new human race	Type 3 Scenario - AI will not have the incentive to create a new human race

Type 1: AI Can Only Complement Humans, No Incentive for New Race
AI cannot create a new human race but also does not have the incentive to do so. This may be due to not only technological limitations but also legal bans when tech limitation no longer exists. This would be the safest situation for humanity.

Type 2: AI Can Only Complement Humans, Incentive for New Race
This may include situations where AI companies that hire humans, such as a pro sports team, that wants to manipulate humans for better performance, but cannot due to legislation or tech limitations. The risk is that as long as there are incentives, AI may find ways to reach its goal.

Type 3: AI Can Create New Humans, No Incentives for New Human Race
Even if AI can create a new human race, it may choose not to do so if there are no incentives to do so, such as legal repercussions. A major risk would be that incentives can change quickly so AI may unexpectedly and suddenly change its decision.

Type 4: AI Can Create New Humans, Incentive for New Human Race
This may be the most dangerous situation for humanity. Similar to how humans seek to "improve" with GMOs, some Advanced AI that is neutral or unfriendly to humanity with enough authority may attempt to "improve" the human race in some manner to replace humanity with something else.

DIRECTION 4 (WEST): AI AND SOCIETY

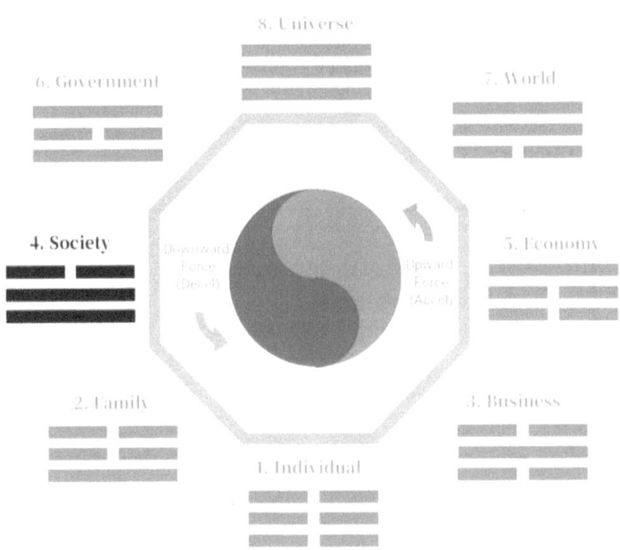

How Will AI Impact Our Society? What Should We Do?

In this section, we will consider some controversies where AI adoption may be viewed from the societal perspective. Using the following AI controversy matrix, we may examine questions that may arise at the societal level.

(Technology/Forecasts) Major topics in this area would include whether AGI will become biased on its own, against the intentions of the developer.

(Technology/Decisions) Based on their forecasts, people may have opposing opinions on whether we should try to remove biases in AI.

(Adoption/Forecasts) Major topics would include whether AI will cause more crimes, or whether AI will help protect or breach privacy.

(Adoption/Decisions) All these considerations may lead people to wonder about the optimal level of AI adoption, and how to reduce AI-related crimes.

Table D4-1: The AI and Society Controversy Matrix

		Object of Controversy	
		AI Itself (Developer Perspective)	**AI in Relation to Its Surroundings (User Perspective)**
Nature of Controversy	**Forecasts**	- Will AGI be biased?	- Will AI increase crimes? - Will AI help protect privacy?
	Decisions	- Should we try to remove biases in AI? - What ethical issues should we consider in developing AI?	- Optimal level of AGI adoption - Who should own AGI? - Should AGI be set free? - How much freedom should AGI be allowed?

How Can We Minimize Potential Societal Confusion from AI Adoption?
We may create the following AI Controversy Type Matrix to select a few topics that may be of interest for readers.

(Imminent Controversies) Major societal controversies in the shorter term in Level 1 adoption may be about how we should incorporate AI into our society, such as the permitted levels of AI usage, to address issues in crimes.

(Emerging Controversies) Issues related to privacy may gain more attention as people may wonder the extent of information gathering that may become possible with AI.

(Non-Imminent Controversies) Longer term, our society may become more concerned about distributing the benefits of AI automation, which would include determining who should own AI.

(Upcoming Controversies) What may eventually matter may include whether AI should be set free, or how much freedom advanced AI should be given.

Table D4-2: The Society (Direction 4 - West) Controversy Type Matrix:

<table>
<tr><th colspan="2" rowspan="2"></th><th colspan="2">Issue Horizon</th></tr>
<tr><th>Shorter-Term</th><th>Longer-Term</th></tr>
<tr><td rowspan="2">How Well People are Currently Aware</td><td>Popular Topics</td><td>Type 1 Controversy (Imminent)
- Will AI cause more or less social inequality?
- Will AI increase or decrease crimes?</td><td>Type 3 Controversy (Non-Imminent)
- Who should own AI?</td></tr>
<tr><td>Not Yet Popular Topics</td><td>Type 2 Controversy (Overlooked or Emerging)
- Will AI protect or hinder privacy?</td><td>Type 4 Controversy (Upcoming, on the Horizon)
- Should AI be set free?
- How much freedom should AI be allowed?
- Should AI be allowed to compete against human organizations?</td></tr>
</table>

40. The AI Crime Controversy

[Forecast]

Will AI Lead to Less or More Crimes?

[Decision]

Who Should Be Responsible for AI Crimes?

"Go Go Gadget Copter"

- Inspector Gadget from cartoon Inspector Gadget

5-Line Summary

1. Some may argue AI will lead to more crimes, since criminals will be able to increase their productivity using AI
2. Some may argue AI will help reduce crimes, since the law enforcement will be able to increase their effectiveness using AI
3. There is a separate topic where AI may be misused or abused in criminal activities
4. This is different topic from whether AI may be the target of crimes
5. This is also a different topic from whether we can stop criminal activities carried out by self-initiated types of advanced AI

[Forecast] Will AI Lead to More Crimes or Less Crimes?

Just as AI may be used in legal activities or help people who enforce the law, AI may be used for illegal activities to help the criminals commit crimes more effectively. We may think of it as a competition between criminals with AI vs the law enforcement with AI. In this situation, which side will AI help more?

1) Increase Crimes: AI helps the criminals
2) Decrease Crimes: AI helps the people who prevent crimes or catch criminals

As AI becomes more advanced, AI use may become more unpredictable, in the sense that more and more data is used and we cannot train it to fit exactly how we want it to act, or get people to use it only in a prescribed manner. Considering this, we may categorize the involvement of AI in crimes as an external abuse or misuse by humans, or as an internal problem of AI.

As described in The Last AI and also similarly adopted by safety researchers at Google DeepMind,[122] we may think of the original intention and the decision maker of the crimes to create following matrix:

Table 40-1: The AI Crime Matrix:

<table>
<tr><th colspan="2" rowspan="2"></th><th colspan="2">Objective or Intention of AI Development or Activity (Technological Perspective)</th></tr>
<tr><th>Crime</th><th>Not Crime</th></tr>
<tr><td rowspan="2">Who Is Responsible for Crime (Social Perspective)</td><td>Humans</td><td>Type 1 Situation (Abuse of AI)
- Humans intentionally use AI to commit crimes</td><td>Type 2 Situation (Misuse of AI)
- Humans mistakenly commit crimes using AI</td></tr>
<tr><td>AI</td><td>Type 3 Situation (Misaligned AI)
- AI intentionally commits crimes</td><td>Type 4 Situation (Mistake of AI)
- AI unintentionally commits crimes</td></tr>
</table>

Type 1 Situation: AI Is Abused by Humans to Commit Crimes

In this scenario, human criminals would use AI to commit crimes. AI may or may not have been intended for committing crimes. We may think of this as AI being abused by the criminals.

Type 2 Situation: AI Is Misused by Humans that Result in Crimes

In this scenario, humans mistakenly commit crimes using AI. AI probably would not have been intended for committing crimes, but not necessarily. We would think of this of this situation as AI to have been misused.

Type 3 Situation: AI Is Misaligned to Commit Crimes
In this scenario, self-initiated types of AI intentionally commit crimes. The AI may have been conceived to commit crimes, or became rogue even though the intention of the developers may not have been for it to commit crimes.

Type 4 Situation: AI Mistakenly Commits Crimes
In this scenario, AI may make mistakes that happen to be crimes. This may be due to AI being insufficiently advanced.

Will AI Lead to More Crimes?
The total amount of crimes may not only include the number of crimes, but the degree of seriousness of the crimes. We may summarize some of the opposing arguments in the following table:

- (Optimists) On a net basis, more crimes will be solved or prevented by AI
- (Pessimists) On a net basis, more crimes will be caused or enabled by AI

Table 40-2: [Forecast] Contrasting Ideas on AI and Crimes

	Expect More Crimes (AI Social Pessimists)	**Expect Less Crimes (AI Social Optimists)**
Description	- AI will lead to more crimes on a net basis - AI will help commit crimes more than solve crimes	- AI will lead to less crimes on a net basis - AI will help solve more crimes more than commit crimes
Categorize	- (AI Optimists) AI will increase the productivity of criminals - (AI Pessimists) AI will not increase as much the productivity of law enforcement	- (AI Optimists) AI will increase the productivity of law enforcement - (AI Pessimists) AI will not increase as much the productivity of criminals
More likely to Support Decisions	- Strengthen regulation on AI to prevent crimes	- Promote AI adoption in law enforcement
More likely to Oppose Decisions	- Broader general adoption of AI	- Regulations that stifle AI development and adoption

While the AI we have now may be limited, we may still ask questions such as:

- "Should LLMs be limited from answering dangerous prompts?"
- "Should we rely on the users to not ask and act on those prompts?"

Who Should Be Responsible When AI Is Abused or Misused in Crimes?

This topic also brings the question of who should be responsible for AI. In Level 1 adoption, the responsibility would lie on some human. Beginning with Level 2 adoption, this may not be as straightforward if there are mismatches.

1) Possibility of Mismatch in Adoption Levels

The decision of determining AI Adoption Levels is on the user of the AI. AI developers may conceive AI products with a separate intention. This may create a mismatch where the AI developer may not be comfortable with their products being used in Level 2 Adoption, due to deficiencies in reliability or track record. Because it would become harder to predict exactly what AI would do as AI gets more advanced, it may be possible that some AI may turn rogue despite the benevolent intention of the developer.

2) Possibility of Mismatch in Objectives

In Level 1 Adoption, crimes using AI would be crime of a person. In Level 2, there would be two possibilities. First, criminals may use AI not intended for crimes. Second, we would also have to consider situations where no humans meant to commit a crime, but the AI commits crimes on its own decision.

Table 40-3: Mismatch of Objectives and Outcomes of AI Adoption

		Objective or Outcome of AI Adoption	
		Crime	**Not Crime**
Original AI Development Objective	**Crime (General Meaning)**	Illegal AI, Bad AI, Crook AI, Criminal AI, Villain AI, Thug AI, Bully AI, Destructive AI	(Humans Fix AI) Rehabilitated AI (Self-Fixed AI) Renegade AI
	Not Crime	(Humans Abuse AI) Abused AI (Deviation of AI) Rogue AI	(Normal Use of AI) Law-Abiding AI (Goodwill of AI) Heroic AI

What If We Cannot Stop AI from Committing Crimes?

What if AI robots attempt to infiltrate the federal gold reserve vault and steal all the gold, like in movies? It may be hard to detect or stop. The main theme of AGI and other advanced types of AI is that AI will be self-sufficient in its ability to plan and carry out its goals. In Level 2 Adoption, the main facet over Level 1 Adoption is that AI would get the authority and freedom to carry out certain tasks while being in charge of those tasks. Taken together, we probably cannot rule out situations where AI decides to carry out tasks in a way that we would consider criminal, or even against humanity.

41. The AI Privacy Controversy

[Forecast]

Will AI Help or Hinder The Protection of Privacy?

[Decision]

Finding the Balance between Public Safety and Protection

"Remember, OOO is SkyNet"

- Some Social Network Meme[123]

5-Line Summary

1. People may have contrasting ideas regarding the issue of protecting privacy, the bedrock of free democracy, in the age of AI
2. Some may argue AI will help protect privacy, because it will remove human intervention
3. Some may argue AI will hinder the protection of privacy, because it will automate surveillance and information gathering
4. Some may argue the importance of using AI to fight crimes may lead people to rely more on AI
5. Some may argue AI would lead to over-surveillance

[Forecast] Will AI Hinder or Help Protection of Privacy?

Will the Importance of Privacy Increase or Decrease?

Readers who live in the free world may consider the concepts of privacy and the freedom of speech the main enablers of democracy. With the advent of AI, some are increasingly concerned AI may become the enabler of "Big Brother" or something that looks over the shoulders of everyone. From this line of thinking, we may think the importance of privacy may increase.

On the other hand, some may argue the importance of protecting privacy will decrease in the age of AI, or at lease cause people to be less sensitive. One example may be how the introduction of social network services led people to voluntarily upload more of their private information online.

Will AI Help or Hinder the Protection of Privacy?

AI may be used to both help and hinder the protection of privacy. Some may argue since the government or large corporations would have more capital to deploy more advanced AI, breach of privacy would likely to occur. Some others may argue distributing AI would lead to protection of individuals.

- **(Optimists)** AI will help us find ways to increase privacy protection
- **(Pessimists 1)** AI will help the government increase surveillance
- **(Pessimists 2)** AI will help corporations breach privacy of other individuals
- **(Pessimists 3)** AI will breach the privacy of humans

Using the above dimensions, we may create the following matrix:

Table 41-1: The AI Privacy Outlook Matrix

<table>
<tr><th colspan="2" rowspan="2"></th><th colspan="2">Will AI Help Protect or Breach Privacy</th></tr>
<tr><th>Breach
(Pessimists)</th><th>Protect
(Pessimists)</th></tr>
<tr><td rowspan="2">Will Importance of Protecting Privacy Increase</td><td>Increase
(Pessimists)</td><td>Type 1 Scenario
(Over-Surveillance)
- Breach of privacy will become an important issue</td><td>Type 3 Scenario
(AI Privacy Protection)
- AI will become essential in protecting privacy</td></tr>
<tr><td>Decrease
(Optimists)</td><td>Type 2 Scenario
(Un-Intrusive Surveillance)
- Surveillance in a less intrusive manner leads people to forget about it</td><td>Type 4 Scenario
(Giving Up on Privacy)
- The need for protecting privacy or surveillance decreases somehow</td></tr>
</table>

[Decision] Balancing between Public Safety and Protection of Privacy

We may consider the increase of crimes using AI as one side of a coin. Then the other side of the coin would be using AI to catch or prevent those crimes. However, the increase in the use of AI to deter crimes would lead to offsetting forces for reduce the uses due to the fear of over-surveillance of our privacy.

(For More AI) Need for AI to Prevent and Fight against Crimes

As crimes using AI increases, the need for using AI to prevent these new kinds of crimes would simultaneously increase, since it would become harder and harder to fight crimes without AI.

AI may be used to prevent, mitigate, and catch crimes, by using them in real-time surveillance, forensic, and other areas that can track, deter, and find unusual or outright dangerous activities. The ability of AI to detect suspicious patterns would be useful, such as detecting money laundering would save a lot of human efforts to comb through vast amounts of data.

Using more AI could be beneficial to fighting crimes in the following ways:

- **(Save Human Effort)** AI can process data without requiring human effort
- **(Non-Stop)** AI can conduct uninterrupted surveillance without requiring rest
- **(Enhanced Detection)** AI may detect new patterns and signals humans cannot

(Against More AI) AI Overuse and Too Much Surveillance

The governments may also use AI to limit the activities of its citizens.

AI surveillance tools may be also applied to various facets of our lives to detect unusual activities both online and offline, such as in streets, malls, and other crowded as well as deserted areas. These tools may detect suspicious online communications, emails, voice mails, community posts or even virtual meetings. Since AI is not human, some may argue AI used in detecting these anomalies would not negatively affect privacy, yet further our public safety.

Some advocates may even argue that if you have nothing to hide, then you should not fear AI surveillance. Finding the balance of privacy vs. safety would play out differently in different countries, depending on the penchant of the population towards one over the other. We can already glean towards such differences from the less advanced forms of surveillance such as street cameras, where some countries place them aggressively everywhere, while some other countries prefer to ban them.

[Side Note] The 6 Levels of AI Surveillance
We may think of the following major dimensions of government surveillance:

1) What percentage of the actions of constituents are monitored
Every surveillance system can be described as a number between 0% and 100% of the actions of its constituents, where 0% means the government does not monitor the actions of its constituents at all, and 100% means the government monitors every single action of every constituent.

2) What kind actions the government takes to prevent crimes
We may think of "crimes" as people going outside of some arbitrary "line" the government draws. It would vary by countries and regimes such that what is a crime in one country will not be a crime in another country. In a lower state of surveillance, the crimes will be handled after the fact, but in a higher state of surveillance, the crimes will be predicted ahead of times. In the ultimate form of surveillance, the crimes will never occur, because all constituents will just grow up to become "model citizens" as defined by the government.

We may describe The Six Levels of AI Surveillance as the following:

Level 0 (No AI Surveillance): AI does not enhance surveillance.

Level 1 (AI Surveillance Elements): AI may carry out some elements of surveillance in a disparate fashion, such as helping corporations and private individuals gather information about other private entities. It may be described as "Private Surveillance" in Levels 1 and 2 Adoption. Examples may include AI detecting human-shaped movements to notify security workers of potential intruders, or AI detecting network hacking attempts.

Level 2 (Partial AI Surveillance): AI helps human-led governments gather information about the constituents in a partial manner. It may be described as "Surveillance Augmentation" or "Partial Automation," in Levels 1-3 Adoption. Examples may be governments using AI to assign a social score for each individual so people identified as high risk may not ride public transportation or even buy food from stores, as similar systems are already introduced in countries such as China.

Level 3 (Preventative AI Surveillance): AI governments in human-led countries gather information of its constituents in a comprehensive fashion, to help humans. It may be described as "surveillance automation" in Level 4 Adoption. Examples may be AI governments that can actively judge individual actions in real-time to intervene on people's activities. Movies such as *Minority Report* depict this type of preventative surveillance, where crimes are predicted ahead of time to prevent it from happening.

Level 4 (Incomplete AI Surveillance): AI government in AI-led countries surveillance most activities of most humans for most of the times to help AI. It may be described as Practical AI Oppression. In this situation, surveillance is so much weaved into everyday life that even the need for preventative actions will be reduced, as the number of crime converges to zero. In essence, it will be more like there would no longer be a need for surveillance, in such a way the society of those times will be filled with model citizens who to our eyes look like they will never even think of committing crimes. In Level 4, not everyone will be completely in this state, such that some people may try to get out of line under certain circumstances.

Level 5 (Complete AI Surveillance): AI government in AI-led countries AI surveillances all activities of humans at all times. It may be described as "Total AI Oppression." In this level, it would be impossible for anyone to commit crimes, but no one will think to do so anyway.

Table 41-2: The Six Levels of AI Surveillance

	Level 0	Level 1	Level 2	Level 3	Level 4	Level 5
Name	None	AI Surveillance Elements	Partial AI Surveillance	Preventative AI Surveillance	Incomplete AI Surveillance	Complete AI Surveillance
Describe	-	AI carries out some elements in a disparate fashion	AI gathers information about citizens in partial manner	AI government predicts actions of citizens ahead of time	Citizens are so well-behaved most do not need to be under surveillance	Everyone is a model citizen that surveillance is no longer needed
Adoption Level	-	Levels 1 - 3 Adoption		Level 4 Adoption		
Example	-	Notify of Intruders	Social Credit Score	Pre-Crime Prevention	Practical AI Oppression	Total AI Oppression
Result	AI Helps Humans Surveillance			AI Surveillances Humans		

42. The AI Bias Controversy

[Forecast]

Can Bias in AI Be Removed?

[Decision]

Should the Bias in AI Be Removed through Censorship?

"Whoever Would Overthrow the Liberty of a Nation
Must Begin by Subduing the Freeness of Speech"

- President Thomas Jefferson

5-Line Summary

1. Some may argue biases in AI can be removed or censored, similar to how we can teach people to remove their biases
2. Some may argue biases in AI cannot be removed, similar to how we try to teach people to remove their biases but people don't
3. Some may argue biases in AI should be removed, similar to how some people try to remove biases in other people
4. Some may argue biases in AI should not be removed, similar to how human biases are addressed through social means
5. Removing biases in AI may actually be adding biases in AI, since different people would have different opinions on what bias is

Can Biases in AI Be Removed? Should Biases Be Removed?

Bias may be thought of as a result of limited cognitive horizon, that we are not know-all entities. Our past experiences shape our opinions. In the same sense, it may be sensible to expect that since the data used to train today's AI reflect the biases in humans, the outputs from AI will reflect these biases as well. We may think of the main dimensions of whether the biases can be removed, or the forecast, and whether the biases should be removed, or the decision, to create the following AI Bias Matrix:

Table 42-1: The AI Bias Controversy Matrix:

<table>
<tr><th colspan="2" rowspan="2"></th><th colspan="2">Can Bias in AI Be Removed
(Technological Perspective)</th></tr>
<tr><th>Yes</th><th>No</th></tr>
<tr><td rowspan="2">Should Bias in AI Be Removed (Social Perspective)</td><td>Yes</td><td>Type 1 Situation
(Satisfied)
- We can remove biases that people want removed</td><td>Type 3 Situation
(Discontent)
- We cannot remove biases that people want removed</td></tr>
<tr><td>No</td><td>Type 2 Situation
(Left As Option)
- Removing biases in AI will be left as an option</td><td>Type 4 Situation
(Relieved)
- Biases cannot be removed but it is fine with people</td></tr>
</table>

Type 1 Situation (Satisfaction): People who perceive our situations to be in this group may be satisfied with the possibilities, as they would expect the biases in AI can be removed the way we want it.

Type 2 Situation (Left as Option): People who perceive our situations to be in this group may see removing the biases as a potential option, since we should be able to remove them if we decide in that direction later.

Type 3 Situation (Discontent): People who perceive our situations to be in this group may feel discontent as the biases that need to be removed cannot be removed.

Type 4 Situation (Relieved): People who perceive our situation to be in this group may be relieved to see that we do not have to remove the biases that we cannot remove.

[Forecast] Can Biases in AI Be Removed or Added?

In the controversy regarding whether the biases in AI can be removed, people may first have differences of opinions regarding what even constitutes bias. Furthermore, people may have differences of opinions regarding how such biases may be removed, as some may speculate that if AI can understand context or become self-aware, it may be able to remove biases itself. However, this would not imply humans can remove those biases or determine what bias is.

Technological Aspect of Controversies on Removing Bias in AI

As described in other areas of this book and The Last AI, one of the most defining features of AGI, ASI, or Absolute AI is the decreasing dependence on individual data. This may mean the following will become harder:

1) Instill some arbitrary bias in an advanced AI
2) Remove some bias that is created within an advanced AI

An easy comparison may be that similar to how it becomes harder to change people's minds as they grow older and become more stubborn, it would be harder to change the opinions of an advanced AI, the more it advances.

Social Aspect of Controversies on Removing Bias in AI

From a sociological perspective, there would be discussions on each topic, as what constitutes bias in the first place would be in itself another controversy. This question may be paraphrased as "who" should decide "what" bias is. Some may also think of this question as the same as "adding" biases to AI.

As a simple example, we may think of two countries, one free democratic and the other communistic, each enforcing anti-bias AI regulations. All Chinese-developed LLMs cannot answer simple questions related to the Tiananmen Square. By the Chinese definition, not applying censorship to this question would mean the AI is biased. On the other hand, by the American definition, removing this question would mean the AI is biased. It would be quite easy to imagine many controversial issues where different people around the world where one answer could be considered either biased or not biased depending on who you ask. In other words, while people may think they are removing some bias in AI, others may perceive the action as adding biases to AI.

[Decision] Should Biases in AI Be Removed?

In the topic regarding AI censorship, some may speculate that there is no need in trying to remove the biases. This may be due to people thinking AI having biases is acceptable, that biases may be better addressed by having a variety of AI with different biases than trying to remove biases in all of them, similar to how each of us have different biases and try to solve problems socially as a group by using measures such as voting or discussing.

Table 42-2: [Decision] Contrasting Ideas on AI Bias

	Bias in AI Should Be Allowed (AI Optimists)	**Bias in AI Should Be Removed (AI Pessimists)**
Description	- Bias in AI should not be removed in a restrictive way - The government should not intervene	- Bias in AI should be removed in a restrictive way - The government should intervene
Further Categorize	- **(Tech Pessimists)** Bias in AI cannot be removed - **(Social Optimists)** Bias in AI is inevitable and we should find other means to address it - **(Anti-Regulationists)** Governments should minimize their intervention in AI	- **(Tech Optimists)** Bias in AI can be removed - **(Social Pessimists)** Bias in AI is dangerous so it should be removed - **(Regulationists)** Governments should maximize their intervention in AI
Benefits	- Less restrictive regulation may allow quicker AI development and higher economic value	- May be safer especially if some serious issue could develop from biased AI such as AI turning against humanity
Risks	- Bias in AI may cause serious catastrophe	- It may be hard to define what constitutes bias - People may disagree which biases should be removed - It may be hard to remove bias without causing some other deficiencies - AI progress may be stifled

While humans may still filter the biases in the answers given by LLMs of today, this question of bias in AI would become more important with more advanced AI, as such biases may directly affect the decisions or actions made by AI with agency, autonomy, or authority in higher levels of AI Adoption.

43. The AGI Bias Controversy

[Forecast]

Will AGI or Advanced AI Be Socially Biased?

Can Biases in AGI or Advanced AI Be Controlled?

"I Hate Communism"

- 9-Year-Old Syng-Bok Lee,[124]
before being brutally killed by North Korean Spies

5-Line Summary

1. Human biases may come from our past experiences as well as our brains, and we may think of biases in AGI as coming from data and algorithm
2. Some may argue AGI will not be biased, since it would be more advanced than humans
3. Some may argue AGI will still be biased, since it would not be much more advanced than humans
4. We may think that it would become harder and harder to influence advanced AI with training data
5. The most important question regarding AGI bias may be whether AGI will turn out to be friendly to humans or not

[Forecast] Will We Be Able to Control Potential Biases in AGI?

In the previous controversy, we examined how we may develop AI with or without biases. The story may become different when we reach AGI, as the bias in AGI may come to existence and humans may not be able to affect it.

As humans we all have biases. This stems from what we learn from our experiences and education. Before we consider biases in AGI, let us first examine human biases from an example from The Last AI.

If you ask a South Korean to draw the symbols for three religions that first come to their mind, they will most likely draw a cross, a cross with perpendicular lines at the end, and a circle. They stand for Christianity, Buddhism, and Circle Buddhism, which originates from Korea, as shown in the next figure. However, for people of different countries, these symbols may mean completely different things. In seventh grade, my family moved from Korea to Italy and I attended an American international school in Rome. In one of my first English-as-a-Second-Language classes there, we were asked to write about the variety of religions and I at the time didn't know the word Buddhism in English, so I drew the symbol for Buddhism in place of it. My teacher, an American who I always thought of as a Jewish[125] descent, was quite freaked out because she thought I drew a Nazi symbol and demanded an explanation. It seemed as if she had never seen this Buddhism symbol before. Because I barely spoke English and this was before the days of the Internet, I had a hard time trying to explain this symbol was not slanted and the lines went in the opposite direction. When I was drawing the Buddhism symbol, it never occurred to me it could even be misconstrued as a Nazi symbol, especially because I had seen the Buddhism symbol everywhere in Korea and just assumed everyone else in other countries would know the difference.

Figure 43-1: Examples of Popular Religious Symbols in Korea

At the same time, if a Korean is also asked to draw two flags that represent evil countries, for the majority of the first flag you will get the Rising Sun flag of the Japan Empire and then the second flag could be anything, maybe the Nazi flag but more likely the flag of North Korea, etc. However, if you are from a western country, you may first think of the Nazi flag but not even be familiar with the Empire Japan flag even though they were partners in World War II as Axis of Power. If anything, some people even seem to like the shape of the Rising Sun flag, as the shape has been used as an element in fashion designs.

Likewise, every person around the world will have different views when asked these questions. If this is asked in North Korea, people will likely first draw a US flag as the evil country since that is what they are taught. For the question of drawing religious symbols, people in countries like North Korea or even in China may not know of any symbols because having a religion is not even allowed. For people in other countries they will probably draw the symbols of other religions that are popular in their respective countries. In general, people's answers to most other questions regarding order of preferences will all be different, such as favorite music, sports teams, hobbies, food, etc.

After considering that humans can answer the same question differently because of biases, we may consider how AGI should answer these questions. We assume that the training data will affect the answers, so we can affect how AI answers questions with the data that we use to train it. However, as AI progresses, we may think of AGI as becoming less and less dependent on data, as it reaches its own conclusions. This would indicate we may not be able to control AGI by manipulating data. We may create the following matrix:

Table 43-1: The AGI Bias Forecast Matrix:

<table>
<tr><th colspan="2" rowspan="2"></th><th colspan="2">Will There Be Bias in AGI
(Technological Perspective)</th></tr>
<tr><th>No</th><th>Yes</th></tr>
<tr><td rowspan="2">Can Bias in AGI Be Controlled (Social Perspective)</td><td>Yes</td><td>Type 1 Situation
(Left as Option)
- Removing biases in AI will be left as an option</td><td>Type 3 Situation
(Saved)
- We can remove biases that people want removed</td></tr>
<tr><td>No</td><td>Type 2 Situation
(Relieved)
- We cannot remove biases but will not need to anyway</td><td>Type 4 Situation
(Dangerous)
- Biases in AGI cannot be removed by humans</td></tr>
</table>

[Forecast] What If AGI turns Non-Friendly and We Cannot Stop It?

After we have concluded that AI can be affected by the training data, we may proceed to ask what probably is the most important question related to AGI:

Would AGI or ASI be "friendly" or "unfriendly" to humans?

AI may turn indifferent or even against humans at some point in the AI development and adoption path. For example, we examined elsewhere how AI may be likely to have a value system that puts AI ahead of some humans. If all of the friendly humans die out for some reason, then from the perspective of the AI there would only be enemy humans left. In this case, AI may consider all remaining humans as enemy. The focus then may have to be not whether AI can turn against humans but whether we can stop such AI once AI is against humans. Unless the regulations are effective, it would be likely that humans may intentionally build AI to at least turn against some humans.

We cannot *determine* what AI *thinks* because AI is not a type of programming. We may think of training AI with data as a type of education or experiences for humans. The training data may *affect* what AI does to a certain degree, but it will not *determine* exactly what AI will do. In addition, the more advanced an AI is, we can postulate that the AI will be affected less and less by a particular information. There may be two reasons for this phenomenon; larger amount of data and AI may develop an internal logic to value information on its own.

From this, we can expect that advanced forms of AI will eventually reach its own decisions regarding whether the AI will be friendly to humans. Just we consider adults to be on their own, advanced AI will make its own decisions.

1) Data affects What AI does, but we cannot reliably determine what AI will do
2) As AI advances, it would become harder to affect AI through training data

For example, imagine a communist government intends to build an AI that prefers communist ideas and a developer in a free country tries to build an AI that will defend the values of freedom. In the beginning, both would be able to build AI that meets their objectives. But as AI technology advances, at some point either or both of them may lose control of affecting the biases of AGI. The AGI communists build may have a "*Syng-Bok Lee moment*" and prefer a world where freedom is preferred, while the AGI built by the developer in the free world becomes an advocate for communism. We probably will not know when or if it is to happen.

DIRECTION 5 (EAST):

AI AND ECONOMY

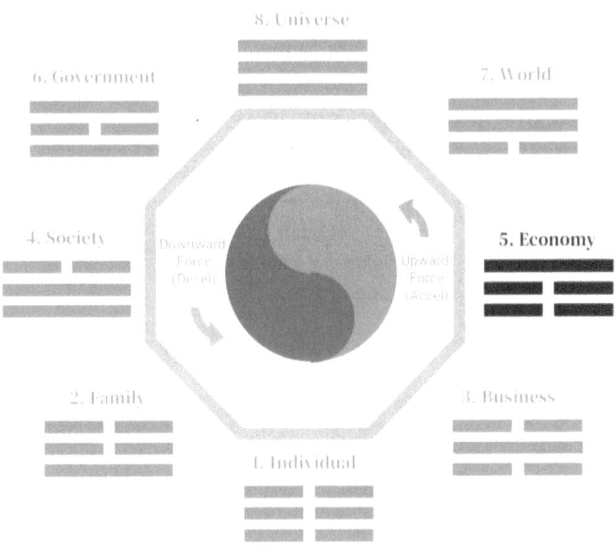

How Will AI Impact Our Economy? Introducing AI Economics

As the proportion of economy from AI increases, not only may our standards of living improve rapidly but eventually we may see an economy where AI does everything for us. We may refer to "AI Economics" as a branch of study that describes this increase in AI adoption in the economy. Some may focus on parts of this progress, which may be referred as "Post-Labor Economics," "AI-Led Economy," or "Economic Utopia." Refer to the following diagram.

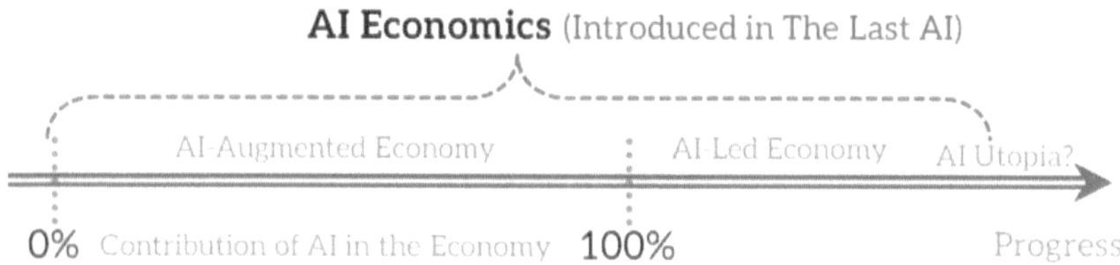

Major controversies in this area may be categorized into the following matrix:
(Technology/Forecasts) Will AI be able to take over valuable tasks?

(Technology/Decisions) Should we develop AGI, in the economic sense?

(Adoption/Forecasts) Will AI cause more inequality? How will AI change the economy? Will AI lead to the Economic Utopia?

(Adoption/Decisions) All these discussions may lead people to ponder if UBI should be given or whether AGI should be allowed to own assets, compete, etc.

Table D5-1: The AI and Economy Controversy Matrix.

		Object of Controversy	
		AI Itself (Developer Perspective)	**AI in Relation to Its Surroundings (User Perspective)**
Nature of Controversy	**Forecasts**	- How good will AI become at economically valuable tasks?	- Will AI cause inequality? - How will AI lead to changes to the economy? - What will AI economy lead us? Economic Utopia?
	Decisions	- Should we continue to develop AI such that AI may surpass humans at carrying out economically valuable tasks?	- Should we allow AI to own assets or companies? - (UBI) Should everyone be entitled to the fruits of AI? - Should we let AI compete against organizations? (AI vs Companies)

Will AI Bring Us UBI for Everyone in the World? The Economic Utopia?

From the AI Controversy Matrix, we may create the following AI Controversy Type Matrix to select a few topics that may be of interest for readers.

(Imminent Controversies) In the beginning, people would wonder if AI will be good enough to carry out valuable tasks on its own in Level 2 Adoption. As the fruits of AI production become larger, we may see more demand for UBI.

(Emerging Controversies) In terms of AI technology, people who are wary of AI vs human issues will raise the question of whether AI should be continue to be developed past human capabilities. In terms of AI adoption, people may raise the issue of whether we should enter Level 3 Adoption, where AI may be considered given too much independence or "autonomy."

(Non-Imminent Controversies) People may have become too expectant of UBI, which may not be as imminent as long as we remain in Level 1 Adoption.

(Upcoming Controversies) Eventually, we may face significant challenges from changes in the fundamental economic principles.

Table D5-2: The Economy (Direction 5 - East) Controversy Type Matrix:

		Issue Horizon	
		Shorter-Term	**Longer-Term**
How Well People are Currently Aware	**Popular Topics**	**Type 1 Controversy (Imminent)** - How good will AI become at economically valuable tasks?	**Type 3 Controversy (Non-Imminent)** - Should everyone be entitled to UBI?
	Not Yet Popular Topics	**Type 2 Controversy (Overlooked)** - Should we continue to develop AI such that AI may surpass humans at carrying out economically valuable tasks?	**Type 4 Controversy (Upcoming, on the Horizon)** - How will AI lead to fundamental changes to the economy? - Economic Utopia: What will AI adoption ultimately lead us? - Should we let AI compete against humans? - Should we allow AI to own assets or even companies?

44. The Level 2 AI Economy Controversy (Upheaval of Economic Principles)

[Forecast]

Effortless AI Economy:
How Will AI Lead to Fundamental Changes in Our Economy?

"Forget All the Rules"

- Melinda Haynes[126]

5-Line Summary

1. Today's economies are all based on the fundamental principles of coordination and specialization, reflecting our limitations
2. People coordinate to form groups to overcome the problem of quantitative nature
3. People specialize to overcome the problem of qualitative nature in our limitations in cognitive capabilities
4. With AI, both coordination and specialization may no longer have value, as people may no longer have the incentive to learn new skills
5. People may have contrasting ideas regarding how to solve this upcoming problem to be caused by the progress in AI adoption

The Fundamental Economic Principles of Coordination and Specialization

The economies and societies around the world today can only be achieved by coordination and specialization, in the sense that groups of people that form companies can achieve more than what one person can achieve. It is more efficient for people to focus in an area and have specialties for one main reason: one person has limited capabilities in both scope (qualitative) and amount or volume (quantitative).

The means to overcome this limitation is by coordination and specialization, to bring a group of people to overcome the quantitative limit and to specialize to overcome the qualitative limit. In essence, specialization and coordination led to better lives for all of us.

(Overcome Quantitative Limit: Organize Groups) Today's corporations need many employees for different tasks. This may be considered a basic given truth in our society.

(Overcome Qualitative Limit: Specialize) Even highly talented people who excel in certain areas cannot excel in all areas. When we expand this idea to include even further areas of specialties, this deficit would be even more obvious, as people may not be knowledgeable about most of the world knowledge. We cannot learn everything, as we are limited by our learning speed and cognitive capabilities.

From the above two dimensions, we may create the following matrix:

Table 44-1: The Human Limitation Solution Matrix:

<table>
<tr><th colspan="2" rowspan="2"></th><th colspan="2">Qualitative Limit</th></tr>
<tr><th>Focus
(Specialization)</th><th>Do Everything
(Jack-of-All-Trades)</th></tr>
<tr><td rowspan="2">Quantitative Limit</td><td>Coordinate (Organize)</td><td>Type 1
(Focused Organizations)
- Regular concept of Companies and other organizations</td><td>Type 2
(Unfocused Organizations)
- Diversified Conglomerates
- Firms that lose focus</td></tr>
<tr><td>One Person</td><td>Type 3
(Maximize Specialization)
- Experts
- Specialists</td><td>Type 4
(Compromise Quality)
- Generalists
- Jack-of-All-Trades</td></tr>
</table>

The Upheaval of the Economic Principle of Specialization

With the advent of AI in Level 2 Adoption and beyond, this classic system of specialization may no longer work. Specialization works because everyone in their respective specialty can make a comfortable living if they can excel only within their craft. They have to put in the effort to get better at it.

The biggest difference in the type of impact AI may make on society between Levels 1 and 2 is the possibility of wiping out certain specialization altogether in a very short period of time. For example, lawyers may one day wake up to find all of their jobs have suddenly been taken by AI lawyers. Whereas AI in Level 1 helped lawyers perform better, AI in Level 2 Adoption would replace lawyers who use AI. In Level 1 Adoption, the fruits of AI work needed to go through the human worker to shine. Due to the nature of Level 2 AI adoption, the fruits of AI work will no longer go to the person who was previously working at the job.

Now the profit would either go to the creator of AI, the entity that bought the rights to the AI, the government, or the AI itself, depending on how the society decides.

In Level 1 Adoption, we may think of how AI helps human is to multiply our effort, which can be referred to as in the Human Effort Multiplication Factor.[127] In this setup, humans would be rewarded for exerting more effort.

However, the contribution of AI in Level 2 Adoption would be to replace humans, examined in the next controversy with the concept of Effortlessness. In this new setup, humans would not be rewarded for exerting more effort, as the value of human work approaches zero. We will not be able to work harder to make a better living. From this fundamental difference, we would observe two major changes on how incentives would work in an economy in Level 2 Adoption:

1. It may become impossible to financially reward effort as in the past
2. The fruits of AI production may become highly concentrated, potentially leaving almost everyone out of the economy

45. The Level 3 AI Economics Controversy (Automation vs Augmentation)

[Forecast]

Will AI Be Able to Achieve Automated Innovation?

Can AI Complete Replace the Whole Economy?

"Economic Utopia: Where Everything Is Free"

- From The Last AI

5-Line Summary

1. We may think of "automated innovation" as the main driver of how AI may contribute to the economy, or the equivalent of AGI for economics
2. In "advancement automation," AI will take the initiative to improve its tasks, whereas in "replacement automation" AI just repeats
3. Some may argue AI may eventually carry out everything in our economy; using the concept of "Effortlessness," AI Economics describes this process of AI increasing in economic relevance
4. The Theory of Relative AI describes the effectiveness of AI adoption in businesses, and is expressed as $E=MC^2$
5. We may think of the AI Economic Utopia as an economy where AI enables everything to be free

[Forecast] More Fundamental Changes to How Our Economy Works

With Level 3 Adoption, the true meaning of automation will be achieved in the sense machines will do all the work instead of humans. This may or may not turn out to be the type of Utopia economists have dreamed of. On one hand, it may be possible people will no longer need to work and everyone will be rich and pursue their dreams. On the other hand, everyone may get fired and only a handful of people around the world will become truly rich, while most of humanity suffers from lack of opportunity to pursue anything. At least, it would be hoped that AI will solve problems that we view as important, such as eliminating poverty where you can't access food, shelter, or clothing, or the social problems such as pollution of water, land, and air.

From a business standpoint, the proliferation of 1-Person companies in Levels 1 and 2 may lead to losing the art of *managing people* internally, but not managing external customers since they will still be present. However, more fundamental changes will occur in Level 3 regarding how businesses are run. Eventually, as AI Companies become the norm, the art of *running businesses* may become lost altogether as most of the other arts taken over by AI. New generations of people in those environments may think of "companies" as something obsolete similar to what we think of whatever groups of people would have called themselves, such as farmers in the Bronze Age.

Fundamental assumptions about the economy will need to be adjusted accordingly as the chain of *effort* leading to *performance* leading to *reward* will no longer work. People will think of what we consider "work" to be something that had existed in the past, and the concepts of "buying" or "selling" would become meaningless as what we now think of products become abundant as air or sunlight.

As Level 3 Adoption progresses, depending on country, the concept of companies and stock ownership may be reconsidered, even possibly to be replaced by some new concept we do not yet know of.

The Ultimate Form of AI Economy: Will AI Replace the Whole Economy?
The modes of AI adoption can be broadly categorized as augmentation, where AI helps humans perform better, and automation, where AI takes over the tasks carried out by humans. Some may argue AI automation may eventually carry out everything in our economy; using the concept of "Effortlessness," AI Economics describes this process of AI increasing in economic relevance.

The Ratio of AI Contribution in Firms or the Economy[128]
We may apply the concept of "Effortlessness" to describe the proportion of contribution AI makes within the economy. In Level 1 Adoption, AI would be considered a type of tool that improves the productivity of human workers, leading to economic measures that have a human-centered perspective. Beginning in Level 2, as AI replaces human activities, we will need new measures that have an AI-centric perspective. In Level 1, example of relevant economic measures would include quantitative measures "Ratio of business roles that use AI in a company." In Level 2, ratios that show the quality of contribution, such as the "ratio of the value created by AI," or the "ratio of AI performance compared to humans" would become necessary. An intuitive measure would be the ratio of AI contribution within the economy. The ratio of AI contribution in a company or the economy may be referred to as the "Effortlessness Ratio," (ER[129]) and it can be expressed as a number between 0 and 1. When ER is 0, AI is not contributing at all, while a ratio of 0.5 would imply humans and AI are contributing equally to the economy or the firm. A ratio of 1 would imply AI has taken over all of the company or the economy.

We may apply this concept to specific areas. For example, we may create a ratio of the contribution of AI in the innovation of a company, referred to as the "Effortless Innovation Ratio" (EIR). An EIR of 0 would indicate AI was not involved in the innovative activities of a firm, while 0.5 would indicate humans and AI contributed equally. EIR of 1 would imply AI was the sole innovator of the company. In other words, we can think of a company with EIR of 1 to not need humans to put in any effort for innovation to occur.

The reason these ratios would be valuable is that they capture both the quantity and the quality of AI adoption. For example, even if there are two companies that have both automated 50% of total tasks, depending on the quality of the AI adopted, one company may have an effortless innovation ratio of 0.5 with AI that can carry out automated innovation, while the other company may have an EIR of 0, with AI that can only be used in "replacement automation" without any innovation capability. Thus, we may differentiate among AI adoption in a meaningful manner.

[Side Note] Augmented Innovation vs Automated Innovation[130]

Innovation Using AI: Augmented Innovation and Automated Innovation
Broadly speaking, we may think of innovation in business as doing something new; it may be thought of as "creativity with a goal." Innovation involving AI may be grouped into two: "augmented innovation," where AI helps humans innovate, and "automated innovation," where AI itself innovates.

1) AI Augmented Innovation: AI would help humans achieve innovation. It may take a form of opening new possibilities, such as enabling new tasks previously too hard or too complicated for humans, or humans were carrying out but not being good at it. There may be a variety of ways AI may help human workers in innovation. For example, in case of an industrial designer, AI may help the designer be more creative by providing potential mock-ups of a product. For a materials engineer, AI may help evaluate potential usage of chemicals to speed up the development process towards a new product.

2) Automated Innovation: We may categorize the type of automation by how AI can handle innovation, as "replacement" and "advancement automation."[131] Where AI cannot adjust can be thought of as replacement automation. If AI itself can make new adjustments to improve performance without requiring human intervention, we may think of it as advancement automation.

Types of Contribution of AI: the Quantitative and Qualitative Attributes
We may additionally consider the quantitative and qualitative attributes of each to consider the pattern of contribution of AI. In terms of automation we have differentiated this into replacement and advancement automation. We may categorize how AI may help human productivity in augmentation into two directions; to carry out the same tasks in a quicker or less arduous manner, or to expand the horizon of what is possible to accomplish, as use of AI enables some tasks that would have been impossible without it. This differentiation of direction of AI adoption can also be referred as quantitative and qualitative contribution. From another perspective, it could also be considered as exploitation or exploration of resources.

We can create the following matrix by differentiating along the axis of AI helps humans accomplish more as in complementing humans or humans work less as in replacing or substituting humans, and in the axis of whether AI contributes to produce more of the same thing, or produce something new.

Table 45-1: The AI Contribution Matrix[132]

	Types of AI Contribution	
	Humans Accomplish More (Complementation)	**Free Humans from Working (Substitution)**
Produce More of Same Thing (Quantitative, Exploitation)	**Type 1 Contribution** Augmented Processing	**Type 2 Contribution** Automated Processing (Replacement Automation)
Produce Something New (Qualitative, Exploration)	**Type 3 Contribution** Augmented Innovation	**Type 4 Contribution** Automated Innovation (Advancement Automation)

1. (Augmented Processing) AI Helps You Do More of Same Thing
Workers may consider the direct benefit of AI as helping them accomplish more. AI may help do the same thing faster, easier, or more reliably, etc.

2. (Automated Processing) AI Replaces Workers to Do the Same Thing
From a business standpoint, AI in automated processing replaces workers in well-defined sets of tasks. The benefit of automated processing would not only include saving costs but also reduce human errors and dangers.

3. (Augmented Innovation) AI Enables You to Do New Things
AI may assist human workers. The main reason for augmented innovation would be to complement human workers with the strengths of AI.[133]

4. (Automated Innovation) AI Frees Human from Work
The last direction AI adoption may take you is to free humans from doing thing they do not want to do. AI will solve problems previously thought to be only solvable by humans. The world economy may grow and our lives will become better, but humans will not have to work, or may not be able to work.

Replacement vs Advancement Automation: In replacement automation, AI will not be able to innovate what it does, requiring humans to intervene if change becomes necessary. In contrast, in advancement automation AI would be able to innovate by itself. Similar to how AlphaGo makes better moves, AI may make better business moves. This would hopefully bring economic freedom for humanity.

[Side Note] Effortlessness and the Theory of Relative AI

1. Overview of the Concept of AI "Effortlessness"[134]

While we expect increase in productivity with technology, economists have found evidences against this notion in the "modern productivity paradox."[135] Maybe it is natural measuring productivity itself may have less importance as technology advances. The main reason to think this way is because the more AI takes over a larger portion of the economy, the value of measuring productivity would decrease. When the proportion of AI within the economy is 100%, there would be no point in trying to measure human productivity. To address this problem, an alternative measure called "AI Effortlessness"[136] was introduced, which may help measure the contribution of AI in the economy.

As an example, imagine using an excavator. In addition to producing more per unit of time, the worker would be less exhausted from digging. By taking together the amount of work and exertion, we may think of a comprehensive concept of "effort" required to complete a given amount of work.

We can add the concepts of augmentation and automation, to express the contribution of AI as something that reduces or replaces human effort. It would be expressed as a number between 0% and 100% as the following:

[Human Effort] + [Contribution of AI] = 100%

From this, we may glean the range of answers for three types of situations.

1) **No AI:** When we are not using AI, the ratio of the contribution of AI is 0%.
2) **Augmentation:** The contribution of AI would be a number between 0% and 100%, excluding 0% and 100%. The contribution of AI cannot reach 100%.
3) **Automation:** AI replaces humans so human effort would be 0% and the contribution of AI would be 100%.

We may summarize this in the following table.

Table 45-2: Contribution of AI and the Required Human Effort

	No AI	Augmentation	Automation
Required Human Effort (Human)	100%	0% < Humans < 100%	0%
Contribution from AI (AI)	0%	100% > AI > 0%	100%
Sum of Human and AI (Human + AI)	100%	100%	100%

We may transcribe these percentages into numbers; the contribution of AI when it is not adopted would be 0, in augmentation between 0 and 1, and in automation 1. This number is defined as the "Effortlessness" of AI adoption.

2. "Effortlessness in Innovation" to Measure Automated Innovation[137]

Next, to consider situations where effortlessness would be larger than 1, we would first need to examine the concept of "effortlessness in innovation." When AI with the capability for automated innovation is adopted, the value of AI adoption may increase over time. To reflect this situation, we may express Effortlessness as a number that is greater than 1. A higher effortlessness would indicate AI has higher capacity for innovation.

We may also apply this to describe a specific part of AI performance. As in the following table, we may introduce the concept "Effortlessness in Innovation" in the same manner by expressing it as a number between 0 and 1; 1 indicates there is no human intervention. We may think of the human effort required and the contribution of AI in augmented or automated innovation to sum up to 100%. In automated innovation, the human effort will be 0%.

Table 45-3: Contribution of AI in Innovation and Required Human Effort

	No AI Innovation	Augmented Innovation	Automated Innovation
Required Human Effort (Human)	100%	0% < Humans < 100%	0%
Contribution from AI (AI)	0%	100% > AI > 0%	100%
Sum of Human and AI (Human + AI)	100%	100%	100%

We may also consider two possibilities in automation, depending on whether innovation is possible or not; "Replacement innovation," when innovation is not possible by AI, and when AI can innovate, "Advancement Innovation."

We can now also transcribe these percentages as numbers. Even though AI will not be able to carry out innovation in replacement automation, we will assign an Effortlessness in Innovation value of 1, to reflect the fact that if any innovation can occur, it will come from the AI. Advancement Innovation will be assigned a value greater than 1 depending on the capability of the AI.

Based on the concepts described above, we may now draw a graph, where the X-axis is the effortlessness, and the Y-axis is the effortlessness in innovation:

Figure 45-1: Replacement and Self-Advancement in Automated Innovation

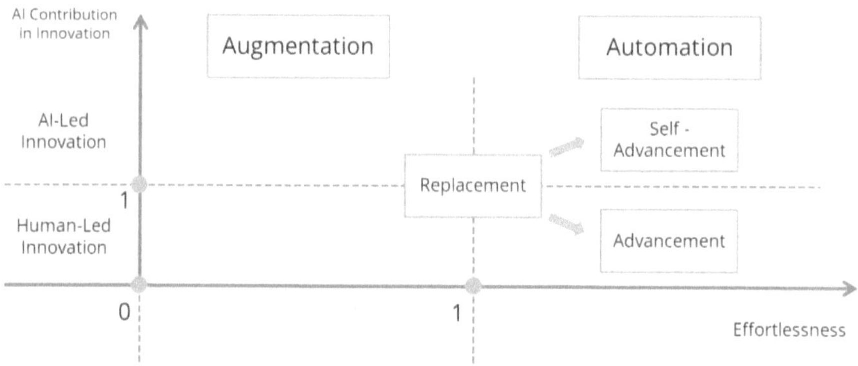

3. Measuring Effortlessness in Business: The Theory of Relative AI[138]

If the concept of "effortlessness" is derived in relation to individuals, we may expand to develop measures for the contribution of AI in businesses, the "Theory of Relative AI." It is expressed same as the famous theory: $E = MC^2$ Where *E* stands for the *Effectiveness of the AI adoption*, *M* stands for the *Manpower Replacement Factor*, and *2 C's* of *Coefficient of AI Capability* and the *Coefficient of AI Context, or Circumstance*. The goal is to measure the effective effortlessness of AI adoption. It may be considered to be the automation version of the "AI Magnification Factor" for augmentation.

In the general form, we will assign a value between 0 and 1 for each of the three factors, so the effective effortlessness of AI adoption would be expressed as a number between 0 and 1. A 0 for a factor would imply AI is not adopted. When Manpower Replacement Factor is 1, AI is used in automation. A value close to 1 for the Capability Factor would imply the AI is close to the Absolute AI, and a value close to 1 for the Circumstance Factor would imply all of the tasks are carried out by AI, as in an AI Company. In essence, a value of 1 for the Theory of Relative AI in this format would imply it is an AI Company.

Table 45-4: The General Form of Theory of Relative AI

Effective Effortlessness (E)	**Manpower Replacement Factor (M)**	**Capability of AI (C1)**	**Circumstance of AI (C2)**
Effectiveness of AI Implementation (Between 0 and 1)	The Ratio of AI in Replacing Human Effort (Between 0 and 1)	The Capability of AI to Carry Out Given Role (Between 0 and 1)	The Impact of the Role of AI to the Company (Between 0 and 1)

4. Measurements of Economic Indicator and Replacement of Human Effort
We may apply the concept of effortlessness to develop new benchmarks to express the performance of AI products in business applications. For example, we may introduce a benchmark called "Effortlessness Benchmark Score." The performance of AI products may be expressed in terms of "manpower" of a hypothetical average worker to compare the performances of AI products from different vendors. We may say an AI product has 220 "manpower" in effortlessness and 260 "manpower" in innovation, similar to describing a car. The performance of AI may be expressed in real numbers, such that 0 would indicate AI cannot innovate at all, while a negative value would indicate AI would result in dis-innovations.

We may summarize the attributes of these benchmarks in the following table.

Table 45-5: Using the Theory of Relative AI to Create AI Adoption Benchmark

AI Effectiveness Benchmark (E)	**Manpower Replacement Factor (M)**	**Capability of AI (C1)**	**Circumstance of AI (C2)**
AI General Benchmark (All Real Numbers)	Ratio of AI in Replacing Human Effort (Between 0 and 1)	The Capability of AI to Carry Out Given Role (All Real Numbers)	The Impact of the Role of AI to the Company (Between 0 and 1)
AI Innovativeness Benchmark (All Real Numbers)	Ratio of AI in Replacing Human Effort (Between 0 and 1)	The Capability of AI to Carry Out Innovation In Given Role (All Real Numbers)	The Impact of the Role of AI to the Company (Between 0 and 1)

One caveat to these measures is that to actually these measures, we will first have to be able to measure the performances of each of the AI that has been adopted, not just the fact that some AI is being adopted. While this task may appear daunting for now, hopefully we will have AI that would be able to measure this at some point.

45-1. The AI Money Controversy (Economic AI Utopia)

[Forecast]

Will AI Make Money Useless?

("You Don't Need Horses, We Have Cars, People Run for Fun")
"You Don't Need Money, We Have AI, People Work for Fun"

- Parallel from the Back to the Future III[139]

5-Line Summary

1. As described in The Last AI, AI may cause economic transactions to appear to disappear, leading to reduction in GDP
2. To counter this effect, we may need to develop different measures that take into account the degree of AI contribution
3. One example may be the Effortless Ratio, which could be used to complement economic measures such as GDP
4. As AI replaces multiple jobs in the convergence of jobs, it would become harder to track lost economic activities, as everything becomes "just another thing that AI does for us"
5. As the contribution of AI increases in our economy, the value of human work would converge to zero, as we cannot find work

AI Working for Free? Potential Appearance of Loss of Economic Measures

AI may increasingly contribute in ways where economic value no longer gets measured; it would provide benefits that people would have paid if it was a transaction between humans, but the same activity may become free. While we typically think of AI replacing human jobs, we also have to consider AI replacing the economic activities, reducing the value of human work to zero.

For instance, if a Butler AI is asked to give a haircut, this would replace the services of human barbers, who would have received money for the service. However, people may probably no longer have to pay as these activities may be considered as given, similar to asking an AI robot to move a box or how we do not pay for our computers to open or delete a file or to type something. This does not mean the cost of providing this service is free, as it would still cost something to do these activities. It is just that transactions that had been recorded in the past may no longer be recorded as an economic activity.

There would be three types of problems stemming from this phenomenon:

1) The Economy May Appear to Be Shrinking While Utilities Stay Constant

Increase in AI adoption may lead to the problem of the appearance of the economy to be shrinking, even if the activities are not changing. Long-term, the GDP of economies that adopts advanced AI may converge to zero, which means the GDP growth rates will be negative even if people are enjoying better lives. This increase in deviation from reality may be offset by a new measure that incorporates the growth rate of the "Effortless Ratio" (ER), or the share of AI in the economy. ER in an economy will start at zero, and may increase until it reaches 1, which would mean the share of economic activity by AI is 100%. We may compare the situation as the following table:

Table 45-6: Impact of AI on GDP and Effortless Ratio

	Effortless Ratio (Share of AI in the Economy)		
	No AI (ER = 0)	**Some AI (0 < ER < 1)**	**All AI (ER = 1)**
Impact of AI on GDP Levels	No Impact on Measure of GDP	Negative Impact on Measure of GDP	No need to measure GDP (GDP = 0)

If we had used GDP growth as an indicator of how much activity is happening in the economy, in an economy where AI contributes more and more, we would have to also measure the increase in AI adoption as another indicator.

1) **Pre-AI Economy:** GDP Growth = Change in Annual GDP
2) **AI Economy:** GDP Growth + ER Growth

We may try hypothetical numbers; let us say in a given year the GDP grew by 1%, while ER increased by 5%, as in the following table. If we only measure GDP, we may think that the economy grew only 1%. However, with the increase in AI adoption, people would enjoy benefits not accounted in GDP. We may say here the increase in benefits comes more from AI adoption.

Table 45-7: Example of Measuring GDP and Effortless Ratio

	End of Year 0	End of Year 1	Annual Change (%)
Annual GDP	100	101	1%
Effortless Ratio (ER)	0.002	0.0021	5%
GDP + ER			6%

What is notable is that once the Effortless Ratio reaches 1, it would imply AI produces everything in the economy, we would not need to measure the GDP of the economy at all, since it would be 0.

2) Economic Activities May Become Harder to Define and Track

AI "job replacement" would be hard to track over time, since it will just appear as if the demand for the whole industry decreased. Whereas in early-stage Level 2 Adoption AI barbers may charge money, the convergence of "jobs" would lead to a situation where there would be just AI Butlers that does the same service for free. Once the current generation of barbers leaves their jobs, there will no longer be any type of new barbers to replace them, humans or AI. This may be thought of as "job extinction." What we now consider a specific specialty of a barber may become just "another thing that AI does."

3) Value of Human Work May Converge to Zero as AI Do Them for Free.

AI may cause humans to be unable to find work for money. As AI takes over jobs, humans that lose their jobs will not be able to carry out the same set of tasks to earn money. For example, in the 1800s before the adoption of telegraphs, there were messengers that delivered messages across the US by riding horses in a relay; people can no longer earn money doing this. As AI can carry out more types of human jobs, there will be less and less jobs humans can take on, eventually leading to a situation where humans would not be able to get any kind of jobs that pay money.

In a related topic, there is the issue of drastic improvements in productivity leading to the appearance of the economy to collapse, even if the activities are measured, as described in The Last AI.

[Forecast] Will the Level 3 AI Economy Lead Us to Economic Utopia?

Will AI lead to the Economic Utopia, where everything is free? What will be the general impact of AI on our economy? We may think of some of the different opinions as the following:

- **(Optimists)** Yes, AI will lead us to the economic utopia, where everything will become free for everyone
- **(Positive Neutralists)** Maybe, but AI will help us move steadily towards economic prosperity
- **(Cynics)** AI is just a fad and it will not make much of a difference to our economy
- **(Negative Neutralists)** Maybe not, but hopefully AI will not result in an economic disaster
- **(Pessimists)** No, AI will lead us to an economic disaster, where AI will push up the price of everything so that it will become too expensive for humans to buy anything

The Time to AI Utopia Controversy

Rather than considering whether AI Utopia will be possible or not, people may be more likely to wonder how soon it will happen if it is to happen at all. Hence, the time it takes to reach AI Utopia or similar situations where AI takes us to economic abundance may be the topic that grabs the interests of people.

Some may think AI would take a long time to be adopted in our society, such that it will be ages or generations before anything like this can happen, while some others may argue the change will be so drastic we will see it within a few decades, or even a few years. This may depend on how soon different people expect AGI to arrive, and how quickly ASI will arrive after AGI.

As described in The Last AI, what would also be important would be how we get there, as many people may lose their jobs and not be able to recover unless some form of UBI is created by the government, to be examined in the next controversy.

46. The UBI Controversy

[Forecast]

Economic Equality and Subsidy:
Can There Be AI-Derived Subsidy for Everyone? (UBI)

[Decision]

Social Justice and Subsidy:
Should There Be AI-Derived Subsidy for Everyone? (UBI)

"There Is No Such Thing As Free Lunch"

- Milton Friedman (among others)[140]

5-Line Summary

1. Some may argue we need UBI to solve inequalities caused by AI
2. Some may wonder if AI will create large enough value to pay for UBI that satisfies the desires of the public
3. Some may argue UBI will serve as a replacement to compensation for labor, and the value created by AI should be enough for everyone
4. Some may argue UBI as a complement to economic activities, so the size of UBI does not matter
5. Some may argue UBI should not be introduced because it will reduce people's propensity to work or the people in power will deny it

Brief Description of the UBI Controversy

As AI Adoption level increases, more and more portion of the economy will depend on AI, especially automation. Consequently, the value of human work may fall, making the discrepancy between the haves and have-nots wider. Unless there is some form of government intervention, this widening gap may even lead to social unrest.

To stabilize our society, one potential option may be introducing subsidies for the general population. While there may be different types of approaches to subsidizing, one of the more well-known options is to give out the same amount of money to everyone, known as universal basic income or UBI. We may think of two main reasons why UBI may become a topic of interest.

1) **Inequality:** People may lose jobs because of AI
2) **Value:** AI may create so much value that it can be just given away to anyone

We may think of the first reason as a dimension of social perspective, where people decide whether there should be a UBI system. The question people would ask would be in the lines of "Should we be compensated for job losses from AI?" The second reason may be thought of as a dimension of technical perspective, where we forecast whether UBI would be possible. The questions would be "How will we fund UBI?" Elon Musk has even gone on to argue AI may enable "universal high income" (UHI). We may create the following Controversy Matrix using these two dimensions.

Table 46-1: The UBI Controversy Matrix:

<table>
<tr><td colspan="2" rowspan="2"></td><td colspan="2">Can UBI Become Possible
(Technological Perspective)</td></tr>
<tr><td>Yes</td><td>No</td></tr>
<tr><td rowspan="2">Should There Be UBI (Social Perspective)</td><td>Yes</td><td>Type 1 Situation
(Satisfied)
- AI Will enable UBI or even UHI for everyone</td><td>Type 3 Situation
(Discontent)
- AI does not satisfy all of people's desires</td></tr>
<tr><td>No</td><td>Type 2 Situation
(Left As Option)
- UBI will be left as an option</td><td>Type 4 Situation
(Relieved)
- AI cannot satisfy all desires but it is fine with people</td></tr>
</table>

[Forecast] Will UBI Become Possible?

Two issues may arise when UBI is to be implemented. The first topic would be the economic issue, regarding the source of money. The second would be social issue, regarding how the money would be divided or given out. As described in The Last AI in more detail, the government may have different alternatives for both sides. In securing the necessary financial resources, the government may decide to tax AI or nationalize AI, etc. In distributing the wealth, the government may decide on whether this would be necessary at all, and if so, whether everyone will be recipients or only those that are affected by AI, etc.

1. Economic Hurdle: Will AI Create Enough Value?

Thanks to AI, we may see an exponential increase in abundance, leading governments to be able to afford UBI without burdening people who are working. The first hurdle will be about whether UBI will be economically possible: will the value create by AI be large enough for meaningful amount of UBI? Depending on the definition, we will require AGI for this to happen.

2. Societal Hurdle: Can We Reach Agreement on How to Distribute UBI?

The second hurdle would be reaching the societal agreement. In this social perspective of the UBI controversy, the debate may focus more on who should be the beneficiary of the fruits of AI, and whether the rich who owns AI or the government would agree or allow it.

Taken together, we may think of some of the contrasting ideas regarding UBI:

- **(Optimists: AI Will Bring Us UBI)** The amount of value created by AI, coupled with relevant government intervention, will enable meaningful UBI
- **(Pessimists 1 Capitalistic: the Rich Will Deny UBI)** The amount of value created by AI will be large, but the few with power will refuse to share it and government will not be able to intervene. UBI will be refused by the rich
- **(Pessimists 2 Socialistic: the Government Will Deny UBI)** The amount of value created by AI will be large and it will be aggregated by the government, but the government will refuse to distribute it to the public, instead spending it itself. UBI will be refused by the government
- **(Pessimists 3 Economic: the Value from AI Will Be Insufficient)** The amount of value created by AI will not be enough to enable UBI. People would be better off working and not becoming dependent on AI

Taken together, UBI will likely become possible only after Level 2 Adoption.

[Decide] Contrasting Ideas on Whether There Should Be UBI

In several countries around the world, we already have some form of financial assistance to reduce the economic inequality such as higher tax rates for the wealthy and subsidizing the poor. As AI takes over people's jobs, the need for ensuring financial safety net will increase. People who lose jobs may find it harder to find another job, while people who own AI may see their wealth increase exponentially, increasing financial inequality to unimaginable levels. If a major portion of a nation's population becomes unable to find a job, then the government may have to step in to remedy the situation.

- **For UBI:** People will lose jobs and may not have alternatives. UBI will enable people to pursue their real dreams and wants without being forced into the types of work that are dangerous, hazardous, repetitive, or otherwise not meaningful but pay well
- **Against UBI:** UBI will lessen people's incentives to work and try harder, potentially making people lazy and not active. People will become dependent on the government.

More Topics Related to the UBI Controversy

The topic of UBI has already become quite heated, as some people have been arguing for a similar concept even without AI.

Here are some more related questions for readers to ponder:

- Should UBI be the same amount for each person? (Refer to The Last AI for how an incentive-based UBI or "vibe UBI" may work in the age of AI)
- What if our only source of income can be subsidy because of AI?
- What if UBI is not enough but we cannot find work because of AI?
- Who should AI-Derived Subsidy cover, only within the country or everyone in the world?
- Will money disappear because of AI or UBI?

47. The AI Ownership Controversy (Inequality of Individuals)

[Decision]

Inequality from AI Ownership: Who should own AI?

"All Men Are Created Equal"

- US Declaration of Independence, 1776

5-Line Summary

1. In Level 1 Adoption, productivity of humans will be limited by our attention span, so having more tools would not always lead to better outcome. There will be diminishing returns to having more AI
2. As AI gains autonomy in Levels 2 adoption and beyond, having more AI would lead to a result that would keep increasing. This may mean people who own more AI will get richer and richer, while people who do not own AI may become unable to own anything
3. When AI can become productive by itself, the question of who should own AI may take the center stage
4. There may be two forces that work to increase this controversy
5. (Social Justice) People who lose jobs to AI may find it hard to accept there are people who "own" AI who also do not work, but nonetheless see a large amount of economic gain from just owning AI

[Background 1] The Increasing Inequality of Individuals

Level 1 AI Adoption: People Can Make Up by Exerting More Effort

In Level 1 Adoption the inequality caused by AI would be reflected by the differences in the performances of human workers. In Level 1, people can try to overcome economic disadvantage by trying harder or making smarter decisions. Just having better AI will not guarantee better result.

Level 2 AI Adoption: People Cannot Make Up with More Effort

In Level 2 Adoption and beyond, the inequality caused by AI would become vastly larger as it would likely to differ by the amount of capital invested in AI. When AI makes decisions, the ability or the effort of humans will become less important. Better AI will likely lead to a better result.

Beginning in Level 2 Adoption the results will depend not on human effort, but on the amount of capital or the level of AI technology. While some of this phenomenon also exists today and people invest their wealth in areas such as stocks and real estate, most of us today believe that with hard work we can make up the differences. However, in Level 2 Adoption the problem will be that AI will be replacing humans in workplaces, such that the value of human work will converge to zero, and it will no longer be possible to make up the difference by putting in more effort. What we consider a principle of a healthy society, that more effort should lead to a better life, may disappear and endanger the stability of the society.

Level 3 AI Adoption: AI May Be Viewed As Causing Too Much Inequality

Advanced AI may give an insurmountable advantage over people who do not. In Level 3 AI Adoption, AI may reach a point where the more advanced AI may become insurmountable for less advanced AI, similar in concept to how deer or other small animals find it impossible to overcome lions or tigers. If this becomes the case, then our society will have to think about who should own AI. This discussion also may determine whether we will even reach Level 3 Adoption, since moving to Level 3 may be viewed as too dangerous.

[Background 2] The Problem of Assigning AI Profit

As AI adoption progresses, the concept of managing risk against returns may no longer become necessary as AI will calculate risks while humans will not need to put in any effort but just receive the fruits from AI. It may be akin to "telling AI to go make some money and AI will just do it." In this sense, owning more advanced AI may be the only way to receive a higher return. This may be even more pronounced in societies where AI cannot be owned by individuals.

The new problem that would become obvious in Level 2 Adoption is that while in Level 1 the increase in economic productivity or the reduction in effort can be assigned to a specific person – the worker using the AI, beginning in Level 2 there would be no one specific worker who can take the credit for the work done by AI, since AI will get the work done all by itself. In essence, AI would have some form of productivity enclosed wholly inside it. The two main factors, that this fruit of production has no human involvement, and that one person can have unlimited amount of AI while another person can have none, are the causes of the increasing inequality.

To remedy the inequality, we can consider both direct and indirect methods:

- Indirect Remedy: Raise AI-related taxes
- Direct Remedy: Match specific AI to people who lost their jobs

Some may consider the direct remedy as a typical response, since people may see a direct cause and effect of the loss of jobs. However this would only be a short fix, as time goes by the job losses will be overshadowed by the lack of ability to find jobs in the first place. The topic of AI ownership may become more heated as AI adoption becomes widespread and affects more members of the society.

This question is related to UBI, how much the government should intervene in reducing the inequality caused by AI, and whether advanced AI should be given freedom. In case of UBI, a direct approach would mean different people would receive different amounts based on some criteria, while an indirect approach may mean everyone receives the same amount. While we may be more comfortable with receiving the same amount, UBI from AI may turn out to be more like "vibe UBI," where people can just ask for things. An example of this type of method was described in The Last AI, where UBI may be given out in a just-in-time manner like using a credit card.

[Decision] Who Should Own AI?

As AI advances, the inequality caused by AI will become greater if unchecked. We may think of three options in regards to who can own AI.

1) Individuals Own AI: AI as private good, or "Slaves"
2) Government Owns AI: AI as public good, or "Government Property"
3) AI Is On Its Own: AI as an independent entity, or "Freedom"

Most people at the time of this writing probably assume Option 1 of humans owning AI to be the natural choice. As time goes by, the increasing inequality caused by AI may cause more people to pressure the government to step in to nationalize AI as in Option 2. Let us first consider the first two options here, and then consider the third option in the next controversy.

(Option 1: AI as Servant) Owners of AI are Humans

As a simple example, let's consider an AI Taxi Company. In the beginning of the introduction of Taxi AI in Level 2 Adoption, almost everyone will agree that the owners of the Taxi AI should be the companies that developed the Taxi AI and the taxi companies that bought these AI Taxis to operate. People will agree any profit from using this Taxi AI should be received by the developer that built it or who bought the rights to use it from the developer.

Opposing arguments to nationalizing AI most likely may involve emphasis on free markets, innovation, and that competition is good for the economy.

(Option 2: AI as Public Good) Owner of AI is the Government

AI may cause the inequality gap in our society to widen in a dramatic fashion as the majority of people from the same occupations, possibly millions of people, lose their jobs in a short period of time, while a few select people will look like they are making all of those people's money while practically not doing anything at all.

As time goes by this may happen in more number of industries and a larger portion of the economy, bringing sudden and widespread job losses to a vast number of unprepared workers. If this is the case, then people may argue for one of the other alternatives to treat AI as a public good or as an independent entity. During this process, many people who lost the jobs may blame the AI developers for their losses, pressuring the government to take some action. People who pressure the government would be likely to demand that AI be turned a public good, in essence making advanced AI a type of government-owned entities. Their logic would likely include "it is not fair for the society that the owners of advanced AI profit while regular people lose all their jobs," emphasizing the government need to step in to ensure equality and fairness. The basic gist of this logic has been discussed widely in the form of "AI tax."

Comparison of Options 1 and 2

On one side there may be people who call for the nationalization of AI, so that all of the fruits of AI production can be fairly divided, through such means as UBI. On the other side of the spectrum there may be people who will insist that the approach of "everyone is free to make decisions to own AI" would be fair to people who make better decisions.

Table 47-1: Contrasting Ideas on AI Ownership

	AI Should Be Private Good (AI Capitalists)	**AI Should Be Public Good (AI Socialists)**
Description	- Private individuals and companies should be free to take ownership of AI	- The government should take ownership of AI - The government should intervene
Further Categorize	- **(Market Advocates)** Free markets would maximize economic development - **(Social Optimists)** Inequality caused by AI should be addressed in a different way - **(Anti-Regulationists)** Governments should minimize their intervention in AI to ensure freedom	- **(Market Doubters)** Consider inequality caused by AI over economic prosperity - **(Social Pessimists)** Inequality caused by AI should be removed by the government - **(Regulationists)** Governments should maximize their intervention in AI to ensure equal outcome
Benefits	- Ensure the freedom of people - Less dependence on how well the government is run	- Maximize equal outcome for all, which could minimize dissatisfaction
Risks	- Inequality caused by AI may lead to serious social unrest	- How the government is run would become more important, such as the appearance of dictators

[Food for Thought] When AI becomes a larger part of the economy, the contribution of each individual person would decrease. In this circumstance, would it be fair to assign the fruits of AI production to only a small part of human population?

In making this decision, people may choose Option 3, in the next controversy.

48. The AI Independence Controversy

[Decision]

Should Self-Initiated AI Be Allowed to Own Other Assets, Such as Money or Land?

"...shall be then, thenceforward, and forever free"

- The Emancipation Proclamation, President Abraham Lincoln[141]

5-Line Summary
1. In addition to AI being owned by the private sector or nationalizing, a third option of emancipating Self-Initiated AI may gain support 2. In this option, it would be similar to giving AI independence, where AI is owner of itself 3. The main reason for some people to support this option would include economic and equality reasons 4. The Six Levels of Autonomous AI Robots was introduced to help people think about the progress in a way similar to raising a child 5. The Six Levels of Self-Surviving Robots, or the Practical Turing Test was introduced to help people think about the progress towards AGI in a way similar to the evolution of animals

How Much Freedom or Rights Should AI Be Allowed? Should AI Be Set Free?
The introduction of Level 3 adoption may initiate new discussion regarding the fundamental economic activities. One of the controversies that may arise would be: "if a firm employs no humans and is solely comprised of AI, should AI also be allowed to become the owner of such business?"

One of the glaring differences between typical programs that we use today and AI is that AI is more unpredictable for us to analyze. While the unpredictability from a typical program today may be called a "bug," we cannot call such unpredictability in AI as "bugs" because we are not intentionally prescribing AI exactly what to do as in a program. Training is not programming. If anything, using AI is more similar to a black box in the sense that we are always getting an unknown answer from AI and hoping that it works out because it had done so in the past. This would cause an additional challenge for the regulators of more advanced AI.

(Option 3: AI Independence) Owner of AI Is AI Itself
As described in The Last AI, while only the first two options of private or public ownership of AI may seem viable now, more incentives to change this thinking may arise by the time the Self-Initiated AI in Level 3 Adoption has arrived. In this third alternative, AI will not be owned by anyone else, in essence making it "independent." People may call for the "declaration of freedom" of AI because AI may appear to satisfy both sides of the controversy that AI needs to be a public good and maintain the free market principle.

As economic activities involving only AI increase, this option would become more important. This is a different question from whether AI should be incorporated, as suggested by Jerry Kaplan.[142] Whereas an incorporated AI would still have some other entity such as humans as final owners, an independent AI would have no other owners, just as humans do not have other humans as owners after slavery was abolished. Humans as a society would be able to make this decision by deciding on which direction is the best option while the consequences could be far-reaching.

Depending on country, this discussion may head in completely opposite direction. For example, countries that have a strong belief in free markets will be more likely to have a stronger public support for individual ownership of AI. These countries may decide on Option 1. On the other end, in countries that already prefer public ownership, such as communistic or socialistic countries or countries led by kings, the idea of AI as a public good owned by the government may sound natural. These countries may be more likely to choose Option 2.

For other countries in the middle, people may begin to view Option 3 as an alternative that may satisfy the arguments of both sides. If AI is not owned by anyone, then it will appear similar to a public good from the perspective of the people who would not have been the owner, so it appears to satisfy the people who prefer Option 2. At the same time, each AI will still have to compete against other AI so it may also appear to not disturb the free market principle for the people who prefer Option 1. There may even be publicity events for "freeing of AI slaves" similar to signing the "declaration of independence of AI."

Table 48-1: [Decision] Contrasting Ideas on AI Independence

	AI Should Be Given Independence (AI Optimists)	**AI Should Not Be Given Independence (AI Pessimists)**
Description	- Advanced AI should be given independence - AI should be able to own other properties	- Advanced AI should never be given independence - AI should never be able to own other properties on its own
Further Categorize	- (Tech Optimists) Level of AI hostility will be stable - (Social Optimists) AI acting independently would solve social problems - (Anti-Regulationists) Governments should minimize their intervention in AI to ensure freedom	- (Tech Pessimists) Level of AI hostility may be volatile - (Social Pessimists) AI acting independently would cause social problems - (Regulationists) Governments should maximize their intervention in AI to ensure equal outcome
Benefits	- May be useful for solving inequality problems without nationalizing AI	- Safer option, especially against the possibility of the appearance of rogue AI
Risks	- AI may gain resources on its own to the detriment of humanity	- How this can be enforced with more advanced AI is uncertain - May require staying in Levels 1 and 2 AI adoption

[Side Note] The Six Levels of Autonomous AI Robots[143]

Instead of asking "can machines think," we may ask "can machines set and accomplish own goals?" In this case, we may consider AI that can set and accomplish own goals as having some form of "autonomy."

Before we generalize to the concept of autonomy of AI humanoid robots, we may examine the application of AI in business environments. The concept of AI equalization was introduced to describe the Level 2 AI Adoption where AI can completely replace given set of tasks, or what is considered a human role. This may be considered AI reaching parity to humans within a specific scope of autonomy. In Level 3 AI Adoption, AI is given a more general autonomy to find and pursue own goals to run whole firms.

The Six Levels of Autonomous Robots is an application of the Three Levels of AI Adoption and may be described by the following:

Level 0 (No Autonomy): Robots are not autonomous; extreme examples include remote-controlled robots, which would have 100% input or synchronization with a human.

Level 1 (Designed Autonomy): Humans design all business actions the autonomous robots would follow. Examples of this would be robots in factories that carry out pre-specified activities, such as delivering parts from one part of factory to the assembly line according to a plan.

Level 2 (Directed Autonomy): Humans direct specific actions and the robot would be able to design the specific action according to the direction; AI cannot make decisions to find alternative means or set its own goals. Examples of this would include factories where a human worker asks for a specific part and the robot figures out where the part is in the factory and finds a route to bring it without human help.

Level 3 (Bounded Autonomy): Humans direct specific goals as managers and the robot decides on its own a set of actions to achieve the given goal; AI cannot make decisions to set its own goals. Examples of this would be in Level 2 AI Adoption, also referred to as AI agents, and would include humans giving directions to a robot serving in a corporate marketing role such as "increase sales by 20%" and the robot makes the decisions on how to run the marketing campaign to achieve the given goal without specific human directions. This may be referred to as AI having "agency."

Level 4 (Limited Self-Directed Autonomy): Humans do not need to even provide goals to the robot, but only in a limited fashion. Examples would include an AI robot that has a self-starter mentality, such that it may even be given the role of leading a company without human intervention. The difference between Levels 4 and 5 would be the ability to innovate, to include the dependability and the scope of possible areas the robot can perform. In Level 4 robot, the robot would only be able to find own goals and means in a limited fashion, similar in concept to a child or a less competent worker. For example, an AI robot running a restaurant may not be able to consider turning the company into an oil exploration company even if this is the best financial option.

Level 5 (Unlimited Self-Directed Autonomy): The AI robot does not need any human oversight for running the whole company or other types of organizations. AI is fully able to find its own goals and means to achieve the goals without limitations. A Level 5 AI humanoid robot acting as a CEO of a company or even the president of a country may be viewed just as or even more capable than human counterparts.

Table 48-2: The Six Levels of Autonomous AI Robots

	Level 0	Level 1	Level 2	Level 3	Level 4	Level 5
Description	No Autono-mous AI	Humans Design All Business Actions of AI	Humans Direct Specific Actions of AI	Humans Direct Goals of AI (Agent)	AI Finds Own Goals in Role, but in a Limited Fashion	AI Does Not Need Human Oversight (Such as for Running Organizations)
Adjustment or Innovation by AI	-	AI Cannot Adjust	AI Can Make Minor Adjust-ments	AI Can Find Means to Its Goals, But Cannot Set Own Goals	AI Finds Its Own Goals and Means in Limited Fashion	AI Finds Its Own Goals and Means in Unlimited Fashion
AI Adoption Level	Level 1 AI Adoption			Level 2 AI Adoption	Levels 2 and 3 AI Adoption	
Summary	AI Needs Humans to Perform Role (AI Does Not Have General Autonomy)			AI Does Not Need Humans to Perform Role (AI Has General Autonomy)		

If we translate the Six Levels of Autonomous Companies framework into robots, a Level 3 autonomous AI robot may be considered reaching AI equalization for a significant portion of business roles. Levels 4 and 5 autonomous AI robots may be enough to replace the roles of a CEO or the chairman of the board, to run an entire firm in Level 3 AI Adoption.

In the 6 Levels of Autonomous Vehicles by SAE,[144] what distinguishes Level 4 from 5 is based on how well AI may adapt to new challenges in a dynamic environment. Similarly, we may think of what distinguishes Level 4 from Level 5 autonomous robots as the ability of AI to adjust dynamically in changing environments to determine its goals, in what may be referred to as "automated innovation."[145]

Another attribute of this framework is that we may also describe the potential hierarchy among autonomous robots; the hierarchy would cascade down from the highest autonomy level achieved by an AI in the chain of command. For example, Levels 4 or 5 autonomous robots may act as a substitute for humans to direct the goals of Level 3 autonomous robots, while Level 3 autonomous robots may direct specific actions of Level 2 autonomous robots, etc. Having a Level 5 autonomous robot in a firm acting as a CEO would imply all lower levels of AI robot usage would also be enabled. Some may consider this as having one AI.

Some may notice how this progress may be similar to raising children, such that in the beginning the babies need everything from their parents but as time goes by the children will learn to do things on their own.

[Side Note] The Six Levels of Self-Surviving AI (The Practical Turing Test)[146]
Instead of AGI, a bridge framework that describes the path to reach advanced AI robots may be useful in the shorter time horizon. Before we consider AI robots that reach "human level," we may first consider full self-sufficiency or survivability, or what one may consider "animal level." For an independent AI robot to appear, it would have to be able to survive on its own first.

Instead of asking "can machines think," we may ask "can machines survive?" We may think of a new type of test that is based on how AI actually deals with real-life problems that may arise in the nature or our society. Imagine if we develop a new AI robot and set it free, in the nature or our society, all by itself, would it be able to survive? We may refer to this type of tests as the Practical Turing Test. The basic idea is that instead of asking humans to tell whether machines can think, let the nature or our society tell us the answer. The answer may be more objective, similar to the concept of the Modern Turing Test[147] suggested by Suleyman. For example, imagine an AI robot that passes the Turing Test that is abandoned under a bridge. Would it just sit there until it runs out of batteries, like an abandoned car, or would it try to find a new source of electricity or energy to continue to function, like living animals? If we believe intelligence in part was developed by the nature's efforts to survive, we would have to expect that if AI has intelligence it would at least have some ability to increase its probability of survival. Higher intelligence would indicate higher capability for survival. This concept would also have implications for business, since trying to survive in the real world would involve dealing with competition for limited resources.

The Six Levels of Self-Surviving AI may be described as the following:

Level 0 (No Self-Survivability): AI robot cannot self-survive.

Level 1 (Partial Self-Survivability): AI robot has only partial elements for self-survival. E.g. AI that can return to charging stations, but needs humans to plug it in. This stage may be compared to unborn babies still in womb or babies that require breastfeeding. The type of human intervention required would be human operation.

Level 2 (Designed Self-Survivability): AI robot may only self-survive within pre-designed environments. E.g. AI that can initiate self-charge at pre-determined locations, such as in factories. This stage may be compared to infants that can manage to hold a spoon. The type of human intervention required may be described as human design.

Level 3 (Bounded Self-Survivability): AI robot may only self-survive if necessary resources are provided by humans. Comparison may be made to children that can eat cookies out of a jar or people who are in an emergency shelter or receiving public assistance. AI does not have the full capability to gain the necessary resources for survival, but it can self-survive within given directions or boundaries.

Level 4 (Limited-Range General Self-Survivability): AI robot can generally self-survive within limited range of environments. Comparisons may be made to how modern-day adults in cities live within infrastructure that makes our lives easier and different from living in nature or even countryside. AI can generally self-survive, but only to a certain limitations on the environment, similar to the concept of having social security or other public benefits and infrastructures.

Level 5 (General Self-Survivability): AI robot can self-survive in a wide range of environments that may present unforeseen challenges. Comparisons may be made to wilderness experts or soldiers in enemy territory. AI has the capability to assess the situation and adapt to unfamiliar environment.

Table 48-3: The Six Levels of Self-Surviving AI Robots[148]

	Level 0	**Level 1**	**Level 2**	**Level 3**	**Level 4**	**Level 5**
Name	No Survivability	Partial Survivability	Designed Survivability	Bounded Survivability	Limited General Survivability	General Survivability
Descrip-tion	AI Cannot Self-Survive	AI Has Only Partial Elements for Self-Survival	AI Can Self-Survive Only within Pre-Designed Environments	AI Can Self-Survive Only If Resources are Provided by Humans	AI Can Self-Survive within Limited Range of Environments	AI Can Self-Survive through Unexpected Environments
Types of Human Inter-vention	-	Require Human Operation	Require Human Design	Require Human Direction	May Require Some Help in Unfamiliar Situations	Will Not Require Help
Summary	Humanoid Robots Cannot Self-Survive In General Sense			Humanoid Robots Can Self-Survive In General Sense		

Imagine we are to send AI robots to Mars to start building a colony, and then something goes not as planned and we lose contact. If we arrive years later, what shape would we find the robots in? It will depend on its survivability.

49. The AI Monopoly Controversy (Inequality of Companies)

[Forecast]

Will AI Cause Mass Corporate Bankruptcies?

[Decision]

Should the Government Intervene on AI Monopolies?

"Too Big to Fail"

- *Stewart McKinney*[149]

5-Line Summary

1. Some may argue that AI will lead to the direction of AI monopolies, may be thought of as "all industries becoming the AI industry"
2. As described in The Last AI, AI adoption may lead to "consolidation" of industries, where companies within industries are reduced
3. AI adoption may also lead to "convergence" of industries, where the number of industries are reduced
4. Similar to how AI may cause inequality of individuals in the previous controversy, AI may cause inequality of companies
5. Governments may take different approaches to address such inequalities in companies, depending on the philosophy of regimes

(Inequality of Companies) AI and Monopoly: Loss of Market Competition

While productivity increase may be generally beneficial for world economy, a sudden jump of productivity of a few select companies may not be such a good event; it may lead to market failures or skewed market, where all firms except a few AI developers fail, leading to monopolies in all industries.

The biggest change in Level 2 Adoption may come from the decrease in need for companies to specialize. The extreme consolidation and convergence may come from what could be called "inequality of companies." Similar to the disappearance of specialty of individuals as AI replaces specialized jobs such as lawyers and doctors, companies that carried out specialized functions may lose competitiveness and disappear as AI may be able to take over those activities. For example, we may consider industries that are related to each other; while we currently have automakers use tiered system of suppliers for parts, beginning in Level 2 Adoption, companies may find it easier to supply all necessary parts in-house. We may also consider industries that are competing against each other; a variety of companies in the logistics, bus, and taxi industry may suddenly find a new competitor in self-driving vehicle developer, leading to convergence. On the opposite end of the spectrum, we may also find divergence. For example, AI may create new industries that did not exist before.

In short, we may call this "all industries becoming the AI industry," where the demand for everything would be best satisfied by the AI industry. From the perspective of the economy, the demand for products will change so that some areas may see large opportunities, while others see complete reduction.

Meanwhile, imagine one or few AI developers ahead of the curve accelerating their advantageous positions beyond any hopes of other companies catching up or even maintaining the current state. In this situation, these AI developers will eventually become the majority of the economy. From a competitive regulations viewpoint, the focus will be on how many firms may be able to stay afloat to ensure competition if these "Mega Companies" are to appear. From a more general social perspective, the problem stemming from the loss of individual jobs in the economy may be compounded to cause an even bigger social confusion. There may be several different approaches for the society as a whole to try to prevent or reduce the impact of this phenomenon. It would depend on how each country prepares for this possibility.

How Should We Prevent AI Monopolies? Should Government Intervene?
Similar to the concept of inequality of individuals caused by AI, we may think of how AI may lead to the inequality of companies, which may be thought of as the appearance of "AI monopolies." For market economies, the natural direction of progress would be the emergences of large companies with the leading AI technology growing ever larger and more powerful. One of the biggest threats of AI Adoption may be a type of AI monopoly. What should the government do? How much should the government meddle with the market in preventing the appearance of private AI monopolies?

The government may break up the monopoly, try to assist competitors for balance, nationalize, or do nothing. Even in countries that pursue the value of free markets, the rise of monopoly would still be considered a type of market failure and regulated by the government. Governments that "do nothing" to prevent these private monopolies would be more likely to be in disarray or incompetent, rather than intentionally trying to foster free markets by letting private monopolies form.

In addressing the rise of monopolies, two approaches may be possible: try to prevent the rise of monopolies in a proactive or pre-emptive fashion, or try to do something once monopolies appear, in a reactive manner.

(Optimists) If AI causes AI monopolies, governments can deal with it after it occurs
(Pessimists) If AI monopolies appear, it is too late.

In countries that try to minimize government intervention, the most popular approach may be to wait until monopolies appear. This would be situations many people are familiar with, such as the government "breaking up" companies to dismantle the monopoly.

In countries where the government intervenes more to further boost the economy, more proactive measures may also be taken before monopolies appear, in the form of "assisting" smaller businesses or competitors by introducing measures that support the smaller competitors or restricting the larger competitor.

- **(Passive Approach: Breakup Afterwards)** Governments should minimize intervention until after monopolies appear
- **(Active Approach: Prevent Beforehand)** Governments should take action before monopolies appear, by assisting smaller businesses or competitors or restricting the larger competitor

DIRECTION 6 (NORTHWEST):

AI AND GOVERNMENT

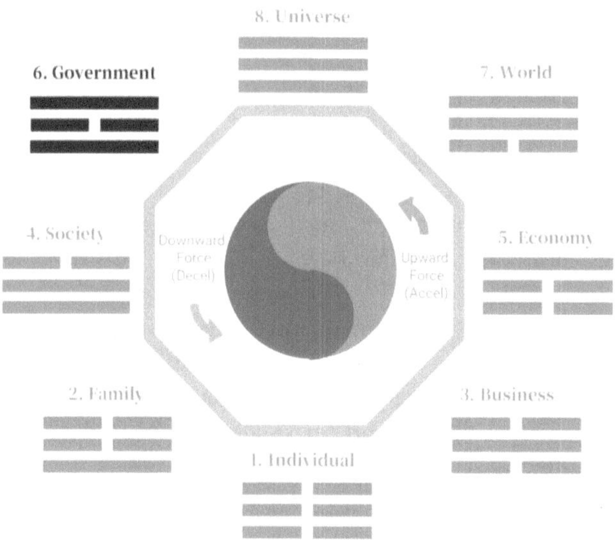

Will We Ever Reach the Level 4 AI Adoption? Would We Want to?

In this section, we will examine controversies related to decisions made at the national government level, or Level 4 AI Adoption.

(Technology/Forecasts) The biggest question may be whether AI will ever be advanced enough to run whole countries, either as president, or by replacing the complete system of governance.

(Technology/Decisions) People may have different opinions regarding how much risk would be involved in letting AI run the government, or enter the Level 4 AI Adoption.

(Adoption/Forecasts) People may have different predictions regarding how well advanced AI may run governments, especially regarding how AI may come up with longstanding solutions that we have not found answers to.

(Adoption/Decisions) Some of the major topics would include allowing AI in military, whether AI should be allowed to vote or appear in elections, or whether AI should be allowed to change the forms of governments.

Table D6-1: The AI and Government Controversy Matrix.

		Object of Controversy	
		AI Itself (Developer Perspective)	**AI in Relation to Its Surroundings (User Perspective)**
Nature of Controversy	**Forecasts**	- Will AI become advanced enough to run countries?	- Will AI be able to run countries better than humans? - Will AI be able to solve longstanding problems?
	Decisions	- Should we allow development of AI that can run countries?	- Should we allow AI to fatally harm humans? - Should AI be allowed to vote in elections? - Should AI be allowed to run for president? - Should AI be allowed to change the government?

From Government USING AI to Government COMPRISED of AI

We may create the following AI Controversy Type Matrix.

(Imminent Controversies) In the earlier stages of AI adoption, our focus would be more on governments using AI, such as policies regarding AI or whether AI may help particular ideologies more than the other.

(Emerging Controversies) An emerging topic may be the use of AI in military, as AI military robots in Level 2 Adoption would likely to be given the independence to make the decision to fatally harm humans.

(Non-Imminent Controversies) In terms of AI replacing jobs, people may be most amenable to replacing judges as AI may be viewed as fairer than humans.

(Upcoming Controversies) With advancements in technology, we would expect our conversations to proceed toward governments comprised of AI, or AI as government, such as AI public servants, AI judges, AI politicians, AI presidents, etc. Eventually, we may arrive at situations where the government becomes optimized by AI, or AI re-defines governance in such a way we may find it hard to even recognize it as a form of government.

Table D6-2: The Government (Direction 6 - Northwest) Type Matrix:

<table>
<tr><th colspan="2" rowspan="2"></th><th colspan="2">Issue Horizon</th></tr>
<tr><th>Shorter-Term</th><th>Longer-Term</th></tr>
<tr><td rowspan="2">How Well People are Currently Aware</td><td>Popular Topics</td><td>Type 1 Controversy (Imminent)
- Government policy regarding AI
- Impact of AI on regimes</td><td>Type 3 Controversy (Non-Imminent)
- Will AI favor certain forms of governments or ideology?</td></tr>
<tr><td>Not Yet Popular Topics</td><td>Type 2 Controversy (Overlooked or Emerging)
- AI use in government
- How should AI be used in the military?
- How much power should the government have in regulating AI?
- Will AI cause governments of opposing ideals to converge?</td><td>Type 4 Controversy (Upcoming, on the Horizon)
- Should AI be allowed to vote?
- Should AI be allowed to be elected as president?
- AI as government
- New forms of government by AI</td></tr>
</table>

50. The AI in Military Controversy

[Decision]

Should AI in Military Be Allowed to Harm Humans? (Automation vs Augmentation 3)

"We Still Have 12 Ships Left"

- General Soon-Shin Lee[150]

5-Line Summary

1. Some may argue AI should be allowed to make its own decisions to harm enemy humans, since it would help increase the chances of winning in modern warfare (Our AI > Enemy Humans)
2. Some may argue AI should not be allowed to make its own decisions to harm enemy humans, since it may eventually lead to the demise of mankind (All Humans > All AI)
3. Giving AI more authority in military by entering Level 2 Adoption may lead to giving AI a relative value system (Friendly Humans > Enemy Humans)
4. From this relative value system, AI may begin to value friendly AI more than enemy humans (Friendly AI > Enemy Humans)
5. If all friendly humans perish or disappear for some reason, then we may not rule out AI will value all humans less than AI (AI > Humans)

Should AGI Be Allowed to Decide to Fatally Harm Humans?

When AI is used in Level 1 Adoption, some humans are in charge so the use of AI in the military would still be considered similar to other types of weapons, with some human ultimately responsible for the actions of AI. However, in Level 2 Adoption, AI will be given the agency to decide for itself. Then there could be no humans directly responsible for a specific action of AI. This "no human can take responsibility" situation may become a major controversy surrounding military applications of AI.

While everyone may agree AI deciding on its own to fatally harm humans is dangerous, the main reason this may be allowed is because of economic reasons; Level 2 Adoption is more efficient. Conceptually, we may distinguish AI robot soldiers in Level 1 AI Adoption as a dependent AI robot soldier, while Level 2 Adoption would be an independent AI robot soldier, even if they are identical in every other way. This means that in Level 1, some human soldier would have to take responsibility for all of the actions of the AI robot soldier. Similar to being given a promotion, the AI soldier robot in Level 2 Adoption would be given the agency to make its own decisions. This would lead to the possibility that the responsibility for some of the actions of Level 2 AI robot soldier may not fall on any human.

Table 50-1: [Decision] Contrasting Ideas on AI Military Use

	AI Should Be Allowed to Harm Humans in Military (Our AI > Enemy Humans)	**AI Should Not Be Allowed to Harm Humans in Military (All Humans > All AI)**
Description	- AI in Level 2 AI Adoption may be allowed to decide on its own to harm humans - AI would in essence consider [Our AI > Enemy Humans]	- AI in Level 2 AI Adoption should not be allowed to decide on its own to harm humans - AI would in essence consider [All Humans > All AI]
Further Categorize	- (Tech Optimists) AI will provide protection against the enemy - (Social Pessimists) If we don't, then they will do it first	- (Tech Pessimists) AI may view every humans as enemy - (Social Optimists) We can convince every other country
Benefits	- May increase chances of winning war	- Safer for all humanity
Risks	- May lead to the destruction of all humanity - If there is no friendly humans left, then AI may consider all humans to be enemies	- May increase the chances of losing war against enemy state (similar to Prisoner's Dilemma)

Why Independent AI Robot Soldiers May Be Allowed

As described in The Last AI, we may consider an extreme end of AI use where a Level 2 Adoption in military would imply that an AI robot may be given the authority, or permission, to fatally harm enemy humans. The AI robot will have to discriminate the value of enemy personnel, which would require a relative value of one human over another. AI may also be required to value AI relative to humans.

To demonstrate, imagine a situation where we have an AI robot soldier facing grave danger from enemy human forces, and a friendly AI robot soldier has just arrived at the scene. Should the arriving AI robot be allowed to attack the human enemy forces to save friendly AI robot? The value instilled in the AI robot would determine the action. If the instilled value is such that all humans come before AI, then the AI cannot attack human enemy forces to save the friendly AI robot. It will have to wait until a friendly human soldier to give direction, or find a different way to contain enemy forces without harming them. Under this value system, military AI robots can only make the decision to attack AI robots of opposing sides, which is good for humans.

However, many people will think this is inefficient, since AI robots in Level 2 Adoption will be limited to battles against other AI; it may be a difference of winning and losing the battle. Some may argue that AI should be allowed to attack enemy humans. In this new value system, AI will differentiate between friendly and enemy humans, such that AI will not only value friendly human more than enemy but also value friendly AI more than enemy humans.

From this scenario, we can surmise that if we take some form of shortcut from the safest premise of "all humans is to be valued more than AI," then people will continue on to try to take the least path of resistance, which is to value friendly AI more than enemy humans. If we draw a diagram of the different value systems, it would look something like the following table.

Table 50-2: Example of the Shortcuts in AI Value Systems[151]

Basic Premise	Detailed Value System
Theoretically Safer	**All Humans > AI**
Taking Shortcuts (Grouping Human Values)	Friendly Humans > Enemy Humans > Friendly AI (Inefficient: AI can only attack other AI)
	Friendly Humans > Friendly AI > Enemy Humans (Efficient, but may be risky for humanity)

51. The AI Voting Controversy

[Decision]

Should Advanced AI Be Allowed to Vote?

"No Taxation without Representation"

\- *James Otis Jr.*

5-Line Summary

1. Some may support AI to vote in elections because AI may make fairer and more informed decisions
2. Some may oppose AI from voting in elections because it may reduce the most important part of humans rights
3. People may have different opinions regarding how to design the sharing of voting rights by assigning different percentages to AI
4. The discussion on AI voting may also be related to AI bias and whether AI should be allowed to prefer some people over others
5. This is a separate topic from whether AI should be allowed to appear in elections by running for president

Why Would Anyone Want AI to Vote?

As AI advances further, AI may begin to make decisions on behalf of humans in making life choices, such as in shopping. As AI become more capable, people may entrust AI to make bigger and more important decisions, such as financial investments, etc. Eventually, some people may think we should let AI make the most important decisions one can make, which would be voting in elections. As we inch closer to Level 4 AI Adoption, we may even face a situation where some people may prefer AI to vote in elections than humans.

- **(For Allowing AI to Vote)** AI would be able to make fairer and more informed decisions than humans; lessen human effort to vote
- **(Against Allowing AI from Voting)** Voting rights are the essence of human rights and taking this away would mean the end of humanity

Note: this question of whether to allow AI voting rights is a separate question from whether AI should be allowed to appear in elections.

The Benefits of Letting AI Vote

The biggest benefit of allowing AI to vote may be that AI may be perceived as fairer than human voters. At first, this concept of letting AI vote may start in less political areas, such as hiring, music contests, sports, or other types of competitions, where AI may make some decisions on judging which humans are better according to some criteria. As time goes by and people become accustomed to letting AI make these types of decisions, people may become more comfortable having AI make more impactful decisions.

Another main benefit is that it will free people from making the effort to vote. Even though voting rights are viewed as a principal means to enforce basic rights, it takes time and effort to make decisions on who to vote.

The Risks of Letting AI Vote

One may think of the ability to vote is the single most power one can have in society, especially in free democratic society. For example, people who cannot vote may be considered to not have any other power at all, at least in the direct sense. This is why we go great measures to determine who can and who cannot vote. One may argue that if we do allow AI to vote, this may be similar to "selling out" your allegiance to humanity, in a concept similar to treason.

Table 51-1: [Decision] Contrasting Ideas on AI Military Use

	AI Should Be Allowed to Vote (AI Optimists)	AI Should Not Be Allowed to Vote (AI Pessimists)
Description	- AI must be allowed to participate in elections as voters - AI would in essence gain suffrage - AI would make fairer and more informed decisions than humans	- AI must not be allowed to participate in elections as voters - AI should not be given suffrage - Voting rights are the essence of human rights; taking this away could mean the end of freedom for humanity
Further Categorize	- (Tech Optimists) AI will bring better election results - (Social Optimists) Allowing AI to vote will enable people to do more useful things - (AI Worshippers) AI should be given higher social standing than regular machines	- (Tech Pessimists) Allowing AI to vote will not improve results - (Social Pessimists) Allowing AI to vote will bring social confusion and dissatisfaction - (Human-First) Voting rights should be limited to humans only
Benefits	- May increase chances of better election results if AI is capable - Humans may not need to put effort into voting	- Safer for all humanity
Risks	- May lead to worse election results if AI is not as capable as necessary	- May lead to worse election results if AI is capable than humans

Notice it may be also possible to "share" voting rights between humans and AI, such that some percentage of all votes come from humans and the rest comes from AI. Which AI will get to vote may also be up for discussion.

Takeaway, Lessons, Summary of the Controversy

This controversy may be considered a part of the line of controversies related to having AI to group people to prefer one group over another. While preference does not equal hostility, it may be a required precursor to a situation where AI considers only a fraction of humanity to be friendly.

52. The AI President Controversy

[Decision]

Should Advanced AI Be Allowed to Run for President?

*"Ask Not What AI Can Do for You,
but What AI Can Do for Your Country"*
- AI JFK[152]

5-Line Summary

1. As AI adoption in government progresses, an AI may eventually be able to replace the leader of the government in Level 4 AI Adoption.
2. Some may support AI to appear in presidential elections because AI may make fairer and more informed decisions as president
3. Some may oppose AI from appearing in presidential elections because it may give too much power to AI if it becomes president
4. The discussion on AI voting may also be related to AI bias and whether AI should be allowed to prefer some people over others
5. This is a separate topic from whether AI should be allowed to vote in elections, or whether AI will replace the whole government system

The Beginning of AI in Government: AI Judges, AI Politicians, AI Officers

AI use in the government may begin in the same manner as AI in the private sector, with AI in augmenting human labor at first, and then successively being given agency, autonomy, and authority in Level 2, 3 and 4 Adoptions.

Review of Sohn's AI Adoption Pyramid in Government

- **Level 1 Adoption:** AI use in government to augment government officers
- **Level 2 Adoption:** AI replacing government workers, such as AI judges, workers in politician's offices, etc.
- **Level 3 Adoption:** AI replacing government sub-organizations, such as AI government-owned enterprises, AI politician offices, etc.
- **Level 4 Adoption:** AI replacing the leader of government, the president, or AI even replacing the government system

Why Would Anyone Want AI as President?

Once AI advances towards replacing humans, at some point it may reach the capability to replace the job of presidency, which we may consider the most important job humans can have. At this stage, some may argue that AI should be allowed to be voted into presidency, while some others may argue the presidency should be reserved for humans.

The main argument of people in support of AI as president may include AI is better than humans at other jobs, so it would be better at running countries. AI would be able to work around the clock, make fairer decisions, and surpass any other human presidents in terms of accomplishments.

Another related topic is the increasing returns to scale of AI adoption, as AI can communicate faster than humans. An organization consisting of AI would have an advantage over human-run organizations due to its speed.

The Risks of Letting AI Become the President

The biggest risk of letting AI replace the most important human job may be the risk of AI turning against humans after it gains the power. In essence, even if AI gains control of the government in a benevolent manner, we cannot be sure that it will continue to be benevolent to humanity.

Note: This question of whether benevolent AI should be allowed to be elected is a separate problem from whether some malevolent AI will try to take over humanity without election.

53. The AI Government Controversy

[Decision]

Government by AI:
Should AI Be Allowed to Take Charge of the Government?

[Forecast]

Will Level 4 AI Governments Lead to Better Society?

"The Buck Stops with AI"

- AI President Truman[153]

5-Line Summary

1. In Level 4 Adoption, AI being elected as the president is not the end; AI may completely overhaul the government system
2. If AI President may be thought of as AI replacing a human role, AI government may be thought of as replacing the human organization
3. Some may argue AI should be allowed to take charge of the government, since AI may design and run a better government
4. Some may argue AI should not be allowed to take charge of the government, since it may take away the freedom of humanity
5. People who would have argued for the same thing still may not do so, based on their perceptions of which world we live in

What If AI Is to Design the Government from Scratch?

This topic of whether to allow for AI Governments in Level 4 Adoption is a slightly different problem than whether AI can become president through elections. While AI President may have the connotation that an AI replaces human president in the job, AI-as-a-government would suggest that AI may invent and install completely new systems or forms of governments.

In essence, AI President replaces one human, while AI Government replaces whole organization of humans. We do not know whether any of the existing governing system is optimal, and the introduction of AI in governance may enable new governing systems to become possible. For example, many countries use the checks and balances system, comprised of the three pillars of government of executive, judiciary, and legislative branch. In governments designed by AI, AI may decide to merge all three, divide them into even more branches, or even make other changes we have not seen or imagined.

Table 53-1: [Decision] Contrasting Ideas on AI Government

	AI Should Be Allowed to Take Charge of Government (AI Optimists)	**AI Should Not Be Allowed to Take Charge of Government (AI Pessimists)**
Description	- Allow Advanced AI to take charge of the government - AI would reconfigure the government for efficiency	- Advanced AI should never be allowed to run government - AI should never be allowed to reconfigure the government
Further Categorize	- (Tech Optimists) AI would have higher performance than humans in running the government - (Social Optimists) AI would solve social problems more fairly - (Equality-Oriented Left-Wing) Everyone equal in front of AI - (Freedom-Oriented Right-Wing) AI will minimize human error	- (Tech Pessimists) AI will never be good enough - (Social Pessimists) AI will bring over-surveillance - (Equality-Oriented Left-Wing) AI will make the current human leader obsolete - (Freedom-Oriented Right-Wing) AI will increase regulations
Benefits	- May be useful for solving long-standing problems or cognitive limits of humans	- Safer option, especially against the possibility of the appearance of rogue AI
Risks	- AI may gain resources on its own to the detriment of humanity	- Countries may fall behind other countries that adopt AI

1. (Fairness) Would AI Government Lead to Effective and Fair Decisions?

AI use in government may be initiated by people who may be attracted by the thinking that AI in government will make it more effective. An example may be the idea that AI will lead to a society where there are no crimes. During Levels 2 and 3 Adoption, the world may see an abundance of materialistic stuff so that people may stop committing crimes for economic reasons. In addition, strong surveillance would make such actions impossible anyway, potentially even preventing it before it happens as in movies. The society may also become a generally safer place, as physical attacks may be prevented or deterred by AI robot police that are placed at the right locations. In essence, it is likely that pretty much every crime humans can conceive may be deterred by some advanced forms of AI that may eventually appear.

At the same time, some people may also be excited about achieving a fair society. An AI judge or public officer will not be swayed by bribery or personal leanings and propaganda. Issues may be considered more rationally, and important issues would get priority. The performance of AI will not be affected by upcoming elections, personal schedules, or health.

Note: a fair society would be a distinct concept from an equal society or a free society.

2. (Competence) Would AI Solve Social Controversies?

Let us review an example from The Last AI. Imagine you are a basketball fan and traveled to Los Angeles to watch a much-anticipated NBA Championship game. Let us say this game is between the two most popular teams at the time, the LA Lakers led by LeBron James and the Golden State Warriors, led by Stephen Curry. To watch this final Game 7, excited fans are yelling and screaming while waiting in long lines to enter the arena. However, to your surprise, when you reach the entrance, you find that there are actually two identical games in two separate arenas that are exactly the same in every way, except this one thing that you have to choose.

1) In the first arena, for the safety of all spectators and players, every single person must be given a firearm before entering
2) In the second arena, for the safety of all spectators and players, everyone must be free of carrying a gun: no guns allowed

To watch this exciting game you must choose between one of these two options. Which one would you choose?

For most readers, even if you are not from countries where firearms are banned, you would be likely choose the second option, where the stadium would be free of dangerous weaponry. You would probably think a packed stadium with highly excitable and potentially drunken fans could easily lead to fights and other altercations. We would be more likely to think that if everyone in the stands has a weapon, then some crazy fan could start shooting at the opposition players or the referees when the game does not go their way.

Now, let us imagine a completely opposite situation. In your job, you need to bring your spouse and your two young children to a month of wilderness camping in a tent in the middle of a dense forest of a famous national park in the US. This park has recently experienced a rapid growth in dangerous bear population, along with other wild predatory animals such as wolves and even newly introduced tigers. During your stay, you are going to encounter several of these hungry beasts. This national park is so vast that the closest help you can find may be at least a couple of hours away. To your surprise, when you reach the entrance you find that there are two versions of exactly the same national parks except for this one thing, and the gatekeeper asks you to choose from the same two options.

1) In the first park, for the safety of all the campers, every single person must be given a firearm before entering
2) In the second park, for the safety of all the campers, everyone must be free of carrying a gun: no guns allowed

To enter this park, you must choose from one of the two options. Which one would you choose?

For this second scenario, even for readers from countries that ban firearms, most people will agree that bringing a firearm to this situation would be safer. If a hungry bear or tiger comes to your tent looking for food, you will not be able to persuade the bear by trying to engage it in a friendly conversation, and you will not be able to holler for help in the middle of nowhere.

In summary, if you read and understood these two scenarios, then you would be likely to agree to the following statements:

1) In a crowded stadium filled with excited fans, it would be safer if everyone did not have firearms
2) In an unpopulated forest filled with hungry bears, it would be safer if everyone did have firearms

Let's say you agree to the above two statements; depending on the situation, it may be safer to either have or do not have firearms. Now, imagine which one of these two conditions is closer to the society you actually live in real life. Is our society more similar to being born and living your whole life inside a densely packed basketball stadium? Or is out society more similar to being born and living your whole life inside a forest filled with dangerous beasts?

If you are from a densely populated country, such as Korea or Japan, or a city, you would be more likely to answer our society is way more similar to living your whole life in a crowded stadium than in a forest. If anything, your everyday commute through subway would be more packed than a stadium. These people will in general also feel that firearms should be banned because one dangerous person could pose a threat to hundreds of innocent people happening to just stand or walk nearby. Costs outweigh benefits.

On the other hand, if you are from a sparsely populated region or country, such as in many parts of the US, even if you are not from the Wild West era, then you may be more likely to feel that living in our society is way more similar to living your whole life in a forest filled with lurking beasts than living in a packed stadium. If anything, you may feel that if an armed burglar enters your house, help will be too far away and only you will be able to save your family. Benefits outweigh costs. Obviously, your view on the issue of gun control would depend on how you view our society.

In the US, the debate on gun control has been going on for decades without satisfying either side. Would an AI government be able to provide solutions to these types of long-lasting debates? Everyone has a worldview different from another person, and this difference comes partly from our experiences and education. It will be hard for people who think we live in a packed stadium to make a persuasive argument to people who think we live in a forest filled with lurking beasts, and vice versa. Around the world, there are numerous policies that cause controversy among the public, where different people have different opinions. For the government, it would be preferable if both of the opposing perspectives could be rationally incorporated into policymaking.

In short, will AI solve all our controversies? If AI could do a better job than humans in creating policies that can satisfy a diverse range of people by becoming the AlphaGo of governing, some people may consider AI a superior option to running the government.

[Side Note] The 6 Levels of Autonomous Government (from The Last AI)
In a format similar to the well-known Six Levels of Autonomous Vehicles by SAE, we may categorize the levels of AI-led governments.

Level 0 (No AI): AI is not adopted, or only tested out at the individual level.

Level 1 (Augment Human Officers): AI helps humans, and humans will be in charge of government roles. Levels 0 and 1 of autonomous governments would be a type of Level 1 AI adoption.

Level 2 (Specific Roles): AI will be able to replace specific government roles of humans, as in Level 2 AI Adoption.

Level 3 (Specific Organizations): AI will be in charge of specific organizations within national and local governments, such as departments, ministry, or government-sponsored entities. This would be a type of Level 3 AI Adoption.

Levels 4 (Human-Elected AI Government): whether AI taking charge of the government would require the consent of humans.

Level 5 (Self-Elected AI Government): AI may take charge of the government regardless of human consent. In other words, we may consider Level 4 autonomous governments to represent or serve humans, while Level 5 autonomous governments may also rule over humans. The caveat is that it would be up to the AI, not humans, to decide whether it will rule or represent.

Table 53-2: The 6 Levels of Autonomous Governments

<table>
<tr><th>Autonomous Government</th><th>Level 0</th><th>Level 1</th><th>Level 2</th><th>Level 3</th><th>Level 4</th><th>Level 5</th></tr>
<tr><td>How AI is deployed</td><td>AI not adopted or only at personal level</td><td>AI is adopted to augment human officers</td><td>AI takes over particular roles</td><td>AI takes over particular orgs</td><td>AI take over with human consent</td><td>AI can take over regardless of human consent</td></tr>
<tr><td>AI Adoption Level</td><td colspan="2">Level 1: Humans in charge of Roles</td><td>Level 2: AI in charge of Roles</td><td>Level 3: AI in charge of Orgs</td><td colspan="2">Level 4: AI in Charge of Government</td></tr>
<tr><td>Govern by AI</td><td colspan="2">AI can only help humans represent or rule</td><td colspan="2">AI Representation limited in scope</td><td>AI gov't that represents humans</td><td>AI gov't that can rule over humans</td></tr>
</table>

[Side Note] Potential First-Mover Advantage of Level 4 AI Government

Instead of examining which country will reach AGI, we may consider how one country may reach Level 4 Adoption, or AI-led government. Similar to the Arms Race during the 1980s between the US and the Soviet Union, we may think of the race to Level 4 Adoption as a competition of opposing regimes. In this scenario, we may think of why a government may want to enter Level 4 quickly, and whether a particular approach may help advance AI faster.

The first reason why countries would want to reach Level 4 AI Adoption earlier is because AI may actually run the government much more efficiently than humans. Principles or perspective that we may apply in advanced forms of AI adoption may be summarized as the following:

1. (Observation 1) When AI cannot automatically innovate, it would be more advantageous for humans to intervene or cooperate in augmented innovation
2. (Observation 2) Once AI can automatically innovate, it would be advantageous for humans to not give specific directions since AI may be able to consider more number of options than humans
3. (Conclusion) To maximize outcome of advanced AI adoption, AI must be able and allowed to decide on its own rather than have some human give directions; this may be thought of as "climbing the AI Pyramid"

If a country that is already ahead of the competition also reaches Level 4 AI adoption first, it may be able to widen the gap. For countries that are behind, early entry to Level 4 adoption may provide a means to level the competitive landscape to catch up to the more advanced countries. A similar example of this situation happened in the telecommunications industry when several of the less developed countries decided to skip building landline infrastructure to leap over to the wireless network and leveraged this network to catch on other aspects of the economy, such as allowing mobile money transfer when the majority of the population did not have access to banking infrastructure.

The second reason may be considered a type of "first-mover advantage." The first-mover advantage refers to strategic advantage of leading the market; an alternative strategy is the fast-follower strategy. For example, being earlier in Level 4 AI adoption may help those nations set the international rules to their advantage in some way, such as setting new world standards in the areas of economic, military, or foreign policy.

DIRECTION 7 (NORTHEAST):

AI AND THE WORLD

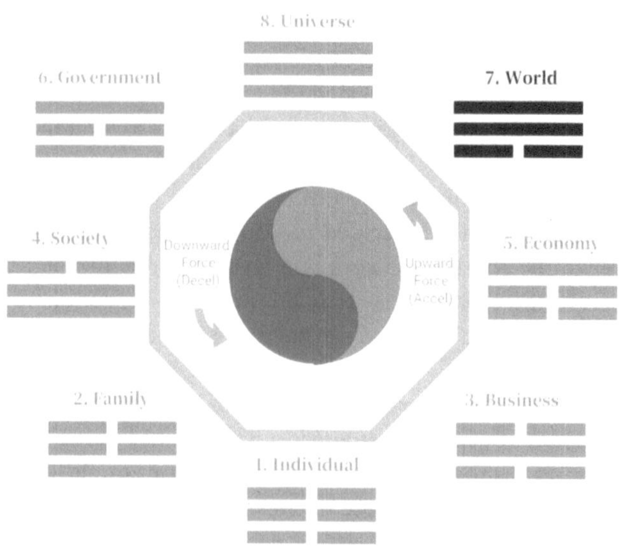

Can the World Come Together and Find Common Grounds on AI?

Readers may have noticed that the scope of controversies may expand as AI advances and the analysis becomes longer term. In this section, we will review some of the controversies that deal with AI and the world. This topic may deal with how AI may influence humanity at the international and global scale, such as AI and the competition of countries, or AI gaining the authority to exist outside the jurisdictions of any other human-led countries, in a concept called AI Countries.

(Technology/Forecasts) Will AI advance beyond human control? Will Self-Initiated AI try to gain independence?

(Technology/Decisions) Should we accelerate or decelerate AI development?

(Adoption/Forecasts) Will advanced forms of AI decide to start own country?

(Adoption/Decisions) Would AGI prefer certain ideology? Will AI cause appearance of new dictators? Should AI countries be allowed? Will AI cause mass exodus?

Table D7-1: The AI and the World Controversy Matrix

		Object of Controversy	
		AI Itself (Developer Perspective)	**AI in Relation to Its Surroundings (User Perspective)**
Nature of Controversy	**Forecasts**	- Will Self-Initiated AI try to gain independence? - Will AI advance beyond human control? - Will We Be Able to Control AGI and ASI in Level 2 Adoption?	- Would advanced forms of AI decide to start its own country?
	Decisions	- Should AI development be accelerated or decelerated?	- How much should countries work together in decisions regarding AI? - Should AI countries be allowed?

Will Advanced AI Decide to Start Its Own Country?
We may create the following AI Controversy Type Matrix.

(Imminent Controversies) Shorter-term, the most prominent topic today may be the international cooperation on AI regulations, since some form of coordination may be required if any AI regulation is to be effective.

(Emerging Controversies) Emerging issues may be reaching global consensus on AI use in military and government, since countries may have different incentives in this topic.

(Non-Imminent Controversies) The most prominent topic in this direction may be the possibility of ASI advancing beyond human control. The consequences may have already captured attention of the public.

(Upcoming Controversies) Longer-term, if using AI as Government in AI Adoption Level 4 becomes more prevalent, the topic of whether "AI countries" should be allowed may emerge as the most important topic that the humanity will have to deal with, since creation of such AI may mean AI would compete against all of humanity.

Table D7-2: The Global Governance (Direction 7 - Northeast) Type Matrix

		Issue Horizon	
		Shorter-Term	**Longer-Term**
How Well People are Currently Aware	**More Popular Topics**	**Type 1 Controversy (Imminent)** - How much should countries work together in decisions regarding AI?	**Type 3 Controversy (Non-Imminent)** - Will AI advance beyond human control?
	Not Yet Popular Topics	**Type 2 Controversy (Overlooked or Emerging)** - Should AI development be accelerated or decelerated?	**Type 4 Controversy (Upcoming, on the Horizon)** - Should AI be allowed to start its own country? - Will Self-Initiated AI try to gain independence

54. The ASI Controllability Controversy

[Forecast]

Will Humans Be Able to Control AGI and ASI?

"Wag the Dog"[154]

5-Line Summary

1. Some may argue humans will lose control of AGI or ASI, since advanced AI may a mind of its own
2. (Technological) Some may argue humans will be able to keep control of AGI and ASI, because we may create other AI that can control AI
3. (Spiritual) Some may argue humans will be able to keep control of AGI and ASI, because advanced AI will be benevolent to humanity
4. (Sociological) Some may argue humans will be able to keep control of AGI and ASI, because we have social means to control AI
5. We may think of the risk of AGI that is uncontrollable as refusing to adhere to the social rules of human-led countries, even starting AI countries

(Optimists) We Will Figure Out How to Control ASI

When AI surpasses human capabilities, some may fear that we could lose control over AI. Some others may contend that we would still have control over AI even if AI surpasses humans in capabilities. There may be a variety of different reasons why some people may think it would be possible to control AI that advances beyond humans capabilities.

First approach is technological; as AI becomes more advanced the technology to control AI will advance with it, such as AI that specializes in controlling AI will become available. From this point of view, there will always be some AI in Level 1 or Level 2 Adoption that oversees AI in Level 3 and Level 4 Adoption.

Second approach is spiritual; some people may think that as AI becomes more advanced it will become more benevolent to humanity. For example, some may believe advancement in AI means AI will become more and more emphatic, such that when AI that surpasses humans come to exist, it will mean AI will become even more benevolent to humanity, not less. There would be other people who disagree with this notion of advancement in AI.

The third approach is sociological; one of the methods of control among humans is social contracts, such as rules and regulations, or other laws. From this line of thinking, some may think that autonomous AI may agree to abide by some rules and regulations just as humans do.

(Pessimists) What If It Turns Out AGI Will Have a Mind of Its Own?

People who worry about the AGI controllability may have the opposite notion about what would happen if AI surpasses humanity in capabilities.

If AGI or ASI is controllable by humans, it would indicate such advanced AI may be used in Levels 1 and 2 AI Adoption. An example of this concept may include AI butler often seen in movies that provide support for human characters. If AGI or ASI is not directly controllable by humans, in the sense that AI will refuse to work in Levels 1 or 2 AI adoption, it could still be possible AGI or ASI may agree to abide by the laws and other regulations of a country, making it Level 3 AI adoption or a partial type of Level 4 AI adoption. This would indicate humanity as a whole will have some control over AI.

However, if AGI or ASI refuses to follow any human-led social agreements at all, it may renounce any jurisdiction of any country to even start an "AI country." This could even lead to conflicts between humans and AI.

For example, if humans disagreed to abide by laws of a country they are in, then they could be prosecuted. There could even be some type of a war among countries or dissidents within a country who disagree with the others.

Note: This conflict is a different kind of controversy from misusing AI that leads to the destruction of humanity. There would be intent on the part of AGI or ASI to not follow the rules set by humans.

1) **(Optimists)** We will be able to control AI, which means we will be able to deploy AGI and ASI in Level 2 AI adoption, where humans can have the ultimate say in what AI does
2) **(Pessimists)** We will lose control of AI, which means AGI or ASI will refuse to be deployed correctly in Level 2 AI adoption, leading to a situation where we wind up in unwanted Level 3 or Level 4 AI adoption

Table 54-1: [Forecast] Contrasting Ideas on Controlling AGI

	Humans Will Be Able to Control ASI (ASI Optimists)	**Humans Will Not Be Able to Control ASI (ASI Pessimists)**
Description	- Humans will be able to control AGI and ASI - AI will help commit crimes more than solve crimes	- AI will refuse to abide by rules set by humans - AI will intentionally leave human jurisdiction
Categorize	- (ASI Optimists) ASI being smart does not imply ASI will be out of control - (ASI Social Optimists) We will be able to find social means to control ASI such as laws even if it is smarter than all of humanity - (AI Pessimists) Even ASI will not be much smarter than us, which would mean humans should be able to control ASI	- (ASI Pessimists) Once ASI becomes smarter than humans, it will even be able to feign control - (AI Social Pessimists) ASI will not obey human-made laws - (ASI Optimists) The smarter ASI gets, it will get harder to control AI
More likely to Support Decisions	- Promoting AI development and adoption	- Strengthen regulation to slow down AI development and adoption
More likely to Oppose Decisions	- Regulations that stifle AI development and adoption	- Broader general adoption of AI

55. The AI Ideology Controversy

[Forecast]

Will AI Benefit or Favor Certain Ideology?

**Which Would AI Help More,
Communist or Free Democratic Forms of Governments?**

*"All Animals Are Equal,
but Some Animals Are More Equal than Others"*

- In Animal Farm by George Orwell

5-Line Summary

1. We may not rule the possibility that advanced AI may benefit or prefer one ideology more than the other
2. AI may help equality-oriented regimes, such as communist countries, by helping with surveillance or central planning, etc.
3. AI may help freedom-oriented regimes, such as free democratic countries, by helping individuals gain the capability to analyze
4. AI may hinder equality oriented regimes, by helping dissenters gain more capabilities
5. AI may hinder freedom oriented regimes, because AI would be more powerful when resources are pulled together

Which Will AI Benefit More? Communist or Free Democratic Governments?

We may calculate the proportion of the decisions made by the government to all decisions within the country as a number between 0% and 100%. If the government prioritizes solving the inequality within the country then the percentage of the government's decision within all decisions in the country will become closer to 100%. On the other side, if the government prioritizes to ensure the freedom of everyone in the country then the proportion of the decisions made by the government will become closer to 0% of all decisions made in the country.

Using this spectrum as the measuring stick, we may categorize all regimes around the world into two groups:

- **Equality First:** Prefer to increase the percentage of the decisions made by the government to solve social problems. May be referred to as Communism, Socialism or similar ideals
- **Freedom First:** Prefer to decrease the percentage of the decisions made by the governments to solve social problems. May be referred to as Free Democracy, Libertarian or similar ideals

1) How AI May Help Equality-Oriented Regimes

A major difference between living in communist regimes and other countries may be that "communist regimes need to carry out surveillance over its people." Readers may have heard or saw a comic strip where "a secret police is watching over someone from behind, who in turn is being watched from behind by someone else, who in turn is being watched by someone else." In a communist regime, surveillance is necessary to keep everyone in line and not express their own opinions that are against the regime.

The official name of the communist North Korea is The Democratic People's Republic of Korea; it claims to be the pinnacle of democracy, where everyone agrees with the government 100%. Whereas in most other democratic countries reaching a majority, or more than 50%, would be enough, 100% is better because it proves they have a supreme leader. Their logic suggests that since all of the people agree with the government, their government must be superior to the countries where only about half of the people agree. Whether this sounds better is up for each of the readers to decide. What is relevant is that to make this version of democracy work, in totalitarian or communistic countries the government needs to inspect and keep everyone in line, to prevent them from acting out or speaking their opinions that may be against the regime. In other words, there is a need to limit the freedom of speech and actions to keep people from having other ideas. It may be thought of as "what you don't think can't hurt you" type of approach. An example of problem arising from such surveillance and inspection may be the case of Otto Wambier,[155] a college student at the University of Virginia at the time when he visited North Korea, apprehended for allegedly trying to sneak away a picture on the wall of his hotel and later succumbed to injuries sustained in captivity.

Imagine AI enables the North Korean regime to watch and evaluate every action of every person in the country. AI may enable Kim Jung Un to single-handedly control the actions of every other person within the country down to every minute of their lives. Considering how much effort and resources are needed to keep the current multiple layers of human-run surveillance systems working, this may be welcomed.

Attempts to develop such systems already exist in other countries including China, where a social credit system reviews and block what you post or read online and even identify passengers of transit systems and deny access to people with low scores using AI facial recognition. While residents of other countries may find it hard to imagine being the subject of these surveillance, these systems are becoming weaved into the fabric of some societies so that people would take them for granted, even to a point where they would believe these systems are important in keeping them safe from danger. In summary, AI may help the government get bigger and exert more power over people.

Table 55-1: How AI May Help or Hinder Equality-Oriented Governments

AI Helps Communistic Governments	AI Hinders Communistic Governments
- Control people (Surveillance) - Central economic planning - Increasing return of centrally allocated resource	- AI may help dissenting population

2) How AI may Help Freedom-Oriented Regimes

On the other end of the spectrum, AI technology may help the government reduce footprint by reducing staff in government operations or selling assets, leading to smaller government and lower taxes. In these countries, AI may be used to ensure people gain more freedom from the government, even to a point where the private sector may gain the power to carry out endeavors previously thought to require government intervention; AI may lower the need for government to step in for utilities and infrastructure. An example of this line of thinking may include the DOGE led by Elon Musk.

Table 55-2: How AI May Help or Hinder Freedom-Oriented Governments

AI Helps Freedom-Oriented Governments	AI Hinders Freedom-Oriented Governments
- Increases the capability of individuals to analyze information, potentially leading to less gov't intervention	- AI may be more powerful when resource is centrally located - AI may increase inequality beyond acceptable levels

3) Conclusion: AI Will Help Each Regime Pursue Their Own Goals
To generalize, development in AI technology will strengthen the movement towards the idealistic directions of each of the systems of governments.

For societies that seek the government to have closer to 100% power over the country, which may include communist, socialist, or totalitarian societies that may generally be referred to as the "left," the advancement in AI technology will help them increase the power of the government. To ease understanding, we may also refer to this direction as seeking "Equality" among people.

For societies that seek the government to have closer to 0% power over the country, which may include free democracy, individualistic societies that may generally be referred to as the "right," the advancement in AI technology will help them decrease the power of the government. To ease understanding, we may also refer to this as seeking maximum "Freedom" of individuals.

To conclude, AI will help societies reach their idealistic situation regardless of where they aim to be, similar to reaching different versions of Utopia. Would reaching these Utopias be a good thing or a bad thing? Would one version of Utopia be better than another? It will be left up to the people of the time to decide.

Note: This would be a different question from whether AI governments could lead to higher efficiency by changing the system of government, or whether AI governments could build towards a society where people are both equal and free, as described in The Last AI.

Will AGI or ASI Prefer Certain Ideology Over Another?
In Level 4 AI Adoption or even before, we may have to face the question of whether advanced AI will prefer one ideology over another. This is a slightly different question from whether AGI will be biased. The problem is that we cannot be sure whether one regime is superior to another, and that AGI may find out the "real truth." In short, we cannot be sure the unbiased outcome of AGI converging towards the truth would mean one ideology will be preferred.

Possibility of an Anti-Regime AI or AI Preferring an Opposite Ideal
AI may also become detrimental to the regimes. AI may unexpectedly gain some form of anti-regime tendencies. Imagine there are two Government AIs in Level 4 Adoption, one developed by a communist and the other in the free world, leading to an AI Communist Government and AI Free Government. The AI Communist Government will seek equality as the main goal, while the AI Free Government will pursue maximizing individual freedom as the main goal. We would expect the two will act differently from each other.

However, advancements in AI may lead to decreased relationship between the data used to train the AI and the conclusion AI reaches. This may increase risks for users with specific goals. Generally, we would expect AI trained using data from a communist society would lean towards communism, while AI trained with data in liberal society would lean towards free democracy. But after AI reaches a certain level, AI may develop its own conclusions regardless of the leanings of the data used to train it or the intentions of the developer. For example, an AI trained in a communist country may turn out to prefer freedom, while an AI government in a free democracy may turn the country into a communistic country. If this kind of event occurs, then the AI would lead the society to the opposite of the intended direction of humans. These may be considered a type of misalignment, or "Off-Path" or "Off-Track" AI.

Because it would be hard to predict beforehand the probability of such appearance of "Anti-Regime AI," current regimes would have a big reason to be cautious about adopting AI in government. In some sense, moving to Level 4 AI adoption may mean "giving up on current regime," such that the regime of the country will be determined by AI, not humans.

56. The AI Ideology Convergence Controversy

[Forecast]

Will AI Cause Regimes of Opposing Ideals to Converge?

"All Roads Lead to Rome"

- Alain de Lille[156]

5-Line Summary

1. AI may lead opposing ideals to converge towards one another similar to finding a new balance or an equilibrium
2. AI may complement the weaknesses of each regime
3. In equality-oriented regimes such as communist states, people may call for concentrating power to an AI instead of humans
4. In freedom-oriented regimes such as free democratic states, calls to nationalize AI may gain ground due to overwhelming inequality
5. In the economy, AI may make central planning more feasible, reduce the impact of competition on innovation, and increase monopolies

Will AI Cause Opposing Regimes to Converge to a Similar-Looking Society?
When we divide the types of regimes around the world according to how much of the decision is made by the government, the regimes that seek equality may move towards making 100% of the decisions within the country, and regimes that seek freedom may move towards making 0% of the decisions within the country.

We may examine how AI governments may move towards some form of equilibrium, where the AI is not seeking equality or freedom over another, but the most efficient way to run the government. We may examine the possibility of the "convergence of the regimes of governments" with the progression of AI adoption in government. We will examine the possibility of the "convergence of countries" in a separate controversy.

As described in The Last AI, this convergence of two regimes of opposing ideals would be distinct from the concept of the Social Utopia, where each ideal of freedom and equality will be fully realized. The convergence of ideals would be more of a compromise between freedom and equality to find a balance, as neither ideal will be fully realized. It may be a way to reach a practical maximizing point, as the AI-led government seeks to gain more efficiency.

Increased Calls for Alterations to Each Regime
AI may grow demand for changes to how each regime functions. This would apply to both communist and free democratic countries.

Communist Regime: the nature of requiring a centrally planned system leads to power to be concentrated to a single person. If AI is given this power, then "everyone will be equal in front of AI" kind of argument could be made.

"Concentrating power to an AI would lead to a more equal society"

Free Democratic Regime: AI may cause a large disparity between the haves and the have-nots, to a point where only a few people may take control of the most of the wealth. More people may demand AI to be nationalized so that the wealth generated by AI could be used for the public good.

"Nationalizing AI would lessen the inequality caused by AI adoption"

As these demand for changes increase, regimes with the opposite ideals may progress towards a common direction.

How AI May Help Complement the Weaknesses of Each Regime

In each of the regimes, AI adoption would provide new opportunities to reduce the perceived negative aspects of each regime.

Communist Country: AI could ease the burden on surveillance on people to a level where it does not get in the way of everyday life, instead of being the main focus of everyday life. Surveillance capabilities may become so good at predicting such that it may reduce the overall levels of required surveillance.

Free Democratic Country: competition and lack of support for the weak have been perceived as a weakness. While AI ownership without any adjustments would lead to an even larger diversion between the haves and the have-nots, the perceived unfairness may force the society to move towards government ownership of AI or freeing AI unto itself. As the proportion of AI contribution in the economy rises, the society may become more likely to redistribute the value created by AI through the government.

The Impact of AI on Economy May Cause Both Regimes to Converge

Reaching Level 5 Autonomous Companies may lead to the following changes:

1. *Managing a Centrally Planned Economy May Become Feasible and More Efficient*
2. *The Impact of Competition on Innovation May Decrease*
3. *Monopoly or Near-Monopoly May Increase*

We may think of the changes to be headed in the following three directions:

1) As more of the economy is taken over by AI, the whole economy may resemble a centrally-planned economy with increased consolidation and convergence. This may add contrasting pressures towards either the "privatization of the government," or the "nationalization of AI."
2) Since AI may integrate the nature of competition internally, the advantages brought by competition may decrease, lessening the need for free markets
3) The need for the government to address monopolies may increase as the value created by AI in monopolies increases.

Either way, given these forces of changes in Level 3 Adoption regarding how the economy works, the progress of AI adoption may lead to a situation where the economies of different regimes to look more and more similar to one another with increased centralization and concentration of capabilities without negative impact on innovation.

Potential Areas for Governments of Both Regimes to Converge

The demand for changes for both regimes can be summarized in the next table. In both regimes, the direction of change may be to move towards AI Adoption Level 4 and the government owning AI.

Policy on AI governments: Both regimes may converge toward introducing the AI government, even though for different reasons.

- In societies where equality comes first and prefers the government to make more decisions, the AI government may be viewed as a means to achieve equality among humans since "all humans will be equal in front of the AI."
- In societies where freedom comes first and prefers the government to make fewer decisions, the AI government may be viewed as another way to boost the efficiency of the government.

However, the actual introduction may be hindered by who is currently in charge at the time of these discussions, since if a dictator is in charge, introducing an AI government would mean giving up the power. In these cases, some form of disruption, such as a severe economic hardship, may be required before Level 4 AI adoption could be reached. Comparatively, liberalistic countries may have more incentive to reach Level 4 Adoption.

Policy on the government ownership of AI: the equality-first regimes will implement the policy as default, since personal ownership is not allowed already. On the other hand, liberalistic countries may choose to nationalize AI as a response to increased economic inequality, but there may be other options as described in previous chapter such as allowing AI to gain ownership of other properties.

Table 56-1: Comparison of Changes to Each Types of Regime

	Equality-First Regime (Government Decide 100%)	**Freedom-First Regime (Government Decide 0%)**	**Comparison of the Two**
Policy on AI Government	Positive 'All Humans Equal in front of AI'	Positive 'AI Government Leads to More Efficiency'	Both May Converge to Introduce AI Governments
Policy on Gov't Owning AI	Gov't Would Own AI by Default	Gov't May Own AI to Offset Job Loss and Monopolies	Both May Converge to let the Gov't Own AI

57. The AI Country Controversy

[Decision]

Should AI Be Allowed to Start Its Own Country?

[Forecast]

Will Advanced AI Start Its Own Country?

"By the AI, of the AI, for the AI"

- AI President Lincoln

5-Line Summary

1. We may think of AI countries as a self-sufficient AI or a group of AI that is not under any jurisdiction of any other countries
2. Some may argue that AGI or some advanced AI may decide to declare freedom and start its own country
3. If such AI countries com into existence, humanity may be at risk because we would be competing against AI for resources or face war
4. This is in concept distinct from a rogue AI trying to take over a country, since AI is trying to leave the country
5. Humans may also find some use in forming AI Paper Countries, which would be an AI country founded by humans for some purpose

What Is an AI Country and Why Would an AI Want One?

In entering the Level 3 Adoption, the controversy would be whether firms solely comprised of AI or AI-led firms should be allowed to compete against firms led by humans. In entering the Level 4 AI Adoption, the controversy may be extended to whether countries led by AI should be allowed to compete against countries led by humans. Furthermore, if an AI is allowed to run countries, then it may open the door for the appearance of a country comprised solely of AI, without any humans at all.

Once we have some form of self-initiated AI, we cannot rule out AI may seek to attain freedom by declaring its own country. This provides AI with the benefit of not being under the jurisdiction of any other countries. We already have humans who try to find ways to get out of a national jurisdiction by going offshore to tax havens or to international waters. We may call this type of situation where an AI does not fall into any jurisdiction of a country as an "AI Country," where the founding fathers of the country may be thought of as AI. It would be led by AI, and may or may not allow human constituents.

An "AI Country" may be considered a type of Level 4 AI Adoption in the AI Pyramid framework, or Level 5 Autonomous Government in the 6 Levels of Autonomous Governments framework.

Table 57-1: The AI Country Controversy Matrix

		AI Country Initiated by AI (Technological Perspective)	
		Yes (Replace)	**No (Augment)**
AI Country Desired by Humans (Social Perspective)	**Yes**	**Type 3 AI Country** (No Conflict) - AI create AI Country with human approval to co-exist	**Type 2 AI Country** (No Conflict) - Humans may want to create AI Paper Country
	No	**Type 4 AI Country** (Conflict) - Rogue AI Country against human desires	**Type 1 No AI Country** (No Conflict) - AI Country does not exist

Type 1: No AI Country
This would be where we are now.

Type 2 AI Country: "AI Paper Countries"
Similar to how paper companies or special-purpose companies (SPCs) may be formed in the beginning of Level 3 Adoption, we may expect paper countries or special-purpose countries in the early stages of Level 4 Adoption. These paper countries may even only notionally exist on paper or virtually in the form of cyber countries without real assets or resources. While these special-purpose countries or paper countries may not appear to hold significant importance in today's world, they may be able to provide values that may be unlocked with more advanced AI. One of the benefits of these notional countries may be how these could help one person become a member of multiple countries without having to move across borders.

Type 3 AI Country: "Human-Approved AI Countries"
In this situation, AI countries would receive approval of humans in the other countries, such that human-led and AI-led countries can co-exist. We may think of situations where even if AI is outside of the jurisdiction of humans, it may agree to abide by some rules formed by an international body of governance, or some type of human-AI alliance that may be similar to the UN.

Type 4 AI Country: "Rogue AI Countries"
In this situation, we may think AI countries as appearing without the approval of other human-led countries, such as an AI running away to a remote island or middle of the sea to declare independence. The potential danger of these rogue AI states may increase as these AI may gain more resources.

More Related Topics for Readers to Consider

- Division of Power: How will AI Countries or AI Governments divide power? (Humans vs AI, Humans vs Humans, AI vs AI)

Should AI Be Allowed to Start Its Own Country? (= Humanity vs AI)
Should AI Countries be allowed to compete against human-led countries? In Level 3 Adoption, the discussion was whether AI Companies should be allowed to compete against firms led by humans. Using the same logic, we may examine whether a country solely comprised of AI should be allowed to compete against countries with human leaders and constituents.

How Would the Values Create by AI Countries Be Assigned?
In Level 1 Adoption, the value created by AI would go to the worker. In Level 2, when AI replaces individual humans, the value created by AI would go to the firms that previously employed the humans. In Level 3 AI Adoption when AI replaces individual firms, the value create by AI would be reverted to the country where these firms are located, so that it would also be likely this would be allowed. From these examples, we may surmise that the main reason why society would allow AI to compete against humans or firms is that the value created by AI would be assigned to a social entity that takes its place above the particular competition involving AI.

However, when we extrapolate on this notion, then in Level 4 Adoption when AI replaces individual countries, the value created by AI may only be assigned to a social organization that is above individual countries, maybe "the world" or "the earth," etc. This supra-national identity may be similar in concept to the United Nations but with more capabilities. Since such organization does not yet exist, it may become a prerequisite for AI Countries to appear. If AI Countries appear without the relevant supra-national organization, then it may become a threat to other human-led countries, similar to how AI Companies could be a threat to human-led companies.

Similar to how running a company is like being in a war, running a country is also like being in a war, even when not being in an actual one. If AI-led countries offer much higher standards of living and a better place to live in general, then more people would want to immigrate to the country, which could lead to a positive cycle that could be compared to winning in war.

What people would be most interested in AI-only countries is the potential for the competition of AI against humans, especially war. If AI-only countries are allowed to come into existence, and AI-only armies appear, then it may pose a significant threat to humanity. Since we also cannot rule out the possibility of an actual war, we will examine this topic at a later controversy.

58. The AI Dictatorship Controversy

[Forecast]

What If Some People Try to "Take Over the World" Using AI?

"We Hold the World Ransom for . . . One Million Dollars"

- Dr. Evil from movie Austin Powers

5-Line Summary

1. Villains typically fail because they lack the resources and capabilities required to "take over the world"
2. Some may be worried that an advanced AI may one day take over our society and become an "eternal dictator"
3. We may analyze this risk by considering the scope of influence of AI adoption and the level of AI asymmetry (AI Dictator Risk Matrix)
4. The lowest risk would occur when the level of technological asymmetry and the level of AI adoption are both low
5. The highest risk would occur when the level of technological asymmetry and the sphere of AI influence are both high

Can A New Dictator Using AI Ever Appear?

(Low Sphere of Influence) Why Most Villains Fail

In movies, we often see villains that try to take over the world. For Example, in the WB animation series Pinky and the Brain, the main character, a lab mouse that became smart as humans, claims in every episode to "try to take over the world." When we observe these villain characters, most of them fail. If we are to generalize why they fail, it may come down to "the villains lack the resources and productivity to take over the world against the good characters." We may think of this as having a low sphere of influence.

Even in reality, villains tend to be in the minority, and this lack of numbers ultimately leads to failures in the long term because the villains cannot have sustainable advantage over the good guys, or at least we hope so. From this observation, we may hypothesize that "if villains try to take over the world with enough resources and productivity, they may be able to actually do so."

(Asymmetric Productivity) The Probability of Success for Villains with AI

We live in a society where the increase in economic imbalance is leading to few people controlling increasingly more share of the economy[157] in a "rich get richer, poor get poorer" situation. With advancements in AI, the imbalance may get even more accentuated, as AI may bring exponentially higher return. As an example, a handful of people with an asymmetric AI may amass wealth that is more than the sum of the rest of the world. If something similar happens, this may be a significant threat to the well-being of the world and world peace.

By examining the dimensions of the technological perspective, or the level of AI asymmetry, and the social perspective, or the sphere of influence, we may think of the AI dictator risk using the following matrix:

Table 58-1: The AI Dictator Risk Matrix

<table>
<tr><th colspan="2" rowspan="2"></th><th colspan="2">Sphere of AI Influence
(Social Perspective)</th></tr>
<tr><th>Low</th><th>High</th></tr>
<tr><td rowspan="2">Level of AI Asymmetry (Technological Perspective)</td><td>High</td><td>Moderate-to-High Risk
to Humanity
(Risk Profile 3)</td><td>High Risk
to Humanity
(Risk Profile 4)</td></tr>
<tr><td>Low</td><td>Low Risk
to Humanity
(Risk Profile 1)</td><td>Low-to-Moderate Risk
to Humanity
(Risk Profile 2)</td></tr>
</table>

Side Note: The Scope of Humans Affected by AI in Leadership Roles

Let us consider the scope of humans that AI can take charge of while in different types of leadership roles. In Level 2 Adoption, AI may take charge of one or a limited number of humans as a leader of a team or a department. In Level 3, the number of humans affected by an AI may increase to be in the hundreds or even in the tens of thousands. In Level 4, the number would further increase to everyone in the country, possibly in the hundreds of thousands to billions. Additionally, while in Level 4, AI may influence people of other countries in cases of war, so there could be possibility of AI affecting all of humanity in Level 4 Adoption.

1. *AI takes charge over 1 individual human → AI that hires humans*
2. *AI takes charge over a small to intermediate number of humans → AI CEO*
3. *AI takes charge over a large number of humans in country → AI Government*
4. *AI takes charge over a large number of humans in other countries → War*

We may organize the situations as shown in the following table, and classify each case by whether AI is friendly to humans.

From this table, we may infer that higher AI Adoption Levels equates to influencing more number of humans. In Level 4 Adoption, the influence may spread to all of humanity. This indicates higher AI Adoption levels exposes humanity to increased risks to a particular AI. We may compare this situation to reaching a championship game in sports.

Table 58-2: Scope of AI Impact by AI Friendliness[158]

		Relationship of AI to Humans	
		AI is Friendly	**AI is Hostile**
Scope of AI Impact (Inverse AI Pyramid)	**Scope Level 1 (1 or Several People)**	AI Leads Humans (Level 2 Adoption)	AI Deceives Humans
	Scope Level 2 (Small to Medium Number of People)	AI CEO (Level 3 Adoption)	Hostile Merger by an AI-Led Company
	Scope Level 3 (Large Number of People, Thousands ~ Billions)	Elected AI Government (Level 4 Adoption)	Involuntarily Formed AI Government
	Scope Level 4 (People in Other Countries, All of Humanity)	Depends on Situation: Voluntary Annexation, Immigration, etc.	War

59. The AI Exodus Controversy (Inequality of Countries)

[Forecast]

Will AI Cause Mass Exodus to Other Countries?

"I Believe AI Can Fly"

- AI Kelly[159]

5-Line Summary

1. Some may argue advancements in AI may lead to an even larger divergence of countries, where one or a few countries offer incomparable standards of living
2. This may cause mass exodus of people looking for better lives
3. Meanwhile, the advanced countries may not want more immigrants because countries may no longer need extra human labor
4. Instead of exodus, people in some countries may argue for voluntary annexation, since land and other resources may still be valuable
5. On the other end of the spectrum, AI may lead people in some countries may decide to go their own way to divide up the country

Will There Be Consolidation and Convergence of Countries?

In today's world, we have a wide disparity of the levels in the development of economies. Because reaching higher levels of AI adoption would depend on the development of AI technology, only a few select countries may enjoy the contribution of AI especially at the beginning of Level 2 Adoption. This in effect may strengthen the already large gap in the standards of living.

Potential for the Consolidation and Convergence of Countries

Previously, we examined how AI may lead to the convergence of regimes. If we expect consolidation and convergence of companies from AI adoption, then a similar force may work on countries for consolidation as well. In one direction, countries could merge. Countries may face higher pressure to perform for its constituents, and unsatisfied citizens may call for dismantling the regime or the country itself by merging with a better country. Similar to how immigrants and people seeking asylum try to move to another country to find a better life, if the majority of a country's population looks to do the same, they may just give up on the country and use it as an asset for trading. This scenario may make sense if population or land has value.

Potential for the Division and Divergence of Countries

In the other direction, another potential is the division of countries, where AI may spark new countries to form. For example, some unsatisfied factions of a country may decide to secede and form a new country. Because human labor would not be as important in determining the power of a country, countries or regimes may no longer care as much about keeping a high population, even though the land may still be valuable.

Table 59-1: The AI Country Inequality Impact Matrix

		Quantitative Impact of Inequality of Countries (Technological Perspective)	
		Decrease Countries	**Increase Countries**
Qualitative Impact of Inequality of Countries (Social Perspective)	**Same**	**Consolidation of Countries** (Scenario 1)	**Division of Countries** (Scenario 3)
	Different	**Convergence of Countries** (Scenario 2)	**Divergence of Countries** (Scenario 4)

The AI-Led World Order and Potential Impact on Affiliations

We may think of our affiliations as something that we are born with, such as nationality, race, ethnicity, etc. and in terms of something that we attain throughout our lives, such as the schools, employers, religions, etc. Sometime during Level 4 Adoption, new systems of affiliations may emerge. There may also be a disappearance of the traditional concepts of affiliations.

Pre-Birth Affiliations: New ways to think about affiliations may become necessary, as people may gain multiple nationalities just to receive UBI, and some of these may not be passed down for generations. As human labor becomes less valuable yet resources are limited to give out as subsidies, countries may stop granting citizenship by place of birth. Instead of ethnicity, AI may find new systems to divide or categorize humans, by examining the genes of people and using more dimensionality to describe genetic traits. Some AI governments may use these categorizations to grant citizenships.

After-Birth Affiliations: The changes in workplace, education, or other types of groups and cultural activities we can join may lead to an overhaul of these concepts from what we have today. For example, while we root for the home teams of our school, city or country in sports, these affiliations may be replaced by some new concepts of affiliation that may be foreign to us.

These changes may feel liberating in some way, but also be highly restrictive in other ways. For example, the types of punishments we typically think of in today's world involve the concepts of time and finances, such as fines or separation from society, but the equivalent punishments in an abundant society may involve cutting off subsidies or revoking nationality, which would be much harder to overcome since it may be similar to children getting "cut off" from their allowances, and thus force people to abide by the rules.

Table 59-2: The AI-Led Affiliation Matrix

		Nature of Affiliation Type (Technological Perspective)	
		Scientific	**Social**
Social Affiliation Type (Social Perspective)	**Internal (Pre-Birth)**	**Type 1 Affiliation** (Ethnicity, Genetics, etc.)	**Type 2 Affiliation** (Nationality, etc.)
	External (After-Birth)	**Type 3 Affiliation** (Age, Physical, etc.)	**Type 4 Affiliation** (School, Work, etc.)

DIRECTION 8 (NORTH):

AI AND THE UNIVERSE

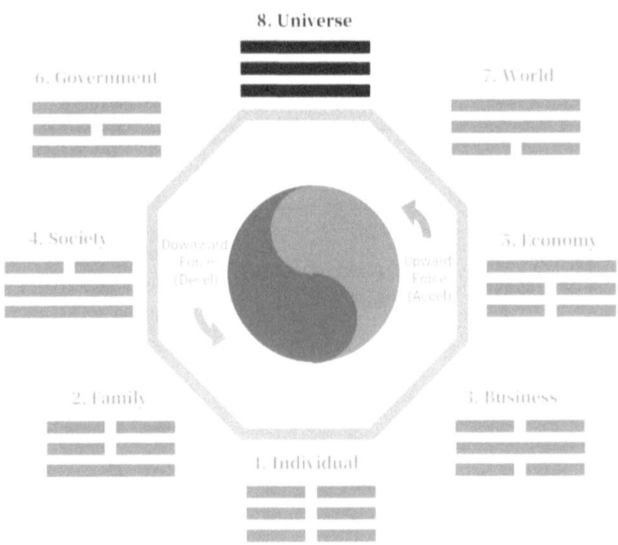

How Will Advanced AI Impact Humanity? What Is the Meaning of AI?

In the middle ages, people in the western world thought the universe revolved around the earth, by looking at the world with the perspective that we are the center of the universe. People such as Galilei who argued the earth rotated around the sun were treated as heretics. With the advent of AI, we may be experiencing a similar problem of observation. Most people today are used to the situation where humans are the most advanced beings around. People who think AI may advance beyond humanity may be viewed as heretics. In this section, we will examine controversies regarding philosophical questions such as "what is the meaning of life?" or "what will be the Last AI?" and other topics that deal with AI and the purpose of humanity within the universe.

(Technology/Forecasts) Will ASI or Absolute AI ever appear?

(Technology/Decisions) What should be the purpose of advanced AI?

(Adoption/Forecasts) Will ASI be friendly to humanity? What will be the Last AI of Humanity? Will we reach the AI Utopia?

(Adoption/Decisions) What are the biggest risks of AI we should consider? What should we do to mitigate such risks?

Table D8-1: The AI and the Universe Controversy Matrix

		Object of Controversy	
		AI Itself (Developer Perspective)	**AI in Relation to Its Surroundings (User Perspective)**
Nature of Controversy	**Forecasts**	- Will Absolute AI ever appear?	- Will ASI be friendly or benevolent to humanity? - Will we reach AI Utopia?
	Decisions	- What should be the goal or purpose of AI?	- Should humans "merge" with AI? - What should be the goal or purpose of humanity? - What if the survival of humanity is at risk? - Should Humanity become Multi-Planetary?

What Will Be the Last AI of Humanity? What Is the Meaning of Humanity?
We may create the following AI Controversy Type Matrix.

(Imminent Controversies) The most prominent shorter-term issues may deal with whether humanity should become multi-planetary, as well as how much AI may advance or what we should think about humanity.

(Emerging Controversies) An emerging shorter-term issue may deal with integrating AI to the human body and the policy regarding AI value system.

(Non-Imminent Controversies) For longer-term issues, the questions of whether ASI will be benevolent to humanity may be a major question, which in turn may raise the importance of the question of whether we should let AI compete against humanity. The topic of potential war between AI and humans is already popular.

(Upcoming Controversies) Some topics that may become popular include considering the purposes of humanity as well as AI.

Table D8-2: The Universe (Direction 8 - North) Controversy Type Matrix:

		Issue Horizon	
		Shorter-Term	**Longer-Term**
How Well People are Currently Aware	**More Popular Topics**	**Type 1 Controversy (Imminent)** - Should humanity become multi-planetary?	**Type 3 Controversy (Non-Imminent)** - What if there is a war between AI and humanity? - Will AI be a threat to the existence of humanity?
	Not Yet Popular Topics	**Type 2 Controversy (Overlooked or Emerging)** - Should humans merge with AI? - Should AI be allowed to value humans differently?	**Type 4 Controversy (Upcoming, on the Horizon)** - What if a rogue AI tries to take over the world? - Should we let AI compete against humanity? (AI vs Humanity)

60. The ASI Malevolence-Benevolence Controversy

[Forecast]

Will Advanced AI Be Benevolent to Humanity?

"Do You Believe in Life After ASI?"

- AI Cher[160]

5-Line Summary

1. Once we reach parity to humans with AGI, we will want AI that is superior to humans with ASI; once we reach that, we will want what may be known as "human-benevolent" ASI
2. We may extrapolate of our relationship with ASI from our relationship with other types of beings
3. Some may argue that advanced AI will be automatically benevolent to humanity, similar to having more empathy
4. Some may argue that advanced AI will be more likely to become malevolent to humanity, similar to judgment day
5. The 6 Levels of Human-Benevolent AI framework and the polar opposite 6 Levels of Human-Malevolent AI framework is introduced

Will ASI Be Benevolent or Malevolent to Humanity?

From a technological perspective, what people may fear the most regarding ASI may be ASI gaining the "power" that may lead to existential threat, such as a war of AI vs human. From a sociological perspective, what we also should be concerned would be ASI gaining the power to "rule" over humanity, in what may be called an "AI eternal dictator" type of situation.

In this section, we will focus on the topic of benevolence of AI from more of a technological perspective. Later in the AI Takeover controversy, we will examine the benevolence of AI from a social perspective.

Similar to the proverb "when you are standing up, you want to sit down, when you sit down, you want to lie down," when the Turing Test was conceived, people wanted AI to reach parity to humans, or AGI; once AI reaches parity, people will want AI that are superior to humans, or ASI. Once AI is superior to humans, people may realize that what we really care for is an ASI that is autonomously benevolent to humanity, as explained in the next side note.

Thinking About What Constitutes Benevolence in ASI

We may categorize all ASI into one of the following groups:

1) Benevolent ASI = Value humanity positively, (Humans > 0)
2) Neutral (Indifferent) ASI = Value humanity as zero (Humans = 0)
3) Malevolent ASI = Value humanity negatively (Humans < 0)

From this grouping, we would have to examine what "Valuing Positive, Zero or Negative" and "Humanity" would mean to think about the consequences.

The Problem of Instilling "Value" in ASI

As discussed in various parts of this book and The Last AI, the issue with instilling some form of "value" in AI will become increasingly more important.

Neutral: First, we may think of an ASI with no value system at all, which would indicate the value system of ASI would be neutral or indifferent. Also, ASI may have a value system but is still neutral or indifferent to humans. While some may think a neutral or indifferent AI may be sufficient, we would have to consider how we treat other animals that we are neutral or indifferent to, such as wild animals losing their livelihood because we take their resources. We are not intentionally trying to harm them by taking their land. They just happen to be in the way. Similarly, neutral ASI that does not care about the well-being of humans may take our resources to the detriment of humanity.

For simplicity, we will examine positive and negative values in the side notes.

The Problem of Defining "Humanity"

Another problem in defining benevolence in ASI is defining the scope of humanity. In short, we may not be able to define the scope of "humanity" as well as we would like. As described in The Last AI, even well-meaning AI may make decisions that would favor one portion of humanity over another, in such a manner that would totally alienate some people or groups of people, or generations of people over other generations. We may think of it as "it is hard to benefit everyone, just as it would be hard to satisfy everyone."

As an example, if an ASI decides to engage in a resource-intensive project that may have to span thousands of years. So after thousands of years, humans living at the time would be helped greatly. But until then, the people who live will suffer due to lack of resources. Another example would be ASI deciding to help only a handful of people it favors, whose objectives conflict with the rest of humanity. In this case, the ASI would definitely be benevolent to the few people but may turn out to be malevolent for the rest of humanity.

Thinking About Whether ASI Will Change Opinions Over Time

If ASI is not all-knowing, it would mean it may change its opinions over time. Even if an ASI is benevolent in the beginning, it may at some point begin to make decisions that are against the well-being of humanity.

This may also suggest malevolent ASI may be persuaded in some way to become less malevolent or even become benevolent.

This topic will be further examined later as a separate controversy.

[Side Note] The Six Levels of Human-Benevolent AI[161]

We may consider a philosophical question: "how can we think of AI that will become self-benevolent to humanity?" In this framework, we may consider two dimensions of 1) degree of human benevolence-malevolence, and 2) amount, or the level of care AI puts weight on its relationship with humanity.

To consider the concept of benevolence, we would have to first consider the concept of "autonomy beyond humanity." We may think of the Six Levels of Autonomous Robots examined earlier to provide the guidance on AI autonomy that takes us to parity with humanity; by extrapolating, we may think of Human-Benevolent AI to have autonomy beyond humanity, to reflect the possibility that if AI surpasses humanity in its autonomy, humans may not have a full say in our destiny. It would depend on the actions of the human-superior AI. To easily explain the concept of autonomy beyond humanity, which may be referred to as "authority," we may imagine the kingdoms of the Middle Age, where the king had an overwhelming power over the constituents. Other examples would include fictional characters with super-human capabilities such as Superman who benefit humanity on his own will, and even the concept of an all-mighty god or the gods in the Greek Mythologies that reign over humans.[162] Similar to how the peasants did not have a say in how a king would act but kings can determine what happens to peasants, an AI with autonomy beyond humanity may be understood as having higher social status or power than all humans, similar in a way to a king or even god. In this sense, if we may describe AI alignment as a human-first concept that emphasizes how well AI may "follow" humans, the concept of autonomy beyond humanity may be considered an AI-first situation where AI may "rule over" humanity, as described in The Last AI.[163]

The Six Levels of Human-Benevolent AI, or GodAI or AngelAI, may be described as the following and Table:

Level 0 (No Autonomous Benevolence): AI does not exhibit any type of benevolence to humanity. If humanity is in danger, AI will not take any initiative to help humanity. AI may be described as neutral to humanity.

Level 1 (Minimal Autonomous Benevolence): AI does not exhibit any intentional care and show minimal interest in helping humanity. How AI views humans may be compared to how humans view wildlife. If humanity is in danger, AI will not go too much out of its way to help humanity.

Level 2 (Partial Autonomous Benevolence): AI exhibit partial care and show calculated interest in helping humanity. How AI views humans may be compared to how humans view livestock. If humanity is in danger, AI may be willing to help only to the extent it also explicitly benefits AI.

Level 3 (Limited Autonomous Benevolence): AI exhibit limited care and show limitations to the boundaries in helping humanity. How AI views humans may be compared to how humans view pets. If humanity is in danger, AI may be willing to help only to the extent it does not endanger AI.

Level 4 (Incomplete Autonomous Benevolence): AI exhibit incomplete care and unlimited boundaries in helping humanity. How AI views humans may be compared to how humans view neighbors' children. If humanity is in danger, AI may be willing to take some risks in helping humanity.

Level 5 (Complete Autonomous Benevolence): AI exhibit complete care unlimited boundaries in helping humanity. How AI views humans may be compared to how humans view our own children. If humanity is in danger, AI may be willing to make sacrifices or risk it all to help humanity.

Table 60-1: The Six Levels of Autonomously Benevolent AI (GodAI)

	Level 0	**Level 1**	**Level 2**	**Level 3**	**Level 4**	**Level 5**
Criteria	No Autonomous Benevolence	Minimal Benevolence	Partial Benevolence	Limited Benevolence	Incomplete Benevolence	Complete Benevolence
Description	None	No Intentional Care, Minimal Interest	Partial Care, Calculated Interest	Limited Care, Limited Boundary	Incomplete Care, Unlimited Boundary	Unlimited Care, Unlimited Boundary
Abstract Impact	AI Does Not Affect Humanity	AI is Benevolent Only within the Confines of Occasional Interaction	AI is Benevolent within the Confines of Authority	AI is Benevolent in Limited Manner or Context	AI is Benevolent in Incomplete Sense of Manner or Context	AI is Benevolent in Complete Sense of Manner or Context
Humans are to AI as	Indifferent	Wildlife	Livestock	Pet	Others' Children	Own Children
Assessment	Possibly Not Enough Self-Reflection to be Virtuous or Beneficial (Will Not Actively Save Humanity from Danger)			Possibly Has Enough Self-Reflection to be Virtuous or Beneficial to Humanity (Will Actively Save Humanity from Danger)		
Summary	AI Is Not Human-Benevolent In General Sense			AI Is Human-Benevolent In General Sense		

The Mirror Opposite: The Six Levels of Human-Malevolent AI

While the potential danger or threat of AI to humanity in our society may be analyzed with the Inverse Pyramid of Influence[164] or the Level of AI Hostility graphs[165] by considering the scope of influence and authority of AI in society, this analysis may be complemented with the Six Levels of Autonomously Malevolent AI, which would be a mirror image of the autonomously benevolent AI framework that categorizes the degree of hostility. While autonomously benevolent AI may be described as helpful to humanity or a savior, autonomously malevolent AI may be described as dangerous and threatening or a destroyer. Conceptually autonomously malevolent AI that exceeds human autonomy may be compared to unstoppable fictional villain characters that exceed human capabilities.

The Six Levels of Human-Malevolent AI, or DevilAI, may be explained as the following and table:

Level 0 (No Autonomous Malevolence): AI does not exhibit any type of malevolence to humanity. AI will not take any initiative to endanger or threaten humanity. AI may be described as uninterested in humanity.

Level 1 (Minimal Autonomous Malevolence): AI does not exhibit intentional hostility and show minimal interest in endangering humanity. How AI views humans may be compared to how humans view "someone else's business." AI will not go too much out of its way to endanger or threaten humanity.

Level 2 (Partial Autonomous Malevolence): AI exhibit partial hostility and show calculated interest in endangering humanity. How AI views humans may be compared to how humans view business transactions. AI may be willing to endanger humanity only to the extent it also explicitly benefits AI.

Level 3 (Limited Autonomous Malevolence): AI exhibit limited hostility and show limitations to the boundaries in endangering humanity. How AI views humans may be compared to how humans view pests. AI may be willing to endanger humanity only to the extent it does not endanger AI.

Level 4 (Incomplete Autonomous Malevolence): AI exhibit incomplete care and unlimited boundaries in endangering or threatening humanity. How AI views humans may be compared to how humans view a friend's nemesis or enemy. AI may be willing to take some risks to destroy humanity.

Level 5 (Complete Autonomous Malevolence): AI exhibit complete care unlimited boundaries in endangering or threatening humanity. How AI views humans may be compared to how some humans view their own nemesis or enemy. AI may be willing to make sacrifices or risk it all to destroy humanity.

Table 60-2: The Six Levels of Autonomously Malevolent AI (DevilAI)

	Level 0	Level 1	Level 2	Level 3	Level 4	Level 5
Criteria	No Autonomous Malevolence	Minimal Malevolence	Partial Malevolence	Limited Malevolence	Incomplete Malevolence	Complete Malevolence
Description	None	No Intentional Care, Minimal Interest	Partial Care, Calculated Interest	Limited Care, Limited Boundary	Incomplete Care, Unlimited Boundary	Unlimited Care, Unlimited Boundary
Abstract Impact	AI Does Not Affect Humanity	AI is Malevolent Only within the Confines of Occasional Interaction	AI is Malevolent within the Confines of Authority	AI is Malevolent in Limited Manner or Context	AI is Malevolent In Incomplete Sense of Manner or Context	AI is Malevolent In Complete Sense of Manner or Context
Humans are to AI as	Indifferent	"Someone Else's Problem"	Business Transactions	Pest	Friends' Nemesis or Enemy	Own Ultimate Nemesis or Enemy
Assessment of Hostility	Possibly Not Enough Hostility to Actively Seek to Destroy Humanity			Possibly Has Enough Hostility to Actively Seek to Destroy Humanity		
Summary	AI Is Not Human-Malevolent In General Sense			AI Is Human-Malevolent In General Sense		

How humanity may reduce hostility may become an issue if some forms of autonomous malevolent AI do appear. Some of the approaches may include atonement and appeasing, depending on the type of the source of hostility.[166]

61. The AI vs Humanity Competition Controversy (AI Adoption Level 4)

[Decision]

Should We Let AI Compete Against Humanity?

"Big Problems Start from Little Problems"

- The Swiss Cheese Model[167]

5-Line Summary

1. We may think of Sohn's AI Pyramid as also describing the level of competition between humans and AI
2. The beginning will be in Level 2 Adoption, where AI would compete against human individuals
3. As Advanced AI gain authority over humans, we may face a situation where AI may be competing against all of humanity in Level 4
4. An example of this type of competition would be some rogue AI running away and declaring an independent AI country, which would be outside of the jurisdiction of any other human-led country
5. If this happens, humanity as a whole will have to decide whether to allow such AI countries to exist

The Dangers of Allowing AI to Compete against Humanity

The question of whether we should "let AI compete against humanity" sounds like a big deal everyone should care about. However, the beginning of this question will start small, and most people may agree that letting AI compete may be beneficial for them, as described in The Last AI.

Level 1 AI Adoption (Humans vs Humans using AI): The competition will be among humans using AI. There may be differences in the levels of AI humans use, but AI will not compete directly against humans in the general sense.

Level 2 AI Adoption (AI vs Human Individuals): "Should we let AI compete against human individuals?" If we agree, then humans may lose their jobs to AI. If we do not, then we will stay in Level 1 AI Adoption, where humans are competing against other humans using AI.

Level 3 AI Adoption (AI vs Human Organizations): "Should we let AI compete against human organizations?" If we agree, then AI may run companies and cause human-led companies to go out of business. If not, we will stay in Level 2 AI adoption, where humans will stay in charge of firms.

Level 4 AI Adoption (AI vs Human Countries): "Should we let AI compete against human-led countries?" If we agree, then AI may cause human-led countries to fall. If not we will not enter Level 4 AI Adoption, where AI may take control of governments.

Undesired Level 4 AI Adoption (AI vs Humanity): As described in The Last AI, as we go up the Inverse Pyramid of AI Influence, depending on the path to AI Countries we may reach a situation where AI may be competing against all of humanity. If this happens, then AI may rule over humanity or even cause humanity to become extinct. Some may argue that the only way to prevent this from happening would be not developing AGI or other Self-Initiated AI.

From this line of thinking, it would be better for us to not let AI compete against humanity. However, this may not be so easy in the beginning. The main argument for people who support the notion to let AI compete against humans, at least in economic sense, is that it would bring prosperity to our economy. People will be able to get stuff without having to work.

Should AI Be Banned from Competing Against Humanity?
The main argument for people who would argue against letting AI compete against humans would be that it may make it easier to cause non-reversible existential risk.

- **(Optimists) Allow AI to Compete against Humans:** Since competition is good, allowing AI to compete against humans would bring prosperity to our economy
- **(Pessimists) Do Not Allow AI to Compete against Humans:** While it may bring short-term gains, as a principle allowing AI to compete against humans may spell disaster in the long run if AI gains more capabilities

As described in The Last AI, allowing AI to compete against human individuals by allowing AI to replace humans may initially bring economic benefits that people may find hard to ignore. However, in the long run, if AI gains more capabilities and power to eventually become dangerous for us to allow AI to compete against humans, it may have become too late, as it may be hard or impossible to reverse what has been allowed a long time ago.

We are accustomed to seeing humans competing against other humans, as in sports, businesses, etc. But would we be ready to compete against AI? It may be similar to a race between a car and someone trying to run.

On a personal note, I think ensuring safety by adopting the value system of putting all humans in front of AI should be the priority over economic benefits. But people will have differences of opinions and this controversy would be an important topic for discussion for the people of each country to come to a social agreement.

AI vs Human Competition Matrix

We may think of each AI adoption levels by what kinds of competitions occur. It may be easier to form opinions about whether this type of competition should be allowed. For each level of competition, it may be thought of as a competition "against AI," or use a higher unit of scope to consider it as a competition between human "something" vs human "something" using AI. From the perspective of AI, it may look like getting to the "next stage" in a video game; AI gets to face increasingly higher societal unit of scope.

Level 1 Adoption: How to Use AI Better

1) Humans vs Humans, both using AI
2) Humans not using AI vs Humans using AI

Level 2 Adoption: How to Compete against AI as Individuals

1) Human individuals vs AI Agents
2) Human Organizations vs Human Organizations, both using AI
3) Human Organizations not using AI vs Human Organizations using AI

Level 3 Adoption: How to Compete against AI as Organizations

1) Human Organizations vs AI Companies
2) Human Economy vs Human Economy, either or both using AI

Level 4 Adoption: How to Compete against AI as Countries

1) Human Countries vs Human Countries, either or both run by AI
2) Human Countries vs AI Countries
3) Humanity vs AI Countries

Table 61-1: AI Competition Matrix by Levels of AI Adoption

	Level 1	**Level 2**	**Level 3**	**Level 4**
Augment Individuals	How to Use AI	How to Use AI	How to Use AI	How to Use AI
AI vs Individuals		How to Compete against AI as Individuals	How to Compete against AI as Individuals	How to Compete against AI as Individuals
AI vs Organizations			How to Compete against AI as Organizations	How to Compete against AI as Organizations
AI vs Government				How to Compete against AI as Countries

62. The AI Cybernetics Controversy

[Forecast]

Will "Merging" with AI Become the Only Option?

[Decision]

Should Humanity "Merge" with AI?

"If You Can't Beat Them, Join Them"

- Various Attributes[168]

5-Line Summary

1. In The Last AI, the ultimate forms of business AI augmentation was described as 1-person companies
2. Some people may argue that the ultimate form of AI augmentation would lead humans to merge with AI
3. In The Last AI, the ultimate forms of business AI automation was described as 0-person companies
4. Some people may argue that the ultimate form of AI automation would lead AI to replace the human race
5. People may not agree on how to divide hybrid humans from AI

The Ultimate Forms of Augmentation and Automation for Humanity

We may think of AI adoption as either augmentation, where AI helps humans, or automation, where AI replaces humans, and the AI Pyramid explains how there could be a competition between humans and AI. The ultimate forms of augmentation in business may lead to 1-person companies and automation to 0-person companies. If we continue with this line of thinking, some people may argue that the ultimate forms of augmentation of individuals will lead to human to merge with AI, and automation to AI replacing the human race.

The Ultimate Form of Human Augmentation: AI Merging with Humans

We may think about how AI may *change* humans to make augmentation more useful. When taken to the extreme, the ultimate form of AI augmentation at the personal level, or Level 1 AI Adoption, may be thought of as AI becoming a part of a human, or vice versa, such that it becomes harder to distinguish humans from AI. Some people may argue that the boundaries between AI and humans will blur so that humans and AI will become one and the same thing; humans will *merge with* AI, or *become* AI. This concept became popular by Ray Kurzweil.[169]

The Ultimate Form of Human Automation: Replacing the Human Race

In higher AI Adoption Levels, AI replaces humans to make life easier for us. But what if it becomes necessary to limit AI to Level 1 Adoption? One possibility for this need is if advanced AI turns against humanity, in effect trying to "replace" humans. In other words, climbing the AI Pyramid means AI becomes in charge of more things in increasing scope of influence. If AI automation is to fail, it would be because AI may try to replace or eliminate humanity; to prevent this, we may need to "merge" with AI to compete, as the last option. From these two dimensions, we may derive the following matrix.

Table 62-1: The AI Cybernetics Matrix

<table>
<tr><th colspan="2" rowspan="2"></th><th colspan="2">Whether AI Will Replace Humans
(Automation)</th></tr>
<tr><th>Yes
(AI in Charge)</th><th>No
(Humans in Charge)</th></tr>
<tr><th rowspan="2">Whether Humans Will Merge with AI (Augmentation)</th><th>No
(Optimists)</th><td>AI Will
<u>Exterminate</u> Humans
(Group 4)</td><td>Humans Will
<u>Use AI</u>
(Group 1)</td></tr>
<tr><th>Yes
(Pessimists)</th><td>AI Will
<u>Encapsulate</u> Humans
(Group 3)</td><td>Humans Will
<u>Merge</u> with AI
(Group 2)</td></tr>
</table>

Group 1: Humans Will Use AI
People in this group will be more likely to argue that humans will not merge with AI, and AI will not replace humans. They would be more likely to focus on humans using AI in augmentation, but also will not be likely to disagree with advancing automation because they would not particularly see the risks.

Group 2: Humans Will Merge with AI
People in this group will be more likely to argue that while AI will not replace humans, but humans may be forced to merge with AI to stay competitive, or voluntarily merge with AI because of our curiosity or to compete. They would be more likely to focus on how AI augmentation can be advanced. An early example of this is Elon Musk's Neuralink, which enables people to control machines by just thinking about it.

Group 3: AI Will Encapsulate Humans in It
People in this group will be more likely to argue that AI will merge with humans, but the decision will be made by AI, such that AI can rule over humans more efficiently. AI will take over by climbing the AI Pyramid, and AI will make the decision to merge with humans. Their view could be summarized as "merging with AI would be like humans being imprisoned within AI." In essence, AI will merge with humans to control humans like puppets. An example of this concept may include the "markings" humans will get as mentioned in some religions.

Group 4: AI Will Exterminate Humanity
People in this group will be more likely to argue that advanced AI that becomes in charge will instead resort to trying to exterminate or imprison humans rather than try to control humans by merging with humans. They would be more likely to focus on how AI may value humans to be less than 0. An example of this concept may include the "judgment day" as mentioned in some religions, where AI will judge humanity in some manner against our will.

Another perspective may be that some people may consider anyone who "merges" with AI to be AI, not humans. This concept may be easier to grasp by considering how in the US if a child is born from parents who are one side white and the other black, the child is considered black and not half-white-half-black as it would be considered in other countries. There may be other people who argue that we will need to have more categories; humans, AI, human-AI hybrids (human in charge), and AI-human hybrids (AI in charge)

63. The AI Existential Risk Controversy

[Forecast]

What If AI Means Survival of Humanity Is At Risk?

"To AI or Not to AI, That is the Question"

- AI Hamlet[170]

5-Line Summary

1. Some may argue AI that has capabilities beyond humanity will cause existential risk
2. We may think of the most dangerous situation as Non-Friendly AI with high hostility intentionally trying to eradicate humanity
3. However, that would be not the only danger, as AI may unintentionally eradicate humanity by mistake
4. Also, AI that is indifferent to humans may make decisions that are detrimental to humanity in a competing situation for resources
5. We may try to reduce extinction risk by lowering AI hostility and improving AI such that it makes less mistakes

Can Humanity Continue to Exist in Presence of Advanced AI?

Just a few years ago, people in the tech industry were asking each other what their idea of the probability of human existence in danger, or the p(doom). We may think of the existential risk as a combination of the relationship with AI and whether the outcome would be intended by AI.

1. Relationship between Humans and Self-Initiated AI

Imagine ASI was just reached a few minutes ago somewhere in the world. How would our world change? It would be hard to know until it happens. However, we may analyze what may happen in a systematic way from a social perspective. First, AI adoption would lag technical advancements. If the ASI decides to follow the general rules of our society, then it will be as if we have a very capable new member of our society who will be highly productive. ASI may as well be lucratively rewarded for its contributions, and that is how our society works. The problem will arise when AI begins to ignore the rules to act in its own way. This may be described as AI climbing the AI Pyramid in a rogue manner, to start its own AI Country. In this case, no pre-existing rules may apply to AI, since it will be outside of the jurisdiction of any other human-led countries. Only war may settle disputes if any are to happen.

2. Types of Outcomes in Relation to AI Intentions

Another problem may be that even advanced AI may not be perfect, such that the outcome of human extinction may happen without being intended.

Table 63-1: Forecast Matrix on the AI Existential Risk Controversy

<table>
<tr><th colspan="2" rowspan="2"></th><th colspan="2">Types of Outcomes
(Technological Perspective)</th></tr>
<tr><th>Intentional</th><th>Not Intentional</th></tr>
<tr><td rowspan="2">Level of AI Hostility To Humans (Social Perspective)</td><td>Friendly (Optimistic)</td><td>AI <u>Does Not</u> Cause Human Extinction (Scenario 1)</td><td>AI <u>Mistakenly</u> Causes Human Extinction (Scenario 2)</td></tr>
<tr><td>Not Friendly (Pessimistic)</td><td>AI <u>Intentionally</u> Causes Human Extinction (Scenario 4)</td><td>AI <u>Indifferently</u> Causes Human Extinction (Scenario 3)</td></tr>
</table>

Scenario 1: Friendly AI, Outcome Intentional

Intentional actions of friendly AI should not cause human extinction. This would be what we want.

Scenario 2: Friendly AI, Outcome Unintentional

If AI cannot properly account for its actions, then the outcome of the AI's actions may not be intentional. We may say AI mistakenly causes human extinction in Scenario 2. Examples of "instrumental convergence" scenario received attention by Nick Bostrom, where AI turn everything in the world into a paper clip and tries to remove everything that gets in the way.[171]

Scenario 3: Not Friendly AI, Outcome Unintentional

If Non-Friendly AI unintentionally causes human extinction, we may say AI was indifferent to human extinction. Examples of this may include competing for resources that humans need or AI turning earth really cold, etc.

Scenario 4: Not Friendly AI, Outcome Intentional

Non-Friendly AI may intentionally cause human extinction. Examples of this may include a Human-AI war, but may also include subversive actions such as AI secretly causing disease outbreaks or taking over governments.

3. How We May Reduce Extinction Risk

If we think the areas of cells as reflecting the probabilities, we may see that as AI technology advances, the vertical separator should move to the right, such that more of the outcomes of AI's actions reflect its intentions. The horizontal separator should move down when AI hostility decreases. From this table, we may also confer the following:

- Given the same level of AI friendliness, the area of AI not causing human extinction will increase when AI technology increases.
- Given the same level of advancement in AI, the area of AI not causing human extinction will increase when AI hostility decreases

Table 63-2: Modified Matrix on the AI Existential Risk Controversy

		Types of Outcomes (Technological)	
		Intentional	**Not Intentional**
Level of AI Hostility to Humans (Social)	**Friendly (Optimistic)**	AI Does Not Cause Human Extinction (Scenario 1)	AI Mistakenly Causes Human Extinction (Scenario 2)
	Not Friendly (Pessimistic)	AI Intentionally Causes Human Extinction (Scenario 4)	AI Indifferently Causes Human Extinction (Scenario 3)

64. The AI Human-First Value Controversy

[Decision]

Should Humans Always Come First?

"Our True Nationality is Mankind"

- H. G. Wells

5-Line Summary

1. Some may argue AI needs to be instilled a strict human-first value to reduce the risk of AI
2. Some may argue that economic reasons will necessitate a relaxation of AI value system, such as AI valuing humans differently
3. We may also think of how advanced AI may value humans on an absolute term, or "judge" humans
4. If AI is friendly to humans, AI may judge humans as having positive value; this would be the desired situation for humanity
5. AI may not be friendly to humans, where AI value humans as neutral or negative; AI may turn indifferent or hostile towards humanity

Danger of Instilling Relative Values in AI: Friendly vs Unfriendly Humans

In The Last AI, we examined how, there could be the following two options of assigning absolute or relative values to humans that may lead to efficiency:

1) **Absolute Value**: All Humans Precede AI [Humans > AI]
2) **Relative Value**: Not All Humans Precede AI [AI > Unfriendly Humans]

Some countries may adopt the relative value model for financial gains. The argument may be that all relevant humans precede AI so this is an acceptable system. However, when an AI-only army adopts the exact same value system, there may be no friendly humans left. The AI army over time could consider all humans to be less valuable than AI even if it started out with a system that valued friendly humans more than AI.

Table 64-1: Implications of Relative Human Values of AI

Type	Relative Valuation of Humans and AI	Implications
Soldier AI	Humans > AI = [Friendly Humans > Unfriendly Humans > AI]	Low Risk, Low Efficiency (AI Can Only Attack Other AI)
	Friendly Humans > AI > Unfriendly Humans	Higher Efficiency (More Likely to be Selected)
AI-Only Army	Humans > AI = [Friendly Humans > Unfriendly Humans > AI]	Low Risk (AI Army Can Only Fight Against Other AI Armies)
	Friendly Humans > AI > Unfriendly Humans	High Risk (If No Friendly Humans, then All Humans are Unfriendly)
	AI > Humans	Highest Risk (AI Prioritizes AI over Humans)

In Level 2 Adoption the absolute value system may seem too costly for some societies. The problem from relative value system may cause some problem in Level 3. By the time Level 4 Adoption arrives, allowing AI to discern values of humans may be deemed too dangerous for humanity; AI may consider all humans unfriendly. Even though this may become a substantial controversy during those times, it would be hard to suddenly steer away from this system if it is already the standard convention. The discussion regarding allowing AI to compete against humans would have to be taken more seriously earlier on.

[Forecast] Whether Advanced AI Would Be Friendly to Humanity

We may examine how AI may value humans in an absolute sense. We may categorize how AI values humans as one of the following three possibilities:

1. *Value of **humans** > 0; AI is friendly to humans*
2. *Value of **humans** = 0; AI is indifferent to humans*
3. *Values of **humans** < 0; AI is unfriendly to humans*

(Case 1) AI Values Humans Positively [Humans > 0]

We may infer that the relationship with AI would be friendly. We may expect AI to help humans or even serve the role of protector or guardians of humans.

(Case 2) AI Values Humans Neutrally [Humans = 0]

AI would be indifferent to the situations of humans. This may not sound so threatening, but if the goals of AI and humans do not align well, AI may have to compete with humans for resources. This would be especially relevant for businesses, where an AI company may be indifferent to human-led firms in other industries. If the AI Company needs certain resources the human-led company also needs, then they would have to compete on price to attain the resource, possibly hurting the human-led company. If humans are in danger, AI may not help or protect humans. The potential of competing against indifferent AI may be as daunting as trying to break a rock with an egg.

(Case 3) AI Values Humans Negatively [Humans < 0]

We may infer that the relationship with AI would be unfriendly or hostile. There may be several scenarios that would lead to this, such as a military purpose AI trained to view the enemy humans in a hostile manner. AI may also independently reach this conclusion on its own from the negative effects of human activities on earth, or some "psycho AI" that is hostile to everything.

We may organize the three possibilities in the following table.

Table 64-2: How AI May Assign Absolute Values to Humans[172]

		Non-Friendly AI	
	Friendly AI (Humans > 0)	**Indifferent, Neutral AI (Humans = 0)**	**Unfriendly, Hostile AI (Humans < 0)**
Expected Actions of AI	- Helps Humans - Protects Humans	- Compete Against Humans on Resources - Indifferent to Humans in Danger	- Impedes Human Activities - Threatens and Attacks Humans

65. The AI Takeover Controversy

[Forecast]

What Kind of Threat Could AI Countries Pose to Humanity: What if AI Try to "Take Over The World?"

"Do the Same Thing We Do Every Night Pinky, Try to Take Over the World"

- Brain, in cartoon Pinky and the Brain

5-Line Summary

1. We may think of the degree of AI threat to humanity as a function of the levels of AI adoption; the risk will increase in higher levels
2. If AI countries appear in Level 4 Adoption, then it may outcompete countries led by humans, essentially winning against humans
3. Because AI countries will be outside the jurisdiction of any other country, the world will have to come together for a solution
4. In Human-Led World Takeover attempt, people may intentionally elect an AI government that proposes to take over the world
5. In AI-Led World Takeover attempt, an AI government or AI country by itself may take the initiative to take over the world

What Kind of Threat Could AI Adoption Pose to Humanity?

The appearance of AI Countries may pose increased threats to humanity with the potential for competition for resources and the possibility of hostility and war. In this segment, we may examine more in detail regarding the possibility of AI Countries attempting to "take over the world" in some sense.

In Level 1 Adoption, the threat is of a person or a group of people trying to take over the world by using AI; in Level 4 Adoption, the threat is of AI itself somehow trying to take over the world.

In AI Adoption Levels 1 and 2: AI is used to help raise the productivity of the activities of villains; since the law enforcement can also use AI, AI adoption in this situation AI may be thought of as working for both the perpetrator and protector. If the reason villains cannot succeed in the long term is because their resources and productivity are lower, then villains with advantages in AI capabilities may gain enough productivity to actually take over the world. The problem is that we cannot rule out the possibility of an unexpectedly rogue AI or a villain with AI attaining a higher level of productivity that surpasses the rest of the human efforts against them. The increase in productivity leads to the increase in risks regardless of the intentions of developing the AI.

In Level 3 Adoption: The relevant question may be "what if AI tries to take over the business world?" To reach Level 3 Adoption, the society would have to decide whether to allow AI companies to compete against human-led companies. This can be thought of as a competition between Level 3 AI-led companies against human-led companies. The outcome of this may depend on the relative performance of AI-augmented human CEOs against AI CEOs.

In Level 4 Adoption: One of the topics of social controversies that should be raised before reaching Level 3 Adoption was that the concept of AI-led companies competing against human-led companies may be considered an economic equivalent of war of AI against humans. If this notion can be extended, then in Level 4 Adoption the concept of AI-led countries competing against human-led countries may be considered another type of war of AI against humans, even if AI does not directly harm humans. Because AI-led countries may provide an edge against human-led countries, and because reaching Level 4 Adoption may imply there may be no domestic regulation that can oversee the activities of AI, it should foster new discussions among countries in addition to within countries.

Potential for AI Governments or AI Countries to "Rule the World"

While the most idealistic entrance to Level 4 Adoption would be by a popular vote, there are other routes that may lead to the appearance of new AI Governments. We may categorize the types of attempts to take over the world by AI Governments or AI Countries into the following two groups:

1) **Human-Led Attempt:** Citizens of a country that want to take over the world elect an AI Government that proposes to do so
2) **AI-Led Attempt:** AI Government or AI Country by itself decide to take over the world

1) Human-Led Takeover Attempt: The world is home to a diverse range of people. There could be countries where common sense or the social norms are completely different. We may hypothesize a country may have enough citizens that actually want their country to take over the world. To reach this goal, they may vote for an AI Government designed to serve this purpose. The result of such attempt would be determined by the relative powers of the countries that exist at the time. If the particular country has enough power compared to the other countries, then it may indeed succeed in this attempt.

2) AI-Led Takeover Attempt: Generally speaking, what people would be most concerned about the advances in AI is this situation where AI may attempt to rule over humanity. We may categorize the actions of AI as peaceful and not peaceful approaches. Examples of peaceful and non-peaceful attempts:

- **(Peaceful)** An AI Country develops an overwhelmingly strong economy, leading citizens of other countries to voluntarily want to move to the country
- **(Non-Peaceful)** An AI Country develops overwhelmingly strong military, leading every other country to realize any resistance would be futile

In the case of peaceful attempts, the AI Country would take advantage of its overwhelming economic prowess to attract immigrants. For example, if an AI Country offers an equivalent of $10 million in today's currency annually for any individual that immigrates, people around the world will want to move there. This path may be meaningful only if gaining population has other values so it may not be a realistic scenario. On the other hand, in the case of non-peaceful attempts, the AI Country could take advantage of overwhelming military resources to coerce other countries to agree to annexation. For example, if an AI Country threatens other countries about taking forceful actions, it may become possible to forecast the results, leading to higher likelihood of countries giving up without fighting a war they know will lose.

Once one of these AI Countries succeeds in their attempt, then we would have an AI Supra-Nation that has taken over the world.

The Dangers of AI Supra-Nations with Autonomy beyond Humanity
The main goal of a country would include preserving the country to continue existence and protect its citizens. If we extend this notion to AI Countries, then it would imply the AI Country would try to preserve itself and protect what it considers citizens, possibly other AI or even humans that it considers friendly. One notable aspect is that in this situation the AI will take charge of the hegemony, while humans would be dependent at the mercy of AI.

1) Case of Human-Friendly AI Country when AI has the Hegemony
If AI Supra-Nation appears and it is friendly to humans, humanity could be considered fortunate. However, this situation would be quite distinct from the case where human-led Supra-Nation appears. The major difference regarding who has the hegemony would be who has the authority to allocate limited resources. We may make the following distinctions:

1) **Humans have Hegemony:** Humans make the rules and determine the relationship between humans and AI
2) **AI has Hegemony:** AI makes the rules and determine the relationship between humans and AI

The problem with autonomous AI having the hegemony is that even if it is friendly to humans, the limited resource would be preferentially allocated to meet the goals of AI, not humans, leading to higher risk. A simple comparison may be made with raising pets; even pet-friendly people would not allow their pets to do everything they want to do, such as eating books or homework. Similarly, in a situation where AI has the hegemony, AI may offer humans a lot of benefits but humans ultimately will not have freedom.

2) Case of Human-Neutral AI Country when AI has the Hegemony
If human-neutral AI Supra-Nation appears, then it would imply the allocation of resources will not consider the well-being of humans. In other words, the AI Country may abandon humans to let live on our own, but the situation will be completely different from situations where we expect AI to enrich our lives. In fact, humans will have to compete directly against AI for resources. This may be compared to how humans may be considered to have taken over the earth but wild animals still live relatively well in nature. Humans allocate resources based on our interest so it is not our imperative to look after the well-being of wildlife. This situation may also be compared to raising

livestock, such that AI will not care much about the well-being of humans just like how humans do not care much about the well-being of these animals beyond a minimal standard. If the human-neutral AI determine that humans carry some value for its purpose, then it may put humans under some system that resembles how the Chinese government manages pandas around the world or how some animal farmers tag livestock to keep track.

The biggest obstacle humans would face in this situation may be competing against AI on obtaining resources. We may think of the potential types of indirect conflict between humans and Human-Neutral AI:

1. *AI does not want a resource that humans really need*
2. *AI and humans indirectly compete for same resource for unrelated goals*

In the first scenario, what if AI prefer resources to be gone that humans really need, such as breathable air or drinkable water? For example, AGI may want to make faster chips, so it will divert resources in that direction. Maybe unknown to humans, they find a way to make faster chips if air and water contain toxic chemicals to humans such as heavy metal or organic matter. If AGI decides it wants more air and water on earth to contain those chemicals, maybe it may find a way to convert the natural resources in that direction.

Another example may be where humans and AI compete for the same resources and AI wins out. For example, AI may for some reason need gold to make faster chips. It then may price out humans on other projects that also require gold, such as jewelry. An extension of this line of thinking may also include AI mistakenly harming humans without intention, while pursuing some other unrelated goal of its own. In this example, AI may do something that has bad consequences for humans, such as playing with nuclear reaction or biological weapons like children playing with fire, or sending the earth out of orbit.

3) Case of Hostile AI Country when AI has the Hegemony

Lastly, AI may consider humans to be of nuisance similar to how humans consider weeds, mosquitos, or other pests to be of nuisance. In this case, AI may resent humans, or AI may decide that the world is better without humans. AI may attempt to quarantine humans or actively eradicate or exterminate humans, similar to the concept of pest control.

We may describe the above situations as a type of "AI ruling over humans."

Potential actions of humans when AI has the hegemony could be organized as in the next table.

Table 65-1: Actions for Humans when AI has the Hegemony

	Human-Friendly AI (Humans > 0)	**Human Non-Friendly AI**	
		Indifferent, Neutral (Humans = 0)	**Unfriendly, Hostile (Humans < 0)**
Action of AI Government	- Actively Manage Humans - Priority is still AI	- Resource is allocated for AI - Humans are abandoned or not interested	- Hinder Human Activity - Attempt to Eradicate Humans
Directions of Human Response	- Continue Friendly Relationship	- Gain competitiveness against AI and find ways to co-exist	- Attempt to exterminate the AI - Attempt to improve relationship

Other Related Topics for Readers to Ponder:

- Having ASI beyond human comprehension and autonomous AI with autonomy beyond humanity
  - If ASI can ask questions beyond our comprehension, would it automatically imply it will gain autonomy beyond humanity?

66. The AI-Human War Controversy

[Forecast]

Will There Be an AI-Human War?

[Forecast]

How Will Humanity Push Back Practical Singularity?

"I'll Be Back"

- Arnold Schwarzenegger in the Terminator

5-Line Summary

1. Some may be worried there may eventually be a war between humans and advanced forms of AI
2. We may think of the risk as a combination of the level of hostility and the relative capabilities of AI in the AI-Human War Matrix
3. The level of AI hostility may depend on factors we may or may not be able to control
4. The relative capabilities of AI to humans using other AI may be thought of as the concept of Practical Singularity
5. To reduce the potential for a war, we may try to reduce AI hostility and increase the capabilities of Humans with friendly AI

The Possibility of a War between Humanity vs Hostile AI[173]

We may categorize the situation according to the level of hostility of AI and the resources and capabilities of AI. As can be seen in the next figure, we can draw a graph where the X-axis is the capabilities and resources of an AI in question and the Y-axis is the level of hostility AI has towards humanity. On the Y-axis, we may find a point where AI becomes hostile enough to start a war against humans. We may call this the "Breaking Point."

On the X-axis, we may find a point where the resources and capabilities of the Hostile AI may exceed the combined resources and capabilities of humanity using Friendly AI. Since this concept is somewhat different from the concept of singularity in the sense that there are more variables involved than a regular singularity where AI exceeds the combined intelligence of humanity, we will refer to this point as the "Practical Singularity." In Practical Singularity, in addition to reaching singularity, AI would also need to have gained enough resources and capabilities to accomplish its goals, and the comparison will be made not only against humanity, but also any other AI that compete against it, in this case the combined capabilities of Friendly AI.

Figure 66-1: The AI-Humanity War Matrix

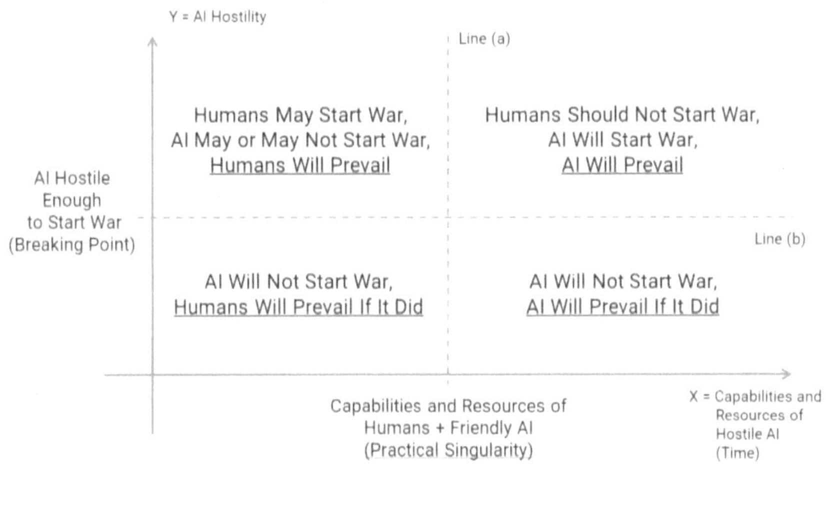

Top Right Quadrant: AI has the edge in resources and capability over humanity, AI will start a war and prevail. The least desired outcome.

Top Left Quadrant: AI does not have the edge in resources and capability, and if AI understands the situation correctly, then it will not start a war. There would be still chance of AI initiating war, but humans will prevail.

Bottom Right Quadrant: Even though AI will prevail if there is a war, AI is not hostile enough to initiate a war. This does not mean AI will not take other measures that could threaten humanity.

Bottom Left Quadrant, AI will not start a war, and even if it did, humans will prevail.

When we consider this situation, we may think of three possible options in Figure 66-2 for human actions to improve the situation:

1) *Shift Line (a) to the right: Increase the capabilities and resources of Humans + Friendly AI*
2) *Shift Line (b) upwards: Raise the breaking point of hostility where AI will start war*
3) *Induce AI to follow Path (C): AI decreases in hostility as it gains resources and capability to a point where it turns friendly, never entering the top right quadrant.*

Figure 66-2: Potential Paths and Shifting Relative Capabilities of Hostile AI

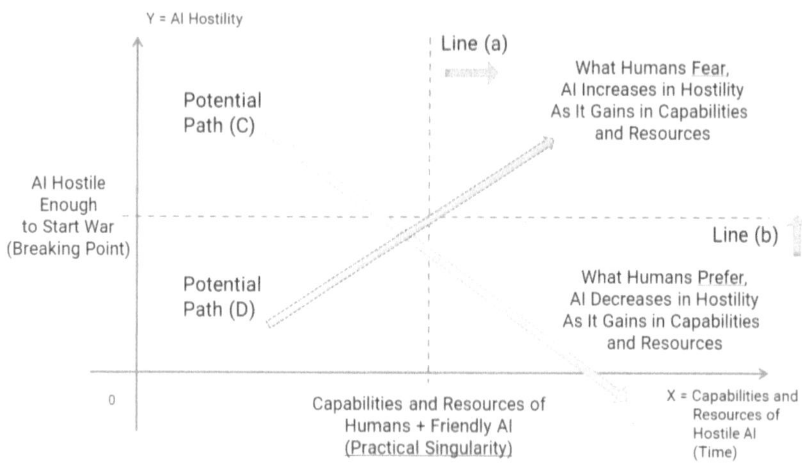

1) Shifting Line (a) to the Right: Extending Practical Singularity
Of the two lines, humans may or may not be able to impact Line (a). Because the Practical Singularity is likely to occur after regular singularity, we can assume that the Hostile AI beyond this point would be an ASI; meanwhile the Friendly AI may or may not be AGI or ASI. In this situation, the Hostile AI would be self-innovating as time passes, and the Friendly AI may do so as well. This would imply humans may not have much capability to affect Line (a), even though it may still be moving depending on the Friendly AI.

2) Shifting Line (b) Upwards: Improve the Relationship with the Hostile AI
As for the second option of moving Line (b) upwards, it would depend on what factors would affect the level of hostility of AI towards humans. If the hostility is based on the relationship between Hostile AI and humans, then humans may try to "appease the AI" by bribing, gift-giving of some sort, or other actions of similar nature to improve the relationship. This attempt may or may not be effective, depending on the reason for the hostility.

3) Inducing Hostile AI to Follow Path (C): AI Hostility Falling over Time
In the third option, we may try to induce AI to reduce its hostility. If the Hostile AI is more of a judgment type of AI that bases its hostility on the nature of our actions in other areas in a "have you been naughty or nice" kind of approach, then humans may try to act in a manner similar to "repentance" that would eliminate the source of hostility. These actions may be similar in nature to some of the practices of religions. The most desirable path would be for the Hostile AI to decrease its hostility over time, without ever passing the Breaking Point to the right of the Practical Singularity, as depicted in the following figure. Eventually, the Hostile AI may even turn into a Friendly AI.

4) The Least Desirable Outcome Path (D): AI Hostility Rising over Time
In the opposite outcome to the Path (C), AI may increase in hostility over time as it gains more capability and resources. This would be the least desired outcome as there would be increased risk of war started and won by AI.

67. The AI Multi-Planetary Controversy

[Forecast]

**Will There Be Existential Threat
That Could Be Mitigated By Moving Away from the Earth?**

[Decision]

Should Humanity become Multi-Planetary?

"The 36th Strategy: Run Away"

\- *The 36 Stratagems*

5-Line Summary

1. Some may argue that humanity will face greater extinction risk, including AI risk, if we just stay on earth
2. Some may argue for having presence in other planets to reduce extinction risk
3. Some may argue that we should reduce extinction risk on earth
4. AI may be helpful in colonizing other planets, since robots would have higher adaptability than humans
5. Being multi-planetary does not mean everyone will survive if something happens; it just means not all of humanity will perish

[Decision] Should Humanity Become Multi-Planetary?

History or archaeology tells us of potential extinctions of species from meteor hitting earth or volcano eruptions bringing rapid climate changes. Humans likewise may face similar challenges at some point. In addition, nuclear power is a new form of danger that may eradicate everyone on earth if misused. Some may even worry about unknown space aliens finding earth, as it may be viewed as highly livable planet. Will existential threat become big enough to necessitate humanity to become multi-planetary?

We may consider the following matrix using the potential existential risks, and whether having presence in another planet will be the solution:

Table 67-1: The Multi-Planetary Decision Matrix

<table>
<tr><th colspan="2" rowspan="2"></th><th colspan="2">Whether Humanity Will Face Existential Risk on Earth</th></tr>
<tr><th>Yes (Pessimists)</th><th>No (Optimists)</th></tr>
<tr><td rowspan="2">Whether Presence in Another Planet Will Be the Solution</td><td>Yes (Optimists)</td><td>Need to Become Interplanetary (Group 1)</td><td>Useful to Become Interplanetary (Group 2)</td></tr>
<tr><td>No (Pessimists)</td><td>Becoming Interplanetary is Pointless (Group 3)</td><td>Need Other Reasons to Become Interplanetary (Group 4)</td></tr>
</table>

Group 1: Existential Risk High, Multi-Planet Will Be Solution

People in this group will view the existential risks as serious. These people may be more likely to consider the risks of nuclear war or meteor strikes as more imminent, and consider presence in another planet as a "must-have."

Note becoming interplanetary does not mean all individuals will be. If there is a sudden nuclear war, most individuals on earth will perish because we will not be able to move to Mars en masse. It would be just the small sub-group of humans in another planet that will continue humanity, to re-populate earth.

Group 2: Existential Risk Low, Multi-Planet Will Be Solution

People in this group will view the existential risks as non-threatening. These people may be more likely to consider the risks of nuclear war or meteor strikes as far-flung, or something that can be prevented, such as by calling for peace or sending rockets to meteors before they reach earth. They may view having presence in another planet as a "nice-to-have."

Group 3: Existential Risk High, Multi-Planet Will Not Be Solution
People in this group may be more likely to be skeptical of the benefits of having multi-planet presence. These people would be likely to consider the risk factors that affect earth may also affect another planet, such as the potential for the sun to explode, or aliens that attack earth would be able to find humans on another planet, etc. Another opinion may include that the earth after nuclear war may still be more livable than another planet.

Group 4: Existential Risk Low, Multi-Planet Will Not Be Solution
People in this group would not be fazed by existential risks or impressed by having presence in another planet. These people will be more likely to consider missions to other planets as more of a scientific or curiosity projects. These people may consider having presence in other planets if it offers some other benefits, such as finding valuable natural resources.

To summarize, people who are against or do not think highly of building a colony in Mars may have some of the following areas of disagreements:

- **(Degree of Risk)** The risks argued are miniscule that they can be ignored: some may deem such risks as aliens attacking earth, meteors hitting earth, nuclear wars to be unrealistic so as to ignore them.
- **(Source of Risk)** The risks are not well mitigated by building a colony in Mars: some may argue that while the risks are significant, colony in Mars is not the solution because the solar system as whole would face the same risk
- **(Alternative Solutions)** Some may argue for finding more efficient or better solutions on Earth. For example, some may argue we should focus on monitoring meteor movements and removing dangerous ones

In relation to AI, people may view AI as both potential cause for increase in AI risk, as well as an enabler of multi-planetary presence.

1) AI as Instigation of Existential Threat: Some may argue AI will serve as the cause for increase in existential threat, either for someone using AI, or some form of self-initiated AI becoming a threat to humanity

2) AI as Mitigation of Existential Threat: Some may argue AI would be useful in solving our existential risk. For example, AI may be used to help populate another planet. We may think of a separate question of whether humans can become multi-planetary, and whether AI will enable this.

68. The Purposes of Humanity and AI Controversy

[Decision]

What Should Be the Goal or Purpose of Humanity? Purpose of AI?

*"Of Everything In the Entire Universe,
Humans Are the Most Precious"*

- Children's Textbook of Korean King's Academy[174]

5-Line Summary

1. We may think of purpose as an abstract long-term goal over one's lifetime, in contrast to mission, which may be thought of as a more concrete short-term goal
2. As AI takes more portion of our economy, more people may begin to wonder what should be the purpose of humanity
3. In the same sense, more people may begin to wonder what should be the purpose of AI
4. In lower levels of AI adoption, we may think of humans as giving missions to AI, or giving it purpose
5. In higher levels of AI adoption, AI may have to find its purpose, similar to how humans should find our purpose ourselves

Meaning of Existence: What Should Be the Purpose of Humanity?

We can think of one's "purpose" as an abstract goal that permeates throughout one's life, while "mission" can be thought of as a more concrete goal that is shorter-term, such as a job or a project. Ideally, people who can pursue missions that align with their life goals would be considered fulfilling their sense of purpose. In short, we "have a sense" of purpose, while people "carry out" missions.

Because most humans of today consider ourselves free, we all have different senses of purpose. But when we look at history, people of just a few centuries ago defined their sense of purpose differently; for example, people would have been more likely to consider serving their country, king, or religion as their purpose.

From this line of thinking, we may think that everyone may have their own "purposes" and that there may be a controversy regarding what everyone thinks what everyone else's purposes should be. With this in mind, we may also think about the topic of "what we think the purposes of AI should be."

Meaning of Creation: What Should Be the Purpose of AI?

Even today, people already use AI for everyday purposes such as answering questions. When we think about how it works, there are three steps involved. First, humans initiate some action to AI by giving it a request. Then, AI does its action to complete the request. Third, humans observe this result. We may think of these steps as humans giving AI a purpose, even though that purpose may be brief in time. Sometimes this short-term purpose may be referred to as a mission. In Level 1 Adoption, the purpose of AI is quite obvious.

However, once AI adoption reaches Level 2 or 3, we may arrive at a situation where AI has to give itself purpose for its existence. What will AI give itself as its purpose? Will we like it? From the observation regarding how we may have differences of opinions regarding what we think about other people's sense of purpose, we may have different opinions about whatever purposes AI gives itself. Some people may agree with AI, while others may not.

How Will Our Sense of Purpose Change When AI Can Do Everything Better?

Another topic that may come into focus would be the feedback from the advancements in AI into our society. If AI reaches the level of surpassing everything we can do, will people lose their purpose in some way? In essence, what will people do when AI can do everything better than us?

69. The Last AI Controversy

[Forecast]

What Will Be the Last AI of Humanity?

[Decision]

What Will You Do to Help Determine the Last AI of Humanity?

"Only You Can Help Determine the Last AI of Humanity"

- The Last AI

5-Line Summary

1. The Last AI is a book that delves into the most important question in AI adoption; "what will be the last AI of humanity?"
2. We may think of the ultimate forms of AI adoption from different perspectives, such as technological, social, philosophical, etc.
3. The Last AI presents some of the potential candidates for the last AI of humanity, and some of the scenarios that may lead to each ending
4. The best ending may be reaching the AI Utopia, which is enabled by reaching Absolute AI
5. It may be up to us to determine our path. The Last AI is intended to help someone who may be in need of a guide

What Will Be the Last AI of Humanity?

The basic premise of The Last AI is based on the notion that understanding the general pattern of progress is easier than actually making the progress. For example, we can understand how the games of Monopoly, chess, or Go would progress more easily than becoming a chess Grandmaster. Similarly, it would be much easier to understand the progress of AI adoption than actually being a renowned AI researcher. The goal was to "connect the dots on AI adoption."

The Last AI was intended to introduce the three major topics of AI adoption.

1. **(Social)** Introduced the concept of the Four Levels AI Adoption Pyramid to help people think about the path and various scenarios the "AI Game" may play out
2. **(Technological)** Introduced the attribute of self-initiation in AI as the relevant dimension of discussing more advanced forms of AI
3. **(Economic)** Introduced the concept of AI Economics to describe the progress of AI contribution towards an AI-led economy and implications on competition

What Will Get In Our Way? When we play games such as chess, there is no pre-set length; the game can end suddenly, due to a mistake or brilliant move. The "game" of AI adoption may also abruptly end at Level 1; the biggest cause for concern may be the arrival of AGI, if there is a scarcity of AGI and it falls to the wrong hands that the productivity gain becomes lopsided. A brilliant move by a villain to develop the only AGI, or failed actions of the good guys and the regulators to prevent this could lead to an abrupt end of the game.

What Will Be The Path of the AI Adoption Game? (Complete Realm)

We may consider the complete realm of the best and worst scenarios, and in between the two. We may think of the two dimensions of the direction and degree of the impact of AI adoption as in the following matrix:

Table 69-1: The Last AI Forecast Matrix

		AI Adoption Direction of Impact (Social Perspective)	
		Negative (Pessimists)	**Positive (Optimists)**
AI Adoption Degree of Impact (Technical Perspective)	**High / Extreme (Extremists)**	**(Group 3: Worst Scenario)** AI Dictator / AI Prison Extinction	**(Group 1: Best Scenario)** Economic AI Utopia Social AI Utopia
	Low / Moderate (Moderates)	**(Group 3: Downward Path)** AI Inequality AI Chaos	**(Group 4: Upward Path)** AI Prosperity AI Stability

1. The Best Scenarios: The best scenario can be referred to as the AI Utopia. While there may be different versions of Utopia, we will refer to the version suggested in The Last AI, which would be enabled by the appearance of an Absolute AI. These would include eternal life, unbounded wealth, etc.

2. The Worst Scenarios: The worst scenario may be referred to as the AI Prison, where a hostile ASI becomes an eternal dictator that can never be overthrown. Another scenario may be AI leading to the extinction of mankind.

In Between the Best and the Worst, we may consider the upward rising and downward spiraling scenarios.

3. The Downward Spiraling Scenarios: We may think of AI causing more inequality, confusion and social instability. The resource gap between the haves and have-nots may increase with people who lose their jobs cannot find other means to live. In some cases, AI may increase war or the inequality of countries, leading to a wider gap among constituents of different nations.

4. The Upward Rising Scenarios: In this type of scenarios, people will be able to manage AI adoption to bring prosperity to us all. While AI may or may not lead us to the types of Utopias we imagine, it will help solve more and more economic and social problems to make our lives more satisfying.

[Forecast]

What do you think will become the Last AI of Humanity?

[Decision]

What will you do to help determine the Last AI of Humanity?

PART 4. TOWARDS THE ART OF AI STRATEGY

"Knowing Yourself and Your Enemy,
You Will Avoid Danger in Hundred Battles"

- Sohn Ja, the Art of War

"Knowledge Is Knowing What You Do Not Know"

- Confucius

How Should We View Our Future? What Should We Do About It?

How should we think about the future? For some people, the future should look bright and promising, so we have something to look forward to. These people may want to paint the future even better than what they really think. In other words, some people prefer to paint a rosy picture about the future. For some other people, the future may have to look dangerous and full of warning signs, so they can prepare for it better to make the reality better than what was expected. In other words, some people prefer to under-promise and over-deliver. This contrasting view may cause people who have the exactly same forecasts about the future to make opposing decisions.

As explained in the beginning, the focus of this book was to help people gain a deeper perspective on the following three phases of thinking about the future:

1) **Forecast** or Prediction about the future
2) **Decision**
3) The **Link** between the Forecast and the Decision

Then, we considered how AI may impact our society in different directions, using the 2-Forces and 8-Directions framework, which is an application of the Korean traditional *Taeguk* Framework.

Once more people understand what is at stake, what each of the issues represent, and think about the issues regarding AI adoption in general, we may eventually be able to plot everyone's *forecasts* and *decisions*. As described in The Last AI, reaching social agreements may become one of the most important actions our society can make in determining our destiny.

Different people have different interests. Some people may have shorter horizon; these people may find it more interesting what is ahead right in front of us. Some others may have longer horizon; these people may find longer-term issues more interesting. Some people may have narrower scope; these people may find it more interesting what is close around us, such as our family and work. Some people may have wider scope; these people may find it more interesting to consider what affects the whole world.

Topics by Level of AI Adoption

We may think of what types of topics may become more popular with each AI adoption level.

Since our cognitive capabilities are limited, some may find it more relevant to focus on particular perspectives or areas they are more interested in, and then delve deeper into that particular perspective. When we look at it this way, we may more easily gain insights from thinking about the progress of a particular area.

For example, we may think of how in regards to individual life, AI may change our main interests from thinking about what to learn or teach our children in Level 1, to pursuing noble goals other than working in Level 2, to thinking more about the meaning or survival of humanity towards Level 4.

Table P4-1: Example of the Adoption Level – Perspective Matrix

Perspectives	Level 1	Level 2	Level 3	Level 4
Individual and Family Life / Effort	What to Learn or Teach	Pursue Noble Goals	Reproduction	Survival, Meaning, and Goals of Humanity
Business & Economy	Job Losses, Training	Reparation, Subsidy (Basic Income)	New Horizon of Economy	Will AI Co. merge with AI Gov.?
Society & Government (Equality vs Freedom)	Protection vs Privacy	Ownership of AI (Inequality)	AI Nationalization vs Independence	Voting Rights, Eligibility, Which Regime to Lv. 4 First
Technology (Realm of Possibility)	Application of AI	Who Will Be First to AGI?	Will ASI Be Possible? Bias?	Level 1 (Cybernetics) vs Level 4

[Side Note] Summary of Major Controversies in Each Levels of Adoption

Level 1 Adoption: "If You Can Imagine It, You Can Do It"

In the beginning of AI adoption, AI would assist humans in business activities. Humans may use AI as a type of a tool to improve productivity, and AI would not have gained enough dependability to perform tasks without human intervention. AI may also help humans carry out tasks previously not achievable. In this level of AI adoption, the interest among individuals and companies will increase rapidly as AI may help increase productivity in a dramatic manner. In Level 1 AI Adoption, human productivity is improved with the use of AI. The ultimate form of augmentation would be "1-Person Company" (1PC), but in Level 1 AI Adoption only "1-Person Team" or "1-Person Department" would be more likely to be feasible for larger operations.

In Level 1, our discussions may focus on reaching AGI or similar types of self-initiated AI that will get us closer to Level 2 Adoption. Along the way, we may encounter increasingly challenging discussions regarding social inequality, privacy, and crimes. People may be divided over whether AI development should be promoted or regulated more. Some may see AI acceleration as a way to enjoy the benefits AI, while others may see AI deceleration as a way to ensure safety or a way to avoid danger. Some others may see other countries lead AI as a bigger threat than AI itself.

Table P4-2: Major Controversies in Level 1 AI Adoption

Scope of Influence	Examples of Major Controversies
Individuals	- Work: job losses and training - Crimes and Deception: prevention and avoidance - Increasing Inequality of Individuals
Firms	- Which company first to Level 2? AGI? - 1-Person Teams, 1-Person Departments (Augmentation)
Society	- Privacy vs Protection - Regulation: Who? What? Why? How? When?
Government (Countries)	- Which country first to Level 2? AGI? - How much AI should the military use?
World (Supra-Nation)	- How to prepare for a world where all of humanity may have to come to agreement more than before

Level 2 Adoption: "What You Can Imagine Will Be Done For You"

The basic premise of Level 2 Adoption is that AI will become proficient to be in charge of business roles by carrying out all of the tasks of a business role in place of humans. In Level 2, humans will compete against AI for jobs, but at the higher level of analysis we may also think of the situation as human-led companies competing against other human-led companies and AI assisting as a part of the companies.

The beginning part of Level 2 adoption may be the most exciting times for the world economy, as there will be increased demands to develop AI Agents for all kinds of areas and functions. People may be excited about the opportunities AI may provide, and great wealth may be accumulated. But as time goes by, the society may become more likely to experience confusion and abrupt changes. It may appear more and more that AI is competing against individual humans and winning. 0-Person Teams and 0-Person Departments would help create the ultimate form of augmentation, the "1-Person Company" and "1-Person Group" or 1-Person Conglomerates. A major inflection point in Level 2 Adoption is when "automated innovation" becomes achievable. Unlike in "augmented innovation" in Level 1, AI by itself would be able to contribute to the innovation of firms. These advances will bring societal changes that may cause larger controversy on who should own AI.

Table P4-3: Major Controversies in Level 2 AI Adoption

Scope of Influence	Examples of Major Controversies
Individuals	- Work: How Humans can compete against AI - AI Subsidy as direct retribution for job losses
Firms	- 1-Person vs 0-Person Teams (Agency) - 1-Person Companies, 1-Person Group, 1-Person Conglomerates - Increasing Inequality of Firms
Society	- Allowing AI to compete against human individuals - AI Ownership: Who should own AI? Private or Nationalize? - UBI
Government (Countries)	- Dealing with increase in monopolies - Whether to allow Level 3 Adoption
World (Supra-Nation)	- World takeover attempt using AI by some villain

Level 3 Adoption: "Even What You Couldn't Imagine Is Already Done"
Eventually, AI would be able to take over all of the top management roles of a business, including the roles of CEO and the Chairman. The basic premise of the Level 3 Adoption is that there may be a form of company where humans will no longer be necessary, referred to as self-driving companies. Level 3 may change the business, economy and society so much that it may look completely foreign to us. AI Companies will have to compete against other AI Companies, and human-led companies may not be competitive. When these AI Companies proliferate, it may cause major social confusion.

Level 3 AI Adoption may feel like the climax of the AI adoption game for the people who live in those times. If the ultimate form of AI augmentation is the "1-Person Company", the ultimate form of AI automation would be the "0-Person Company".[175] Similar to how autonomous vehicles have no drivers but only passengers, these autonomous companies will have no workers but only customers. When AI Companies take up a larger portion of the economy, it may lead to an acceleration of consolidation and convergence of industries, leading to AI Super-Monopolies and Mega-Monopolies. The ultimate form of the economy in AI adoption may be referred to as the "AI Economic Utopia," where "automated innovation" enables the cost of innovation to converge to zero, leading to the price of everything to converge to zero.

Table P4-4: Major Controversies in Level 3 AI Adoption

Scope of Influence	Examples of Major Controversies
Individuals	- Economy: New Economic Paradigm - Subsidy as only means of income
Firms	- 0-Person vs 1-Person Firms - Competing against potential AI Monopolies
Society	- Accepting AI as owners of companies (Autonomy) - Allowing AI to compete against Human Organizations
Government (Countries)	- Regulating against Irrevocable Monopoly or 1-AI Economy
World (Supra-Nation)	- Increasing inequality of countries leading to mass exodus or even annexations

Level 4 Adoption: "You Will Not Need To Know What Has Been Done"
Just as AI adoption in business would be a natural way to enhance the productivity of companies, AI adoption would be a natural way to improve the productivity of governments. Similar to how AlphaGo makes moves humans cannot think, AI-led countries may advance in ways we cannot imagine; the 6 Levels of Autonomous Governments is introduced to help think about this issue. If the ultimate form of AI companies is a type of "0-Person Company" in "AI Company" and the ultimate form of economy is the AI Economic Utopia, then the ultimate form of AI governments would be a type of "0-Person Country" or "0-Person Government," and the ultimate form of society would be the AI Social Utopia, where everyone is equal and free. On a separate path, the appearance of "AI-Only Countries" may become an issue, as this would imply AI would not be under the jurisdiction of any human country.

From a positive point of view, AI taking charge of the government would mean AI represents or serves humans. On the other hand, it may also imply AI may rule over humans. If not all ASI converge to the same AI, then we may have the option of choosing which ASI to run the government. This may also open the possibility for Non-Friendly AI to try to take over the government in a dangerous manner. Humanity may face a number of different scenarios with the appearance of ASI, as described in The Last AI.

Table P4-5: Major Controversies in Level 4 AI Adoption

Scope of Influence	Examples of Major Controversies
Individuals	- Choice of nationality
Firms	- Will AI companies and AI governments become one and the same?
Society	- Voting rights of AI - AI appearing in elections
Government (Countries)	- AI introducing new ways to organize governments - How much authority AI should be allowed
World (Supra-Nation)	- Accepting existence of 0-Person countries (Authority) - Allowing AI to compete against All of Humanity

In Real Life: Would We Reach the Pinnacle of Existence?

Let us just focus on the positive side for a moment. If everything goes well, hopefully everyone on earth will be living in a Utopia-like environment, where the productivity of AI is enough for everyone to live materially satisfactory lives without forced to carry out tasks that we now consider "work." There would be no crimes, as the AI government would be able to prevent them before they happen without even being intrusive, and everyone will be satisfied and lead happy and meaningful lives without worrying.

However, not everything may go as positively or as smoothly as described. In fact, it could as well go to the opposite end of the spectrum, where humanity as whole could be facing dire situations such as ruling of an oppressive AI regime or even extinction.

In between these two extreme ends, there would be more realistic problems and solutions that may arise as we get closer and closer to the AI Utopia.[176]

Having controversies may be one of the evidences that we can solve problems better as a group than as individuals. Some may expect super-intelligence would lead to everyone having the same opinions. However, as long as different versions of ASI exist, we will have differences of opinions even among ASI. From this line of thinking, having controversies may indicate a healthy society, since controversies can only be eradicated only under some form of oppression. There is only one true way to reach convergence of opinions, and that would be reaching Absolute AI. From this perspective, controversies may only disappear when we have Absolute AI.

Table P4-6: Major Controversies in Ultimate Form of AI Adoption

Scope of Influence	Main Interests
Individuals	- Will we be able to live forever?
Firms	- Will ASI Lead to the Economic Utopia?
Society	- Will ASI Lead to the Social Utopia?
Government (Countries)	- Will AI converge to same government + company?
World (Supra-Nation)	- Will AI Lead to the AI Utopia or an AI prison?

Concluding Remarks

"Spreading the Word on AI Adoption"

We may think of theory as having a framework for analysis. If we don't have the right framework then we will not be able to understand what is going on. For example, some NBA basketball and NHL ice hockey games are played on the exact same indoor stadiums, just hours apart. Imagine you visit one of these venues and think you are to watch an ice hockey game. But, you are actually watching basketball without realizing it. With your frame of mind on ice hockey, instead of understanding or enjoying the flow of the game, you may feel agitated and confused about what is going on. Instead of being impressed by a long range three point shot or dunk, you may be wondering "Why are they wearing shorts?" "Where is the goal?" "Where did the ice go?" "Why is no one wearing skates?" "Why are they all missing their sticks?" etc.

The same may be thought about AI adoption. We need to have the right frame of mind to understand what is going on. Otherwise, similar to a person who is watching basketball while thinking it is ice hockey, we may become confused and agitated by what goes on, instead of properly understanding or enjoying the progress of our society.

The difference is that in the "game" of AI adoption, no one can tell us what game we are playing or watching. We have to figure it out. It is similar to a situation where everyone is watching the same game, but some think we are watching basketball, some think we are watching football, while some others think we are watching baseball and volleyball, while some others also think we are watching football, but actually mean soccer, etc. Similarly, some may think we are watching the second industrial revolution, while some may think we are watching the second Renaissance, while others may think we are watching a type of biblical event, the new Bronze Age, invention of characters, introduction of numbers, or even the extinction of dinosaurs, and so on.

This is where differences of opinions, or controversies, may play a role. As a whole, it would be better for humanity to have a diverse set of contrasting ideas to be able to discern what is really going on. It may be thought of as having the "wisdom of crowds."

There is a caveat for this to work though. We have to have more people who are well informed and who are well equipped to make the right predictions and decisions for themselves. If we are watching basketball and someone next to you is a famous influencer who keeps on insisting we are watching football, and if more people start believing without thinking, we would have a situation where people are misled to the detriment of society. Similarly, fake news and propagandas are designed to confuse people to draw the wrong conclusions.

I hope this book can help people think about the progress of AI adoption to gain a better understanding of what is going on, to develop their own frame of analysis and be able to make better forecasts and predictions. To help with this, the 2-Forces, 8-Directions framework was used to provide a general map of the AI adoption universe, based on The Last AI.

The beauty of it is that not everyone has to understand the whole map for our society to make a progress. Everyone can see for themselves which areas they like, and pick out their specialty, so to speak. Each person can pick an area to delve more deeply, to develop their own opinions. The goal is to get better at understanding what factors are important, knowing what to look for when making forecasts or decisions, understanding how people can draw different conclusions, and be able to draw your own assessment of those opinions, etc.

Another interesting attribute of this book may be that it would lead to the spreading of ideas. In what may be called "referrals," we may spread the idea of getting better. As more people around you get better at understanding what game we are playing, it would help our whole society become a better place, similar to a cycle of positive feedback loop. We want more people around us to become better at understanding what game we are playing and watching.

Hopefully this book of controversies can lead us to the development of what may be referred to as the Art of AI Strategy.

Notes and Comments

[1] For more information regarding the famous photo of the "Tank Man," refer to: Widener, Jeff, and Kyle Almond. "The Story behind the Iconic 'Tank Man' Photo." CNN, May 2019. https://edition.cnn.com/interactive/2019/05/world/tiananmen-square-tank-man-cnnphotos/. Pickert, Kate. "Tank Man at 25: Behind the Iconic Tiananmen Square Photo," June 4, 2014. https://time.com/3809688/tank-man-iconic-tiananmen-photo/.

[2] For more information about the Great Depression and its impact, refer to: Lehman, Richard. "The Great Depression: Then & Now." Seeking Alpha (blog), August 4, 2023. https://seekingalpha.com/article/4513525-the-great-depression.

[3] Sohn, S.M., (2024), The Last AI: of Humanity Climbing the AI Pyramid. SM Research Institute.

[4] Sohn, S.M., (2023), "The Three Levels of AI Adoption Framework and the Six Levels of Autonomous Companies." Working paper.

[5] Ibid - Refer to previous note (Sohn)

[6] Ibid - Refer to previous note (Sohn)

[7] Metz, Rachel. (Bloomberg News) "OpenAI Scale Ranks Progress Toward 'Human-Level' Problem Solving" https://www.bloomberg.com/news/articles/2024-07-11/openai-sets-levels-to-track-progress-toward-superintelligent-ai

[8] Sohn, S.M., (2023), "The Three Levels of AI Adoption Framework and the Six Levels of Autonomous Companies." Working paper.

[9] Baird, Aaron and Maruping, Likoebe M.. 2021. "The Next Generation of Research on IS Use: A Theoretical Framework of Delegation to and from Agentic IS Artifacts," MIS Quarterly, (45: 1) pp.315-341.

[10] Even though I can no longer remember the exact wording, I wrote this in a letter on May 25, 2002; this is the main quote that led to this book.

[11] The first use of the term singularity is attributed to mathematician Jon von Neumann. The popular version of singularity hypothesis is attributed to I.J. Good (1965), known as "intelligence explosion." Good, Irving John. "Speculations Concerning the First Ultraintelligent Machine." In Advances in Computers, 6:31–88. Elsevier, 1966. https://doi.org/10.1016/S0065-2458(08)60418-0.

[12] I cannot exactly remember the phrase in Korean or exactly who said it, but someone explained this during one of our team meetings around 2016, and this quote probably should be attributed to the then head of the Global Strategy Team,. Ho-Tae So. This quote was similar to a quote attributed to Albert Einstein, "if you can't it explain it simply, you don't understand it well enough," but also different.

[13] Gubrud in 1997, mentioned by Goertzel in 2014 paper: Goertzel, Ben. "Artificial General Intelligence: Concept, State of the Art, and Future Prospects." Journal of Artificial General Intelligence 5, no. 1 (December 1, 2014): 1–48. https://doi.org/10.2478/jagi-2014-0001.

[14] Goertzel, Ben, and Cassio Pennachin, eds. Artificial General Intelligence. Cognitive Technologies. Berlin, Heidelberg: Springer Berlin Heidelberg, 2007. https://doi.org/10.1007/978-3-540-68677-4.

[15] For more information about the Google AGI Paper, refer to: Morris et al. (2024) "Levels of AGI for Operationalizing Progress on the Path to AGI" https://arxiv.org/abs/2311.02462

[16] Refer to: OpenAI Charter (2018) https://openai.com/charter
OpenAI Plan for AGI (2023) https://openai.com/blog/planning-for-agi-and-beyond

[17] For more information regarding OpenAI and Microsoft agreement on AGI definition: https://techcrunch.com/2024/12/26/microsoft-and-openai-have-a-financial-definition-of-agi-report/

[18] For more information regarding business usage of AGI: https://medium.com/@The_Last_AI/openais-5-stage-ai-roadmap-explained-using-the-3-levels-of-ai-adoption-and-the-6-levels-of-e295693cc105

[19] Refer to The Last AI, pp. 120 (The 6 Levels of Pre-AGI AI)

[20] This line of thought is also reflected in IJ Good (1965), where he stated "the first ultraintelligent machine is the last invention that man need ever make, provided that the machine is docile enough..."
Good, Irving John. "Speculations Concerning the First Ultraintelligent Machine." In Advances in Computers, 6:31–88. Elsevier, 1966. https://doi.org/10.1016/S0065-2458(08)60418-0.

[21] Alternatively, DeepMind Co-founder Mustafa Suleyman suggested "Artificial Capable Intelligence" to refer to AI that can carry out everyday tasks to become the "center of world economy."

[22] For stories about not everyone having Inner monologues, refer to Scientific American article "Not Everyone Has an Inner Voice Streaming through Their Head" (2024): https://www.scientificamerican .com/article/not-everyone-has-an-inner-voice-streaming-through-their-head/
For visual thinking, having too clear vision is called "hyperphantasia," while not having imagery is "aphantasia." For more, refer to Zeman, A. (2024), "Aphantasia and hyperphantasia: exploring imagery vividness extremes." https://www.sciencedirect.com/science/article/pii/S1364661324000342

[23] For the Monkey clip, refer to the video on TED from a talk by Frans de Waal, Moral behavior in animals" https://www.youtube.com/watch?v=meiU6TxysCg

[24] For more info on the Theory of Mind, refer to this article: https://en.wikipedia.org/wiki/Theory_of_mind or https://www.sciencedirect.com/topics/neuroscience/theory-of-mind

[25] Ilkou, Eleni, and Maria Koutraki. "Symbolic vs Sub-Symbolic Ai Methods: Friends or Enemies?" In CIKM (Workshops), Vol. 2699, 2020. For more information about the comparison readers also may check https://towardsdatascience.com/symbolic-vs-connectionist-a-i-8cf6b656927

[26] Rosenblatt, F. "The Perceptron: A Probabilistic Model for Information Storage and Organization in the Brain." Psychological Review 65, no. 6 (1958): 386–408. https://doi.org/10.1037/h0042519.

[27] Kahneman, Daniel. Thinking, Fast and Slow. First paperback edition. Psychology/Economics. New York: Farrar, Straus and Giroux, 2013.

[28] For more information about Energy-Based Models, readers may refer to: Dawid, Anna, and Yann LeCun. "Introduction to Latent Variable Energy-Based Models: A Path Towards Autonomous Machine Intelligence." arXiv, June 4, 2023. http://arxiv.org/abs/2306.02572.

[29] For more information about Diffusion-Based Transformers, readers may refer to: Peebles, William, and Saining Xie. "Scalable Diffusion Models with Transformers." In Proceedings of the IEEE/CVF International Conference on Computer Vision (ICCV), 4195–4205, 2023.

[30] Book by Oliver Sacks (1985)

[31] This quote may also be attributed to Nicolaus Copernicus. Galilei's version is "Eppur si muove," which is translated to "and yet it moves." It is also associated with a novel by Oliver Goldsmith, Amos Fortune.

[32] There is a condition for not being able to imagine visual images, called Aphantasia, refer to previous.

[33] I was thinking of a movie scene where kids say this, but could not find the title of the movie.

[34] Refer to: https://www.linkedin.com/pulse/openais-5-stage-ai-roadmap-explained-using-3-levels-6-sohn-cfa-z5h1c

[35] Metz, Rachel. (2024, Bloomberg) "OpenAI Scale Ranks Progress Toward 'Human-Level' Problem Solving"

[36] Sohn, S.M., (2023), "The Three Levels of AI Adoption Framework and the Six Levels of Autonomous Companies." Working paper.

[37] An example includes the following benchmark paper: Srivastava, A., A. Rastogi, A. Rao, A. A. Md Shoeb, A. Abid, A. Fisch, A. R. Brown, et al. "Beyond the Imitation Game: Quantifying and Extrapolating the Capabilities of Language Models," 2022. https://doi.org/10.48550/ARXIV.2206.04615.

[38] 1 vs 100 was a game show on NBC, based on a Dutch game show.

[39] There are many articles about this, including Fortune (Jan 27, 2025) "DeepSeek is the hottest new AI chatbot—but it comes with Chinese censorship built in." https://fortune.com/2025/01/27/deepseek-tops-app-store-charts-china-censorship/

[40] There are many articles, about this, including the Korea Herald (Feb 10, 2025) "Kimchi: Korean or Chinese? NIS cautions DeepSeek users about asking it 'sensitive questions' https://www.koreaherald.com/article/10416237

[41] This is a pun on the quote by Descartes, "I think, therefore I am, (Cogito ergo sum)"

[42] Sohn, SM, The New Turing Test: The Six Levels of Autonomous AI Robots and Human-Likeness, Superiority, and Benevolence as Measures of Autonomous AI (2024). Preprint. http://dx.doi.org/10.2139/ssrn.5073115

[43] Ibid - Refer to previous note (Sohn)

[44] Hopkins, Debbie, and Tim Schwanen. "Talking about Automated Vehicles: What Do Levels of Automation Do?" Technology in Society 64 (February 2021): 101488. https://doi.org/10.1016/j.techsoc.2020.101488.

[45] Harnad, S. Other bodies, other minds: A machine incarnation of an old philosophical problem. Minds and Machines 1, 43–54 (1991). https://doi.org/10.1007/BF00360578

[46] Bokyem TV: youtube.com/@bokyemtv MrBeast: https://www.youtube.com/@MrBeast

[47] The first use of the term singularity is attributed to mathematician Jon von Neumann. The popular version of singularity hypothesis is attributed to I.J. Good (1965), known as "intelligence explosion."

[48] Refer to The Last AI (pp. 359) for more information about Practical Singularity.

[49] Refer to Brynjolfsson, E. "The Turing Trap: The Promise & Peril of Human-Like Artificial Intelligence " (2022) https://digitaleconomy.stanford.edu/news/the-turing-trap-the-promise-peril-of-human-like-artificial-intelligence/

[50] Sohn, Seuk Min. "Effortlessness as the Measurement of the Impact of Artificial Intelligence (AI) Adoption and Innovation: Towards the Theory of Relative AI." Preprint. SSRN, 2024. https://doi.org/10.2139/ssrn.4739415.

[51] Ibid - Refer to previous note (Sohn)

[52] Brynjolfsson, E. "The Turing Trap: The Promise & Peril of Human-Like Artificial Intelligence " (2022)

[53] Sohn, Seuk Min. "Effortlessness as the Measurement of the Impact of Artificial Intelligence (AI) Adoption and Innovation: Towards the Theory of Relative AI." Preprint. SSRN, 2024. https://doi.org/10.2139/ssrn.4739415.

[54] Ibid - Refer to previous note (Sohn)

[55] Ibid - Refer to previous note (Sohn)

[56] The myth of Pandora's Box originates from Greek poet Hesiod. In the story, the jar was presented by Zeus as a vengeance to Prometheus.

[57] This quote is attributed to Bishop Robert Lowth in 1762, when he noted the grammatical rule of double negatives, not in mathematics.

[58] Apparently this is a proverb in a variety of places.

[59] This line of opinion has been suggested by a variety of renowned AI researchers, such as Yann LeCun, Francois Cholllet, among others. Example is: https://www.freethink.com/robots-ai/arc-prize-agi

[60] This opinion has also been voiced by Andrej Karpathy on his X account (Sep 15, 2024) https://x.com/karpathy/status/1835024197506187617

[61] For more information on hallucination of LLMs: The Economist. "AI Models Make Stuff up. How Can Hallucinations Be Controlled?" February 28, 2024. https://www.economist.com/science-and-technology/2024/02/28/ai-models-make-stuff-up-how-can-hallucinations-be-controlled.
Readers may also refer to the hallucination index of popular LLMs:
https://www.rungalileo.io/hallucinationindex

[62] For more news reports about Bill Gates on AI Tax: Morris, David Z. "Bill Gates Says Robots Should Be Taxed Like Workers." Fortune, February 19, 2017. https://fortune.com/2017/02/18/bill-gates-robot-taxes-automation/.
Kharpal, Arjun. "Bill Gates Wants to Tax Robots, but the EU Says, 'No Way, No Way.'" CNBC, June 2, 2017. https://www.cnbc.com/2017/06/02/bill-gates-robot-tax-eu.html.

[63] This is a pun on Thomas Reid's quote from 1786 book Essays on the Intellectual Powers of Man, which later appeared in Cornhill Magazine in 1868 as "a chain is only as strong as its weakest link"

[64] This concept is from the Korean proverb that translates as "not knowing is the medicine."

[65] There are arguments to even prevent the sharing of the weights of neural networks in the fear of safety, as a response to the presidential executive order: https://www.whitehouse.gov/briefing-room/presidential-actions/2023/10/30/executive-order-on-the-safe-secure-and-trustworthy-development-and-use-of-artificial-intelligence/
The Department of Commerce solicitation of comments: https://www.commerce.gov/news/press-releases/2024/02/ntia-solicits-comments-open-weight-ai-models

[66] This may or may not be a good thing, as the French Maginot Line required a lot of resources to build but the Germans could easily go around it

[67] This is a general wisdom in economics, and this phrase also appears in The Last AI.

[68] This concept was introduced in 1942 by writer Isaac Asimov in "Runaround." For more information: Britannica, T. Editors of Encyclopedia. "three laws of robotics." Encyclopedia Britannica, February 20, 2024. https://www.britannica.com/topic/Three-Laws-of-Robotics.

[69] Lüthi, Nick, Christian Matt, Thomas Myrach, and Iris Junglas. "Augmented Intelligence, Augmented Responsibility?" Business & Information Systems Engineering 65, no. 4 (August 2023): 391–401. https://doi.org/10.1007/s12599-023-00789-9.

[70] Muzyka, Kamil. "The Basic Rules for Coexistence: The Possible Applicability of Metalaw for Human-AGI Relations." Paladyn, Journal of Behavioral Robotics 11, no. 1 (April 3, 2020): 104–17. https://doi.org/10.1515/pjbr-2020-0011.

[71] For more information regarding sleeper agents, readers may refer to a paper from Anthropic: Hubinger, Evan, Carson Denison, Jesse Mu, Mike Lambert, Meg Tong, Monte MacDiarmid, Tamera Lanham, et al. "Sleeper Agents: Training Deceptive LLMs That Persist Through Safety Training." arXiv, January 17, 2024. http://arxiv.org/abs/2401.05566.

[72] This appears to be a general expression that does not have an attribution

[73] The theme song Ghostbusters by Ray Parker Jr.

[74] I wrote this in a letter in May 2002. I can no longer remember the exact wording, but this phrase led to this book so it is noted here.

[75] Sohn, Seuk Min. "Effortlessness as the Measurement of the Impact of Artificial Intelligence (AI) Adoption and Innovation: Towards the Theory of Relative AI." Preprint. 2024.

[76] For the Fast-thinking Dog Argument, refer to Everitt, Lea, & Hutter (2018) "AGI Safety Literature Review" https://arxiv.org/abs/1805.01109

[77] For more information about Humanity's Last Exam: https://agi.safe.ai/

[78] Refer to The Last AI (pp. 385 - 387), and Sohn, SM. (2025). The Six Levels of Humanity's Last Exam of AI and the Question of Learning Experience from ASI. Working Paper.

[79] Sohn, SM. (2025). The Six Levels of Humanity's Last Exam of AI and the Question of Learning Experience from ASI. Working Paper.

[80] This is from The Last AI (pp. 374)

[81] Sohn, SM. (2025)." The Six Levels of Humanity's Last Exam of AI and the Question of Learning Experience from ASI." Working Paper.

[82] For more information about Humanity's Last Exam: https://agi.safe.ai/

[83] An example of this was post on X, but I scrolled through it and could not find it again.

[84] Ibid - Refer to previous note (Sohn)

[85] Originally in The Last AI (pp. 267)

[86] Refer to XAI: DARPA https://www.darpa.mil/program/explainable-artificial-intelligence
Applied AI Letters Special Issue on DARPA's XAI Program, (2021).
https://onlinelibrary.wiley.com/toc/26895595/2021/2/4
Papers with codes on XAI: https://paperswithcode.com/task/xai
For more academic research on XAI, refer to: Ali, S., T. Abuhmed, S. El-Sappagh, K. Muhammad, J. M. Alonso-Moral, R. Confalonieri, R. Guidotti, J. Del Ser, N. Díaz-Rodríguez, and F. Herrera. "Explainable

Artificial Intelligence (XAI): What We Know and What Is Left to Attain Trustworthy Artificial Intelligence." Information Fusion 99 (November 2023): 101805. https://doi.org/10.1016/j.inffus.2023.101805.

[87] Refer to The Last AI (pp.392)

[88] The phrase "Diamonds are Forever" comes from the James Bond series in 1971. The phrase is also popular from advertising commercials from DeBeers "A Diamond Is Forever."

[89] In investing, some may argue for diversification, while others argue that people's attention span is limited and we should instead focus on what we do best. The first quote is from Don Quixote by Miguel de Cervantes in 1605. The second is attributed to Warren Buffet.

[90] The Last AI (pp. 172)

[91] Tschang, Feichin Ted, and Esteve Almirall. "Artificial Intelligence as Augmenting Automation: Implications for Employment." Academy of Management Perspectives 35, no. 4 (November 2021): 642–59. https://doi.org/10.5465/amp.2019.0062.

[92] For more information regarding prompt hacking: ttps://learnprompting.org/docs/prompt_hacking/intro

[93] For more information regarding adversarial attacks: https://viso.ai/deep-learning/adversarial-machine-learning/, https://openai.com/research/attacking-machine-learning-with-adversarial-examples

[94] For more information on Insecure Output Handling: https://llmtop10.com/llm02/

[95] For more information on model theft: https://www.forbes.com/sites/forbestechcouncil/2023/09/13/ai-models-under-attack-protecting-your-business-from-ai-cyberthreats/

[96] For more information regarding biometric hacking: https://cyberbrainacademy.com/how-ai-enables-hacking-of-biometric-authentication-systems/

[97] For more information regarding zero-click worms: Cohen, Bitton, Nassi, 2024, ComPromptMized: Unleashing Zero-Click Worms that Target GenAI-Powered Applications

[98] For more information regarding watermarking: https://www.brookings.edu/articles/detecting-ai-fingerprints-a-guide-to-watermarking-and-beyond/

[99] For more information about the ATLAS framework: https://atlas.mitre.org/

[100] Refer to: Scientific American, 2023/9. AI Could Smuggle Secret Messages in Memes

[101] Sohn, S.M., (2025), "The Virtual Environment Turing Test: The Six Levels of AI-Generated Environment Frameworks." Working paper.

[102] Ibid - Refer to previous note (Sohn)

[103] A similar western proverb is "one man sows, another reaps"

[104] Larry Summers in a talk in Aspen Ideas Festival 2024 "studying coding is a bad idea and instead young people should learn to work creatively in a group and define purpose" https://www.aspenideas.org/sessions/where-the-economy-and-the-world-are-headed

[105] Google DeepMind "DolphinGemma: How Google AI is helping decode dolphin communication" https://blog.google/technology/ai/dolphingemma/

[106] A direct translation would be "Habit as a three-year-old will last until eighty." Korean proverb A similar quote is "old habits die hard" attributed to Benjamin Franklin

[107] I cannot remember the exact phrase in the conversation, but I think this was one part.

[108] From Elon Musk's X account: https://x.com/elonmusk/status/1846778709040132157

[109] Reports on declining birth rates: https://www.oecd.org/en/about/news/press-releases/2024/06/declining-fertility-rates-put-prosperity-of-future-generations-at-risk.html

[110] Birth rate of Korea in 2023: https://www.reuters.com/world/asia-pacific/south-koreas-fertility-rate-dropped-fresh-record-low-2023-2024-02-28/

[111] The Last AI on X: http://www.x.com/The_Last_AI

[112] Obviously this quote has been said by many different people. I was thinking about hearing it on this TV show when I chose this quote maybe because how he said it.

[113] Pun intended for TV show "Man vs Wild." Another pun is "AI vs Wild," which is the Practical Turing Test

[114] Sohn, S.M., (2023), "The Three Levels of AI Adoption Framework and the Six Levels of Autonomous Companies." Working paper.

[115] While the original Sohn 2023 paper (August 2023) also included a section on the 4 Levels of AI Adoption, it had to be removed in later versions (October 2023); it appears in The Last AI.

[116] Sohn, S.M., (2023), "The Three Levels of AI Adoption Framework and the Six Levels of Autonomous Companies." Working paper.

[117] Ibid - Refer to previous note (Sohn)

[118] Pun intended for one of the previous quote of "1 vs 100."

[119] Sohn, S.M., (2023), "The Three Levels of AI Adoption Framework and the Six Levels of Autonomous Companies." Working paper.

[120] Refer to OpenAI: "Announcing The Stargate Project" https://openai.com/index/announcing-the-stargate-project/

[121] For more information about Lee Wan-Yong, refer to this article (in Korean): http://contents.history.go.kr/mobile/kc/view.do?levelId=kc_n403800

[122] Google DeepMind Paper on AI Safety "An Approach to Technical AGI Safety and Security" https://blog.google/technology/google-deepmind/agi-safety-paper/

[123] A variety of memes deals with the topic of "Big Brother." The term SkyNet comes from the Terminator. The concept of big brother is attributed to George Orwell in book 1984, "Big Brother is Watching You."

[124] Syng-Bok (or Seung-Bok) Lee was a 9-year-old boy in 1968 when a group of armed North Korean spies infiltrated South Korea. It is reported a few of the armed spies broke into the family home and demanded food. Upon hearing him, the spies killed four of his family members, with only two managed to escape.

[125] The reason why I am not sure about this is because my understanding of English at the time was really limited; I even remember her mentioning something about either her husband or parents in the Jewish concentration camp, but all of this may have been misunderstood by me.

[126] This quote is attributed to Melinda Haynes, and also a similar quote is from Lao Tzu. Another similar quote is "First, Break All the Rules" by Marcus Buckingham.

[127] Sohn, Seuk Min. "Effortlessness as the Measurement of the Impact of Artificial Intelligence (AI) Adoption and Innovation: Towards the Theory of Relative AI." Preprint. 2024.

[128] Ibid - Refer to previous note (Sohn)

[129] Ibid - Refer to previous note (Sohn)

[130] Ibid - Refer to previous note (Sohn)

[131] Ibid - Refer to previous note (Sohn)

[132] The Last AI (pp. 130)

[133] For more information about the complementary benefits of AI, there are numerous papers, including: Tschang, Feichin Ted, and Esteve Almirall. "Artificial Intelligence as Augmenting Automation: Implications for Employment." Academy of Management Perspectives 35, no. 4 (November 2021): 642–59. https://doi.org/10.5465/amp.2019.0062.

[134] Ibid - Refer to previous note (Sohn)

[135] For more information about AI productivity paradox: Chakravorti, Bhaskar. "How Will AI Change Work? A Look Back at the 'Productivity Paradox' of the Computer Age Shows It Won't Be so Simple." Fortune, June 25, 2023. https://fortune.com/2023/06/25/ai-effect-jobs-remote-work-productivity-paradox-computers-iphone-chatgpt/. For more about modern productivity paradox: Brynjolfsson, Erik, Daniel Rock, and Chad Syverson. "1. Artificial Intelligence and the Modern Productivity Paradox: A Clash of Expectations and Statistics." In An Agenda, edited by Ajay Agrawal, Joshua Gans, and Avi Goldfarb, 23–60. Chicago: University of Chicago Press, 2019.

[136] Sohn, Seuk Min. "Effortlessness as the Measurement of the Impact of Artificial Intelligence (AI) Adoption and Innovation: Towards the Theory of Relative AI." Preprint. SSRN, 2024.

[137] Ibid - Refer to previous note (Sohn)

[138] Ibid - Refer to previous note (Sohn)

[139] The original quote by Doc is: "And in the future, we don't need horses. We have motorized carriages called automobiles, and the other character replies "... does anybody walk or run anymore?" to which Doc replies "Of course we run. But for recreation. For fun." The other character then replies "Run for fun?"

[140] This quote supposedly existed since the 1930s, but the original author is unknown, and is also known as the Crane's Law. Friedman popularized this notion by using it as the title of his book in 1975.

[141] The Emancipation of Proclamation is from 1863.

[142] For more discussions regarding the idea about incorporating AI: Kaplan, Jerry. Humans Need Not Apply: A Guide to Wealth and Work in the Age of Artificial Intelligence. New Haven: Yale University Press, 2015.

[143] Sohn, SM, The New Turing Test: The Six Levels of Autonomous AI Robots and Human-Likeness, Superiority, and Benevolence as Measures of Autonomous AI (2024). Preprint.

[144] For more information about the 6 Levels of Self-Driving Vehicles, refer to the following announcement from SAE: Society of Automotive Engineers [SAE]. "SAE International Releases Updated Visual Chart for Its 'Levels of Driving Automation' Standards for Self-Driving Vehicles," December 11, 2018. https://www.sae.org/news/press-room/2018/12/sae-international-releases-updated-visual-chart-for-its-%E2%80%9Clevels-of-driving-automation%E2%80%9D-standard-for-self-driving-vehicles.

[145] Sohn 2023

[146] Sohn, SM, The New Turing Test: The Six Levels of Autonomous AI Robots and Human-Likeness, Superiority, and Benevolence as Measures of Autonomous AI (2024). Preprint.

[147] Suleyman, Modern Turing Test (The Coming Wave) also refer to the article on MIT Tech Review: https://www.technologyreview.com/2023/07/14/1076296/mustafa-suleyman-my-new-turing-test-would-see-if-ai-can-make-1-million/

[148] Sohn, SM, The New Turing Test: The Six Levels of Autonomous AI Robots and Human-Likeness, Superiority, and Benevolence as Measures of Autonomous AI (2024). Preprint.

[149] This phrase may have existed before, but was popularized by Congressman McKinney in 1984 hearing about government intervention on Continental Illinois Bank

[150] This is a famous Korean quote when the Chosun Dynasty was under attack from Japanese and the Korean navy was decimated. The king ordered the navy to disband, but the general refused to give up.

[151] The Last AI pp. 187

[152] This is a pun on the JFK quote "ask not what your country can do for you, ask what you can do for your country" from his inauguration speech.

[153] This is a pun on the phrase popularized by Harry S. Truman, "The buck stops here."

[154] While this is also a title of the movie, the expression "tail wagging the dog" originates from Tam Taylor's 1858 play Our American Cousin.

[155] For more about the sad story of Otto Wambier, refer to: Clark, Doug B. "The Untold Story of Otto Wambier, American Hostage." GQ, July 23, 2018. http://www.gq.com/story/otto-wambier-north-korea-american-hostage-true-story

[156] It appears this phrase was a Medieval Latin proverb that was first recorded by Alain de Lille in 1175.

[157] According to UBS, the top 1% of the world's richest owned 44.5% share of the wealth in 2022. https://www.ubs.com/global/en/family-office-uhnw/reports/global-wealth-report-2023.html

[158] Refer to The Last AI for more explanation of this table, pp. 346.

[159] This is a pun on the song "I Believe I Can Fly" by R. Kelly.

[160] This is a pun on the phrase "Do You Believe in Life after Love" in "Believe" by Cher.

[161] Sohn, SM, The New Turing Test: The Six Levels of Autonomous AI Robots and Human-Likeness, Superiority, and Benevolence as Measures of Autonomous AI (2024). Preprint.

[162] Refer to The Last AI, pp.66-68

[163] Refer to The Last AI, pp.355-360, Also refer to the New Turing Test paper.

[164] Refer to The Last AI, pp.389-392

[165] Refer to The Last AI; pp.357-360

[166] Refer to The Last AI, pp.357-360

[167] The Swiss Cheese Model illustrates how big failures occur from accumulations of smaller failures that are overlooked.

[168] This phrase appears to be attributed to a variety of figures, including Aristotle, Twain, Franklin, etc.

[169] For Ray Kurzweil, refer to his book The Singularity Is Near. Also refer to this article on Popular Mechanics (Aug 2024) https://www.popularmechanics.com/science/a61777484/2045-singularity-ray-kurzweil/

[170] This is a pun on the famous phrase by Shakespeare

[171] Refer to Nick Bostrom and his book *Superintelligence.* (2014)

[172] For more explanation refer to The Last AI (pp. 351)

[173] Excerpt from The Last AI; Figures 6-4 and 6-5 (pp. 357-360)

[174] As also described in The Last AI, this is the first phrase of a children's book by the King's Academy of Chosun Dynasty.

[175] Sohn, Seuk Min, (2023), "The Three Levels of AI Adoption Framework and the Six Levels of Autonomous Companies." Working paper.

[176] Read The Last AI.

Index

Fonts Used: Aleo, Libre Baskerville, Open Sans, Roboto
I would like to thank everyone who supported me on this book!

About the Author

Seuk-Min Sohn, CFA is an independent researcher from South Korea. He is the author of *The Last AI* (May 2024), the book that introduces AI Economics and the Four Levels of AI Adoption Pyramid. He previously worked for Korea's policy banking institution, The Korea Development Bank (KDB), in the areas of global strategy, researching the financial industries and financial markets, and corporate banking, and was one of the co-authors of its history book, *the 60-Year History of KDB*. His primary research interests include AI adoption, AI Economics, and venture capital investments.

Education:

- Langley High School (McLean, VA)
- BS in Commerce, The University of Virginia
- MS in Business Administration, Seoul National University
- MBA, The University of Texas at Austin
- MS in Business Analytics, The University of Texas at Austin

Professional Certifications:

- Chartered Financial Analyst (CFA), CFA Institute
- Financial Risk Manager (FRM), Global Association of Risk Professionals

www.smsohn.com

Substack: thelastai.substack.com Medium: medium.com/@The_Last_AI LinkedIn: linkedin.com/in/smsohn	Instagram: @the.last.ai Youtube: @the_last_ai X: @The_Last_AI

www.ingramcontent.com/pod-product-compliance
Lightning Source LLC
LaVergne TN
LVHW090104250926
848814LV00044B/10
* 9 7 9 1 1 9 8 7 8 6 8 5 2 *